THE SECOND
JEWISH BOOK
OF
WHY

THE SECOND JEWISH BOOK OF
WHY

by
Alfred J. Kolatch

 Jonathan David Publishers, Inc.
Middle Village, New York, 11379

THE SECOND
JEWISH BOOK OF WHY

Jonathan David Publishers, Inc.
68-22 Eliot Avenue
Middle Village, New York 11379

Library of Congress Cataloging in Publication Data

Kolatch, Alfred J., 1916-
   The second Jewish book of why.

   Bibliography.
   Includes index.
   1. Judaism—Customs and practices. I. Title.
BM700.K593 1985   296.7   84-21477
ISBN0-8246-0305-2

Printed in the United States of America

FOR THELMA
AS WE CELEBRATE OUR
45TH WEDDING ANNIVERSARY

רַבּוֹת בָּנוֹת עָשׂוּ חָיִל
וְאַתְּ עָלִית עַל־כֻּלָּנָה

"Many women have performed valiantly,
but you have outperformed them all."

—PROVERBS 31:29

In Appreciation

Thanks are due many colleagues and friends—Orthodox, Conservative, and Reform—who in the course of the past three years that this book has been in preparation have read all or part of the manuscript. I am particularly grateful to the following for their insightful comments and suggestions:

Rabbi Ephraim Bennett of Netanya, Israel; Dr. Anthony Buono of Jamaica, New York; Rabbi Solomon Freehof of Pittsburgh, Pennsylvania; Rabbi Harold Kamsler of Oyster Bay, New York; Rabbi Stephen C. Listfield of Washington, DC; Rabbi Arthur Kolatch of San Francisco, California; Dr. John C. McCollister of Ormond Beach, Florida; Dr. Herbert Ribner of Long Beach, New York; Rabbi Sidney Schulman of Oakhurst, New Jersey; and Rabbi Isaac Toubin of New York City.

I am deeply indebted to my sons, Jonathan and David, who spent numerous hours discussing and editing the manuscript. As a result of their critical efforts I am certain the text has been considerably enhanced.

My appreciation also is extended to Nettie Herzog for her very capable proofreading. And to the staff at Jonathan David Publishers—particularly to Marvin Sekler, vice-president, and to my two devoted secretaries, Florence Weissman and Mary McGee—my profound thanks.

Contents

General Introduction

The enthusiastic response that greeted the publication of *The Jewish Book of Why* three years ago was somewhat unexpected and most encouraging. That volume answered some 500 questions, but it also provoked many new ones, and these questions are treated here.

The Jewish Book of Why deals with fundamental questions about the Sabbath and holidays; the dietary laws; synagogue practices; and the various milestones in the life of the individual, including birth, circumcision, Bar and Bat Mitzva, marriage and divorce, death and mourning. While *The Second Jewish Book of Why* occasionally touches upon the same or similar themes, it does so only to expand, provide commentary, or offer totally new information. In the main, it deals with more complex, controversial, and far-ranging subjects, including the attitudes of Jewish legal scholars toward such issues as abortion, conversion, birth control, artificial insemination, organ transplants, smoking, proselytizing, intermarriage, traveling on the Sabbath, and Jewish-Christian relations.

Since many of the subjects under discussion in this volume involve basic Jewish law, it is important to indicate how the law developed and how the rabbinic mind works.

THE PRIMARY AND SECONDARY LAWS

The Bible is the basic source of all Jewish law, custom, and tradition. While most of its attention is devoted to the early history of the Jewish people and to the exploits of its heroes and heroines, it is first and foremost concerned with man's relationship to God and to his fellow man. The purpose of the Tora is to teach man how to lead a godly life. The commandments (*mitzvot*) set forth within it are the directives one must follow if one is not to stray from the path that leads to God.

The reason for Israel's existence, according to the Bible, is to demonstrate and prove the holiness of God. "Ye shall be holy, for I the Lord thy God am holy" (Leviticus 19:2). This is the leitmotif of the Bible. The admonition to be holy and to emulate God is an ever-recurring biblical theme.

Holiness—to be a holy nation—was at the heart of the Covenant established between God and Abraham (Genesis 12:1-3), later confirmed at Mount Sinai (Exodus 19:6ff.) and reconfirmed in the final address of Moses to the Children of Israel (Deuteronomy 29:9ff.). Israel thus became God's Chosen People.

For Israel to fulfill itself as God's people, it had to remain loyal to the teachings of the Tora. Since the biblical prescriptions and proscriptions are not always sufficiently clear or specific or enforceable, however, the Rabbis interpreted the Bible and presented what they considered to be the true meaning of the text. Of the works that have been produced to explain the Bible, the Talmud is undoubtedly the most important.

The first part of the Talmud, known as the Mishna, consists of the teachings of the *tannaim,* meaning "teachers." The *tannaim* were scholars and sages who lived prior to 220 C.E. In compiling the Mishna, Judah the Prince (135-220), his co-editor Nathan, and their associates sifted through, evaluated, and edited a vast number of legal opinions that had been expressed over the centuries in the academies of learning, primarily in Palestine.

The second part of the Talmud, known as the Gemara, is a commentary on the Mishna. The scholars whose views are presented in the discussions in the Gemara are known as *amoraim,* meaning "interpreters" or "speakers." For the most part they lived in Babylonia, where the great academies were situated following the destruction of the Temple and the continuing Roman occupation of Palestine. The Gemara of the Babylonian scholars was edited and finalized by Rabina and Ashi and their associates around the year 500 C.E. Together with the Mishna it comprises the Babylonian Talmud.

A second Talmud, the Palestinian (or Jerusalem) Talmud, was also created. The Mishna of Rabbi Judah the Prince is the central text of this work as well. However, the Gemara of the Palestinian Talmud consists of the discussions that took place among the *amoraim* in the academies of learning in Palestine. The academies that continued to flourish in Palestine, primarily in Tiberias, during the Roman occupation in the early centuries C.E. were not equal in stature to those of Babylonia, and the Palestinian Talmud therefore enjoys a lesser status than the Babylonian Talmud.

The Palestinian Talmud, which is often called by its Hebrew name, Yerushalmi, meaning "of Jerusalem," is only about one-third the size of the Babylonian Talmud, which is often referred to as the Bavli, meaning "of Babylonia." It should be noted that only in recent centuries have scholars begun to study the Yerushalmi.

The Talmud is encyclopedic. Within its pages is information covering almost every conceivable area of human interest—information presented specifically in order to help Jews understand their legal and moral responsibilities as proclaimed in the Bible and discussed, commented upon, and interpreted by rabbis and scholars over a period of about one thousand years—from the time of Ezra, who lived about 450 B.C.E., up until the end of the sixth century C.E. The overriding purpose of the interpreters of the Bible was to preserve the uniqueness of the Jewish people, to make sure that they remained loyal to the Covenant by observing all the laws (*mitzvot*) of the Tora. To the Rabbis of the Talmud this meant that a system of law had to be established that would train Israel to carry out the mission of being a holy, godlike people. Jews would have to be protected from alien influences that might lead them away from God.

The discussions and rulings of the Rabbis did not always exist in the written form we know today. Since it had been contrary to established tradition to commit formally to writing anything but the Tora itself, the arguments and opinions of the Sages had been passed on by word-of-mouth from father to son, from scholar to disciple, from teacher to pupil. These spoken teachings came to be known as the Oral Law, in contradistinction to the Bible, which was called the Written Law.

By the second half of the fourth century C.E., because it was feared that the massive body of knowledge that comprised the Oral Law might be forgotten, the ban was lifted and the Oral Law was finally put into written form.

THE EARLY POST-TALMUDIC SCHOLARS

The Talmud, which is in reality the first code of Jewish law, presents problems to the student because its subject matter is not logically arranged. The issues under discussion are often extremely complex, and the final decision on a particular law is often difficult to pinpoint. It was these factors that prompted the writing of many commentaries on the Talmud.

For the first five hundred years following the final editing of the Talmud—from the years 500 to 1000—great scholars, particularly in Babylonia, continued the process of interpreting the Bible. They also explained and commented on the Talmud and gained new insights from its teachings. This period is known as the geonic period and its scholars are called *geonim* (singular, *gaon*, meaning "his eminence"). Among the better-known *geonim* are Hai, Sherira, and Amram, each of whom headed an academy of learning in a Babylonian city.

These scholars, as well as those who followed them for approximately the next five centuries—until about the middle of the sixteenth century—were known as the *rishonim,* meaning "the early ones." In addition to studying and analyzing the Talmud, they wrote commentaries on it and answered questions addressed to them by rabbis and teachers from all over the world.

Among the more celebrated scholars of the post-geonic period (after the year 1000) was the North African Isaac ben Jacob of Fez (1013-1103), better known as the Alfasi or by the acronym Rif; the French-born Solomon ben Yitzchak (1040-1105), better known by the acronym Rashi; his grandson Rabbenu Tam (1100-1170); Moses ben Maimon (1135-1204) of Spain and Egypt; Moses ben Nachman (1194-1270) of Spain, also known as Nachmanides and by the acronym Ramban; and Meir ben Baruch of Rothenburg, Germany (1220-1293).

The Mishneh Torah

Undoubtedly the most outstanding of these talmudic authorities was Moses ben Maimon, better known by the acronym Rambam or by his Greek appellation, Maimonides. Maimonides, along with some of his contemporaries, not only explained and interpreted the law but also codified it. His *Mishneh Torah* is the most comprehensive code ever written. In this fourteen-volume compendium, Maimonides organized all the material in the Talmud by subject matter, thus creating order out of what was previously a loosely organized admixture of law, history, folklore, philosophy, legends, and miscellany. He included the laws that applied to the Temple sacrificial system because he expected that one day the Temple would be rebuilt and the duties of the Priests reinstituted.

In the *Mishneh Torah,* Maimonides, unlike other codifiers of the law, does not present the varying viewpoints of talmudic scholars on any one issue. Rather, he records only that which he believes to be the established law. Maimonides does not list the talmudic sources for his conclusions, and he was criticized severely for that in his lifetime.

The Rosh and His Son

Following the death of Maimonides, the two most outstanding codifiers of Jewish law were Asher ben Yechiel (1250-1327), popularly known as the Rosh, and his son Jacob (1270-1350). The Rosh was an outstanding pupil of Meir of Rothenburg, and he succeeded him as the spiritual leader of Germany. He is famous for his legal compendium, *Piskay Harosh* ("Legal Decisions of the Rosh"), as well as for his responsa.

Asher ben Yechiel's son, Jacob, collected the decisions of the scholars who preceded him, principally those of his father. He published them under the title *Arba'a Turim* ("The Four Rows"), a name derived from the Bible (Exodus 39:10). Jacob himself came to be called by the nickname "Baal Haturim." His compendium of Jewish law consists of four parts:

- Orach Chayim, which deals with the laws of prayer and man's daily conduct.
- Yoreh Deah, which deals with the dietary laws, laws of ritual purity, and laws of mourning.
- Even Haezer, which deals with personal and family matters, including the laws of marriage and divorce.
- Choshen Mishpat, which deals with civil and criminal law and the administration of justice.

Another of the prominent codifiers of this period was the German scholar Jacob ben Moses Halevi Molln (or Mollin) (1360-1427), popularly known as Maharil. He was regarded as the leading authority on Jewish customs and liturgy, and his responsa, collected by a disciple, were published in *Sefer Maharil,* a standard work that is often quoted.

Caro and Isserles

In 1565 Spanish-born Joseph Caro (1488-1575) published his code of Jewish law known as the *Shulchan Aruch* (literally "Prepared Table," because all the laws are set forth in an orderly fashion). The *Shulchan Aruch* is actually an abbreviated and simplified form of the *Arba'a Turim* of Jacob ben Asher. It takes into account the views of previous codifiers of the law, primarily those of the Alfasi,

Maimonides, and Asher ben Yechiel. Where there is lack of unanimity, Caro sides with the two who agree.

Since Joseph Caro as well as Asher ben Yechiel, his son Jacob, Maimonides, and the Alfasi were all Sephardic scholars, Caro was charged with ignoring the views of French and German legal authorities. As a result, Moses Isserles (1520-1572) of Poland, known by the acronym Rema or Rama, wrote supplementary notes to the *Shulchan Aruch*, the *Mappah* (meaning "Tablecloth," for the "Prepared Table"). The Notes of Isserles set forth the views of Ashkenazic scholars and present the customs of their communities. On occasion Caro and Isserles do not agree, in which case the Sephardim follow Caro and the Ashkenazim follow Isserles.

The combined Caro-Isserles *Shulchan Aruch* is *the* standard code of Jewish law. Unchallenged for the past four hundred years, it has earned the title *Code of Jewish Law*, and adherence to its laws have become the test of Jewish fidelity. In this book the term *Code of Jewish Law* is used interchangeably with *Shulchan Aruch*.

THE LATER POST-TALMUDIC SCHOLARS

With the publication of the *Shulchan Aruch*, the period of the early scholars (*rishonim*) ended and the period of the *acharonim*, "the later ones," began. From the end of the sixteenth century to the present the *acharonim* have issued authoritative interpretations of the law. Although respected as scholars, they have not achieved the degree of acceptance accorded the *rishonim*.

The views of many of the distinguished *acharonim* are presented in this volume. Among the most famous of these rabbinic scholars are

- Solomon Luria (1510-1573) of Poland, also known by the acronym Maharshal. A contemporary and severe critic of Joseph Caro, Luria was displeased that, in determining which laws were to be included in the

Shulchan Aruch, Caro relied on the works of earlier codifiers rather than on the original source—the Talmud.

● Ezekiel Landau (1719-1793) of Prague, famous for his collection of responsa, *Noda Biyehuda.* He became so identified with his acclaimed book that he himself was referred to as the Noda Biyehuda.

● Moses Sofer (1762-1839) of Hungary, a vocal opponent of the Reform movement and of all innovations in Jewish religious practice. *Chatam Sofer* is the title of Sofer's distinguished legal work. It contains not only his creative legal insights but his responsa as well. This six-volume *halachic* work was so popular that Sofer himself was often referred to by its name.

● Russian-born Isaac Elchanan Spektor (1817-1896), founder of a famous *yeshiva* in Kovno and the author of several commentaries on the Talmud and the *Shulchan Aruch.* He was particularly concerned with the plight of the *aguna,* the "abandoned" wife, and he wrote 158 responsa on the subject. Many institutions of higher learning, including the Rabbi Isaac Elchanan Theological Seminary in New York, are named after him.

● Rabbi Abraham Kook (1865-1935), the highly regarded Chief Rabbi of the Ashkenazic community in Palestine in 1921. He organized a *yeshiva* called Merkaz Harav, and dealt in particular with problems concerning Jewish life in an agricultural setting.

There are many contemporary rabbinic scholars of great distinction who undoubtedly fall into the category of *acharonim.* Perhaps the most acclaimed is the Orthodox authority Moshe Feinstein (1895-   ), founder and head of the Tiferet Yerushalayim Seminary in New York City. He is the author of six volumes of responsa, entitled *Igrot Moshe.* A non-Orthodox authority to whom countless questions of law have been addressed over the past fifty or more years is Solomon B. Freehof (1892-   ), rabbi emeritus of Rodef

Shalom Temple, a Reform congregation in Pittsburgh. He is the author of eight volumes of responsa.

THE ELASTICITY OF JEWISH LAW

One of the traditional debates in Judaism is whether the Law—the Tora—is subject to change. This is often a question of semantics, but what becomes clear as we study the teachings and attitudes of the Rabbis of the Talmud and their successors is that when these scholars interpreted the Bible to make it more relevant to their times, they were in effect often actually modifying its laws. Frequently, they found it impossible to insist that the laws be carried out as written literally in the Bible. The Rabbis said more than once, "We do not impose a hardship on the community that the majority cannot endure."[1]

The biblical law of "an eye for an eye" (Exodus 21:24; Leviticus 24:20), for example, reflected the norms of the biblical era. By the time the Talmud was compiled some one thousand years later, this law was considered inhumane and the Rabbis therefore interpreted it to mean that if one causes another person to lose an eye, that person shall pay for the crime not by losing an eye but by making monetary compensation.[2] Although not in accord with the Bible, this ruling became the law.

In like manner, the Rabbis realized that the biblical law (Deuteronomy 15:1-3) that calls for the cancellation of all debts upon the arrival of the sabbatical year (every seven years) penalizes the poor farmer in need of a loan. Who would lend the farmer money as the sabbatical year approached, only to find that the loan would not have to be repaid? So, the great Hillel of the first century B.C.E. introduced a ruling that is known by its Greek name, *prosbul*, meaning "for the court." The lender could stipulate in writing before witnesses that he wished to be able to collect his loan despite the arrival of the sabbatical year. The court in effect then guaranteed that it would collect the debt for him, thus circumventing biblical law.

Another example of bending the law to suit the needs of the individual is the manner in which authorities handled the biblical admonition (Deuteronomy 17:16) that Jews are never to return to Egypt, the land in which they were once enslaved. Moses Maimonides (1135-1204) lists this prohibition in his Mishneh Torah[3] as one of the 365 negative precepts that must be observed. But while emphasizing that one may not settle in Egypt permanently, Maimonides explains that one may settle there temporarily if one's business interests demand it. Maimonides' family came to Egypt for business reasons after spending six months in Palestine, and they remained there for four generations, until the fourteenth century.

A contemporary example relates to the question of whether it is proper for a Kohayn (Priest) to study medicine despite the fact that he will be violating the biblical law which prohibits him from coming into contact with corpses. Some experts consider the laws of Levitical purity as prescribed in the Bible to be as valid today as in early times. Accordingly, they forbid a Priest from coming into contact with a corpse. Other authorities disagree, arguing that Priests (Kohanim) today are only Priests by presumption, since their pedigree can no longer be proven. Hence, they permit the study of medicine by Priests.

The Rabbis felt justified in reinterpreting many biblical laws, such as those mentioned above, because they contended that they were not actually effecting changes in the laws but were merely uncovering what was already implicit in them. They believed that on Mount Sinai God gave Moses not only the Written Law but the Oral Law as well, and that through their oral interpretation they were merely expressing the original intent of the biblical law.

PRINCIPLES OF JEWISH LAW

As the Rabbis of the Talmud engaged in the process of interpreting Jewish law so that it would meet the needs of the individual and of the community-at-large, a number of legal principles of Jewish law evolved, four of which are referred to frequently in this book.

The Lifesaving Principle

The lifesaving principle (*pikuach nefesh* in Hebrew) is undoubtedly the most basic of all principles in Jewish law. Its source is biblical. Leviticus 18:5 says, "Observe my commandments, which if a man do, he shall live by them." And Deuteronomy 30:19 states, "I have set before you life and death, blessing and curse. Choose life so that you and your offspring may live." From these verses, the Rabbis concluded that there is no higher priority than saving a life—one's own as well as that of one's fellow man.[4]

The Rabbis emphasized the importance of this principle through the following legend: When David returned victorious after his battle with Goliath, the women of Israel showered him with their gold and silver jewelry. He set the jewelry aside for future use in the building of the Temple, and even during a three-year period of famine did not use it to purchase food for the needy. Because of this, because David bypassed the immediate needs of the hungry for the future needs of the Temple, Solomon, not David, was granted the privilege of building the Temple.[5]

So important is the lifesaving principle, the Rabbis declared, that "saving a life takes precedence over the Sabbath."[6]

The Rabbis were careful not to leave the impression that an individual's life is more important then the life of his fellow man. The Talmud describes an incident involving Raba, the fourth-century Babylonian *amora*.

A man once said to him, "The governor ordered me to kill someone. He said he would kill me if I did not carry out his order. What shall I do?"

Raba replied, "Let him slay you, but do not take another man's life ... Why must you assume that your blood is redder than his?"[7]

The lifesaving principle has a direct bearing on the subject of organ transplants, discussed in Chapter Five. The question is raised, What proprietary rights does an individual have to his own body, and to what extent may he permit his body to be tampered with in order to save the life of another? While the Talmud warns that a person may not inflict a wound upon himself or upon others, most authorities would consider it permissible to allow a "wound" (operation) to be inflicted on one's body in order to donate an organ for transplant.[8]

The Stumbling-Block Principle

Leviticus (19:14) says, "Thou shalt not place a stumbling block before the blind." Deuteronomy (27:18) adds, "Cursed be he who misleads the blind." The purpose of the law is not merely to emphasize the obvious—that one should not place a physical obstruction in the path of a blind person—for only an outright sadist would act in that manner. The point of the law is to instruct Jews to refrain from deceiving and misleading the weak, the ignorant, and the inexperienced and also from acting in a manner that would lead the unwary to violate the laws of the Tora.

The Talmud asks: "How do we know that it is wrong for a man to offer a cup of wine to a Nazirite [who has vowed never to taste wine and liquor]?" And it answers: "Because it is stated, 'Thou shalt not place a stumbling block before the blind.' "[9] Tempting one to sin is a violation of the stumbling-block principle.

A second example of this principle at work concerns the treatment of children. The Rabbis warned that a man should not punish his grown son by striking him, lest the boy be provoked to strike back. By striking the boy, the parent would be placing a stumbling block before his son, because it might result in the boy speaking or acting disrespectfully, thus violating the positive commandment to honor parents.

In a third case, which goes even further than the above two examples, the Talmud states that if one lends money to another, and witnesses are not present to witness the transaction, the lender is guilty of violating the law against placing a stumbling block before the blind.[10] Why? Because if the creditor does not insist that witnesses be present when he makes the loan, he is tempting the borrower to lie at some future date about having borrowed the money. To prevent this from happening, Jewish law insists that witnesses be present when a loan is made, thus removing the stumbling block from the path of the borrower.

The stumbling-block principle (known in Hebrew as *lifnay iver lo titayn michshol*) would have a bearing on any discussion of the propriety of the "sting" operations conducted by government agencies in recent years. Is it proper to entice (entrap) people into participating in illegal activities of which they are suspected with the purpose of bringing them to trial at some later date?

The Appearance-Factor Principle

This principle, known in Hebrew as *marit a'yin* (literally, "what the eye perceives"), refers specifically to conveying a false impression of one's actions.

Jewish law, for example, would rule that if a Jew were walking down the street and needed to make an urgent telephone call, he should not walk into a nonkosher meat market in order to use its pay telephone. The reason: people who see the Jew in the store might be left with the false impression that he was in the store to make a purchase of nonkosher meat.

A classic example of this same principle at work is seen in a responsum of Rabbi Solomon Luria (1510-1573) of Poland. Luria was asked whether a man who was subject to headaches might, in the privacy of his home, eat his meals without wearing a hat. He replied that it is permissible and stated that there is no prohibition against even praying without a hat. Luria added, however, that he personally would not conduct himself in that manner because of the appearance factor. He felt that eating bareheaded might offend people who believe that the wearing of a hat is essential. It might leave people with the false impression that he was not observing the law properly.[11]

Along the same lines, the outspoken German rabbinic authority Jacob Israel Emden (1697-1776), who was critical of women who wore wigs, wrote in one of his responsa that a woman should not cover her hair with a wig because one might be misled into believing she was exposing her own hair, which is prohibited. Instead, he suggested, a married women must wear a *tichl* (cloth covering).

The Goodwill Principle

In Jewish law certain actions are prohibited *mishum ayva*, "because of hatred." Such actions have the potential for creating disharmony between the Jewish and non-Jewish communities.

The talmudic tractate Taanit[12] mentions that lay representatives (*Anshay Mishmar*) would assemble in their synagogues on Monday, Tuesday, Wednesday, and Thursday when the Priests offered sacrifices. These men would fast and pray for members of the community; but they never did so on Friday, Saturday, or Sunday. On Friday and Saturday they did not fast out of respect for the Sabbath, but why did they not fast on Sunday? The Talmud responds, "Because of the Nazarenes." Christians would be insulted if Jews turned the Christian Sabbath into a fast day.

Maintaining a harmonious relationship with the non-Jewish community is an old, established principle of Jewish law. This is the reason why attending Christmas parties, giving Christmas gifts to non-Jews, and occasionally burying a non-Jew in a Jewish cemetery is given sympathetic consideration in Jewish law.

THE DECISOR IN ACTION

How the various principles of Jewish law and tradition come into play when a decisor, a legal authority (called a *posek* in Hebrew), renders decisions becomes clear as we review a recent decision rendered by Rabbi Moshe Feinstein. He was asked about the permissibility of Jewish graduates attending commencement exercises to be held on a Jewish holiday. The immediate question concerned attendance at the Harvard University commencement exercises to be held on June 7, 1984, the second day of Shavuot.

Feinstein prohibited attendance, basing his decision on three elements of law and tradition.

First, to attend such ceremonies on a holiday would fly in the face of tradition; it would not be in keeping with the spirit of the day.

Second, it would violate the biblical law which states, "Thou shalt not place a stumbling block in the path of the blind" (Leviticus 19:14). Members of the graduates' families who are less meticulous about the observance of Jewish law, and others who are blind to its provisions, might get into their cars and drive to the ceremony, thereby violating the holiday. By attending the ceremony, the graduate would thus in effect be setting up a stumbling block before the blind. He would be causing them to violate the law.

Finally, Rabbi Feinstein argued, attendance at a graduation on a Jewish holiday would violate the rabbinic principle of *marit a'yin*, the appearance factor. Although the graduate may walk to the ceremony and be fastidious about not violating Jewish law, those who notice his presence there might be left with the impression that he did, indeed, violate the law to get there.[13]

In answering the questions posed in *The Second Jewish Book of Why*, many of the sources and authorities mentioned above—the Bible, the Talmud, the writings of the *geonim*, the rulings of the *rishonim* and *acharonim*, the decisions recorded in the *Code of Jewish Law* and in the

Responsa literature—are referred to and quoted. For exact references see the Notes following the text. Information about the books referred to in the Notes is furnished in the Bibliography.

The Index makes reference not only to material covered in this book but also to subject matter discussed in *The Jewish Book of Why*. This will provide easy access to all material on any given subject covered in both volumes.

ALFRED J. KOLATCH

CHAPTER 1

Who Is a Jew?
Who Is a Good Jew?

INTRODUCTION

Before the establishment of the State of Israel in 1948, the question Who is a Jew? was rarely asked, although the question Who is a good Jew? was often debated.

Two eminent Jews who voiced opposing views on the Who is a Jew? question were David Ben-Gurion (1886-1973), first prime minister of Israel, and Yitzchak Halevi Herzog (1888-1959), the former Chief Rabbi of Israel. The Chief Rabbi asserted that according to Jewish law only the offspring of a Jewish mother can be considered a Jew. If the mother is not Jewish and the father is Jewish, a child born to them is not Jewish. And the only way a person can become Jewish if his mother is not Jewish is to convert. For a female conversion, immersion in a ritual bath (mikva) is necessary; for a male, immersion and ritual circumcision are required. The natural-born Jew and the converted Jew, the Chief Rabbi declared, are Jews for all time.

Ben-Gurion argued that anyone who declares that he is a Jew, lives a Jewish life, and is interested in the welfare of the Jews is to be considered a Jew, regardless of the faith of the mother. His reasoning was as follows:

> We have been Jews without definition for the last 3,000 years and we shall remain so . . . By one definition the Jews are a religious community . . . There is a definition that Jews are a nation . . . There are Jews

17

without any definition. They are just Jews. I am one of them. I don't need any definition. I am what I am . . .

To Ben-Gurion legal status is not the sole criterion for determining who is a Jew. One's emotional connection with Judaism as well as how one is perceived by his fellow Jews and by non-Jews must also be considered. This view, shared by many Jews, is summarized in Professor Raphael Patai's *The Jewish Mind*. He states that to be a Jew involves "a state of mind." To be a Jew, he says, one has to think or know or feel that he is a Jew and he must be considered by others to be a Jew. Being born of a Jewish mother is not the only determining factor. In recent years Reform and Reconstructionist Jews have advocated the legitimacy of patrilineal descent in determining who is a Jew.

Two events in modern history demonstrate how these two perceptions of what constitutes a Jew operate in Jewish life.

In 1817, when Benjamin Disraeli was thirteen, instead of taking him to the synagogue to become a Bar Mitzva, his father, Isaac, took him to church to be baptized. Isaac Disraeli gave as the reason for his action the displeasure he felt over the way the synagogue conducted itself. This was merely a pretext because he himself never converted. Undoubtedly, Isaac Disraeli, like many nineteenth-century Jews, believed it essential to be part of Christian society in order to achieve success. Submission to baptism was seen as the first necessary step toward that goal.

But despite an experience that must have been shattering to a boy of thirteen, Benjamin Disraeli never ceased to proclaim his sympathy for and admiration of the Jewish people. He developed a sense of pride in what he referred to as "the destiny and genius of the Jewish race." This attitude was in particular evidence in 1874 when Disraeli became prime minister of England and was befriended by Queen Victoria. The queen once inquired of him, "What are you?" Disraeli walked up to the Great Bible displayed on a mahogany lectern in the room where they stood and turned the pages until he reached the dividing point between the Old and the New Testaments. Then, pointing to the blank, white page, he said, "This is what I am!"

If Disraeli were alive today, would he be entitled to Israeli citizenship under the Law of Return, which grants citizenship to any Jew who wishes to become a citizen of the State of Israel? Under Jewish law, he should be, because it is technically impossible for a Jew (meaning, one born to a Jewish mother or one converted to Judaism) to ever renounce his Jewishness. This principle, stated in the Talmud (Sanhedrin 44a), declares that a Jew is a Jew forever, even if he sins. As a sinner he might forfeit some privileges, but he does not lose his basic rights as a Jew.

But more than Jewish law is to be considered when discussing the question Who is a Jew? As Ben-Gurion and others have viewed it, the attitude of Jews toward fellow Jews is of great importance. How do Jews, as individuals, react to someone who has defected, who has converted to another religion, who has forsaken the ways of his ancestors?

The Israeli High Court was confronted with this issue in 1962 when Brother Daniel (whose original name was Oswald Rufeisen), a member of the Carmelite Order, requested citizenship under the Law of Return. Daniel was born to Jewish parents in Poland in 1922. He had been an active Zionist during World War II and had helped save Jewish lives. In 1942 Daniel became a Christian, but he continued to consider himself a Jew as well. He then became a monk and, because he loved Israel and had yearned for it since his youth, joined an order that had a chapter in Israel.

When Brother Daniel's application for citizenship under the Law of Return was rejected, he appealed the decision, claiming his rights as the child of a Jewish mother. The High Court, headed by Judge Moshe Silberg, rejected the appeal and emphasized that although according to *halacha* (Jewish religious law), Daniel is technically a Jew, in the eyes of

Jews he is not a Jew. The majority of the justices of the High Court argued: When so many Jews throughout history have sacrificed their lives for their faith, how could one who turned his back on his faith be considered a Jew? The decision of the court was not in strict keeping with Jewish law, but it did express the will of the people.

The questions in this chapter deal with facets of the issues outlined above as well as with the question Who is a *good* Jew? What are the determining factors in ascertaining who is a good Jew? Must one observe all the *mitzvot* (commandments) meticulously to be called a good Jew, or can one be a good Jew even if he or she is not totally observant?

These questions are not easily answered, for the term "good Jew"—that is, properly observant Jew—is defined differently by the Orthodox and non-Orthodox communities and by the various segments within those groups. As one example, during the mourning period following the death of a loved one some modern Orthodox rabbis permit a mourner to listen to mood music or turn on the television for information programs. Others, however, especially the ultra-Orthodox, condemn such activity. For another example, while modern Orthodox rabbis participate alongside non-Orthodox rabbis in community and rabbinic organizations, the ultra-Orthodox condemn such joint participation.

Within the non-Orthodox community the same dichotomy exists. While Conservative Judaism considers the Law (Tora) to have been revealed to Moses by God and therefore to be authoritative and immutable, it does allow its Committee on Law and Standards to issue majority and minority opinions, either of which may be followed by local rabbis and their congregations. Thus, while on the question of permitting travel to a synagogue on the Sabbath a majority report expressed approval, the committee also issued a minority report opposing such travel. In another instance, a minority report was issued allowing congregations that are so inclined to observe Jewish holidays for the same number of days as they are observed in Israel (one day less for Passover, Shavuot, and Sukkot).

Reform Judaism does not consider the Law either revealed or binding. The earliest Reform rabbis sought to free their followers from ritual observance and concentrated instead on promoting the ethical and universal ideals of the religion. As a consequence, they declared that all the laws of the Sabbath were no longer to be observed; the day was to be marked primarily by attendance at one or two religious services. The laws of *kashrut* were no longer to be binding, as were many other Jewish practices. In recent years Reform Judaism has changed its attitude toward ritual observance and does not discourage any of its members who wish to adhere to some or all traditional practices. For example, whereas Reform Jews as a group have never worn headcoverings at a Reform service, today large numbers of individuals do. And whereas in the past few Reform Jews observed dietary laws, today many do to one degree or another.

Reconstructionism takes the middle road between Conservative and Reform Judaism, and in its eyes one is a good Jew if he expresses his Jewishness in any of a variety of ways. Since Reconstructionists consider Judaism a civilization of which religion is but one aspect (peoplehood, the Hebrew language, the Land of Israel, music, dance, and social action are among the others), a Jew can be a good Jew whether or not he observes Jewish ritual. Reconstructionism encourages its members to search for ways in which they may adopt ritual observance to meet the needs of this day.

Given the wide diversity of opinion among Jews as to what constitutes proper religious behavior for a member of the Jewish faith, answering the question Who is a good Jew? is not a simple matter. Many concrete examples of how each group views specific Jewish laws and observances will be found in this chapter and throughout the book. These constitute part of each group's answer to the question Who is a good Jew?

———————□———————

Why are Jews known as "Covenant People"?

One of the cardinal teachings of Judaism is that God made a covenant with the Jewish people. In an agreement between God and Abraham described in Genesis 12:1-3, God in effect says: Go forth and spread My name throughout the world, and as a reward I will bring blessings to you and your descendants forever.

In the last address of Moses to the Children of Israel, the covenant is confirmed (Deuteronomy 29:9ff.):

> You stand this day before the Lord . . . to enter into the Covenant which the Lord your God is concluding this day . . . to the end that He may establish you this day as His people and be your God as He promised you and swore to your fathers, Abraham, Isaac, and Jacob . . . I make this Covenant not with you alone . . . but with those who are not here this day . . ."

In Jewish tradition, the Covenant is regarded as a permanent link between the past and the present. It can never be dissolved. All Jews come under its umbrella by virtue of the fact that they are of the "seed of Abraham." The Jewish people thus became the "holy seed" (in Hebrew, *zera kodesh*), and the members of this holy fellowship became known as the Covenant People. It matters not whether an individual Jew remains fully observant of Jewish law. Membership in the holy fellowship cannot be denied one who is of the seed of Abraham.[1]

Why are Jews called the "Chosen People"?

The idea that Jews are the Chosen People of God, that they stand in a special relationship to Him, stems from the Bible. The Book of Deuteronomy (7:6) describes this relationship: "For thou [Israel] art a holy people unto the Lord thy God; the Lord thy God has chosen thee, from among all the peoples on the face of the earth, to be his treasured people."

This "treasured people," referred to as "Chosen People" in popular parlance and as *am segula* in Hebrew, is mentioned in Exodus 19:5 and repeated in Deuteronomy 14:2. According to scholars such as Martin Buber, *segula* ("treasure") is derived from the Akkadian word meaning "cattle" or "property." Just as cattle was man's treasured property in nomadic times, so was Israel considered by God to be His treasured possession.

Wny was Israel chosen above all peoples? In the Talmud,[2] the first-century leader of Palestinian Jewry, Rabbi Yochanan, says that Israel was not actually chosen by God. Israel, he says, did the choosing. He bases this view on verses in Deuteronomy (33:2) and Habakkuk (3:3) which he interprets to mean that God offered the Tora to every nation and they refused it. He then offered the Tora to Israel and they accepted it. Thus, Israel chose God.

Rabbi Dimi ben Chama, a fourth-century Palestinian scholar who lived during the time when Constantine ruled Rome (327-330) and controlled the Church, introduced another explanation of how the Jews became the Chosen People.[3] Unlike Rabbi Yochanan, who believed that Israel chose God, Rabbi Dimi believed that God chose Israel, which in fact made it God's Chosen People. Israel, he said, was not willing, at first, to accept the Tora and the many commandments it contained, but God imposed His will upon it. Rabbi Dimi based this conclusion on his interpretation of the verse in Exodus (19:17), "And Moses brought forth the people out of the camp to meet God, and they [Israel] stood *at the foot* of the mountain." The fact that the Tora mentions that Israel was brought to meet God at the foot of the mountain teaches us, says Rabbi Dimi, that God wanted Israel close to the mountain so that he might suspend the mountain over them like a dome and say to them, "If you accept the Tora, it will be good with you; if not, this [place] will be your grave."

Regardless of which of the above interpretations students of Jewish tradition have accepted over the centuries, few have expressed the opinion that the notion of chosenness implies that Jews are a superior people or that special privileges have been conferred upon them. On the contrary, chosenness means that the people of Israel bear special responsibility to lead exemplary lives. The Prophet Amos (3:2) said, "I have known you [Israel] of all peoples on the earth; therefore I will visit your iniquities upon you [punish you for your sins]."

The chosenness of Israel and the responsibilities that go with that chosenness are deeply rooted in Jewish history. Throughout the centuries, Jewish philosophers have clung to the idea of the election (chosenness) of Israel despite charges by non-Jews that this smacks of an attitude of superiority. Even the enlightened Jewish philosopher of the modern age, Moses Mendelssohn (1729-1786), who was in close contact with the Christian community, espoused the idea. Because of the revelation at Mount Sinai, Mendelssohn explained, Jews were singled out as the Chosen People. As such, they have the obligation to be bearers of that revelation to the rest of the world. Chosenness carries with it responsibility; it does not imply superiority.

Why do some Jews believe that the idea of a Chosen People should be discarded?

In the view of most Jews, the belief in Israel as God's Chosen People has contributed immeasurably to Jewish survival. It has enabled Jews to carry on in times of adversity. Some Jews, however, consider the Chosen People concept an expression of unwarranted pride and self-importance, one that ought to be discarded. They argue that we really do not know what the Bible originally meant when it used the term *am segula,* "Chosen People." (See the previous question.)

Opponents of the Chosen People idea also believe that retaining this concept is detrimental to Jewish interests because it leads to a false sense of superiority that invites contempt from non-Jews and denies the democratic idea of equality for all men, which Judaism espouses.

Reconstructionists in particular, led by their founder, Professor Mordecai M. Kaplan (1881-1983), have long urged that Jews not continue to regard themselves as the Chosen People because of the ring of arrogance that the concept carries with it. Accordingly, this movement omits from the traditional Tora blessing the words "Who has chosen us above all peoples . . ." and substitutes "Who has *brought us closer to His service.*" In their view, this modification in the prayer expresses the idea of responsibility rather than superiority.

Opponents of the Chosen People concept often point out that the idea has not been considered basic to Judaism by all authorities. Moses Maimonides' Thirteen Articles of Faith, for example, does not allude to the chosenness concept. Nevertheless, all Jewish religious denominations other than Reconstructionism continue to subscribe to the traditional view that Jews are the Chosen People.

Why do some Jews consider Judaism more than a religious community?

Rabbi Mordecai Kaplan, founder of the Jewish Reconstructionist Society (1922), coined the phrase "Judaism as a civilization" and in 1934 published a book under that title in which he proposed that Jews are more than just a religious community. They are a "people" who share a common heritage—one that includes a religion, a history, a language, customs (folkways), a great literature, and a promising future. A Jew need not subscribe to all facets of Judaism to be considered a good Jew. Kaplan taught that the laws, customs, and traditions of Judaism were not handed down by God to Moses on Mount Sinai in a supernatural fashion, but that they developed over many centuries and ultimately became hallowed as "God's commandments."

Over the past two decades the Reconstructionists have founded a federation of congregations and fellowships comprised of synagogues in sympathy with the teachings of Dr. Kaplan. In 1967, the Jewish Reconstructionist Society established a rabbinical college in Philadelphia, where men and women are prepared for the rabbinate and ordained.

Why in Jewish law is it only the mother's lineage that determines whether one is a Jew?

The Talmud[4] states that a child born of a Gentile father and a Jewish mother is Jewish. Rashi reinforces this view: "Since the mother of the child is Jewish, he [the child] is to be counted as one of our brothers."

To support the position that it is the mother's, not the father's, lineage that counts in determining whether a child is Jewish, the Rabbis cited the verse in Deuteronomy (7:4): "He [the non-Jewish idolator who is the father of the child] will wean your son away from me [God]." In this verse, say the Rabbis, the words "your son" clearly refer to the child of a Jewish mother, and we must therefore conclude that at all times and in all cases your son is Jewish if he is the offspring of a Jewish woman.[5]

A second reason advanced in support of the view that it is the mother's lineage that counts in determining the Jewishness of a child is that at the time of birth one is always positive of the identity of the mother of the child, but one cannot be positive of the identity of the child's father. Jewish law therefore established that if a child's mother is Jewish, the child is Jewish, and that Jewishness is passed on to all future generations until the end of time.[6]

In the fifteenth century, talmudist Rabbi Solomon ben Simon Duran of Algiers declared categorically that the offspring of a Jewish mother and a Gentile father is Jewish "for all time." A century later, this opinion was codified as law.[7]

Why do some believe that one should be considered a Jew if the father is Jewish but the mother is not Jewish?

Owing in part to the Holocaust, in part to the fact that Jewish families are not reproducing at the same rate as in the past, and in part to assimilation, the number of Jews in the world is dwindling. The 1983 Jewish birthrate of 1.6

children per couple lagged behind the 2.2 rate for the public-at-large. It is estimated that if this trend continues, the current (1984) population of 5.5 million Jews in the United States will be reduced to 4.2 million by the year 2000. To remedy the situation, many scholars are of the opinion that the law (halacha) should be modified to bring more people into the Jewish fold. A case can be made, they say, for considering as Jewish the children of a Jewish man and a non-Jewish woman.

The argument advanced is that there is much within Jewish law and tradition that identifies a child with his father. The Bible contains a number of instances that point to this conclusion. For example, in taking the census, the Children of Israel were to be counted "by their *fathers'* houses" (Numbers 1:2). Numbers (18:1) also indicates that the Priestly status passes from father to son. And, again in the Book of Numbers (36), we find that the sons inherit the estate of the father.

Additional support for the view that the status of the father is primary is adduced from legislation found in the Talmud:[8]

1. If a *Kohayn* (Priest) marries an ordinary Jewish woman (Israelite), a child born from the marriage is a *Kohayn,* like the father.
2. If an Israelite marries a woman who is a *Kohayn,* a child born from this union is an Israelite, like the father.
3. Jewish law exempts the mother from some parental obligations. If a father fails to provide for his child, the *Bet Din* (court), not the mother, assumes the obligation.

Advocates of the paternity position also cite the statement of Maimonides who, in discussing the biblical laws [of Deuteronomy (25:5ff.)] relating to Levirate Marriage, says that what makes a surviving brother responsible to marry (*Yibum*) or release from marriage (*Chalitza*) his deceased brother's widow is the fact that the two brothers have a father in common. The law of Levirate Marriage does not apply to brothers who have only a mother in common.[9]

It is also pointed out in regard to this same law that the child born as a result of the marriage of the brother to his deceased brother's widow is (legally) not the child of the living brother who provided the seed, but of the deceased brother. The child carries the name of the deceased, not that of the natural father. He also inherits the property of his mother's deceased husband.

In March 1983, at the convention of the Central Conference of American Rabbis (Reform), a large majority (three to one) voted to recognize as Jewish a child whose mother or father is Jewish. The only requirement is that the child be reared as a Jew and be identified formally and publicly with the Jewish faith. Orthodox and Conservative rabbinic groups have repudiated this Reform position, which is also advocated by Reconstructionists.

Why is it not possible for a person to be half-Jewish?

As stated above, in Jewish law a person is either Jewish or not Jewish. If the mother is Jewish, the child is Jewish; if the mother is not Jewish, the child is not Jewish. The religion of the child's father is irrelevant.

So strong is the maternal bond in Jewish law that even if a child is brought up by non-Jews and is not aware that his mother is Jewish or that his maternal grandmother or great-grandmother (and so on) is Jewish, that person is Jewish in the eyes of Jewish law. The maternal lineage is the determining factor. (See previous answer for the non-Orthodox view.)

Why is the family status of a Jewish father who sires a child out of wedlock significant?

While Jewish law (halacha) does not take into consideration the status of the father of a child in determining whether the child is Jewish, it is a factor in other respects. The father's lineage, not the mother's, determines whether a child is a *Kohayn* (Priest), a *Layvee* (Levite), or a *Yisrael* (Israelite). Even if a child is born out of wedlock to a Jewish mother and father, the child is a *Kohayn* if the father is a *Kohayn,* a *Layvee* if the father is a *Layvee,* and a *Yisrael* if the father is a *Yisrael.*

In cases where an unmarried mother refuses to identify the father of her child but states that he is Jewish, she is believed. If she asserts that the father is a *Kohayn,* she is also believed, and all Priestly privileges and obligations are assumed by the child, including pronouncing the *Priestly Benediction (duchening)* and officiating at the redemption of a firstborn son *(Pidyon Haben).*

Why does an adopted infant of unknown parentage have to undergo conversion to be considered Jewish?

Jewish tradition[10] has high praise for one who takes an orphan into his home and raises the orphan as his own. But neither the Bible nor the Talmud addresses itself to the religious status of the "adopted" child. Rabbinical authorities have stated, however, that an adopted child who is not definitely known to be Jewish must undergo formal conversion to be so considered.

Why is loyalty to the Jewish people alone not considered sufficient reason for recognizing a person as a full-fledged Jew?

In the 1950s a young man, the son of a Jewish father and a Gentile mother, wrote a letter to Golda Meir from the *kibbutz* on which he had settled after coming to Israel. Requesting recognition as a full Jew, the boy explained that his father had worn the required yellow Star of David during the Nazi occupation of his native Holland, and that he himself had lost both legs while serving in the Israeli army.

[At that time the Israeli Knesset (Parliament) was debating whether a person whose mother is non-Jewish should be considered a Jew if that is his choice or, in the case of a minor, the choice of both his parents.]

The Knesset Record of 1956 [page 739] records the young man's arguments:

1. Is it fair for Israel to regard the children of mixed marriages (where the father is the Jew) as non-Jews when the Nazis considered us to be Jews?
2. Do you think I was right in coming here? Do you think that there is a place for me here as a "non-Jew"?
3. Was I right in doing what other Jews do, that is, joining the army? Did I lose my legs fighting for a country that I cannot consider my homeland?
4. What shall I do? Shall I remain here and feel ashamed because my mother was not Jewish, or shall I return to Holland and feel ashamed because my father is a Jew?

The answer the young man received was that his heroism and acts of devotion to Israel and his close identification with Jewish life were not sufficient cause to bend the law for him. Traditionally, to be a Jew one has to either have been born to a Jewish mother or have converted to Judaism. This young man did have a way—conversion—of remedying his situation. However, since he did not choose to convert, professing to be a secularist and an atheist, nothing could be done for him.

Why does religious observance play no part in determining who is a Jew?

In traditional Judaism, whether one practices much religious observance or little or nothing at all has no bearing on one's legal status as a Jew, because the Jewishness of an individual is determined by the religious status of the mother. A person is Jewish if one's mother is Jewish. The religion of the father is not a factor. If the father is Jewish and the mother is Gentile, and their children are brought up to observe all Jewish laws and customs, the children would not be considered Jewish unless a formal conversion takes place.

An actual ruling in a case of this type is to be found in the responsa of Rabbi Moshe Feinstein.[11] A woman had been married to an Orthodox Jew by an Orthodox rabbi, and the couple lived Orthodox lives for many years. They raised two daughters and a son, all of whom were observant Jews. When the woman died, it was rumored that she was not Jewish, that her mother was a Gentile who had never converted and consequently this woman and her children were not Jewish. The question in this case was whether the woman could be buried in a Jewish cemetery next to her husband, but in a wider sense the question was the status of the children. Was the fact that they had lived Jewish lives for many years sufficient to consider them Jews? Rabbi Feinstein ruled that if it could be proven through the testimony of reliable witnesses that the rumor was true, that the mother of the woman was a non-Jew, it would be necessary for the children to be converted formally, otherwise they could not be considered Jews. Having lived a full Jewish life up until that point had no bearing on the situation.

Why did the Rabbis of the Talmud improve the status of the *mamzer* (bastard) over the status assigned to it in biblical times?

English dictionaries define a bastard as an illegitimate child, meaning one born of a man and a woman who are not married to each other. In Jewish law, however, a *mamzer* (bastard) is a child born of an adulterous union—specifically, one born to a married woman who has had sexual intercourse with a man who is not her husband. A *mamzer* is also a child born of a woman who has remarried without having obtained a valid Jewish divorce *(get)* from her first husband. And, finally, *mamzer* refers to a child born of a sexual relationship between a couple forbidden to marry because their marriage would constitute incest. (Incestuous marriages, such as those between a brother and a sister, are listed in Leviticus 18.)

The Bible (Deuteronomy 23:3) specifies the status of such a child: "A *mamzer* shall not enter into the congregation of the Lord; even until the tenth generation he shall not enter . . ." This means that only after an extremely long time ("tenth generation" means an indefinite number of years) will the stigma of bastardy be erased. The Rabbis considered this rather harsh treatment for innocent people who were paying for the sins of their parents and ancestors. And so, while they had no power to set aside the biblical law, the Rabbis did find a means of easing it by extending the marital privileges of the *mamzer*. Initially, the *mamzer* could marry only another *mamzer*, but by homiletical interpretation of the biblical texts (Numbers 15:15 and Deuteronomy 23:3, 9) the Rabbis concluded that a *mamzer* may also marry a proselyte.[12] (See next question.)

Why in Jewish law is the status of an individual determined by his educational achievements?

From the beginning, Judaism has equated godliness and piety with learning and wisdom. The Psalmist said, "The beginning of wisdom is the fear of the Lord" (Psalms 111:10). This theme is emphasized often in later Jewish literature. In the first century B.C.E. Hillel said, "An uncultured person cannot fear sin, and an ignorant one cannot be truly pious."[13]

Emphasis was placed on acquiring an education because learning was considered an essential ingredient of the godly life as prescribed by Jewish law. This meant that to be a good Jew one had to learn all about the commandments in the Tora and Talmud in order to be able to carry them out in everyday living. An unschooled person would be ill-equipped to fulfill the commandments.

A reverence for learning has prevailed throughout Jewish history. The Talmud,[14] in a revealing passage, demonstrates the attitude quite dramatically. It says that a Priest takes precedence over a Levite, a Levite takes precedence over an Israelite, and an Israelite over a *mamzer* (bastard), provided that all are equal in learning. However, if a *mamzer* is a scholar and the High Priest is an ignoramus, the learned *mamzer* takes precedence over the ignorant High Priest. The ideal man, to the Sages of the Talmud, is the one who studies Bible and Mishna, attends to the needs of scholars, is honest in business, and speaks gently to his fellow man.[15].

The importance of learning in Jewish tradition propelled Simeon ben Shetach, a first-century B.C.E. leader of Palestinian Jewry,[16] to establish community-sponsored public schools. A century later it motivated Joshua ben Gamala, the wealthy High Priest (about 64 B.C.E.) who was not learned himself, to establish in every town schools for children over five years of age.[17] These were the beginnings of a long tradition demanding excellence in education among Jews—young and old alike. Only through education, it is believed, will God-fearing citizens be produced.

Why did the Rabbis permit a *mamzer* to marry a proselyte?

As pointed out earlier (page 31), the Bible excludes a *mamzer* (bastard) and his descendants from being full-fledged members of the Jewish community. Realizing that this law was overly severe and unfair both to the innocent *mamzer* and his descendants, the Rabbis tried to ease their condition by integrating them into the Jewish community more quickly. Noting that the stigma of proselytism wears off within a generation or so, the Rabbis permitted a proselyte to marry a *mamzer* in order to help the *mamzer* rid himself of the stigma of bastardy more quickly. The Rabbis believed that the offspring of a *mamzer* who had married a proselyte would, within a generation or so, begin to be referred to as a descendant of a proselyte, rather than as a descendant of a *mamzer*. By the sixteenth century the stigma attached to the *mamzer* was fully dissipated and it was ruled that "a *mamzer* may be called to the Tora."[18]

Why is Jewish law unwilling to classify as a *mamzer* a child born as a result of artificial insemination?

In cases where artificial insemination has been performed and it is known that the husband is the sperm donor, all Jewish authorities agree that the baby born has the same status as a child born of normal cohabitation. However, there is much disagreement over the status of the child conceived of semen from a donor other than the husband of the mother. (See Chapter Five, The Personal Dimension, for a fuller discussion.)

In the opinion of some Christian theologians and some Western legislators, artificial insemination by a donor other than the husband is to be condemned as immoral. They consider this tantamount to adultery, and therefore a child conceived by artificial insemination is branded a bastard. Jewish law does not agree. Bastardy (in Hebrew, *mamzerut*), it states, is a label that can be applied only when there has been direct physical contact between a man and a woman. In the case of artificial insemination there is no sexual intercourse, hence Jewish law does not label the resulting offspring *mamzer*.

How did Jewish law arrive at this conclusion?

The ruling is based on the talmudic interpretation of Levicitus 21:14, which requires a High Priest to marry no one but a virgin. And the Talmud[19] says, "Ben Zoma was asked: 'May a High Priest marry a virgin who has become pregnant?'" The question raised was whether the High Priest may marry such a girl (or, if already married, may keep her as a wife) if she claims that despite her pregnant condition she is still a virgin because she has never had actual sexual intercourse with a man. How is this possible? The answer the Talmud offers is that she may have taken a bath in water previously used by a man and into which semen had been discharged. Thus, without her being aware of it, the semen had entered her body, and she became pregnant.

Later authorities established a rule based on this talmudic interpretation, affirming that a virgin who is impregnated by means other than physical cohabitation with a man does not lose her status as a virgin; and that the child born of such pregnancy cannot be called a *mamzer*. There must be *direct* sexual intercourse for the stigma of bastardy to apply.

Why do Jews never lose their Jewish identity, even if they convert to another religion?

Jewish law adopted the view of the third-century Palestinian Rabbi Abba ben Zavda, who said, "Even when Jews sin, they continue to be identified as Jews."[20] He followed that statement with this picturesque comparison: "A myrtle though it stands among reeds is still a myrtle and continues to be so called."

The concept that once a Jew, always a Jew is based upon an incident in the Book of Joshua. Under the leadership of Joshua, the Children of Israel began to conquer Canaan, and the first city taken was Jericho. The Israelites had been warned that after the city was captured, no one was to take any war booty for himself; it was all holy and belonged to the Lord. But some disobeyed the order.

One of the violators of the ban was Achan ben Carmi, and he was to suffer death for his sin. Joshua pleaded with him to confess his sin (Joshua 7:19), and Achan did so, divulging where he had hidden the loot. Although the Bible does not so indicate, the Talmud implies that Joshua convinced Achan that by confessing his sin he would not avoid execution, but he would be assured entry into the next world with a clean slate.

Based on the story of Achan and its talmudic interpretation, a principle of Jewish law was established: one may never think of an errant Jew as being lost to Judaism. There is hope, even until his dying day, that a Jew who has done wrong will confess his sins and repent. For this reason, the door is never closed to his return, and Jewish law insists that a Jew may never be denied his basic rights as a Jew, even if he goes so far as to convert to another religion.

Why can one who defected from Judaism and was baptized in the Christian Church return to Judaism without undergoing a Jewish conversion ceremony?

A Gentile who wants to convert to Judaism must undergo immersion in a ritual bath *(mikva)* and, if a male, undergo the circumcision ceremony *(brit mila)* as well. However, a Jew who abandons Judaism, joins the Church, and then subsequently has a change of heart can return to Judaism without going through the conversion ceremony. The basis for this ruling is that in the eyes of Jewish law a Jew can never forsake Judaism regardless of what he does or professes. He is considered to be a sinning Jew who has forfeited certain rights, but no more than that. A Jew is a Jew forever.

Why do some families sit *Shiva* for a family member who marries outside the faith?

If a Jew marries a non-Jew, he is still a Jew. Although sitting *Shiva* for an individual who marries outside the faith was once a widespread custom among Jews (and is still practiced today to a lesser extent), it is not required by law. The practice can be considered no more than an expression of revulsion felt by Jews toward one who has been disloyal to his people and tradition. (For more information on this subject, see Chapter Six, Death and Dying.)

Why is the term "Oriental Jew" sometimes confused with "Sephardic Jew"?

When the Jewish people was young, all Jews lived in the Eastern part of the world, hence they were Oriental Jews. (The word "Orient" is synonymous with "East.") The Eastern countries inhabited by Jews included Babylonia (now Iraq), which for many centuries was the foremost center of Jewish life, plus Egypt, Palestine, Syria, Persia (now Iran), Yemen, and India.

Over the centuries many Eastern Jews moved north and eventually settled in Spain and Portugal, primarily Spain, and these Jews became known as "Sephardim," Sepharad being the Hebrew name for Spain. At the same time, other Jews moved north and settled in the Germanic countries, in France, and in the neighboring countries of eastern Europe. Since Germany received most of the migrants, these Jews became known as "Ashkenazim," Ashkenaz being the Hebrew name for Germany.

After the expulsion of the Jews from Spain in 1492 and from Portugal in 1497, large numbers of the refugees settled in the North African countries, and they soon became the majority, overshadowing the native Jewish population which had come there from the East. In time the Oriental character of North African Jewry began to fade, and the Jews of North Africa not only adopted Sephardic customs but also came to be referred to as Sephardim. Other refugees from Spain and Portugal settled in Holland, Greece, Turkey, and various other countries.

Today, Jews living in the Eastern (Oriental) countries as well as Jews of Oriental descent are usually referred to as Sephardim (or "Sephardim of the East"), and most even refer to themselves as Sephardim. This probably came to pass because of the similar manner in which both the Oriental and the Sephardic Jews pronounced Hebrew. Scholars, however, have pointed out that in the truest sense only descendants of Jews who once lived in Spain and Portugal may properly be called Sephardim. For this reason, in Israel today the Oriental communities of Jews are not called Sephardim but *Edot Hamizrach,* meaning "Communities of the East."

Why did the Karaites break away from mainstream Judaism?

In the eighth century in Babylonia, under the leadership of Anan ben David, a group of Jews unhappy with the leadership of the *geonim* (the religious leaders of Babylonia who often wielded considerable temporal power) broke away from the mainstream and organized their own community. They called themselves *Karaim,* meaning "adherents to *Mikra"* (the Hebrew word for Bible). The Karaites were displeased with the manner in which the Rabbis of the Talmud and post-talmudic period interpreted and, in effect, changed many of the laws prescribed in the Bible. Consequently, the Karaites defied rabbinic law and denied the authority of the Talmud. They demanded of their followers, who soon were to be found in Persia and Egypt and Palestine, strict adherence to biblical law, because it alone is the word of God. All other laws and regulations were considered rabbinical impositions and hence not valid. Consequently Karaites

- did not burn a fire on the Sabbath for light or heat
- ate cold food on the Sabbath
- did not permit a non-Jew to work for them on the Sabbath
- did not permit circumcisions on the Sabbath (circumcisions were performed at the close of the Sabbath so healing would not begin on the Sabbath)
- did not seek medical help because they took literally Exodus 15:26, "I am the Lord who heals you"
- did not observe Chanuka, which is a post-biblical holiday

Karaism also disapproved of the manner in which the Rabbis mandated the observance of the commandments relating to *tefilin, mezuza, tzitzit,* marriage, and divorce. The rabbinic forms, they argued, were not prescribed in the Bible.

Why have marriages between Karaites and other Jews been declared invalid?

By the end of World War II 7,000 of the 12,000 Karaites in the world lived in Egypt. During the Israeli War of Independence (1948), these Egyptian Karaites imperiled their lives to perform many heroic deeds in behalf of the emerging State of Israel. By 1950 about 3,500 Egyptian Karaites emigrated to Israel, and the State allocated funds for the establishment and administration of Karaite courts that would rule on issues brought by members of the Karaite community. In 1972 there were 10,000 Karaites in Israel, with nine synagogues.

Despite the tacit recognition given the Karaite community, its members are not considered full Jews. Their status in Jewish law was established as far back as the sixteenth century.[21] The basic argument is that over the centuries many Karaites have remarried after having been divorced, but the divorce document *(get)* issued by Karaite courts has never met the requirements of rabbinic law. Hence, when a Karaite woman remarried on the basis of a Karaite *get*, the new marriage was really invalid (because the woman who was remarrying was still a married woman in the eyes of Jewish law), and the offspring of the invalid marriage were *mamzerim* (bastards). In Jewish law, only a proselyte or another *mamzer* can marry a *mamzer*.

The view casting the taint of bastardy on all Karaites has not been shared by all scholars. As far back as the sixteenth century one of the leading rabbis of Safed, Rabbi David ben Solomon ibn Abi Zimra (also known as the Radbaz, 1479-1573), opposed the decision to disallow marriages with Karaites. He offered legal arguments refuting the view of Isserles, and he maintained that it is wrong to lock out a large group of Jews who sincerely want to be one with the larger Jewish community.

In Israel today the issue is not resolved, and debate continues.

Why was there once doubt about the status of the Falasha Jewish community?

The Falashas are a community of black Jews who have lived in Ethiopa (Abyssinia) for centuries. The Falashas believe that after the Queen of Sheba (ruler over the southern Arabian kingdom) visited King Solomon in Jerusalem (described in I Kings 10), she returned to her land full of admiration for the wisdom of the king. Returning with her was a contingent of Jews who subsequently settled in Abyssinia. This contingent was the first of the Falasha community.

There is also the belief among Falashas that they are the descendants of a marriage between the Queen of Sheba and Solomon. More probably, the Falashas are descendants of a tribe that lived in Abyssinia in pre-Semitic times and who adopted Judaism after being exposed to it by Jews who visited and/or settled there.

By the early centuries C.E., it is clear, the Falashas had become aware of the Bible and had accepted its teachings and commandments. However, the rabbinic interpretations and explanations of the biblical laws, which are enunciated in the Talmud, did not reach them in their entirety. They were exposed only to those teachings communicated to them by occasional visitors. Consequently, we find that Falashas circumcise their sons on the eighth day after birth, observe the Sabbath and most holidays, and follow the biblical dietary laws. Yet the sounding of the *shofar* on Rosh Hashana is not customary, the *lulav* and *etrog* are not used on Sukkot, and Purim is not observed at all.

The Falashas call themselves *Beta Israel,* meaning "House of Israel." Their Ethiopian neighbors look upon them as outsiders, however, calling them Falashas, meaning "exiles" in Amharic, the Semitic language used officially in Ethiopia.

The status of Falashas as Jews has been debated for centuries. As far back as the sixteenth century Rabbi David ben Zimri, who for many years was a rabbinical judge and Chief Rabbi in Cairo, accepted as fact the contention that Falashas were descendants of the tribe of Dan. Nevertheless, in one of his responsa he ruled that Falashas were like Karaites: we accept their marriages as valid marriages, but we do not accept their divorces as valid divorces. (See the previous question on Karaites.) With few exceptions, this view is subscribed to by rabbinic Judaism at large and is based on the fact that the marriage ceremony of the Falashas incorporates all the elements necessary for a valid Jewish marriage, even if their divorce document *(get)* does not comply with (satisfy) the demands of rabbinic law.

The current practice in Israel is to accept Falashas as Jews, but to nevertheless require that they go through the conversion process before they can marry a Jew.[22]

Why were the Samaritans read out of the Jewish religious community?

In 530 B.C.E. the Persians conquered the Chaldeans, who then ruled over Babylonia. The benevolent Persian king, Cyrus, allowed the Jews who had been exiled to Babylonia in 586 B.C.E. to return to Palestine. Many, but not all, returned.

When the exiles arrived in Palestine, they found among the inhabitants descendants of Jews who had not left Palestine with the exiled Jews. Many of the Jews who had stayed behind lived in Samaria, in an area today called Nablus.

Samaria (Shomron) was the capital city of the northern kingdom of Israel, and its inhabitants were known as Samaritans *(Shomronim)*. Upon the return of the exiled Jews, the Samaritans offered to help rebuild the Temple, but the offer was refused on the ground that during the years of the Babylonian Exile the Jews who had remained behind became idol worshippers and followed the customs and rituals of the Chaldeans. The returning exiles refused to accept the Samaritans as Jews, and a great hatred developed between the Samaritans and the rest of the Jewish population—a hatred that lasted for centuries, making reconciliation with the larger Jewish community impossible.

Maimonides categorized the idol-worshipping Samaritans as Gentiles, and to the present they are not recognized as Jews. They consider Mount Gerizim, overlooking Nablus, to be the holy mountain on which the intended sacrifice of Isaac (known as the *Akeda*) was to have taken place. In

332 B.C.E., having been granted permission by Alexander the Great, the Samaritans built a temple on Mt. Gerizim. The temple was later destroyed by John Hyrcanus, but to this day, on this mountaintop, a few hundred remaining Samaritans still celebrate Passover each year in the manner prescribed in the Bible—by offering the Paschal lamb as a sacrifice. Like the Karaites, the Samaritans do not accept post-biblical, rabbinic law as valid.

Today, despite the fact that the Samaritans are not recognized in Israel as a separate religious community, the government does contribute funds to support their religious needs.[23]

Why is a Jewish heretic sometimes called an *apikoros* and at other times an "apostate"?

The Greek word *apikoros*, meaning "disbeliever, skeptic, heretic," is derived from the name of the fourth-century B.C.E. Greek philosopher Epicurus, who inspired the Epicurean school of thought, which taught that the goal of man is to attain pleasure but the search for pleasure must be governed by morality and moderation. The followers of Epicurus disputed the attitudes of Judaism and its belief in one God as the source of the moral law. Because of this, a Jew who denied the validity of Jewish beliefs and practices became known as an *apikoros*, that is, an apostate, a heretic.

The word "apostate" is the accepted English translation of both the word *mumar*, meaning "one who changes," and the word *meshumad*, meaning "one who destroys." The Tosefta,[24] which is a supplement to the Mishna and was composed in Palestine, uses the word *meshumad*, while the Babylonian Talmud[25] uses the word *mumar* in the same quotation.

Although the Talmud in general defines an "Israelite apostate" as a Jew who has turned to idol worship and because of this is to be equated with one who has abandoned the whole Tora, in later times the word apostate took on the meaning of a Jew who abandons Judaism for another religion, not necessarily idol worship.

Why in Jewish tradition is one considered to be an apostate if he continues to believe in God but refuses to practice the ritual forms?

In theory, Jewish tradition considers a Jew to be an apostate if he becomes an idol worshipper or if he casts God out of his life, saying, there is no God, or God does not govern the universe. In practice, however, the Rabbis believe the real apostate to be a Jew who abandons the practice of ritual law. The Midrash speaks of God saying about Israel: "I would have been satisfied if they [the Jews] abandoned Me but did not forsake My Tora."[26] The idea is that even if a Jew is an atheist, by observing the commandments (mitzvot) of the Tora he will return to a belief in God.

As evidence of the fact that the ritual forms are essential in the Jewish tradition, the Code of Jewish Law[27] classifies as an apostate a Jew who deliberately and spitefully (le hachis) eats nonkosher food or wears articles made of shaatnez (forbidden mixtures of fabrics, such as wool and linen) or the like. The worst of all apostates in the eyes of Jewish law is the Jew who violates the Sabbath publicly.[28]

Why does an apostate lose many, but not all, privileges and rights as a Jew?

The apostate loses much credibility as a Jew, and some privileges, but he cannot be denied all his rights. As stated above, in Jewish law an apostate can range from anyone who abandons Judaism for another faith to one who disobeys the basic biblical commandments.

Depending on the nature of the apostasy, specific privileges are denied the apostate. For example, Orthodox rabbis will not permit the apostate who violates the Sabbath publicly to sign as a witness on a ketuba (marriage contract) or on a *get* (divorce document). But while these privileges may be denied him, he retains all marital obligations and family rights. Before the apostate's wife can remarry, she must be granted a *get* by him. Before the childless widow of his brother can remarry, he must agree to release her through the Levirate Marriage *(Chalitza)* ceremony (Deuteronomy 25:5).

An apostate inherits his father's estate; and if he is a firstborn *(bechor* in Hebrew), he does not lose the rights of the firstborn.[29] A child may say *Kaddish* for an apostate father. And a Priest *(Kohayn)* who became an apostate and then repented has not lost the right to offer the *Priestly Benediction* (known as *duchening* in Hebrew).

Why do all Jewish religious denominations demand of their members that they celebrate the Sabbath?

Although there are sharp differences between the Orthodox and the non-Orthodox as to what specifically constitutes proper Sabbath observance, all agree that to be considered a good Jew one must observe the Sabbath. The Orthodox demand full compliance with the law, while the non-Orthodox demand less, placing more emphasis on the spiritual aspects of the day.

To all groups within the Jewish religious community the Sabbath represents a sacred and inviolable bond made between God and the Jewish people. In the Bible the Sabbath is described as a sign between God and the Children of Israel forever (Exodus 31:13), and he who severs this bond is deserving of death (Numbers 15:32-36). The early Rabbis stressed the importance and uniqueness of the Sabbath: "The Sabbath is equal to all the other precepts of the Tora combined."[30]

Each of the Jewish religious denominations is firmly committed to the centrality of the Sabbath in Jewish life, because in remembering the Sabbath and commemorating it as a holy day they are expressing two of the essential beliefs of Judaism as represented in the Ten Command-ments (Exodus 20:8-11 and Deuteronomy 5:12-15):

1. God created the world in six days and then rested (Exodus).
2. Just as God was the instrument through which the Israelites found freedom from Egyptian slavery, so is He the instrument through which all enslaved peo-ple can achieve freedom (Deuteronomy).

Because these two basic beliefs have always been sub-scribed to by all members of the Jewish religious commu-nity, they became the motif of the *Kiddush* prayer recited on the Sabbath. The Sabbath is ushered in and sanctified with the declaration that God is the Creator and that God sets men free. God and freedom are one.

Why are Jews who violate the Sabbath *publicly* considered the worst kind of sinners?

The Talmud[31] draws a sharp distinction between one who violates the Sabbath in public and one who does so privately. While the appellation *mumar*, "apostate," is ap-plied to both, the public violator is equated with a Gentile, a heathen, an idolator (because by his actions he has seem-ingly denied the faith completely) while the private violator is not so stigmatized.

This point was reasserted by Moses Maimonides in the *Mishneh Torah*, where he equates a person who dese-crates the Sabbath publicly with an atheist and an idolator.[32]

In discussing the blatant violation of the Sabbath, the Talmud emphasizes *public* violation (the Greek word *be-farhesya*, meaning "open, frankly," is used). The Rabbis focused their discussion on public violation because they were aware that the person who violates the Sabbath pub-licly is a much greater threat to Judaism than one who violates it in the privacy of his own home. While the private violator's actions go unnoticed, the actions of the public violator might encourage sinning by others.

Apparently, exclusion of Jews from the Jewish fold for violating the Sabbath in public was a serious problem, and an attempt to mitigate the situation was made from the very beginning. The first indication of this effort is found in the Talmud,[33] where the question is asked, "How many persons must be present for an action to be called a *public* action?" And the answer is, "Rabbi Jacob said in the name of Rabbi Yochanan: 'The minimum is ten.' " The comment is added that all ten must be Jews.

Clearly, since ten Jews had to witness a violation of the Sabbath for it to be labeled a public violation, it is evident that the Rabbis were not anxious, nor did they make it easy, to characterize Jews as apostates for violating the Sabbath.

Why do some rabbis refuse to allow a Sabbath violator to sign as a witness on a *ketuba*?

According to talmudic law a Jew who violates the Sabbath publicly is labeled an apostate—one no longer to be trusted. Rabbis who are adherents to the strict letter of Jewish law will not permit such a violator to sign as a witness on a Jewish marriage contract *(ketuba)*.

Ultra-Orthodox rabbis such as Moshe Feinstein have ruled as invalid marriages performed by Reform rabbis because the Reform *ketubot* must be presumed to have been witnessed by Sabbath violators. In one responsum[34] he allowed an *aguna* to remarry after ascertaining that her first marriage had been performed by a Reform rabbi. (An *aguna* is a "chained woman." She is unable to remarry because it is not known whether her missing husband is dead or alive.) The presumption was that the witnesses to the Reform marriage contract were not Sabbath observers, and hence the marriage was invalid, freeing the woman to remarry.

Why do some Orthodox Jews consider non-Orthodox Jews a threat to Judaism?

Ultra-Orthodox Jews consider nonobservant Jews sinners (particularly because they do not adhere to the Sabbath laws as prescribed in the *Code of Jewish Law)*, and as such they cannot be recognized as complete or reliable Jews. The umbrella organization of the ultra-Orthodox, the Agudat Yisrael World Organization, considers Reform Judaism to be "creating a separate body of Jews into which religious Jews cannot marry."

Rabbi Moshe Sherer, president of the American Agudat Yisrael, labels Conservative Judaism a greater threat than Reform Judaism because it pretends to be traditional and is "more able to mislead the public into thinking it is authentic Judaism."

Probably the most outspoken critic of Conservative and Reform Judaism is Rabbi Moshe Feinstein, who addresses questions on this subject in his six volumes of responsa entitled *Igrot Moshe*.

Among his rulings are:

- Reform marriages are to be deemed invalid because the witnesses to the marriage contracts are presumed to be Sabbath violators (see previous question).
- Conversions performed by Conservative rabbis are not valid because the *Bet Din* (court of three) they convene to attest to the conversion is presumed to have consisted of nonobservant Jews who deny the basic principles of Judaism.
- Orthodox rabbis and laymen should not associate with non-Orthodox Jews even in organizations where issues of *halacha* (law) are not involved.[35]

Modern Orthodox rabbis do not share the views of the ultra-Orthodox. They subscribe to the philosophy of Rabbi Samson Raphael Hirsch (1808-1888), who believed in harmonizing Judaism with the ways of the world [*Tora im derech eretz*] and in maintaining a working relationship with all elements of the Jewish community.[36]

Why do some Jews consider themselves observant even if they fail to observe many of the Jewish laws?

Most Orthodox Jews today refuse to characterize Conservative or Reform Jews as observant, primarily because not all believe in Divine Revelation in its literal sense, nor do all observe the Sabbath and other rules and regulations as mandated in the *Shulchan Aruch* (the accepted code of Jewish law). Nonetheless, many of these Jews do consider *themselves* observant.

There is an historical basis for this. In the talmudic period (the early centuries C.E.) a more tolerant view of religious commitment prevailed. Rabbi Nehemiah said, "Whoever is faithful to [observes] one commandment [*mitzva*] is worthy of having the Holy Spirit rest upon him."[37] He is accepted as a full Jew. Rabbi Akiba made the same point, adding that God considers the observance of even one commandment a fulfillment of the Covenant between Himself and Israel.[38]

Hence, it is argued that it is commitment to God that determines whether one is or is not religious. If one emulates God, as pointed out in the Talmud, he is a godly (religious) person regardless of how careful he is to observe all of the ritual laws. To emulate God, says the Talmud, means to be merciful just as He is merciful, to visit the sick just as He visits the sick, to bury the dead just as He buries the dead, to comfort mourners just as He comforts mourners.[39]

Moses Maimonides reinforced the above view in his commentary on the Mishna, where he states that if a person observes *one* of the 613 commandments *(mitzvot)* properly, with love, he merits thereby life in the world-to-come.

Why are there differing traditions about men keeping their heads covered?

There are no regulations in the Bible that require men to

keep their heads covered. The Bible does not even require headcoverings for men entering the sanctuary or participating in a religious rite or service. Only Priests were required to wear headgear (Exodus 28:4), and this when officiating at the Temple altar or when performing other Priestly functions. Scholars explain that this requirement was introduced in order to distinguish Jewish Priests from heathen priests who offered sacrifices to their deities with heads uncovered.

In talmudic times there was no established practice or binding law with regard to the covering of the head.[40] It seems clear that the custom in Babylonia, where most Jews lived, was for a man, upon rising in the morning, to place a kerchief (called a *sudara* in Aramaic) over his head and to recite the blessing, "Blessed is He who crowns Israel with glory." This would indicate that men did keep their heads covered. Yet, on the other hand, the Talmud also states that the average man did not always keep his head covered.[41]

We also know from the Talmud that Babylonian scholars wore a *special* headcovering which symbolized their status.[42] The learned Rabbi Chia bar Abba, a third-century Babylonian-born Palestinian, once reprimanded his fellow Palestinian scholar Joshua ben Levi for wearing a plain kerchief rather than a scholar's cap on his head.[43] In time, the habit of scholars covering their heads spread to the masses, and it became increasingly common for the average man to wear a headcovering, especially when reciting prayers and studying.

The habit of covering the head that prevailed among the Jews of Babylonia did not prevail in Palestine. In Palestine, a person in mourning generally followed the ancient custom of covering the head, but the Talmud indicates that those who came to comfort him and to recite prayers before him did not cover their heads.[44] The minor talmudic tractate Soferim, which was composed in Palestine, clearly states that a man with uncovered head may serve as the Tora Reader and may lead the congregation in reciting the

Shema, something not permitted in Babylonian synagogues.[45]

This attitude of Palestinian Jewry spread to the Sephardic Jewish communities in the distant countries of Spain and Portugal. In time, the Ashkenazic communities in France and Germany began to follow the Palestinian practice. We know from historian Israel Abrahams that in the thirteenth century "boys in Germany and adults in France were called to the Tora bareheaded."

Rabbi Isaac ben Moses of Vienna (1200-1270), author of *Or Zarua,* tells us that rabbis in France prayed with uncovered heads. This would appear to have been normal conduct, because nowhere in his commentaries or responsa does Rashi (1040-1105) make reference to headcoverings worn by men, although he does mention the fact that women may not appear in public with head uncovered.

One of the leading Polish scholars of the sixteenth century, Rabbi Solomon Luria, better known as the Maharshal, was asked whether a person who suffers from headaches is permitted to eat bareheaded (and hence recite the blessings bareheaded). In his reply he states that he is aware that Rabbi Israel Isserlein (1390-1460), the leading German authority (whom Luria respected greatly), says that it is wrong to pronounce God's name without a headcovering. But he adds that he doesn't understand why Isserlein ruled in that manner, that he himself would not hesitate to utter benedictions with an uncovered head. Luria bases his argument on the Talmud (Soferim 14:12), which says that one may recite the *Shema* with uncovered head. The Maharshal concludes, "Since other teachers have said it is not proper to pray without a headcovering, he will not contradict them and will support their view."

Solomon Luria goes on to explain the reason why he thinks most Rabbis insisted that the head be covered despite the leniency of Jewish law in this regard. It is a matter of public perception, he says. Since many Jews had become accustomed to thinking of anyone who walks around bareheaded as being frivolous and disrespectful of Jewish law, it is best that Jews should not go bareheaded.

The Spanish scholar Joseph Caro, compiler of the *Shulchan Aruch,* acknowledges that some Jews go about bareheaded and even enter the synagogue and pray with uncovered heads. He does not condemn those who follow this practice, but he does suggest that to keep one's head covered is a more pious way of living *(midat chasidut).*[46]

It is clear that according to Jewish law there is no compelling reason for Jews to wear a headcovering. Nonetheless, for the reasons indicated above the Babylonian custom of keeping one's head covered not only during prayer but at all times became accepted by all traditional Jews.

Today, Orthodox Jews generally wear a skullcap *(yarmulke* in Yiddish, *kipa* in Hebrew) at all times, although some do not do so while at work or in certain social situations. Conservative Jews are of various minds. Some keep their heads covered at all times; others only when reciting prayers, studying Bible or Talmud, and at mealtime; and still others only when reciting prayers. Reform Jews do not generally wear skullcaps, but the matter is optional. Many Reform Jews do wear headcoverings during prayer.

Why has the wearing of a headcovering become associated with being a God-fearing (religious) Jew?

There are three references in the Talmud that associate "fear of heaven [God]" with keeping one's head covered.

In the first reference, the Talmud says, "Rav Huna, son of Joshua [a great third-century Babylonian scholar], would not walk four cubits [six to seven feet] without [wearing] a headcovering, for, he said, 'The *Shechina* [God's glory] is above my head.' "[47]

In a second talmudic reference, the same Rav Huna replied to a question by saying that the observance for which he hoped to be rewarded the most was "for never walking four cubits with uncovered head."[48]

The third and most commonly quoted reference in this regard notes that the mother of the prominent fourth-century Babylonian scholar Nachman ben Yitzchak was once told by astrologers that her son would become a thief. In order to foil this prediction, she never allowed her son to go about bareheaded, admonishing him always, "Cover your head so the fear of heaven [God] may be upon you, and pray [for mercy]."[49]

Why has the practice of keeping one's head covered become widespread among Orthodox and some Conservative Jews when not all authorities believe it is demanded by Jewish law?

Despite the preponderance of opinion (as indicated in the two previous questions) that the keeping of one's head covered is not required by biblical or talmudic law, and despite the fact that it was never unanimously espoused by rabbinic authorities, many observant Jews in recent centuries have shown a preference for keeping their heads covered at all times.

Probably the most plausible explanation for this development is that over the centuries Jews were accustomed to seeing Christians going about with head uncovered—particularly in church—and the uncovered head became associated with Christianity. To maintain their integrity as a community, Jews often avoided practices that were current among Christians.

Why do some Orthodox Jews wear a skullcap under their hats?

The practice of wearing a yarmulke (skullcap) under one's hat began in the Middle Ages (seventeenth century), when it was customary in German lands for one to doff his hat to a government official as a gesture of respect. In order not to be without a headcovering for even a moment, Orthodox Jews wore a skullcap under their hats. This practice is still observed by ultra-Orthodox Jews today.

Why do strictly Orthodox women keep their heads covered?

In biblical times women covered their heads with scarves or veils as a sign of chastity and modesty. To expose a woman's hair was considered a humiliation (Numbers 5:18).

In early talmudic times, it became common practice for married women to keep their heads covered.[50] Rabbi Sheshet said, "A woman's hair is sexually exciting."[51] To be out of doors with head uncovered was a serious breach of law and custom, and it constituted sufficient grounds for a man to divorce his wife without being required to pay her any of the monies normally due upon divorce, as stipulated in the marriage contract.[52]

To emphasize the importance of a woman keeping her head covered, the Talmud relates the story of a pious woman named Kimchit. Kimchit was the mother of seven sons, each of whom became a High Priest. When asked why she thought she was blessed to have so many distinguished sons, she replied, "Because the beams [posts] of my house never saw my hair."[53]

Today, only ultra-Orthodox women keep their heads covered at all times. Some wear a scarf (called a *tichl* in Yiddish); others wear a wig (called a *shaytl* in Yiddish).

Why are unmarried women not required to keep their heads covered?

The *Code of Jewish Law* states: "Married women always keep their heads covered; unmarried women do not have to keep their heads covered."[54] The purpose of the legislation is to make perfectly clear to men the marital status of a woman.

Why are there conflicting views about whether one must reside in Israel in order to be a fulfilled Jew?

Jews have always felt a strong attraction and devotion

to the Land of Israel *(Eretz Yisrael).* This is traceable to the covenant made between God and Abraham in which the Land of Israel was promised to Abraham and his descendants (Genesis 12). To live on the Land became a requirement of Jewish law. "A person who dwells in the Diaspora," says the Talmud, "is like one who has no God."[55] And in the same talmudic tractate there is a complementary statement: "Whoever lives outside of Israel may be regarded as one who worships idols."[56]

The great thirteenth-century Spanish scholar Moses ben Nachman (Nachmanides) supported the talmudic position when he affirmed that settling in Israel is a positive Tora commandment. He himself spent the last three years of his life in Palestine.

Throughout the centuries individuals, and occasionally small groups, have taken the talmudic caveat seriously and have returned to the Holy Land. Nevertheless, this activity, known as *aliya,* meaning "going up [to settle in Israel]," was not particularly noticed, nor did it take on great significance, until 1948, when the State of Israel was created.

However, even as far back as talmudic times, many have opposed the concept of *aliya* on grounds that it interferes with the fulfillment of biblical prophecy. Jeremiah said, "They [Israel, the defeated nation] shall be carried to Babylon and shall remain there [in the Diaspora] until the day I [God] remember them" (Jeremiah 27:22). To Rabbi Judah this meant, "Whoever goes up [returns] from Babylon [the Diaspora] to Israel transgresses a positive commandment of the Tora."[57] God must be the instrument through which Jews will return to Israel.

Today, a considerable number of ultra-Orthodox Jews continue to accept the view of Rabbi Judah, believing, as Jeremiah implied, that only through divine intervention can the Children of Israel be returned to Israel. Typical of those who support this position are members of the Satmar chassidic sect, which originated in Hungary. In 1953 Rabbi Joel Teitelbaum (1888-1979) became the leader of the ultra-Orthodox Neturei Karta community in Jerusalem, but he spent little time there. Although he visited the community every few years, he spent most of his time in his Brooklyn headquarters.[58]

Why are Jews sometimes excommunicated?

In talmudic and later times excommunication, known in Hebrew as *cherem* (sometimes spelled *herem*), was employed to control the religious life of the community. The *cherem* was used—and to a much lesser extent continues to be used today—as a means of enforcing Jewish law in general and specific local laws in particular.

The Talmud[59] cites twenty-four offenses punishable by excommunication. Among these are

- insulting a learned man, even after his death
- insulting a messenger of the court
- refusing to appear before the court at the appointed time
- violating the second day of a holiday
- testifying against a fellow Jew in a Gentile court, which has caused him to lose money he would not have lost if the case were brought before a Jewish court
- taking the name of God in vain
- causing others to profane the name of God
- tempting another person to sin
- selling nonkosher meat as kosher meat

These are some of the offenses for which a ban on an individual might be proclaimed. The ban has usually been issued by a rabbinic court after the offender has been duly warned about his offensive conduct. Sometimes the *cherem* was pronounced by an individual rabbi or even a layman who felt wronged by another member of the community. The *cherem*, which might last anywhere from a day to several years, may prohibit members of the community from having not only social dealings with the individual charged but business dealings as well.

Among the forms of excommunication sometimes imposed are denial of eligibility for public office, denial of the right to be called to the Tora, denial of eligibility to be counted as one of a *minyan,* denial of the right to have one's children attend school or one's wife attend synagogue services.

The excommunication ends when the time period that was proclaimed has elapsed and the individual has repented and begged forgiveness. If the offender does not repent, the ban is extended.

One of the most famous contemporary examples of a person being placed in *cherem* was when Rabbi Mordecai M. Kaplan, founder of the Reconstructionist movement, was excommunicated by the Orthodox rabbinate because of his unorthodox views.

Why were the works of Moses Maimonides banned by members of the Jewish community and by the Church?

As explained in the previous question, *cherem* has been an instrument used by the rabbinic leadership of a community to isolate Jews who have strayed from the "right" path. The expectation was that the isolation would force these individuals to reconsider their actions and beliefs. But *cherem* has also been used by segments of the Jewish population to ban the writings of an individual. Rabbi Moses ben Maimon, better known as Moses Maimonides or the Rambam, is a case in point.

Maimonides, one of the giants of Jewish history, was born in Cordova, Spain, in 1135. In 1148, after escaping persecution at the hands of the fanatical Almohades Muslims, Maimonides and his family fled to Morocco, North Africa. Finally, after years of moving about, the family settled in Egypt, where Moses Maimonides (who had studied medicine in the meantime) served as a physician and leader of the Jewish community of Cairo. He died in Cairo in 1204 and was buried in Tiberias, Palestine.

The great literary achievements of Maimonides were his encyclopedic code of Jewish law, the *Mishneh Torah,* and his philosophical work, *Moreh Nevuchim (Guide for the Perplexed).* While these two monumental works earned Maimonides worldwide acclaim, they also brought upon him the scorn of many scholars and the banning of his books by the rabbis of northern France shortly after his death. Objecting to the *cherem* placed on Maimonides, the scholars and communal leaders of southern France and Spain countered by issuing a *cherem* of their own against Maimonides' opponents. Almost two centuries were to pass before the feud fully subsided. Even the Church had become involved: in 1232, convinced that Maimonides was a heretic, the Dominicans burned his books.

Among the opinions expressed by Maimonides that aroused the ire of the northern French rabbis and many leaders of Jewish communities in various countries were these:

- In the Introduction to his *Mishneh Torah* he made the claim that, because of its systematic presentation, his new code of Jewish law would replace the Talmud, and it would therefore be unnecessary to consult it with much frequency in the future. Many resented this claim. They even resented the name of his work, *Mishneh Torah,* meaning "repetition of the Tora." Many chose to call Maimonides' code *Yad Hachazaka,* "the strong hand." They chose the name *Yad* because the numerical value of the Hebrew word *yad* is 14, which corresponds to the number of books in the code.
- He attempted to rationalize and explain away miracles.
- His writings left the impression that he was not affirming the resurrection of the dead as a Jewish belief.
- He did not accept everything in the Bible literally. He conceived of God as not having human form (of not being anthropomorphic).

Why was the philosopher Baruch Spinoza excommunicated by the Jewish community?

Like Moses Maimonides, Baruch Spinoza was looked upon with distrust by certain elements within the Jewish community. He was born in Amsterdam in 1632, just a few years after his parents had fled Portugal. By age 15 Spinoza had become thoroughly acquainted with the teachings of all the great Jewish philosophers and the foremost natural scientists. Reason became his god, and he would not countenance beliefs founded on superstition or faulty thinking.

Spinoza rejected the Mosaic authorship of the Pentateuch and was critical of its internal contradictions. He argued that God and Nature are one, and that God acts only in accordance with the laws of His own nature, which are totally logical. This ruled out belief in miracles or in the supernatural or in God's transcendence. It also ruled out any interplay between God and man.

Slowly Spinoza alienated himself from traditional Judaism. He stopped attending synagogue and began influencing young people to follow his lead. The leaders of the Jewish community in Amsterdam became alarmed upon learning that Spinoza was spreading radical ideas about God and particularly about immortality. Not terribly secure politically, the leaders feared that his teachings, which were contrary to those of the Church, would offend the Christian community. Such blasphemies, they felt, might be used to justify the expulsion of the Jews from Amsterdam, for their presence there at this time was merely tolerated.

The community elders pleaded with Spinoza to recant his heresies, but the rebel refused. As a consequence, in 1656 Spinoza was excommunicated by the Sephardic community. Members of the community ceased all contact with him and even members of his own family turned against him.

Spinoza was not terribly upset at having been placed in *cherem*. Able to earn a living by giving private lessons and later by grinding lenses, he continued his studies and his philosophical writings until his death in 1677. Although Spinoza never recanted and was never formally returned to the Jewish fold, the Jewish community of later centuries harbored no ill-will toward him and his thinking.

Why did Rabbenu Gershom issue a series of enactments revolutionizing Jewish life?

In order to correct many abuses among Jews of Western Europe, about the year 1000 a series of enactments was introduced by Rabbi Gershom ben Judah. These ordinances became known in Hebrew as *Takanot d'Rabbenu Gershom* ("Ordinances of our Rabbi Gershom"), and violators of them were placed in *cherem* (excommunication).

Rabbenu Gershom (965-1040) was the leading rabbi of the century. A brilliant scholar, he founded a number of academies on both sides of the Rhine while serving as the Rabbi of Mainz, Germany. Rabbi Gershom's reputation as an outstanding teacher, plus his fine personal qualities, earned for him the respect of Jewish communities throughout Europe, particularly those in Germany, France, and Italy. Questions were addressed to him from all parts of the Diaspora, and he soon became known as Rabbenu Gershom Meor Hagola, meaning "our Rabbi Gershom, the Light [Luminary] of the Diaspora."

At a meeting of the leading rabbis of Western Europe which he convened, the following ordinances were introduced by Rabbenu Gershom:

- Polygamy was unequivocally banned. While polygamy had been condemned much earlier, not all European Jews had remained monogamous. This was due largely to the influence of Islamic communities in which polygamy was commonplace.
- A ban was placed on unilateral divorces. A man could no longer divorce a wife without her consent. This ancient talmudic law had often been violated.
- A ban was placed on all members of the community

who mocked or mistreated a person who had converted to Christianity under duress and was now returning to the Jewish fold. Rabbenu Gershom further threatened to excommunicate anyone who refused to grant the returnees full participation in the social life of the community.

- A ban was placed on all who cut pages out of books not belonging to them.
- A ban was placed on persons who read letters not addressed to them.

Rabbenu Gershom died in 1040, the year Rashi was born, although some historians note Rabbi Gershom's year of death as 1028.

CHAPTER 2

Judaism and Christianity

INTRODUCTION

Original sin, the virgin birth, the Trinity, and vicarious atonement are among the concepts that Christians embrace but Jews reject. Over the centuries, and particularly in the Middle Ages, the Church has tried to force its beliefs upon Jews. Disputations (organized debates) were set up, and Jews were called upon to send their most illustrious scholars to debate Christian scholars on matters of theology and Church doctrine. Often it was apostate Jewish scholars who represented the Church and even organized these confrontations, the only purpose of which was to prove the superiority of Christianity and embarrass the Jewish community.

One of the first of the public debates was instigated by the converted Jew Nicholas Donin. In 1239, he denounced the "blasphemies" of the Talmud to Pope Gregory IX, claiming that the Rabbis had perverted the God-given teachings of the Bible by reinterpreting them in the Talmud.

The scholar Rabbi Yechiel ben Yosef of Paris was ordered to head a delegation of four prominent French scholars to debate the issue. Predictably, the rabbis lost the debate, and as a result the Talmud was burned in the streets of Paris in 1240.

In 1261, a debate was held before King James of Aragon and his court. The Jewish apostate Pablo Christiani and others presented the Christian case, and Nachmanides was the sole Jewish spokesman. Nachmanides was so convincing in his presentation that the Church, fearing that he might influence Christians and weaken their faith, forced him to leave Spain.

The last great public debate, the Disputation of Tortosa, extended over two years (1413-14), and many prominent rabbis and scholars were compelled by official command to come to Tortosa to participate. The disputation was organized and led by the apostate Joshua Lorki, also known as Geronimo de Santa Fé, and the antipope Benedict XIII. Four Jewish scholars, the most prominent of whom was the Spanish philosopher Joseph Albo from Castille, presented the Jewish argument. His famous work, *Sefer Halkarim (Book of Principles),* sums up the position taken by Jewish scholars at the debate. The ugly atmosphere created by the Disputation of Tortosa led to many anti-Semitic incidents, and many Jews during this period submitted to baptism.

Through the public disputations, the Church was eager to prove the validity of its theological beliefs, and since in many countries the Church held temporal power, the debates assumed quasi-legal status. Nevertheless, no matter what public pressure was applied to Jews, they continued to cling to their own beliefs.

Dr. Otto Piper, Professor of Systematic Theology at Princeton Theological Seminary, understood the "stubbornness of Jews," as the Church characterized it. In his *God in History* (1939), he summed up the reason for Jews maintaining dogged loyalty to their roots: "If Jews were to recognize Jesus as their Messiah and Savior," he wrote, "they would no longer be Jews."

Ludwig Lewisohn was convinced that Jewish strength is derived from "an island within." He explained this as a core of loyalty in each Jew that impels him to turn a stiff neck to all who would not allow him the freedom to make his own choices in matters of religion and conscience.

Despite the long history of confrontation between Jews

and Christians, Jews continue to seek ways of living in peace with the non-Jewish community. They continue to emphasize that the righteous of all peoples, Christians included, have a share in the world-to-come. Jews believe in maintaining goodwill and amity with those with whom they have fundamental differences. Goodwill does not mean obliterating differences but understanding them.

It is this belief that motivated the great German critic and poet Gotthold Ephraim Lessing to write his famous philosophical drama *Nathan the Wise* (1779). Lessing, a Christian, had a good Jewish friend, namely Moses Mendelssohn. In an attempt to moderate the anti-Jewish mood that prevailed in Germany in the eighteenth century, Lessing, through his play, was issuing a plea for understanding and tolerance. His friend Mendelssohn served as the model for the Jew in the play.

In the play's most significant and dramatic scene, at a meeting between Nathan and a friar, the friar, touched by Nathan's beautiful character, cries out: "Nathan! Nathan! You are a Christian! By God, you are a Christian! There never was a better Christian!"

And Nathan replies: "We are of one mind! For that which makes me, in your eyes, a Christian, makes you, in my eyes, a Jew!"

This chapter highlights some of the major differences between Jew and Christian, but in the process the areas of agreement and shared values become clear as well.

———□———

Why does Judaism reject the doctrine of original sin?

St. Augustine (354-430) was the first theologian to teach that man is born into this world in a state of sin. The basis of this belief is the Bible (Genesis 3:17-19) where Adam is described as having disobeyed God by eating the forbidden fruit of the tree of knowledge in the Garden of Eden. This, the first sin of man, became known as original sin.

Many Christians today, particularly members of the Anglican, Roman Catholic, Lutheran, Methodist, and Presbyterian Churches, subscribe to this belief. They maintain that the sin of Adam was transferred to all future generations, tainting even the unborn. Substantiation for this view is found in the New Testament (Romans 5:12) where Paul says, "Wherefore as by one man sin entered into the world, and death by sin; and so death passed upon all men, for that all have sinned." And Paul adds, "By one man's disobedience many were made sinners."

How does man rid himself of the burden of original sin? Christianity answers that it is only through the acceptance of Jesus Christ that the "grace" of God can return to man. A Christian need only believe in Jesus to be saved. Nothing else is required of him.

The doctrine of original sin is totally unacceptable to Jews (as it is to Fundamentalist Christian sects such as the Baptists and Assemblies of God). Jews believe that man enters the world free of sin, with a soul that is pure and innocent and untainted. And while there were some Jewish teachers in talmudic times who believed that death was a punishment brought upon mankind on account of Adam's sin, the dominant view by far was that man sins because he is not a perfect being, and not, as Christianity teaches, because he is *inherently* sinful.[1]

Why do Jews reject the Christian concept of vicarious atonement?

According to Christian teaching (I Corinthians 15:22) the burden of original sin was lifted from man when Jesus died for him upon the Cross. Jesus was the sacrificial lamb through whom man, born into a state of sin, was saved and restored to an untainted state. This concept of vicarious atonement, which Christians believe was foretold in the prophecy of Isaiah (particularly Chapter 53), is at variance with Jewish belief, which holds not only that man was *not* born into sin but that every individual is responsible for his own actions.

Judaism, from the time of Moses, has taught that a third party cannot bring to an individual absolution or salvation. Moses asked God that he alone be allowed to accept the punishment for Israel's sin of worshipping the Golden Calf (Exodus 32:33). God responded that whosoever has sinned shall suffer. This view was reiterated in Deuteronomy (24:16): "The fathers shall not be put to death for the children, neither shall the children be put to death for the fathers; every man shall be put to death for his own sin." The prophets Jeremiah (31:29-30) and Ezekiel (18:2) repeat this concept.

While Judaism definitely opposes the idea of one human being vicariously atoning through another, it does not completely rule out vicarious atonement through animals or objects. The Bible speaks of the *sa'ir laazazel,* the scapegoat that bore the sins of the Children of Israel and was sent out into the desert on Yom Kippur (Leviticus 16:10).

To this day, the practices of *Kaparot*—in which a hen, rooster, or money is used as a medium through which one rids himself of his sins—is still in vogue.

Why do Christians and Jews disagree on which species of fruit Adam and Eve ate in the Garden of Eden?

The Bible does not specify the kind of fruit Eve offered Adam. It merely says (Genesis 3:6), "And when the woman saw that the tree [of knowledge] was good for food . . . she took of the fruit thereof and did eat; and she also gave some to her husband and he ate it." Nowhere in the chapter is the name of the fruit mentioned.

In the Christian tradition, the fruit that Eve offered Adam is an apple. This is how the Vulgate (Latin translation of the Bible) translates the words of the Hebrew Bible. In the Jewish tradition, "the fruit of the tree" is said to be the fig because the following verse (Genesis 3:7) says that as a result of eating the fruit, "the eyes of both [Adam and Eve] were opened, and they realized they were naked; so they sewed together fig leaves and made for themselves aprons." It is reasonable to assume that since a fig tree supplied Adam and Eve with leaves, it was of the fruit of that very tree that they ate.

The Talmud and Midrash suggest other fruits that might have been eaten by Adam and Eve.[2] (These are usually based on homiletical interpretations.) Among the fruits mentioned are the *etrog* (citron) and the carob. Some even go so far as to say that it was wheat that was eaten, because the Hebrew word for wheat, *chita,* is similar to the Hebrew word for sin, *chet.*

Why do Jews reject the Christian dogma of the virgin birth?

Based on Isaiah 7:14, Christians claim that the birth of Jesus was predicted long before the event. The verse reads, "Behold, the *alma* shall conceive and bear a son and shall call him Immanuel [literally, 'God is with us']." Although the Hebrew word *alma* literally means "young woman," when the Gospel of Matthew (1:23) cites the verse from Isaiah, it translates *alma* as "virgin." This translation is useful in supporting the contention that the miraculous birth of Jesus was predicted in the Old Testament.

Although the Septuagint, written by Jews, translates *alma* as "virgin," the concept of a miracle such as a virgin birth runs counter to what normative Judaism can accept as a miracle (see question on miracles in Chapter Seven). Jewish scholars reject the idea of the virgin birth because, they point out, in Isaiah 7:14 the word *alma* is part of the Hebrew phrase *ha-alma hara,* meaning "the *alma* is pregnant." Since the present tense is used, it is clear that the young woman was already pregnant and hence not a virgin. This being the case, the verse cannot be cited as a prediction of the future.

Jewish scholars, supported by many Christian scholars, have also noted that the word *alma* in Isaiah 7:14 cannot mean "virgin" because elsewhere when the Bible wants to specify "virgin," it uses the Hebrew word *betula*.

When the Revised Standard Version of the Bible was issued in 1952, the words "young woman," not the word "virgin," were used for *alma* in its translation of Isaiah 7:14. This upset the Fundamentalist Christian community, which maintains that *alma* in Isaiah refers to the mother of Jesus, who conceived miraculously, without cohabitation with a man. These Fundamentalists expressed their vehement opposition to the new translation by holding burnings of the revised edition of the Bible.

Why is the charge that Jews crucified Jesus without historical foundation?

Crucifixion was a practice begun in Persia and later used by the Romans. The Roman ritual of crucifixion began with a severe beating. Following the beating, the person was hanged on two crossed wood beams by driving nails through the hands and feet. The body of the victim was not permitted to touch—and thereby defile—the ground. The Jewish historian Flavius Josephus, who lived in the time of Jesus, tells of thousands of Jews who were crucified by the Romans. It is an established fact that crucifixion was the Roman way of executing criminals.

The Christian charge that the Jews crucified Jesus can be refuted on a number of counts:

1. By the time Jesus appeared on the scene, the Sanhedrin (the superior judicial body in Jewish life) had lost all authority to pass sentence in capital cases. The authority was held completely by the Romans. The order to execute Jesus could only have come from the supreme Roman authority, namely Pontius Pilate.

2. According to New Testament accounts in Mark (14:54) and Matthew (26:57), the Sanhedrin convened a session on the same night that Jesus was arrested; this was

Passover Eve, which in that year fell on the Sabbath. According to the Talmud,[3] this could not have occurred because (a) capital cases could legally be tried only during the day, and (b) the Sanhedrin would not have heard a case on a holiday and certainly not on a Sabbath. The Gospel of Luke (22:54,66) does not agree with the other two Synoptic Gospels (Mark and Matthew) on this point. Luke says that the Sanhedrin met in the morning of that day.

3. While crucifixion was a method of capital punishment widely used by the Romans, there is no evidence of it ever having been used by Jews.[4] The Jewish methods of execution were stoning, burning, strangling, and slaying by the sword. The first three methods are mentioned in the Bible, and the fourth is mentioned in the Talmud.[5]

Why over the centuries have Jews been labeled "Christ-killers"?

Pontius Pilate, the Roman governor of Palestine in the time of Jesus, is portrayed in the New Testament as a leader without control over events. Although the Book of Matthew describes him as accusing Jesus of being the King of the Jews and hence a threat to Roman authority, Pontius is presented as unwilling to condemn Jesus and sentence him to execution. The blame for the Crucifixion is placed on the "chief Priests and the elders," who cry out, "Let him be crucified" (Matthew 27:11-25). Pontius Pilate then literally washes his hands in public and says, "This blood is not shed by my hands," while the Jews respond boastfully, "His [Jesus's] blood be upon us and our children." Here, Matthew shifts the guilt for the Crucifixion from the Romans to the Jews.

This account is the basis for the twenty-century-old libel which labels Jews as Christ-killers. Some Christian New Testament scholars have explained away Matthew's representation of Pilate as a victim of circumstances rather than as a ruthless ruler responsible for the execution of

Jesus. They point out that when the Gospels were written, relations between the emerging Church and the Jewish community were extremely strained, and new Christians were eager to portray Jews unfavorably.

Why does the Judas incident carry anti-Semitic overtones?

According to the Gospel of Matthew, Judas Iscariot, one of the disciples of Jesus, pointed Jesus out to the representatives of the Jewish community who were looking for him "in order to arrest Jesus by stealth and to kill him" (Matthew 26:4). For this betrayal Judas was paid thirty pieces of silver, which he later, upon repenting, turned over to the Temple treasury. The Temple Priests used this money to buy burial ground for Jesus.

Some students of the Bible believe that the attention that has been paid the Judas incident in Christian theology over the centuries has been part of a conscious effort to attach Jewish responsibility to the death of Jesus. The name "Judas" is so close in sound to "Jews" that when Christians condemn Judas as a betrayer of Jesus, it has the effect of condemning the Jews as well.

When the word "Judas" is used in common parlance, it has the connotation of traitor, money-grubber, one who will sell his soul for money. Whether intended or not, when one hears "Judas," subconsciously or otherwise he thinks "Jew."

Why do Jews not accept the belief that Jesus was a performer of miracles?

The Gospel of John advances the idea that the miracles performed by Jesus are proof of his divine nature. When Jesus heals the incurable, revives the dead, walks on water, transforms water into wine, feeds a crowd of 5,000 for three days with only five loaves of bread and two small fish, raises his friend Lazarus from the grave, and performs some of the other forty miracles attributed to him in the New Testament, he is demonstrating that he is God Incarnate, that is, God in the flesh. John quotes Jesus as having said, "Believe the works [miracles] that you may know and understand that the Father is in me and I am in the Father" (10:38).

Judaism rejects the idea that the laws of nature can be contravened. As far back as early talmudic times, opinions were expressed by the Rabbis that the miracles of the Bible were not breaks with nature but events programmed into nature at the time of Creation. (See Chapter Seven for a fuller discussion of miracles.) According to the traditional interpretation of Scripture, although the Bible does describe a number of "miraculous" occurrences, these cannot be said to be "supernatural" because even God Himself would be unwilling to contravene the natural laws He had established.

This view of miracles is one to which Jewish philosophers generally have subscribed throughout the ages. "Miracle workers" who have appeared on the scene from time to time have never been accepted by mainstream Judaism.

Why were the times ripe in the days of Jesus for Jews to accept him as the Messiah?

For a full century following the death of Jesus, the Jews of Palestine suffered under the yoke of the occupying Roman forces. Their political and military stranglehold left the country in desperate straits, and many among the poverty-stricken population lived in deplorable conditions.

Efforts at rebellion failed and hope for a brighter future waned. Conditions were therefore ripe for the ideas of preachers who promised a better life. Flavius Josephus, the great Jewish Palestinian historian who lived in the first century C.E., records how in the years before and after the destruction of the Second Temple in the year 70 men came forward claiming to be the Redeemer foretold by the Jewish prophets. Jesus was one of those men who through his preaching was successful in attracting a following. He offered the poor and oppressed hope for a better world. But in his lifetime and for many decades that followed, those who claimed that Jesus was the Messiah, the one whose coming the prophets had prophesied, were unable to win over the oppressed Jewish masses.

Why after the death of Jesus were most Jews reluctant to accept him as the Messiah?

Of the Jews living in Palestine in the early centuries following the death of Jesus, relatively few accepted him as the Messiah whose coming, some claimed, was predicted by the prophets of Israel. In Jewish tradition, the arrival of the Messiah was to bring with it the amelioration of oppressive conditions and the restoration of Israel to its former glory. Maimonides summarized what Jews looked forward to in the Messianic Age: "There will be no hunger or war, no jealousy or strife; prosperity will be universal; and the world's chief occupation will be to know the Lord."[6] Since these conditions did not come to pass, the idea of Jesus as the Messiah never took root among Jews, and the followers of Jesus therefore turned to the pagan community in search of converts.

Why do Jewish scholars believe that Jesus did not think of himself as the Messiah?

Many Jewish scholars believe that Jesus considered himself a prophet only. They reject the contention of Christian scholars that when Jesus used the phrase "Son of Man" in his preaching (first mentioned in Daniel 7:13, where the Aramaic phrase *bar enash* is used), he was referring to himself as the Messiah. The phrase "Son of Man," in the Jewish view, is used in the third person, and more likely than not, when Jesus used the phrase he was referring to someone other than himself. Jewish scholars also point to the fact that there is little evidence in the Synoptic Gospels (Matthew, Mark, Luke)—the earliest accounts of the life of Jesus—that Jesus regarded himself as the Messiah.

Why are most Jews unwilling to regard Jesus as a prophet?

Over the years Christian as well as some Jewish scholars and writers have been making the point that although Jews may not be willing to accept Jesus as the Messiah or the Son of God, they should at least accept him as a prophet.

This thesis is rejected because none of the prophets of Israel spoke in his own name; none ever presented himself as the originator of his own prophecies. The Jewish prophets considered themselves the mouthpiece of God. God, they believed, was speaking through them. For this reason, Isaiah, Jeremiah, Ezekiel, and the other Hebrew prophets introduce their prophecies and admonitions with the words, "Thus saith the Lord."

When Jesus introduces his prophecies and admonitions, he does so with the words, "I say unto you," clearly suggesting that he saw himself as *the* authority. This attitude is reflected in many New Testament passages. In Matthew (9:6), for example, Jesus represents himself as "the Son of Man who has power on earth to forgive sins." In John (13:13), Jesus says, "Ye call me 'Master' and 'Lord'; and ye say well; for so I am." Since Jesus portrayed himself as more than a spokesman of the Lord, Jews are unable to accept him as a prophet.[7]

Why do Jews not accept the Christian idea that God became man in Jesus?

The unity of God and His incorporeality is a basic Jewish belief. The Talmud contains many passages reflecting this, and the twelfth-century scholar Moses Maimonides later emphasized it in his Thirteen Articles of Faith. Maimonides condemns anyone who takes literally such biblical expressions as "the hand of God" or "the finger of God" or Moses viewing "the back of God."

The *Yigdal* hymn, which was written by David ben

Judah Dayan in the fourteenth century and which is to be found in all prayerbooks today, is based on the creed of Maimonides. The hymn expresses the Jewish belief that God is spiritual in nature, that He is without body, without human form. This tenet runs counter to the doctrine of incarnation accepted by most Christian denominations, including some of the most progressive. According to the Christian doctrine of incarnation, God transformed himself into human life in the form of Jesus. To Jews, who believe that God is One and unchangeable, this doctrine is unacceptable.

Why do Christians use the term "Old Testament" for the Jewish Scriptures?

In Christian belief, Jesus came to bring a new Covenant that was established through the shedding of his blood just as the Covenant at Sinai had been established with the shedding of sacrificial blood (Exodus 24:8).

When they came to categorize the two Covenants, the word "Testament" was used. Testament was the Latin translation of the Greek *diatheke,* used in the Septuagint for the Hebrew *brit* (covenant). Since the Christians spoke of their writings as a "New Testament," the first Covenant automatically became the "Old Testament." The indications "new" and "old" were simply indications of time. For Christians, the New Testament fulfills the Old Testament.

Why is so little written in the Talmud about Jesus?

Jesus appeared at a time of turmoil in Jewish history, when the Herods and the Roman procurators occupied center stage in Jewish history. Jesus and his small group of followers were relatively insignificant. By the time the Talmud was written down in its final form some 500 years after the death of Jesus, little or no information about him was available. Consequently few references to Jesus appear in the early editions of the Talmud, and as of 1580 the Church forced the Jews to expunge all references to Jesus from future editions. (See next question on Talmud censorship.)

Generally speaking, the Talmud has little to say about events—including some major ones—that occurred during the Second Temple period (approximately 500 B.C.E. to 70 C.E.). For example, minimal reference is made to the important struggle of the Maccabeans against the Syrian-Greeks (second century B.C.E.), and had it not been for the Books of the Apocrypha (Maccabees I and II) and the Greek writings of Josephus, the struggle would not be known of today. In fact, were the Talmud the only source of information about that period, we would not even know that a man named Judas Maccabaeus existed.

Why did the Christian Church censor the Talmud?

As early as the seventh and eighth centuries, the Christian Church, believing that the Talmud contained "blasphemous" material, took steps to prohibit Jews from studying it. These initial efforts failed, but over subsequent centuries, at the urging of educated Jewish converts to Christianity, new attempts at suppression were made. In the thirteenth century, an anti-Talmud campaign was begun, and it reached its height in 1240 with the burning of copies of the Talmud in the streets of Paris by Pope Gregory IX. Such incidents were repeated in many European cities in the years that followed.

In 1564, at a Church synod held in Trent, Pope Pius IV ruled that the Talmud could be distributed on condition that passages considered by the Church as an affront to Christianity be deleted. As a result of this edict, an edition of the Talmud was printed in Basel, Switzerland, under the supervision of censor Father Marco Marino, who ordered many passages deleted on the ground that they were insulting to Christians or various other groups.

Of the numerous changes demanded, the most basic involved the use of the word *Talmud*. For some unexplained reason, *Talmud* was replaced by the word *Shas,* an acronym for the Hebrew words *shisha sedarim,* meaning "six orders [of the Mishna]," or by the word *Gemara,* which strictly speaking is only that part of the Talmud that complements and explains the Mishna. Both words, *Shas* and *Gemara,* are still used today as synonyms for *Talmud.*

Another problem for Christian censors was the word *goy,* which means "Gentile" as well as "nation." Wherever the word *goy* occurred in the Talmud, censors changed it to *akum,* an acronym for the Hebrew words *oved kochavim umazalot,* "worshipper of the stars." When one spiteful Jewish convert to Christianity suggested to the censors that the word *akum* has a derogatory meaning, being the acronym for "worshipper of Christ and Mary," they would not permit it to be used, and other words were substituted for the word *goy.* The most commonly used were *kuti,* meaning "Samaritan," and *kushi,* meaning "Kushite" or "African." These substitutions often left scholars with a text that was confusing.[8]

The censors were particularly watchful for references to Jesus and to Christianity that they sensed were offensive. Most such references were changed or were completely omitted even when they were not actually offensive. For example, in order not to offend celibate monks (and Jesus himself, who was unmarried), one Christian censor of the Talmud changed a text which originally read, "An unmarried man is not a man in the full sense [of the word]," to read, "A *Jew* who has no wife cannot be called a man." Our present editions of the Talmud contain the original wording.[9]

Why are many Jews averse to using the term "Jesus Christ"?

The word "Christ" is from the Greek *Xristos (christos),* meaning "the anointed one [Messiah]." Originally, Jesus was referred to as "Jesus the Christ," but the form was later shortened to "Jesus Christ." Since Jesus Christ means "Jesus the Messiah," many Jews refrain from using the phrase, for to do so would be to acknowledge that Jesus is in fact the Messiah. In Jewish tradition, the Messiah has not yet appeared. (See the next question.)

Why are some non-Jews offended when Jews use the abbreviated form "Xmas" for "Christmas"?

Some Jews prefer to use the abbreviated form "Xmas" so as to avoid writing the word "Christmas." Oddly enough, the use of Xmas for Christmas is not a Jewish innovation, nor is its use confined to Jews. The abbreviation was popularized by the print media to conserve space. Some Christians object to the use of Xmas, considering it a sign of disrespect and an attempt by nonbelievers to rid Christmas of its central meaning. However, Christian scholars have explained that use of the abbreviation should not be thought of as an affront to Christians because "X" is the first letter of the Greek word *Xristos*. "Mas" is the abbreviated form of the word "mass." Put together, they mean "worship for Christ."

Why does Jewish law not consider the Christian belief in the Trinity to be idolatrous?

The Christian belief in the Trinity—the Father, the Son, and the Holy Spirit—has been viewed by Jewish scholars in two ways. To people such as Moses Maimonides (1135-1204), worship of a Trinity is polytheism; he called Christians "heathens," "idolators," violators of the commandment "Thou shalt have no other gods before me" (Exodus 20:3). Maimonides, who was born in Spain but spent most of his life in countries where the dominant religion was Islam, considered only Jews and Muslims to be true monotheists. [10]

Scholars such as the French-born Rabbenu Tam (1100-1171), the grandson of Rashi who spent his life in Christian Europe, accepted the view of Christian theologians, who explained that the Trinity is consistent with the concept of *one* God. To these theologians the three personages are part of the one God; they are not individual gods. Just as spokes of a wheel are not in themselves wheels but components that are integral to the actual wheel, so the three personages are not gods but together they comprise the one God.[11]

Why do Christians often say that Christianity is a religion that preaches love while Judaism is stern and legalistic?

Christianity has always prided itself on being a religion of love and compassion while characterizing Judaism as harsh and inflexible. The most commonly cited proof for this contention is in the Gospels. Matthew 5:43-44 says:

> You have heard it said, "Thou shalt love thy neighbor and hate thine enemy." But I [Jesus] say, "Love your enemy, bless them that curse you . . ."

Matthew 5:38-39 is a second text usually quoted to prove that Judaism is legalistic, vindictive, lacking in love:

> You have heard that it was said, "An eye for an eye, a tooth for a tooth." But I say unto you, "Do not resist one who is evil. But if anyone strikes you on the right cheek, turn to him the other also."

Judaism has responded to the above allegations by explaining that in the first instance Matthew is not quoting the Bible accurately. The source of the first quotation is Leviticus 19:17-18. Verse 17 says, "Thou shalt not hate thy brother in thine heart." Verse 18 says, "Thou shalt love thy neighbor as thyself." Nowhere does the Hebrew Bible say, "Hate thine enemy," as the Gospel of Matthew reports.

Instead, one finds in the Old Testament many references suggesting that one's enemy ought to be treated well. Exodus 23:4, for example, says, "If you see your enemy's ox or donkey going astray, you should surely bring them back."

As to the second allegation, Jewish scholars have pointed out that adopting a turn-the-other-cheek philosophy, as suggested here by Matthew and repeated in the Gospel of Luke (6:29), is an unnatural way of promoting love in the world. Judaism preaches that one ought not be vindictive, that one ought not bear a grudge (Leviticus 19:18), but it does not propose that one *love* his enemy and thereby allow himself to be abused. The Jewish attitude was clearly enunciated in the Book of Proverbs and later in the Talmud. Proverbs (24:17) urges that when man's enemy falls, man should not rejoice and say, "I will do to him as he has done to me" (24:29). The Talmud, expanding upon this admonition, says, "Let not your heart be glad when your enemy falls lest the Lord see it and it displeases Him."[12]

Why do Christians say that Jews insist on "an eye for an eye"?

Scholars have long pointed out that the biblical law known in Latin as *lex talionis*, "the law of retaliation" (mentioned in Exodus 21:24, Leviticus 24:20, and Deuteronomy 19:21), is not a Jewish invention. The law, popularly known as "an eye for an eye," was widely accepted in ancient Mediterranean society. It was first enunciated by the Babylonian king Hammurabi (1728-1686 B.C.E.), who was famous for his code of law.

The Talmud found it inadvisable to follow the "eye for an eye" law literally. Long before the New Testament was written, the Rabbis suggested that the law should be interpreted to mean that if one damages another person's eye, he is to recompense the victim with money; he is not to be punished by having his own eye removed.[13]

Despite the fact that the Jewish Sages clearly state that the law of retaliation is not to be taken literally, the Gospel of Matthew (5:38-39) criticizes the Old Testament law as inhumane, emphasizing instead the "turn-the-other-cheek" philosophy.

Whatever the motivation, through the centuries the Church has continued to teach that Jews believe in *lex talionis.* It has rarely been explained to Christian laymen that the biblical law of "an eye for an eye" was reinterpreted almost 2,000 years ago. As recently as 1982, a statement issued by Pope John Paul II referred to the "cruel" Old Testament [meaning Jewish] law of "an eye for an eye."

Why does Christianity stress faith over action while Judaism believes that action is more important?

Christian theologians have long taught that faith in Jesus is more important than the Law. To Paul (Galatians 2:4), the Law—that is, the Tora—hampered the dissemination of the Gospel (the Good News) and was therefore the enemy of Christianity. The concept that the Law had been superseded by faith was accepted as basic Christian doctrine.

Although there are conflicting views in the Jewish tradition as to which is the more important—faith or action—generally the Rabbis expressed the opinion that action is more important than faith.

The Rabbis in the Midrash portray God as saying to Israel (when they were guilty of being lax in observance), "It would be far better if they [Israel] would abandon Me, but would observe [the laws] of My Tora."[14] The Rabbis felt that if a person would observe the laws *(mitzvot)* meticulously, his faith in God would be restored. In the Talmud, the Rabbis portray what will happen when man appears before God on Judgment Day. He will not be asked about his faith in God. Instead he will be asked how well he observed the Tora, particularly laws pertaining to his relationship with his fellow man.[15]

Professor Abraham J. Heschel summed up the difference between the Jewish and the Christian attitudes by emphasizing that while Christian philosophers such as Kierkegaard advocate a "leap of faith," Judaism demands a "leap of action."

Why did the Christian Church abandon ritual observance of Jewish law even though Jesus himself did not?

During his career as preacher to his fellow Jews in Palestine, Jesus was careful to point out that he had no intention of promoting the idea that observance of Jewish law should be abandoned. The Synoptic Books of the Bible (Matthew, Mark, and Luke) portray Jesus as a practicing Jew. Nonetheless, New Testament scholars have argued that Jesus did not live the life of an observant Jew. As proof, they point to Jesus's defense of his disciples' violations of Jewish law. He defended, for example, their failure to wash their hands before eating (Mark 7:5) and their having plucked ears of corn on the Sabbath (Mark 2:23). Scholars who maintain that Jesus was an observant Jew respond to this argument by saying that although in these instances Jesus defended the actions of his disciples, such defense might be expected from any leader. In itself it does not, however, constitute proof that Jesus endorsed their conduct. In fact, in Matthew (23:3) Jesus urges his followers, "Do and observe whatever they [the Scribes and the Pharisees] tell you to do."[16]

Given Jesus' portrayal as an observant Jew in the Synoptic Gospels, the total abandonment of Jewish ritual by the Christian Church seems strange. It is explained as an attempt by Church Fathers to draw a sharp distinction between Jew and Christian and thereby strengthen the Church. The abandonment is also the result of the great resistance encountered by Paul (and others) in his missionary activity among the Gentile population outside of Palestine. Paul found himself unable to win converts to Christianity when he insisted on adherence to biblical laws such as those pertaining to the Sabbath, family purity, and especially circumcision. Therefore, with regard to circumcision, for example, Paul introduced the idea that the "circumcision of the spirit," not the "circumcision of the flesh," will save man (Philippians 3:3). Paul condemned as his enemy those Christians who continued to follow the Old Jewish law of circumcision, because by their actions, he said, they were shaking the faith of ignorant Christians and were turning away Gentiles from the new message he brought them.

Why did Christians change the day on which the Sabbath is observed from Saturday to Sunday?

The Talmud describes how prayers and fasting by Jewish laymen accompanied the offering of various sacrifices in the Temple on every day of the week except Sunday. Why not on Sunday? Rabbi Yochanan, the leader of Jewry during the trying years of 66-70 C.E., immediately prior to the destruction of the Second Temple, answered, "So as not to offend the Nazarenes." Rashi comments, "They [the Nazarenes or Christians] made Sunday their holy day."[17]

Although it would appear from the comment of Rabbi Yochanan that Sunday became the day of rest for Christians soon after the death of Jesus, it was actually not until the year 321 that it became official. In that year Constantine, the emperor of Rome—the first Roman emperor to embrace Christianity—declared that Sunday is a legal holiday and the official day of worship for all Christians, thus replacing the Sabbath as proclaimed in the Ten Commandments (Exodus 20:8). Henceforth, the Sabbath was to be celebrated on the first day of the week (Sunday), the day on which, in Christian tradition, Jesus rose from the dead. The change of the day of the Sabbath from Saturday to Sunday was a sign of the complete break that was taking place between Christianity and Judaism, its mother religion. It was another way of the Christian community asserting its independence.

Although today most Christian sects observe Sunday as the Sabbath Day, the Seventh-Day Adventists continue to observe the Sabbath on Saturday because they believe that God's commandment, "Remember the Sabbath Day," refers to the seventh day of the week.

Why do Christians call themselves "spiritual Semites"?

The term "spiritual Semites" is used to underline the great spiritual patrimony that has come down to Christians from the Jewish people. In a September 6, 1938, radio message, Pius XI stated: "Through Christ and in Christ, we belong to the spiritual lineage of Abraham. . . . We are spiritual Semites."

Why are many Christians intent on winning over Jews as converts?

Unlike Judaism, which believes that all righteous people will have a share in the world-to-come, Christianity maintains that only through Jesus can one achieve salvation. Living an honest, righteous, God-fearing life is not adequate in itself; it must be accompanied by a belief in Christ as the Savior. To spread this belief, Paul was sent to tell the Gentiles about Christianity, and by the middle of the fourth century his work and that of the other disciples and followers of Jesus brought the entire Roman Empire under Christian rule.

Spreading the Gospel (that is, telling the Good News about Jesus as Savior) has been an essential part of Church activity since the days of the disciples, and Jews have long been a prime object of Christian missionaries. The history of the Jews is filled with stories of attempts made to convert Jews to Christianity. To this day, missionaries continue their efforts with great zeal because they are convinced that the Jews are being unnecessarily obstinate and that their resistance to the acceptance of Jesus as savior is impeding the Second Coming of Christ.

In the late 1960s, the Ecumenical Council was convened by the Catholic Church. Professor Abraham J. Heschel (1907-1972) was the major Jewish consultant. When the Council issued a statement expressing the hope that Jews would eventually join the Church, he took his protest directly to Pope Paul, and the Pope personally deleted the reference to conversion and mission to the Jews. In making his effective protest, Professor Heschel said, "I'd rather go to Auschwitz than give up my religion!"

In summing up his attitude toward Christian attempts at converting Jews, Heschel made this statement in a pre-recorded radio interview on February 4, 1973:

> This great, old, wise Church in Rome realizes that the existence of the Jews as Jews is so holy and so precious that the Church would collapse if the Jewish people would cease to exist. If there are some Protestant sects who still cling to this silly hope of proselytizing, I would say they are blind and deaf and dumb.

Why have the Christian Churches in recent years begun to develop a more positive attitude toward the Jewish people?

Since the Second World War there has been improvement in the attitude of most Christian Churches toward the Jewish people. Some of the factors that have led to this change are:

• The persecution and extermination of millions of Jews by the Nazis prompted an examination of conscience on the part of the Churches and their members.

• The Ecumenical Movement made Christians reassess their relationship with the Jewish people.

• The teachings of the Second Vatican Council about the Church's relationship to Jews emphasized the bonds that linked Christians and Jews and issued a powerful call to active collaboration.

• The State of Israel came to be viewed by many Christians—who are against atheistic communism—as a bastion of Western democracy in the Near East. These Christians, primarily Fundamentalists, began to advocate greater cooperation between Christians and Jews.

Why is America spoken of as a nation founded on the Judeo-Christian Ethic?

The founders of America were devoted to the Bible, the Judeo-Christian Scriptures. They were propelled to this new land by their total commitment to the principles enunciated in these Scriptures. They regarded this undeveloped land as a new Canaan that God had reserved for those dedicated to following his word.

The *laws* drawn up by the new society were based on the Bible as well as on English Common Law and on Roman Natural Law (which was itself Judeo-Christian).

Why are Christian Fundamentalists in favor of a strong Israel?

Christian Fundamentalists take every word of the Bible literally. They believe that the newly established State of Israel is part of God's plan and a fulfillment of Old Testament and New Testament prophecies. They believe that when God promised the Land of Israel to Abraham and his seed (Genesis 12) and established its boundaries (Genesis 15), this constituted an inviolable covenant. Fundamentalists believe that it is their duty to protect and support this Abrahamitic Covenant, which must be fulfilled before the Second Coming of Christ can be realized.[18]

Why does Judaism not share the Christian attitude toward asceticism?

As a means of elevating man to a higher spiritual plane, early Christianity favored abstention from any form of self-indulgence. Accordingly, it encouraged the avoidance and even the renunciation of the desires of the flesh. Abstinence from sex, food, wine, and submission to flagellation were embraced by those who followed the ascetic lifestyle. In Galatians (5:16), Paul says, "Walk in the Spirit, and ye shall not fulfill the lust of the flesh." He then goes on to say that physical cravings are the antithesis of spiritual cravings.

In biblical times, there existed Hebrew sects such as the Nazirites (Numbers 6:1-21) whose members would take vows to refrain from cutting their hair or drinking wine or other intoxicants for a specified period of time. The Bible does not applaud such conduct, for when the period of abstention ended, the Nazir was required to bring a sin-offering to atone for the sin he had committed against his own person. The Book of Jeremiah (35) describes a similar sect called the Rechabites. They lived in tents and drank no wine.

In later years, particularly between the first century B.C.E. and the first century C.E., sects of this kind continued to exist. One such sect was the Essenes, who lived on the western shore of the Dead Sea area of Palestine. They were punctilious about religious observance, studied and prayed a great deal, ate frugal meals, fasted frequently, abstained from sex, and did not marry. (The historian Josephus mentions one group of Essenes who were the exception: they *did* marry for the sole purpose of having children.)[19]

Jewish tradition is generally opposed to the ascetic way of life. The ascetic lifestyle is considered aberrant—in fact, sinful—for it reflects a rejection of the bounty and goodness God intended for man's enjoyment. Maimonides, in his *Mishneh Torah,* forbids a Jew from living a celibate life, eating no meat, drinking no wine, and generally living a life of self-deprivation.[20] This statement of Maimonides represents a summary of the beliefs of the Rabbis of the Talmud. The Jerusalem Talmud expresses the popular rabbinic attitude when it says that man will have to account before God on the Day of Judgment for every legitimate pleasure he denied himself in life.[21] Another tractate is even more direct when it asks of those who aspire to asceticism: "Were not enough things forbidden to you by the Tora that you should want to add to them?"[22]

CHAPTER 3

Jews in a Gentile World

INTRODUCTION

Although many laws in the Bible, Talmud, and later rabbinic writings were designed to limit contact between Jews and Gentiles, other laws were introduced to create a climate of friendship and peaceful coexistence between the two groups. Especially after the Roman occupation of Palestine in the first century C.E., the need for the establishment of amity between Jews and non-Jews became pronounced, and many laws and practices were introduced to help achieve it. In talmudic literature, these laws and practices were explained as *mipnay darkay shalom,* meaning "for the sake of peace," for the sake of maintaining goodwill between the Jewish and non-Jewish communities.

Rabbi Judah the Prince, the most outstanding Jewish scholar and leader of the second century B.C.E., was the first talmudic authority to espouse this policy of harmony between groups. He set the tone for future leaders by carrying on a dialogue with the Roman rulers, and owing to his political astuteness, he succeeded in maintaining goodwill and peaceful relations between the Jews and the Roman occupiers. Many early Jewish leaders followed Rabbi Judah's example. The Talmud states without equivocation: "We feed the poor of non-Jews, we comfort their mourners, and we bury their dead with the Jewish dead for the sake of peace."[1]

The desire for maintaining a positive relationship with the non-Jewish community compelled the Rabbis to be more demanding of Jews in their dealings with non-Jews than with Jews. They ruled, for example, that "it is a more serious breach of law to steal from or to deceive a Gentile than a Jew. Stealing from a Jew," they said, "violates only the law that prohibits stealing. But when one steals from a Gentile, he violates a second law, namely the commandment not to profane God's name [Exodus 30:7]."[2]

Even in medieval times, when oppressive measures against Jews were instituted by the Church, Jews continued to espouse the peaceful coexistence doctrine. Rabbi Isaac ben Moses Arama, the fifteenth-century Spanish philosopher who was forced to flee to Naples, Italy, because of the Spanish Inquisition, still found himself able to write in his famous homiletical work *Akedat Yitzchak,* "Every pious Gentile is equal to a son of Israel." The same attitude was echoed by Joseph Caro in his sixteenth-century work the *Shulchan Aruch,* which has been the authoritative code of Jewish law for over four centuries.

Although Jews have striven to live in harmony with the larger Christian world, this has not always been easy or even possible to achieve. On the one hand, the non-Jewish majority has not always been anxious or even willing to allow Jews to enter its social circles. On the other hand, rabbinic leaders, as guardians of the Jewish faith, have not always been eager for Jews to have unnecessary contact with the non-Jewish community for fear that this might lead to assimilation.

The questions in this chapter concern the relationship between Jew and Gentile. They address the problems Jews face as a minority in a non-Jewish world, and they look at the problems a non-Jew confronts in trying to understand and penetrate the Jewish world.

Why does biblical and early talmudic law prohibit even casual intermingling of Jews with Gentiles?

The Bible (Deuteronomy 7:3) forbids Jews (called Hebrews or Israelites) from intermarrying with members of pagan nations. The purpose: to prevent the monotheistic character of the then emerging Jewish nation from being diluted. In time, however, the biblical prohibition alone was found to be an insufficient deterrent. Intermarriage became increasingly common, particularly in the Greek period, after Alexander the Great conquered Palestine in 333 B.C.E. During the next two centuries paganism made serious inroads into Judaism, and the survival of the religion was threatened. The struggle of the Maccabees revolved about this issue. Adoption by Jews of Greek names such as Menelaus, Aristobulus, Hyrcanus, and Alexander was symptomatic of the insidious Hellenization of Jewish life.

The Rabbis of the early talmudic period, beginning with the second century B.C.E., understood the threat that intermingling with Gentiles posed to Jewish life, and they began the process of introducing precautionary legislation that would prevent further deterioration of Jewish observance. The legislation involved the building of a "fence" around Jewish law in order to maintain its integrity. In Hebrew this became known as establishing a *seyag laTora,* meaning "a boundary around the Tora" which one may not violate.[3]

One such precautionary measure aimed at limiting social contact between Jews and non-Jews involved the handling by Gentiles of wine to be drunk by Jews. Since the wine prepared by non-Jews (heathens in particular) was once used for idolatrous purposes (they poured wine on their altars as a libation), Jews had long been forbidden to drink their wine. The Rabbis reasoned that even though idolatry was no longer the issue, the ban against drinking wine prepared by Gentiles should continue in order to minimize social contact between the groups and thus reduce intermarriage.

Why does Jewish law condemn a Jew who deceives a Gentile?

Equating deceit with theft, the Talmud (Chulin 94a) explicitly condemns anyone who deceives his fellow man. In Jewish law, deceit is called *genevat daat,* which literally means "the stealing of one's mind." And the point is made in the Talmud that the condemnation applies to misleading and deceiving Jew and non-Jew alike.

Moses Maimonides (1135-1204) elaborates on the teaching of the Talmud and says that deception may not be engaged in when selling an article to one's neighbor. The whole truth must be told, even to the extent of informing the buyer of a defect in the article.[4]

A century later, the rabbi-preacher Moses ben Jacob of Coucy, France, expended much effort, traveling as far as Spain in an attempt to encourage Jews to live in accordance with the highest ethical standard. In his popular code[5] he writes that Jews must not deceive anyone, whether Christian, Muslim, or Jew: "God has scattered Israel among the nations so that proselytes shall be gathered unto them. If Jews behave deceitfully toward non-Jews, who will want to join them? Jews should not lie either to Jew or to Gentile, nor mislead them in any matter."

Judaism calls actions that are dishonest or misleading *chilul haShem,* a "desecration of God's name." To deceive a fellow man—Jew or non-Jew—is not only an affront to man but an affront to God.

Why is the supporting of non-Jewish charities by Jews consistent with Jewish tradition?

In the Talmud, particular importance is attached to the fact that in the Bible the command to love, to befriend, to be kind toward a stranger is mentioned no less than thirty-six times.[6] Often the command is coupled with the words "because you were a stranger in the land of Egypt" (Leviticus 22:20, Deuteronomy 10:19). These words, say the Rabbis, emphasize the importance of remembering what it means to be unloved and unwanted. The Rabbis were careful to emphasize that extra consideration must be accorded the orphan and widow.

Caring for all people in need became an integral part of Jewish life. Jews were expected to be kind and charitable, decent and righteous. So intertwined did the concepts of charity and righteousness become that the Hebrew word for righteousness—*tzedaka*—became the Hebrew word for charity. The requirement that Jews care for all who are in need—non-Jews as well as Jews—was expressed by the Talmud in this manner:

> Our Rabbis have taught: We must support the poor among the Gentiles, even as we support the poor of Israel; visit the sick of the Gentiles, even as we visit the sick of Israel; give an honorable burial to the dead of the Gentiles, even as we bury the dead of Israel with honor—all in the interests of peace.[7]

Why may a rabbi officiate at the funeral of a non-Jew?

There are occasions when a rabbi is called upon to officiate at the funeral of a Gentile either because no other minister is available or because the family of the deceased is especially fond of the rabbi. Although the propriety of a rabbi's participation in such a non-Jewish funeral is sometimes questioned, Jewish law permits it for the sake of goodwill. The *Code of Jewish Law*[8] repeats the talmudic law that urges Jews to provide an honorable burial for Gentiles when there is no one else to do so, and to bring comfort to their mourners. This would certainly imply that where the services of a rabbi are required to conduct a burial for a non-Jew, the rabbi is free and possibly obligated to offer them. Naturally, the rabbi cannot be expected to recite prayers that are Christological in nature.[9]

Why do some authorities believe that Jews should not enter church buildings?

A number of contemporary Orthodox authorities are of the opinion that it is absolutely forbidden to enter a church and worship there. Rabbi Moshe Feinstein ruled that it is even forbidden to enter a church merely to view its art and sculpture.[10] Rabbi Ovadya Yosef, the former Sephardic Chief Rabbi of Israel, who left office in 1983, absolutely forbids Jews from visiting churches. He fears that they might be influenced by the missionary activities carried on therein, and he goes so far as to warn tourist guides against allowing groups to enter church buildings. He accepts the view of Maimonides, who believed that Christians are idolators, and concludes that Christian churches are like pagan shrines.[11]

This view of Maimonides does not appear in our editions of the *Mishneh Torah*[12] and was never accepted by normative Judaism. Beginning with Rabbenu Tam, a contemporary of Maimonides, almost all authorities agree that despite their belief in a Trinity Christians are monotheists. Rabbenu Tam notes in his commentary that despite outer appearances Christians truly believe in one God, as do Jews.[13]

There is little discussion in the Responsa literature about whether one may *enter* a church building. There is, however, some discussion as to whether one may *worship* in a church building. The consensus is that there is no inherent holiness in the church structure itself, and Jews may use such a building for worship if all crosses and other religious symbols are removed. This was done during World War II, when Jews and Christians shared the same chapels.

Why is it forbidden for a Jew to be a member of a church choir?

Hymns sung by a church choir often contain references

to the Trinity: the Father, the Son, and the Holy Ghost. These hymns also contain a variety of references to Jesus as the Messiah and Savior, concepts that a Jew does not accept.

Rabbis of all denominations have expressed disapproval of Jews who join church choirs whose hymns articulate religious concepts that run contrary to the spirit of Jewish belief.[14]

Why are most Jewish denominations opposed to having non-Jews as members of a synagogue choir?

The Orthodox and Conservative rabbinate is opposed to having non-Jews as members of a synagogue choir. The Conservative position was set forth by the Committee on Law and Standards of the Rabbinical Assembly. The synagogue choir, says the committee, is an extension of the cantor. Since the cantor who represents the Jewish congregation must be a Jew, the choir members who chant portions of the liturgy must also be Jews. The committee also believes that since many of the Jewish prayers contain phrases such as "our God and God of our fathers," only one whose ancestors are in fact Jews should be reciting them.

Congregations that do permit non-Jews to be members of a synagogue choir are of the opinion that adding beautiful voices, whether those of Jews or non-Jews, to a synagogue choir will only result in the enhancement of the synagogue service.

Why is it sometimes proper for Jews to join non-Jews in celebrating their holidays?

Rabbi Moses Isserles (1525-1572), in his Notes to the Shulchan Aruch of Joseph Caro, writes that for the sake of retaining goodwill and avoiding enmity Jews who find themselves in the midst of a Gentile holiday celebration should join in the festivities. He suggests that Jews should not seek out such celebrations, but he considers it proper for Jews to send gifts to non-Jews on non-Jewish holidays.[15]

This longstanding ruling is of particular significance in modern societies where Jews are invited to attend Christmas parties and celebrations and are expected to exchange gifts with non-Jewish friends in celebration of the holiday. Apparently the problem is an old one.

What applies to Christmas applies equally to other holidays that are basically of a Christian religious nature: Halloween (All Saints' Day), Valentine's Day, and the like.

Thanksgiving, despite its religious overtones, is not a Christian holiday and is celebrated fully by American Jews.

Why do some Jews object to holding New Year's Eve parties?

Holding celebrations on the first day of the new year was common among ancient nations. The Romans, in particular, celebrated the beginning of the new year by giving gifts to each other and especially to the emperor. With these gifts they expressed best wishes for a good year and good fortune. At first, the gifts given by the Romans consisted of products of the forest, such as branches from the bay tree and palm tree; and for this reason the name Sylvester, meaning "from the forest," became associated with the new year. Later, more expensive gifts were brought. When the Romans invaded England (43 B.C.E.), their priests brought with them the New Year gift-giving custom. In England, priests cut off branches of mistletoe that grew on their sacred oaks, and these were handed out to the people as good luck charms.

Not until 487 did New Year's Day become associated with Christianity. In that year it was incorporated into the Church calendar as a holy day to celebrate the circumcision of Jesus. In the fifteenth century, the German scholar Israel Isserlein (1390-1460) noted in his book of responsa[16] that there is no real objection to sending gifts to Christians on the occasion of the New Year, for it is not really a day of worship but primarily a time of wishing friends and neighbors good luck.

Despite the fact that the New Year's celebration has lost its religious significance, and despite the fact that practically all Jews celebrate the holiday today, some authorities oppose holding New Year's parties. In 1981, Bezalel Zolti, Chief Rabbi of Jerusalem, warned hotels not to hold New Year's parties "because Sylvester celebrations may offend the sensibilities of religious people." Almost all hotels complied so that their certificates of *kashrut* would not be withdrawn.

Why do some Jews object to their children celebrating Halloween?

Halloween originated in early Roman times (before the advent of Christianity) as a holiday celebrated by Druids (priests of a religious order in ancient Gaul and Britain). The celebration marked the end of summer, and pumpkins, cornstalks, and similar products of the earth were used in the feasting and merrymaking.

In the eighth century, when the Church saw that it would not succeed in weaning the people away from observing this pagan holiday, it incorporated Halloween into the Christian calendar. The holiday would be celebrated on November the first as a day honoring all saints, hence the name All Saints' Day. The night before (October 31) was called "holy [hallowed] evening," and many of the old pagan Druid practices were retained in its celebration, including the dressing up as ghosts, goblins, witches, fairies, and elves—a variety of spirits who seek to harm humans.

Some authorities object to Jewish children participating in Halloween celebrations on the ground that the holiday is *chukat hagoy,* "a Gentile practice," in violation of the biblical commandment "You shall not follow the customs of the nation which I am casting out before you" (Leviticus 20:33). Many Jews, however, consider the holiday secular in nature and, as with New Year's, its pagan and Christian connections have long ceased to be a factor.

Why was it necessary for many Jewish communities to establish laws regulating extravagance?

From talmudic times through the Middle Ages individual Jews were often criticized by the Jewish community at large for throwing lavish parties, furnishing their homes ostentatiously, and wearing gaudy jewelry.

The Talmud describes the wedding feast Rabina made for his son in the fifth century C.E.[17] The rabbis present were growing merry, so Rabina brought out a very expensive crystal cup (or vase) and threw it to the ground, breaking it before their very eyes. The action and the noise created by it shocked the merrymakers into remembering the value of conducting one's life in a sober and socially acceptable manner.

Rabbi Solomon Luria, the sixteenth-century Polish rabbinic authority known as the Maharshal, condemns unbridled celebrations at Bar Mitzva dinners, which he says are often held "just for the purpose of enabling guests to stuff themselves with food and to carry on in an uninhibited, wild fashion."[18]

The extravagance of individual Jews not only offended the Jewish community, it earned the scorn of many Christians who considered such conduct immoral. Consequently, Jewish communities (especially those in Italy) at various times in history established what came to be known as Sumptuary Laws, which restricted the number of people who could be invited to private parties, the types of food that might be served, the amount of jewelry one could wear, the type and number of wedding gifts one could give, and the like.

Why are most Jews opposed to prayer in public schools?

Most Jews are opposed to prayer in public schools—voluntary or involuntary—not because they are opposed to permitting prayer per se, but because they are fearful of what it might lead to.

Jews recall the experience in early America when they were denied basic political rights because of the influence of the Church. Consequently, all efforts at removing the wall of separation that exists between Church and State is vigorously opposed as being in violation of the Constitution of the United States.

A small minority of Jews favors allowing prayers to be recited in public schools. This segment of the Jewish population believes that the First Amendment to the Constitution, which prohibits the establishment of a state religion, does not intend that religion be totally removed from public life. They point out that the sessions of Congress and of the Supreme Court open with prayer, and that chaplains are paid by the government to serve in all branches of the military. With this in mind, they reason that it is not improper for religion to occupy a place in the program of public schools. These Jews do not accept as legitimate the fear held by many that permitting even voluntary prayer in public schools would be opening the door to the establishment of a state religion.[19]

Why do some Christians resent being called "Gentiles"?

Although the New Testament uses the word "Gentile" often when referring to non-Jews, some Christians today object to its use. The objection is based on the erroneous assumption that the word "Gentile" is the equivalent of the Hebrew word goy, which has been used by Jews in a derogatory sense, although not really with malice.

The Hebrew word goy was first used in the first book of the Bible (Genesis 12:2), where God, speaking to Abraham, says, "I will make you into a great nation, and I will bless you." The Hebrew text uses the word goy for "nation," and throughout the Bible and later Jewish literature the word goy always means "nation" and nothing else. At one point in history, Jews expanded its meaning to include anyone belonging to another religion.

The word "Gentile" is similar to *goy* only in that it refers to someone who belongs to a group or clan other than one's own. The Romans referred to anyone who was not a Roman as a Gentile, meaning "stranger, foreigner, one of a different clan." Mormons today refer to non-Mormons as Gentiles. And in the same manner, without assigning any negative connotation to the word, Jews use "Gentile" to refer to anyone who is not Jewish.

Why is it improper to offer a Gentile a prayer-shawl *(talit)* when he attends a Jewish service?

A Gentile in the eyes of Jewish law is a *ben Noach,* "a descendant of Noah." Noah, who was a righteous man, was not a Jew. And from the Jewish point of view, for a non-Jew to qualify for the rewards of the world-to-come he need only observe the Seven Noahide Laws. For a non-Jew to observe additional laws that apply specifically to Jews is considered improper and ill-advised.

As the prayershawl *(talit)* is donned by a Jew, he recites a prayer that includes the words, "Blessed art Thou . . . who commanded *us* to . . ." The "us" refers to Jews. Gentiles were not so commanded. Therefore, since it is not proper for a non-Jew to recite the blessing that must accompany the action of donning the *talit,* it would be improper for the Gentile to wear the *talit.* Some argue that it might even mislead members of a congregation into thinking that the person wearing the prayershawl is a Jew. None of this implies that non-Jews are unwelcome at Jewish services.

The Conservative movement, taking a slightly more liberal stand on the above issue, permits a Gentile to wear a *talit* only if he has declared his intention to convert. However, he may not recite the blessing until such time as he actually is a Jew—that is, after his conversion has taken place. By and large Reform Jews do not wear prayershawls.

Since one does not ordinarily inquire of visitors to a

synagogue whether they are Jewish, Gentiles by and large are offered *talitot* and do wear them at Jewish services.

Why were the Seven Noahide Laws enacted?

Judaism never expected anyone but Jews to abide by all the laws of the Tora, but it did expect all human beings to live by elementary moral precepts. According to rabbinic tradition,[20] non-Jews are obligated to abide by seven basic laws, called Noachian Precepts or Noahide (also spelled Noachide) Laws, which are based on chapter nine of Genesis.

Maimonides considers a Gentile who observes the Seven Noahide Laws to be a righteous person *(chassid),* and as such he is assured a place in the world-to-come, just as any observant Jew who abides by all 613 precepts of the Tora.[21]

These are the Seven Noahide Laws:

1. To behave equitably in all relationships, and to establish courts of justice.
2. To refrain from blaspheming God's name.
3. To refrain from practicing idolatry.
4. To avoid immoral practices, specifically incest.
5. To avoid shedding the blood of one's fellow man.
6. To refrain from robbing one's fellow man.
7. To refrain from eating a limb torn from a live animal.

In Jewish tradition, Gentiles who abide by these laws are called *chasiday umot haolam,* meaning "the righteous among the nations of the world."

Why is it proper to offer a skullcap to a Gentile attending a Jewish service?

Although in recent years many young Jews have been expressing their Jewish loyalty and identity by wearing a skullcap *(kipa)* at all times—in the street, at work, in the classroom, and in all public places—the skullcap has no religious significance in Jewish law. This has been affirmed over the centuries by outstanding authorities, including Rabbi Solomon ben Yechiel Luria (1510-1573), better known by the acronym Maharshal, and by Elijah ben Solomon (1720-1797), better known as the Vilna Gaon. In our own time, many authorities—even among the ultra-Orthodox— have pointed out that the custom of wearing a skullcap has no basis in biblical or rabbinic law. Consequently, a blessing was never assigned to it. This being the case, and unlike the *talit,* there is no reason for prohibiting a non-Jew from wearing a skullcap in the synagogue or anywhere else. In fact, when non-Jews appear at Orthodox or Conservative functions, religious or social, they are often invited to wear skullcaps.

Why is it permissible for synagogues to accept contributions from non-Jews?

According to Jewish law, it is perfectly permissible, so long as there are no conditions attached, for a Jewish congregation to accept a financial contribution from a non-Jew. Rabbi Moses Isserles, in his Notes to the *Code of Jewish Law,*[22] states that even if the Christian, when offering the gift, does not specify that it is being offered free of all conditions, the gift can be accepted.

Some scholars have inferred from this that a congregation may accept the services of a non-Jew who wishes to contribute his or her talents as a member of a synagogue choir. Orthodox and many Conservative congregations, however, do not feel comfortable with this practice.

Why are non-Jews prohibited from becoming synagogue members?

In Jewish law, one can carry out Jewish religious obligations only if he is in fact a Jew. A non-Jew is not expected, nor is he permitted, for example, to put on *tefilin* and recite the blessings, or to be called to the Tora and recite the Tora blessings, because as a non-Jew these commandments do not apply to him. For this reason a non-Jew cannot be accepted as a member of a congregation of Jews even if he is married to a Jewish woman who is active in synagogue affairs. And all of this applies equally to a non-Jewish woman married to a Jewish man.

While all Jewish denominations do not allow the non-Jewish spouses of their members to become members of their congregations, there is generally no particular objection to a non-Jewish spouse attending services or joining in social activities or attending adult classes. However, synagogue membership is not granted because, it is argued, if a non-Jew were allowed to become a member, what would prevent him from one day holding high office in the synagogue and thus be in a position to set synagogue policy? This could lead to untold problems, and it is generally felt that a non-Jew who feels close to Jewish life should be willing to convert to Judaism if he or she is eager to participate in setting synagogue policy.

Although Reform congregations allow families in which one spouse is a non-Jew to become members of a congregation, the official position of the Responsa Committee of the Central Conference of American Rabbis is that family membership of such mixed marriages should be held in the name of the Jewish spouse, and the non-Jewish member should not be permitted to hold synagogue office.[23]

Why are non-Jewish children allowed to attend some religious schools?

All Conservative and Reform congregations, and many Orthodox ones, permit the unconverted child of a Gentile woman married to a Jewish man to attend their congregational schools. They share the belief that through education the youngster will be drawn closer to Judaism and at some stage accept Judaism formally.

Orthodox and Conservative congregations, however, do not allow a child to celebrate a Bar or Bat Mitzva unless he or she is a born Jew or a converted Jew. The Reform group allows a non-Jewish child to have a Bar or Bat Mitzva if a pledge is made to live a committed Jewish life. The Bar/Bat ceremony is considered his/her actual acceptance of, and conversion to, Judaism.

Those who follow the very strict Orthodox view believe that the son of a non-Jewish father and a Jewish mother (which makes the child Jewish) should not be called to the Tora as a Bar Mitzva, and the occasion should not be celebrated. They suggest that it is best that such children not be admitted to Hebrew school in the first place. The more liberal Orthodox interpretation of the law would permit the child of a Jewish mother married to a non-Jew to attend Hebrew school, but not the child of a Jewish father married to a non-Jewish woman.[24]

Why may a non-Jew who marries a Jew not participate formally in Jewish rituals and ceremonies?

While there is no objection to a non-Jew whose spouse is Jewish attending synagogue services or religious ceremonies, Orthodox and Conservative rabbis generally consider it improper for a Gentile to serve as an *active* participant. They reason that since non-Jews are not bound by Jewish law, their participation in a religious service can have no religious significance, and any prayer they might recite would be a *beracha levatala,* a "wasted [unnecessary] prayer." Moreover, the recitation of a Jewish prayer by a non-Jew would lead an observer to mistakenly conclude that the individual reciting the prayer (the non-Jew) had been accepted as a Jew. This would be clearly misleading and hence a violation of the Jewish principle of *marit a'yin* (a principle which demands that one must avoid any action that might be misleading).

Traditionalists also object to having a non-Jewish father participate in the naming of his child in the synagogue, to his being a formal participant in a Bar or Bat Mitzva ceremony, and to his presence under the *chupa* (canopy) at his child's wedding. Most Reform and Reconstructionist rabbis do not share these views.

Why is it permissible under Jewish law to attend a funeral in a Christian cemetery?

In the Talmud, the ancient custom of visiting the cemetery on fast days is discussed.[25] On these special days in particular, Jews would visit the cemetery in order to pray at the graves of their ancestors. It was felt that praying at graveside would be more meaningful than praying elsewhere.

Apparently this practice continued for many centuries because the sixteenth-century codifier Joseph Caro makes reference to it.[26] Moses Isserles, in his Notes to the text, adds that if there is no nearby Jewish cemetery, one may visit a Christian cemetery. And Abraham Gombiner, author of the Magen Avraham commentary, is even more explicit, adding, "We go there [to the Christian cemetery] to supplicate and plead."

From the writings of these commentators, the extension has been made that if a Jew can pray in a Christian cemetery, he can certainly attend a funeral in one.

Why are Gentiles sometimes buried in Jewish cemeteries?

In early times there were no Jewish cemeteries. The first known Jewish burial site was purchased by Abraham from a man named Ephron, a member of the pagan Hittite nation (Genesis 23). Abraham bought from him a plot of land in a place called Machpelah, near Hebron, and there he buried his wife Sarah. The fact that Sarah's burial site was not a Jewish "cemetery" but a private parcel of land led the Rabbis of the Talmud to declare that a person should be buried *betoch shelo,* meaning "in his own property."[27] They give no indication that the site must be totally separate from the burial place of non-Jews.

At a later point in history the custom of burying Jews in their own cemeteries began. However, since this was custom, not law, Jewish burial practices varied in different communities. Not all agreed when a question arose regarding the burial of intermarried couples. Should the non-Jew be permitted to be buried in the same plot as the Jewish spouse?

Although the Orthodox view, as generally stated, is that a Gentile may not be buried in a Jewish cemetery, the ultra-Orthodox Rabbi Moshe Feinstein in a recent responsa did permit a non-Jewish woman to be buried near her Jewish husband in a Jewish cemetery.[28] The case, which was exceptional but nevertheless sets forth the law, concerned a woman who had been married to a Jewish man by an Orthodox rabbi. The couple had conducted their lives in keeping with Orthodox teachings. They raised three observant children, two daughters and a son.

When the woman died, she was prepared for burial by the Burial Society (Chevra Kadisha) in strict Orthodox fashion. But just before the funeral was to take place, a rumor spread that the deceased was not Jewish, that she was the daughter of a non-Jewish woman and that neither mother nor daughter had ever converted.

The question was brought to Rabbi Feinstein. Was this woman who had lived as an Orthodox Jew all her life to be allowed burial in a Jewish cemetery? The husband insisted that she be buried in the family plot, next to the grave reserved for him.

Rabbi Feinstein ruled that only if two reliable witnesses testify that they know for a fact that the mother of the deceased was *not* Jewish, and that neither mother nor daughter ever converted, then the deceased is to be considered non-Jewish. She may, however, be buried in the family plot provided a space of twelve feet (eight cubits) is left between her grave and the next grave, or if a fence twenty handbreadths high is built around her grave.[29]

The Conservative movement has gone on record as permitting a non-Jew to be buried next to his or her Jewish mate if in life the non-Jew was close to the Jewish community and sympathetic to its attitudes and practices. However, it suggests that a symbolic gesture be made to call attention to the situation. The gesture is to leave one unoccupied grave on either side of the burial site of the non-Jew or to surround the grave with shrubbery or a railing.

The Reform attitude is that close Gentile relatives may, at the request of the family, be buried in the family plot.

Why may non-Jewish funeral parlors be used by Jews?

If there are no Jewish funeral parlors in a city, it is proper to use the services of a non-Jewish undertaker. Christian undertakers will abide by the requirements of Jewish law if requested. They will arrange for knowledgeable Jews to prepare the body for proper burial. Prior to the funeral service itself, the officiating rabbi will make sure that all Christological symbols (such as crosses) are removed from the chapel for the Jewish service.

Why may non-Jews serve as pallbearers at Jewish funerals?

While it is traditional for members of the family or close Jewish friends to carry the deceased to his final resting place, Jewish law does not prohibit non-Jews from acting as pallbearers.

The Talmud speaks of "burying the poor of the heathen along with the dead of Israel for the sake of peace,"[30] and the *Code of Jewish Law* reiterates the importance of maintaining good relations with the non-Jewish community when it says that one must bury the Gentile dead and comfort their mourners *mipnay darkay shalom,* in order to maintain a peaceful relationship.[31]

While the Orthodox rabbinate views the principles of

mipnay darkay shalom as referring to that which Jews do for non-Jews in order to maintain harmony and goodwill, most of the non-Orthodox rabbinate view the principle as reciprocal. Since when non-Jews participate in Jewish funerals they are according honor and respect to the dead *(kevod hamet),* and since interfaith cooperation is not only expected but encouraged by Jewish law, they have no objection to accepting the goodwill of non-Jews who agree to serve as pallbearers at Jewish funerals.

Why, if there is no Jewish cemetery in a city, may a Jew be buried in a non-Jewish cemetery?

The establishment of a separate place for the burial of Jews, although an ancient practice, is not mandated directly in the Bible or Talmud or in the codes of Jewish law. The Bible (Genesis 23) describes the acquisition by Abraham of a private plot to bury his wife Sarah, and the Talmud also calls for burial in one's own family plot *(b'toch shelo).*[32]

In talmudic times, while ancestral tombs continued to be used, public burial plots were already established. In one reference, the Talmud suggests that a righteous man not be buried next to a sinner,[33] which would indicate that burial in communal cemeteries did take place. The sinner the Talmud speaks of is one guilty of a capital offense, which includes the worship of idols.[34] Since idolatry was prevalent among non-Jews, all heathens—and by extension all non-Jews—were placed in the same category. This is probably the rabbinic foundation for insisting that Jews be buried in their own cemeteries.

In theory and in emergencies, however, the law does permit a Jew to be buried next to a non-Jew. Rabbi Yekutiel Greenwald, in his book on mourning,[35] mentions the case of a Jew who lived among non-Jews and who feared that when he died he would be buried in their cemetery. The Jew therefore left word that when he died his body was to be burned. When the man's wish became known, the rabbis ruled that the wish was not to be fulfilled because it is far better to be buried among non-Jews than to be cremated, which is a clear violation of Jewish law.

During World War II, the law committee of the Jewish Welfare Board's Division of Religious Activities, consisting of Orthodox, Conservative, and Reform rabbis, ruled that Jewish chaplains may officiate at military funerals in national cemeteries such as Arlington, where Jewish and Christian soldiers are buried side by side.

Why may *Yizkor* and *Kaddish* be recited for a non-Jew?

The *Yizkor* prayer was introduced into the liturgy during the eleventh century, when much suffering was endured by Jews at the hands of Crusaders who wreaked havoc upon Jewish communities as their armies of Christian fanatics marched from town to town across Europe to free the Holy Land from the Moslems. Basically, the *Yizkor* prayer—which was originally recited only on Yom Kippur but was later introduced as part of the synagogue service on Passover, Shavuot, and Sukkot—expresses the hope that those who lost their lives during the Crusades will intervene with God in behalf of the living and thus bring an end to man's suffering. Since the prayer does not seek an end to Jewish suffering alone, rabbinic authorities are of the opinion that it is proper to recite *Yizkor* for non-Jews.

Similarly, the *Kaddish* is basically a universal prayer that extols God's holiness, although it contains several specific references to the welfare of Israel.

Why is it permissible for a non-Jew to serve as an attendant to the bride or groom at a Jewish wedding?

Nothing in Jewish law prohibits a Gentile from serving as an attendant at a Jewish wedding, even as best man or maid of honor. These honors are purely social, without religious significance. A non-Jew would, of course, not be permitted to sign as a witness on the Jewish marriage contract *(ketuba)*, for the witnesses to any Jewish religious document must be Jewish. In fact, Orthodox rabbis insist that the witnesses be *observant* Jews, and most will allow only strict Sabbath observers to serve as witnesses. Gentile attendants at a wedding may, however, be invited to sign as witnesses on the civil marriage license.

Why may a Jew participate in the wedding ceremony of a non-Jew as best man, bridesmaid, or in some other capacity?

As stated above, since these honors are purely social, without religious significance, most rabbis would have no serious objection to a Jew participating in a non-Jewish wedding if the wedding is held in a setting other than a church. (See questions earlier in this chapter on the propriety of attending and participating in religious ceremonies and services held in a church.)

Why is it permissible to leave a *mezuza* on a house sold to a Gentile?

In Jewish law, a *mezuza* must be affixed to the doorposts of houses occupied by Jews. The general practice is for a Jew to remove the *mezuzot* (plural of *mezuza*) from doorposts of a dwelling he is about to vacate unless a Jew will be occupying the house in the future. The *mezuzot* are removed to eliminate the possibility of their being desecrated.

However, Moses Isserles, the Ashkenazic authority, states in his Notes to the *Shulchan Aruch*[36] that *mezuzot* may be left on the doorposts of a house to be occupied by a Gentile if there is the slightest indication that the new owners might be offended should the *mezuzot* be removed. Twin principles of Jewish law are at work here: situations that may create ill feeling between Jew and non-Jew are to be avoided.[37]

Why is it permissible to invite non-Jews to a synagogue and to allow them to handle a Tora scroll?

In many communities in America it is customary for public school children to be brought to a synagogue to learn about Jewish customs and ceremonies. Very often the Tora scroll is removed from the ark so that the children can inspect it. While some Jews are opposed to this practice, the Talmud notes that a Tora scroll used in the synagogue cannot be made ritually unclean regardless of who handles it.[38] This is emphasized by Moses Maimonides, who wrote that anyone may handle a Tora scroll and read from it, even a non-Jew.[39]

CHAPTER 4

Marriage, Intermarriage, and Conversion

INTRODUCTION

Next to the Sabbath, marriage is the most sacred institution in Jewish life. While the first *Jewish Book of Why* addresses general laws and customs relating to marriage, this chapter examines specific problems that are of concern to many Jews today. Some of these relate to marriages between Jews, but the larger number relate to intermarriage and conversion. There was a time when relatively few Jews were affected by the matters discussed here, but as society has opened up and contact between Jews and non-Jews has grown, problems relating to intermarriage and conversion have become widespread.

The status of an intermarried couple causes much uneasiness in the Jewish family and community. Can such a couple join a synagogue? Will the family be accepted for membership in a synagogue? Will the children of an intermarried couple be admitted to the Hebrew or religious school?

What rights, if any, does the non-Jewish husband of a Jewish wife have? Can he participate in the *brit* (circumcision ceremony) of his son? Can he participate in the boy's Bar Mitzva? May he and should he sit *Shiva* for his wife in the traditional Jewish way?

If a Jewish man, married to a Jewish woman, decides to join the Church, what happens to his wife? Is she free to remarry after obtaining a civil divorce, or does Jewish law make additional demands?

If a person converts to Judaism and his father or mother dies, does the person sit *Shiva* for his non-Jewish parent? Can he participate in the wake or burial?

The process by which a non-Jew becomes a Jew perplexes many people today. A rabbi in a medium-sized American city wrote that not a week passes that four or more people do not confront him with questions relating to the subject. Among the questions most frequently asked are: How does one become a proselyte? What are the requirements and why were they instituted? What are the obligations of a convert toward his former family and the religion that he has abandoned? Why and how do Orthodox, Conservative, and Reform Judaism differ with regard to the admission of proselytes? How are proselytes to be treated? Are they equal to other Jews in all respects?

Subjects such as these, which are among those dealt with in this chapter, are of necessity tied to many of the issues discussed in the first three chapters of this book, which deal respectively with who is a Jew, the difference between Judaism and Christianity, and Jewish-Gentile relations. They are also linked to areas to be discussed in later chapters. What becomes fully evident as one reviews the questions under consideration is that Judaism does not consider itself a race. The bond that joins Jews one to another is not blood but a wide spectrum of ideals, laws, customs, and traditions. Anyone is free to enter the Jewish fellowship regardless of his antecedents, and once he has fulfilled the requirements for admission, he becomes a permanent member of the Jewish community.

Why was the biblical practice of polygamy abandoned?

The Bible does not encourage polygamy; nor does it forbid it. The Book of Deuteronomy (17:17) warns the future kings of Israel against taking "many" wives, but it never limits the number of wives a man can have concurrently. The patriarch Abraham had two wives, Jacob had two wives (plus two concubines who bore him children), David had at least eighteen wives, and Solomon is reputed to have had one thousand wives.[1] (It should be noted that in Jewish law a woman could never have more than one husband. See the next question.)

In the course of time, the practice of polygamy began to wane, but it did not disappear. Scholars such as the fourth-century Rabba of Babylonia frowned upon the practice and sought to limit it. He ruled: "A man may marry other wives, in addition to his first one, provided that he has the means to support them."[2]

The warnings of Rabba and the other scholars did not succeed in eliminating polygamy, and Jews of later centuries, especially those who lived among Muslims (who accept polygamy), continued to take two or more wives. The majority of Jews living in Christian countries, however, were monogamous. The Church steadfastly demanded monogamy, based on statements in the New Testament (Titus 1:6 and I Timothy 3:2,12) that advise all who aspire to be bishops and elders of the Church to lead exemplary lives, and this includes not taking more than one wife.

Rabbenu Gershom ben Yehuda (960-1028) of Germany sought to establish monogamy as the rule of Jewish law. His goal was to avoid conflict with the Church as well as to heal family problems created by polygamous marriages. Rabbenu Gershom convened an assembly of rabbis from various European countries, and a ruling banning polygamy was issued. Anyone who violated the ban was placed in *cherem,* that is, he was excommunicated, and fellow Jews were prohibited from having contact with him.

In time, the enactment of Rabbenu Gershom's assembly became widely accepted by all Ashkenazic communities. Sephardic Jews, however, who lived among Muslims, did not accept the ruling of Rabbenu Gershom. It is interesting that, in his code of Jewish law, Moses Maimonides, a

Sephardi, does not so much as allude to the ban against polygamy.

In 1950, a rabbinic conference convened in Israel by its Chief Rabbis renewed the ban instituted by Rabbenu Gershom—known as the *cherem d'Rabbenu Gershom*—and proclaimed that monogamy is binding upon all Jews. Exceptions were allowed, by special application to the Chief Rabbinate, for immigrants who had come to Israel with several wives from Muslim countries. Marriages that had been contracted before these new immigrants entered Israel were not nullified, but all future polygamous marriages were banned.

Why was polygamy once acceptable for Jewish men but not for Jewish women?

Society in biblical times was male-dominated. The commandment "to be fruitful and multiply" (Genesis 1:28), although actually addressed to Adam and Eve, was considered by the Rabbis of the Talmud to have been addressed solely to man, not to woman. Despite the fact that women bear the children, the Rabbis reasoned that it is man's seed that propagates the race. Man was therefore permitted as many wives at any one time as might bear him children. However, each of the women married to the man was sanctified (set aside) to him and was not to bear the children of any other man. This general rule was first stated in the Talmud.[3]

Why is a childless widow not free to marry until she is released by her deceased husband's brother?

The institution known as Levirate Marriage (called *Yibum* in Hebrew) requires that a man marry the childless widow of his brother in order to produce a child who will carry the deceased brother's name. The reason: so that the deceased brother's name will not be forgotten. So important is the perpetuation of a name that that which is called incest (in this instance marriage to a sister-in-law) and is forbidden in an earlier book of the Bible (Leviticus 18:16) may be engaged in to comply with the law of Levirate Marriage.

Levirate Marriage is detailed in the Book of Deuteronomy (25:5ff.):

> If brothers dwell together, and one of them shall die and have no child, the widow shall not be married to another man who is not his [her husband's] kin. Her husband's brother shall come on her [have intercourse with her], and take her to him as a wife, and perform the duty of a husband's brother unto her. And it shall be that the firstborn that she bears shall carry the name of the brother that died so that his name not be blotted out of Israel.

What happens if the brother of the deceased refuses to marry the widow? Deuteronomy (25:7–10) explains that the wife then must go to the gate of the city where the Elders sit and inform them that her brother-in-law has refused to marry her. The Elders then must call the brother to them, and if he states "I will *not* marry her," the Ceremony of the Removed Sandal (called *Chalitza* in Hebrew) takes place. In this ceremony the widow loosens or removes the brother-in-law's shoe, spits in front of his face, and says, "So shall be done to a man who refuses to build up his brother's house." Only after this symbolic act has been performed is the widow free to marry a stranger.

Today, only the Orthodox continue to require that *Chalitza* be performed, and a widow in that situation may not remarry until this obligation is met.[4]

Why was Levirate Marriage abandoned in favor of *Chalitza?*

Levirate Marriage was performed well into the second century C.E. About that time rabbinic authorities began to question the wisdom of continuing the practice, especially in view of Leviticus 18:16, which declares that marriage between a man and his brother's wife is incest. The Rabbis began to doubt whether a man could really marry his childless sister-in-law purely out of the high motive set forth in Deuteronomy 25:6: to perpetuate his deceased brother's name. They felt this was not likely to happen, free of all sexual overtones, and *Chalitza* rather than *Yibum* became the accepted practice.

However, as long as polygamy was in vogue the problem continued to exist, and it was not until Rabbenu Gershom ben Judah of Germany (965-1028) and his synod placed a ban on polygamy, around the year 1000, that Levirate Marriage was abandoned in favor of *Chalitza*. This was a necessary change because up until that time a brother-in-law could have other wives and still marry his widowed sister-in-law. Once polygamy was banned, however, a married brother-in-law could not fulfill the Levirate Marriage law, for he would then be guilty of bigamy, which was declared a violation of Jewish law. Consequently, *Chalitza* became the normative practice, and the requirement that a childless widow marry her brother-in-law was abandoned in cases where the brother of the deceased was already married.

This was a welcome change in the law because often the brother-in-law was suspected of marrying the widow for financial gain. Even in the talmudic period there was concern among the Rabbis that a brother-in-law's intention in marrying his brother's widow might be to acquire the brother's property through marriage rather than to perpetuate the name of the deceased by siring a child who would carry his name.

During the geonic period (approximately 700-1200), Levirate Marriage was practiced in Sura, Babylonia, but *Chalitza* was practiced in Pumbedita, Babylonia. Maimonides, in the twelfth century, favored Levirate Marriage, and the Sephardic communities in North Africa, Yemen, Persia, and Babylonia followed his lead. However, the grandson of Rashi, Jacob ben Meir (Rabbenu Tam), a contemporary of

Maimonides, favored *Chalitza,* and this became the accepted practice in Ashkenazic communities.

Chalitza, not *Yibum,* is the established practice among
Orthodox Jews today. In Israel in 1953, the Rabbinical
Courts Jurisdiction Law was issued: "Where a rabbinical
court, by final judgment, has ordered that a man be compelled to submit to *Chalitza* by his brother's widow . . . the
Attorney General can compel compliance with the order by
[ordering] imprisonment."

Why do Orthodox rabbis accept marriages but not divorces performed by non-Orthodox rabbis?

It is clearly stated in the Talmud (Kiddushin 6a and 13a)
that only he who is fully versed in the laws of *both* marriage
and divorce may perform these ceremonies. In fact, except
for the ultra-Orthodox, most Orthodox rabbis do accept
marriages performed by non-Orthodox rabbis, although
they do not always accept as valid a divorce executed by a
non-Orthodox rabbi or *Bet Din.* The reason for this is that
the divorce laws and procedures are much more complicated than those pertaining to marriage, and the argument
is made that only Orthodox rabbis are sufficiently trained to
handle divorce proceedings.

An additional reason for the Orthodox accepting marriages but not divorces granted by the non-Orthodox is that
although it is important to have God-fearing and Sabbath-
observing Jews act as witnesses to the marriage *ketuba,* to
the Orthodox it is absolutely *essential* that witnesses meet
these qualifications in order to sign on a divorce document
(get). The reasoning is that when a couple is married they
live in a community and it is evident to all that the couple
residing in their midst is in fact living as husband and wife.
The community-at-large bears witness to the fact. The
same, however, is not true when a couple is divorced, so the
witnesses to the document must be depended upon ex-
clusively.

Why is it not absolutely necessary that an ordained rabbi officiate at a marriage?

In Jewish life, a rabbi is no more important than the average layman. If special accord and consideration is afforded the rabbi, it is only because of his learning. But a learned layman is accorded the same respect as a learned rabbi.[5]

Although Maimonides is reported to have warned the Egyptian community of the twelfth century that an ordained rabbi must supervise every marriage ceremony, Jewish law does not specifically require it. A marriage is considered valid as long as proper witnesses are present who hear a man ask a woman to be his wife, and see her accept from him a ring or any other article of some minimal value as a token of the marriage.

Why is the marriage of a Jewish couple valid even though a religious ceremony has not been performed?

Until the early 1800s European governments did not require couples to go through a civil ceremony in order to get married. The religious marriage ceremony was the only ceremony conducted. When the civil ceremony became mandatory in France, Germany, Austria-Hungary, and elsewhere, many Jews did not bother having a Jewish religious marriage ceremony (known in Hebrew as *kiddushin*) in addition to the civil ceremony.

While all rabbinic authorities of the past and all rabbinic groups today consider civil marriage without an accompanying religious marriage to be contrary to the spirit of Judaism, they nevertheless consider the civil marriage perfectly valid. Children born of such a marriage are full Jews in every sense.

Rabbi Yehuda Lev Zirelsohn (1859-1941), a great Rumanian scholar, in a responsum published in 1922, ruled that a civil marriage between two Jews is valid enough to require that should the two divorce, a Jewish divorce document *(get)* must be issued if either partner is to remarry in a Jewish ceremony.[6] Zirelsohn's reasoning was that if a *get* were not issued, more harm than good would result. In the eyes of the Jewish community the couple was assumed to be husband and wife. They were seen living together for many years. If suddenly they were divorced civilly but a *get* was not issued, the public might think the husband derelict in his duty. Furthermore, should either one, in the future, be remarried by a rabbi, the public might think that the rabbi was conducting a ceremony in which one of the partners was still married.

Why does a widow and a divorcee have to wait three months before remarrying?

The law requires a three-month waiting period after a woman has been widowed or divorced so as to be certain who is the father of a child she may give birth to after her remarriage. If a child is born seven or eight or nine months after her remarriage, there would be a doubt about the paternity of the child. If the divorcee or widow marries *immediately* after her first marriage has ended, a child born seven or eight or nine months later could have been fathered either by the first husband or by the second husband. By waiting three months all doubt is eliminated.

Why does a natural father retain his Jewish legal rights even if his child is adopted by a stepfather?

If a woman remarries and her new husband legally adopts her child, in Jewish law the natural father continues to be regarded as the true father. Even where there is great love between child and stepfather, the legal relationship between the natural father and the child does not change. The child is legally bound to respect and honor his natural father, whereas the honor and respect he bestows upon his stepfather is praiseworthy but not required under the law.

At an adopted boy's Bar Mitzva it is the natural father who is traditionally obligated to recite the traditional benediction, "Praised [be He] who has freed me from the obligation [burden] of this child." It is also the natural father who receives an *aliya,* although there are usually a sufficient number of *aliyot* available so that the stepfather can also be honored.

Why is a Jewish divorce not required to dissolve a marriage between a Jew and a non-Jew?

The Jewish divorce (*get* in Hebrew) was designed to dissolve a marriage entered into "according to the laws of Moses and Israel." A marriage between a Jew and a Gentile could not have possibly been conducted in accordance with the laws of Moses and Israel. As such, the marriage has no validity in Jewish religious law; it is as if no marriage has taken place. This being the case, it would be meaningless to execute a *get* with the purpose of dissolving the marriage.

Why does Jewish law demand that a woman married to a man who was Jewish but who converted to Christianity must nevertheless receive a Jewish divorce from her husband before she can remarry?

In the eyes of Jewish law a Jewish apostate is a Jew until death, and a wife who has been abandoned by the defector is not free to remarry until she receives a Jewish divorce (*get*) from him. This law has been in force throughout Jewish history and still applies today.

The law was severely tested in the eleventh century when a case was brought before Rashi (1040-1105) in which the brother of a man who had died childless had converted to Christianity. Was the widow still required to obtain a release from the brother-in-law in order to remarry as prescribed in Deuteronomy 25 (see earlier questions on this subject)? Rashi answered that although the brother-in-law is an apostate, he does not lose any of the marital rights or obligations of a Jew. The widow therefore may not remarry unless the brother-in-law first releases her by subjecting himself to the *Chalitza* ceremony. Rashi's ruling has become accepted as law and has been cited as the basis for requiring *any* woman whose husband has become a Christian to receive a *get* from her apostate spouse before she can remarry.

Why are mixed marriages prohibited in Jewish law?

The prohibition of marriages between Jews and non-Jews is biblical in origin. Deuteronomy 7:3 sets forth the law clearly: "You shall not intermarry with them; do not give your daughters to their sons or take their daughters for your sons." The reason: so that the Israelites would not be influenced to worship the gods of the seven idolatrous nations whose lands they were about to invade and conquer (Deuteronomy 7:1). The law was precautionary, instituted to prevent the weakening of the newly developed concept of monotheism introduced by Moses and the unity of the recently reconstituted Jewish people.

In talmudic literature the prohibition against intermarriage was reinforced by banning social activity between Jews and non-Jews, lest such activity lead to intermarriage.[7] And despite the fact that in the post-talmudic era (from the early Middle Ages onward) Christians and Muslims were no longer considered idolators,[8] laws prohibiting intermarriage with non-Jews continued in force so as to preserve the integrity and unity of the Jewish community.

Why will some Reform rabbis marry a Jew to a non-Jew without requiring conversion?

A number of the more liberal members of the Reform rabbinate will marry a Jew to a Gentile without demanding that the Gentile first convert to Judaism. They perform the mixed marriage in the hope that the religious ceremony will draw the non-Jew closer to Judaism. The rabbis who follow this practice usually exact a promise from the Gentile partner that the children of the marriage will be raised as Jews. They believe that at some future date—after the non-Jew has become involved in the Jewish community and spent time studying the teachings of Judaism—he or she will request to be admitted as a full-fledged Jew.[9]

In support of this position, rabbis who agree to perform intermarriages cite the talmudic statement that a conversion performed simply for the sake of marriage is invalid. The Talmud puts it this way: "If he [a non-Jew] says to a [Jewish] woman, 'Be betrothed unto me after I become a proselyte, or after you become a proselyte [in this latter case the man is Jewish and the woman is not] . . .,' such a marriage is not valid."[10] These rabbis call attention to the ruling in the *Code of Jewish Law* which states that Jews should not receive converts who come to Judaism merely to marry a Jew and without a deeper conviction.[11]

It should be pointed out that the vast majority of Reform rabbis abide by the 1909 statement of the Central Conference of American Rabbis (reaffirmed in 1947), which condemns intermarriage as being contrary to the traditions and interests of the Jewish religion and hence a practice that should be discouraged by the American rabbinate. The Committee on Jewish Law and Standards of the Rabbinical Assembly (Conservative) does not permit its members to officiate at the marriage of a Jew to a non-Jew, and anyone who does is subject to expulsion.

Why is the non-Jewish father of a Jewish child prohibited from carrying out Jewish religious duties?

In many cases of intermarriage where the wife is Jewish but the husband is not, the wife (and sometimes even the husband) wants the children of their marriage, who are Jewish, to be brought up in accordance with prescribed Jewish rites. She wants a *brit* (circumcision) for her son;

she would like her daughter named in the synagogue; she wants a *Pidyon Haben* ceremony for a firstborn son; she wants a Bar Mitzva for her son and perhaps a Bat Mitzva for her daughter. How can these rites be fulfilled, however, when it is the obligation of the father to carry them out but the father in question is not Jewish?

The *brit* and *Pidyon Haben* in particular involve the participation of the father. It is he who is commanded to circumcise his son (Genesis 17:11), and it is he who must redeem his firstborn son by giving the Priest five *shekalim* as prescribed in Numbers 18:16. (Five silver dollars is generally the amount given to the *Kohayn* today.) If the father is not Jewish, he is not qualified to carry out the commandment and therefore not in a position to recite the prescribed prayers for these occasions, which include the words *asher kideshanu bemitzvotav vetzivanu,* meaning "[God] Who has sanctified us by His commandments and commanded *us* to . . ." Not being Jewish, the father has not been so "commanded" and his prayers would therefore be superfluous and invalid.

In cases such as the above, the Jewish court *(Bet Din)* steps in and acts as though it were the Jewish father.

Why do some congregations confer special status on the non-Jewish spouses of their members?

Because of the growing incidence of intermarriages in which the non-Jewish partner is unwilling to convert but is sympathetic to Judaism and would like to be affiliated with the mate's congregation, special problems have arisen. How is the non-Jew to be regarded? Can he or she serve on congregational committees? Can he or she participate in synagogue activities and functions?

For years, the Conservative, Reconstructionist, and Reform rabbinates have been struggling with these questions, searching for ways to draw the unconverted spouse closer to Judaism. Members of these three movements have found justification for allowing the participation of non-Jewish spouses in synagogue life by pointing to the findings of the historian Joseph Klausner. Klausner cites many examples of the non-Jewish mates of Jews being affiliated with synagogues throughout the Diaspora in Second Temple times (about 500 B.C.E. to 70 C.E.). These spouses were referred to as "fearers of heaven" or "respecters of heaven" *(yiray shama'yim)*. Although they did not convert to Judaism, they were sympathetic to its ideals. Jews treated them respectfully in the hope that one day they would undergo conversion.

Some modern-day congregations cite the above as the basis for extending a warm hand of friendship to non-Jewish spouses. In the Conservative movement they are welcome at all services, but they cannot become members of the congregation. They may participate in all synagogue activities, may serve on committees, but may not hold office or vote. This view is generally shared by the Reconstructionist and Reform groups. The Orthodox do believe in extending a hand of friendship to the non-Jewish spouse, and do welcome him or her to attend synagogue services or functions. The non-Jewish spouse is not, however, permitted to be a formal participant in synagogue life.

Why may Jews who have intermarried be counted as part of a *minyan*?

In Jewish law, a Jew who intermarries does not lose his status as a Jew.[12] It should be noted, however, that over the years there has been an undercurrent of opinion that a Jewish man who marries a Gentile woman should not be counted as one of the ten men who constitute a quorum *(minyan)*. When a man defies the Tora by intermarrying, it is argued, he should be treated as a Jew who has been excommunicated. In earlier centuries excommunication *(cherem)* was an effective instrument used by the Jewish community to maintain control over the religious conduct of its members. Often, an excommunicated person was not counted as part of a *minyan* as long as the ban that had been placed upon him remained in effect. Today, however, the prevailing view is more liberal. Even ultra-Orthodox leaders hold that an intermarried Jew may be counted as part of a *minyan*.[13]

Why does Jewish law recognize sincerity as the only acceptable basis for conversion?

Converts who become Jews for any reason other than that they sincerely want to join the Jewish community are called *gayray ara'yot,* "leonine proselytes," implying that they have converted under threat. The origin of the name can be traced to the Bible (II Kings 17:24ff.). After the Assyrians captured Israel in the eighth century B.C.E., the king of Assyria expelled all the inhabitants of Samaria (northern Israel) and replaced the population with idolators from strange lands. Disapproving of their idolatrous practices, God besieged them with ferocious lions. The strangers took this as sign of God's disapproval and converted to Judaism. However, while they professed belief in one God, they continued to practice idolatry. Because these conversions were obviously insincere, the Rabbis of the Talmud henceforth condemned all conversions that were not purely motivated.

Because the Rabbis were suspicious of the motives of prospective converts, from talmudic times onward the newcomers were not routinely accepted. Those who wished to become Jews were expected to prove their sincerity. The Talmud suggests that when a Gentile expresses a desire to convert, he should be asked, "Why do you want to convert to Judaism? Do you know that at the present time Jews are oppressed, despised, and harassed?" If the Gentile answers that he is aware of all these problems but nevertheless wants to join the Jewish community, he is accepted as a candidate for conversion.[14]

Why were converts to Judaism sometimes treated poorly by members of the Jewish community?

One of the oft-repeated comments in the Talmud concerning prospective proselytes originated with the fourth-century scholar Rabbi Chelbo. He said, "Proselytes are as troublesome to Israel as a sore [scab]."[15] The view of Rabbi Chelbo was shared by many talmudic authorities, because they believed that Judaism was a way of life that included traditions, practices, and associations that could not be acquired unless a great effort was made. They did not want to admit into the Jewish fold individuals who were converting merely to marry a Jew or for some other ulterior motive. Such converts, it seemed, did not serve the Jewish community well and often created problems. For this reason, prospective proselytes were treated poorly so as to discourage them, and those who had already converted were regarded as second-class citizens.

The most famous convert to Judaism was a Catholic priest named Obadiah, who early in the twelfth century (about 1102) was influenced by the conversion to Judaism of the archbishop of Bari (Italy). Obadiah spent his years in several near-eastern countries and wrote religious works, including poems and prayers, notations pertaining to Tora cantillation, and a diary, fragments of which were found in the Cairo *geniza* early in the twentieth century. After his conversion Obadiah was apparently not accepted as a full Jew even by his teacher, and he therefore wrote a letter to Moses Maimonides. In this now-famous letter, Obadiah asked whether the teacher was correct in suggesting that in his prayers Obadiah not use the words, "Our God and God of our fathers," since Obadiah's father was not Jewish.

Maimonides reprimanded Obadiah's teacher sternly and said to the convert, "Go tell your teacher that he owes you an apology. And tell him that he should fast and pray and ask God to forgive him for what he said to you. He must have been intoxicated, and he forgot that in thirty-six places the Tora reminds us to *respect* the convert and that in thirty-six places it admonishes us to *love* the convert. "A convert," Maimonides went on to say, "is a child of Abraham, and whoever maligns him commits a great sin."

Why are converts considered full Jews even though they come from non-Jewish blood?

Judaism is not a race but a community bound together by religion, culture, language, and other interests. The bond that cements Jews is not blood; it is a subscription to a way of life that is far from monolithic.

Members of many religions and nationalities have slipped in and out of the Jewish fold for thousands of years, and these have included men and women of all races. In Jewish law, anyone who adopts Judaism by choice is a full-fledged Jew.

Why is a candidate for conversion to Judaism required to pursue an intensive course of study?

When a Gentile is admitted to the Jewish fold, he enters a world far different from the one he leaves behind. The demands placed upon him as a Christian were minimal. Basically, he was required to attend church services, celebrate Christian holidays, and accept Jesus as the savior and redeemer. The convert to Judaism must learn the Hebrew language, study the Bible and Jewish history, and learn how to observe the many customs, laws, and ceremonies of Jewish life.

The average born Jew does not receive a great deal of formal religious training, but he comes to learn about many of the aspects of Judaism through family, friends, and organizational affiliations. On the other hand, a person who enters Judaism from the outside finds it difficult to compensate for his lack of Jewish experience. He must therefore undergo a course of intensive study.

Why are converts generally named after Abraham, Sarah, or Ruth?

Although there is no legal requirement mandating that a male convert to Judaism adopt the Hebrew name of Abraham or that female converts use Sarah or Ruth as a first name, there is a longstanding tradition to this effect. In most cases, at the time of conversion a male convert is named Avraham ben Avraham Avinu (Abraham the son of Abraham our father), and a female convert is named Sara bat Avraham Avinu (Sarah the daughter of Abraham our father) or Rut bat Avraham Avinu (Ruth the daughter of Abraham our father). The use of "ben Avraham" and "bat Avraham" is generally insisted upon for purposes of identifying the individual as a proselyte.[16]

Two reasons are offered for naming converts Avraham. First, the Bible (Genesis 17:5) speaks of Abraham as being "the father of a multitude of nations," and since proselytes come from diverse peoples and backgrounds, it is appropriate that they be called the sons and daughters of Abraham.

A second explanation, offered in the Midrash, runs as follows: Since the Children of Israel are called God's "friends," as it is written, "the seed of Abraham My [God's] friend" (Isaiah 41:8), and since proselytes are called God's "friends," as it is written, "God is the friend of the proselyte" (Deuteronomy 10:18), it was concluded that Abraham has a special relationship to proselytes. In Jewish tradition, Abraham became known as "the father of proselytes" because once non-Jews have converted to Judaism, their legal connection with their former non-Jewish families is, for the most part, severed, and the family of Abraham is now their family. The Talmud calls them "newborn babies."[17]

(Nevertheless, proselytes are still obligated to fulfill the biblical commandment of "Honor thy father and mother," and therefore the Jewish laws of mourning must be observed by the proselyte when his non-Jewish parents die. The Talmud also indicates that if a proselyte's father dies, he may inherit his portion of the estate along with his non-Jewish brother.)[18]

Offering the convert the name of Abraham is explained by the Midrash to be an expression of deep love. The Midrash says, "God loves proselytes dearly. And we, too, should show our love for them because they left their father's house, and their people, and the Gentile community, and have joined us."[19]

It is, of course, a matter of history that not all proselytes have taken the name Abraham. The scholar Onkelos was a proselyte. Flavius Clemens, nephew of the Roman Vespasian, was a proselyte. The Talmud also refers to a proselyte named Judah the Ammonite.[20]

Female converts take the name of Sarah because she was the wife of Abraham, the first Hebrew, and also because, as tradition has it, she and Abraham were active in "winning souls" (Genesis 12:5) to the worship of God, Abraham converting idol-worshipping men and Sarah converting the women.[21]

Female converts to Judaism also take the name of Ruth because the Ruth of the Bible is regarded as the epitome of loyalty to Judaism, although she was not a convert in the formal sense, not having undergone immersion in a ritual bath (mikva). Ruth is famous for swearing eternal allegiance to her mother-in-law, Naomi, as expressed in the following immortal words from the Book of Ruth (1:16).

> Whither thou goest, I will go,
> Where thou lodgest, I will lodge,
> Thy people shall be my people,
> And thy God my God.

Why have circumcision and immersion become prescribed rites for the admission of converts to Judaism?

In the Bible we find that the Children of Israel (or Hebrews, as they were then called) entered into a covenant with God through three rites: circumcision (brit mila), immersion (tevila), and offering a sacrifice (korban).

Abraham (Genesis 17:1-14) was the first person to accept God, and this acceptance was marked by a "sign" of the Covenant: "Throughout the generations, every male among you shall be circumcised at the age of eight days" (verse 12). When the Bible describes how the Jews prepared themselves for the Exodus from Egypt, and later when it describes how Israel prepared itself for the Revelation at Mount Sinai, circumcision is once again the central symbol. During their enslavement in Egypt, circumcision had apparently not been practiced by the Israelites and, therefore, to prepare them for Passover, Moses circumcised all the males so they could be counted as members of the Covenant People and thus be permitted to eat of the Paschal lamb (Exodus 12:48). The law was thus firmly established that all males who wish to be part of the Jewish people must be circumcised. Circumcision became a sign of identification with the historic Covenant People.[22]

The second rite through which Israel entered the Covenant was immersion. According to the Rabbis of the Talmud, the first instance of immersion occurred in the Sinai Desert before the Revelation.[23] When the Israelites arrived at the foot of Mount Sinai, Moses instructed them to prepare for a great religious experience. They were to "meet" God but, before this could take place, Moses told them to "sanctify" themselves and to wash their garments (Exodus 19:10). The Rabbis equated the word "sanctification" and the washing of garments with immersion in a ritual bath (mikva). Hence, they said, immersion in a ritual bath is required before one is to be admitted as a member of the Covenant People.

The third rite associated with Israel's becoming the Covenant People was the bringing of a sacrifice on the altar (Exodus 24:5ff.).

The Rabbis of the Talmud[24] transferred the three rituals—circumcision, immersion, and sacrifice—that originally applied to all born Jews who affirmed their loyalty to Judaism and applied them to non-Jews who wished to enter the Jewish fold.[25]

The Code of Jewish Law, which gives the details of how

a Gentile is to be converted to Judaism,[26] makes no reference to the requirement of offering a sacrifice upon the restoration of the Temple.

Orthodox and Conservative Judaism requires all male converts to be circumcised and all male and female converts to be immersed in a *mikva*. Reform Judaism today does not require these ceremonies, but it does encourage them.[27]

Why do some non-Orthodox rabbis admit converts without requiring them to submit to the rites of immersion and circumcision?

Some rabbis consider it more important that potential converts to Judaism prove their sincerity by pursuing a course of serious study than by submitting to immersion (required of both males and females) and to circumcision (required of males). Liberal rabbis support this view by pointing out that nowhere in the Bible are these demands made. In fact, the requirements of immersion and circumcision were not instituted until the early talmudic period (first century C.E.).

The original decision of the Reform rabbinate not to require immersion or circumcision was rendered at the second convention of the Central Conference of American Rabbis (1891) and was passed by a vote of 25-5. The argument presented was that neither the Bible nor the Mishna mentions an initiation rite for a proselyte. It is only in the Talmud proper[28] that the need for circumcision and immersion is first introduced and discussed. Various views are expressed there, with the final decision being that a conversion is not valid unless the rites of circumcision and ablutions in a ritual bath have been performed.

It should be noted that in Israel today the school for proselytes established by the Reform movement requires immersion and circumcision of its converts. The Orthodox rabbinate nonetheless does not accept these converts as Jews, nor does it accept conversions performed by any non-Orthodox rabbi in Israel or the Diaspora.

Why is it required that a "court" of three men be present when a convert is circumcised and immersed in a ritual bath?

In Jewish tradition, the process of conversion, culminating in the admission of a proselyte into the Jewish fold, is a legal matter. As such, it requires witnesses to attest to the fact that the ceremonies involved are properly conducted. Three qualified men are to be present at the circumcision *(brit mila)* and immersion *(tevila)* of a male convert. The three men (of whom usually at least one is a rabbi) constitute a legal entity known as a *Bet Din,* a court. There is no indication in the Talmud[29] or in the code of Maimonides that all members of the *Bet Din* must be rabbis or learned men, as is sometimes believed. Average, intelligent, knowledgeable Jews may be members of the court.

The *Bet Din* is required to be present at the immersion of female converts as well. A woman accompanies the female convert into the ritual bath chamber *(mikva).* She then reports to the three men, who wait in an outer room, that the convert has removed all of her clothes and has immersed herself completely, as prescribed by law. From the outer room, the *Bet Din* can hear the convert pronounce the conversion prayer, which is recited while standing naked in the water.

Why does a proselyte who was circumcised in a nonreligious ceremony as a child have to undergo a token circumcision upon his conversion?

Orthodox and Conservative Judaism requires that male converts be circumcised as part of the initiation ritual, just as every male Jew is circumcised on the eighth day after birth. If a non-Jew had been circumcised as a baby, as is routinely done in many hospitals, that circumcision does not satisfy the requirement of conversion since the circumcision was not performed with the *intent* of admitting the child into the Jewish Covenant.

A circumcised non-Jew (whose circumcision was medically but not religiously motivated) must submit to a token circumcision if he plans to become a Jew. The *mohel* (a layman trained as a specialist in circumcision) merely draws a drop of blood from the penis and then pronounces all the blessings normally recited at a *brit* (circumcision). The drawing of the blood is known as *hatafat dam brit,* meaning "drawing the blood of the Covenant."

Why is an Orthodox *Kohayn* (Priest) not permitted to marry a proselyte or a divorcee?

The Book of Leviticus (21:6-7) emphasizes that the Priests *(Kohanim),* descendants of the family of Aaron, are expected to be in a constant state of holiness since they tend the sanctuary and offer sacrifices to God. Special laws were enacted to ensure that the Priests would always be in a state of ritual purity and thus ready to perform their Priestly duties.

The Bible considers it improper for a Priest to marry a divorced woman or a woman who has converted to Judaism: "They [Priests] shall not take a woman that is a harlot, or profaned; neither shall they take a divorced woman, for he is holy unto his God."

To the Rabbis of the Talmud the word "harlot" meant not only "prostitute" but any woman who was tainted for any reason. And since the proselytes in early times came from heathen stock, whose morality was not on a par with the Jewish standard, they were considered tainted. Therefore, a *Kohayn,* who was expected to be as unblemished as the sacrifice he offered on the altar, was not permitted to marry a woman whose past life might reflect negatively upon his character or stigmatize the offspring of the marriage.[30]

The same reasoning forbids a Priest from marrying a divorcee. The Rabbis felt that a divorced woman is blemished and therefore unsuited to be the wife of a *Kohayn.*

Today, only the Orthodox community continues to follow the above rulings. The position of the Rabbinical Assembly (Conservative) is that since today's Priests in general are of uncertain genealogy, the rulings have lost their validity. They also argue that it is unfair and even embarrassing to admit a proselyte to the Jewish fold and then to deny her the right to marry a *Kohayn* because of a regulation that may have had validity when the Temple existed but which is no longer appropriate. The reestablishment of the Temple, they say, is not anticipated. The Reform and Reconstructionist rabbinate share the Conservative view.[31]

Why is a child born to a woman who was pregnant before her conversion considered to be fully Jewish?

There is no question that a child is fully Jewish if the mother is Jewish at the time of its conception. Doubt arises, however, when a Gentile woman converts after she has conceived but before she has given birth. Is the child born to this woman considered fully Jewish as a result of the mother's conversion, or must the child undergo a separate conversion after birth?

Most rabbinic authorities are of the opinion that the child in its embryonic form is part of the mother's body (referred to in the Talmud as *ubar yerech imo*), and as such the conversion of the mother automatically includes the unborn fetus. This view was first expressed by Rashi in his commentary on the Talmud.[32] Later scholars, including Rabbi Moses Isserles (sixteenth century), made the point that the term "convert" is not to be used in reference to these children because they are born Jews in the fullest sense.[33]

Why are proselytes sometimes more enthusiastic about Jewish life and observance than are their mates who are born Jews?

Jews born into a Jewish family usually live in a Jewish milieu and "absorb" Judaism to one degree or another in a very natural, matter-of-fact manner. As a consequence, observance of the laws and customs of Judaism is sometimes routine and automatic.

New converts to Judaism—Jews by choice—do not have that experience and cannot relate to all the facets of Judaism immediately. What they are able to relate to most easily are the "tangible" elements of Judaism, that is, the customs and ceremonies. They can be taught without difficulty to observe dietary laws or to light candles on the Sabbath and holidays. However, the deep-felt ethnic connection that is usually an inborn phenomenon requires many years of association with Jews and Judaism before it is acquired.

In 1979, Professor Egon Mayer, of Brooklyn College, conducted a survey on behalf of the American Jewish Committee to study intermarriage in the United States. He found that proselytes who marry a Jew by birth are more observant than their Jewish spouses. They adhere more carefully to the ritual practices of Judaism than do the born Jews. He discovered, however, that non-Jews who have converted to Judaism tend to be somewhat more religious than ethnic and more behavioral than attitudinal. They are "more adept at acting like Jews in matters of religious practice than they are at feeling or thinking like Jews when it comes to social relations."[34]

Why is a convert to Judaism expected to respect his non-Jewish parents?

Although the Talmud speaks of a convert as being a "newborn babe" who is no longer connected to his former family,[35] this view was not taken literally by contemporary talmudic or later authorities. It was recognized that not only would it be unnatural for a child to ignore his natural parents, but it might also be impractical. The Talmud, for example, rules that a proselyte has not forfeited his right to an inheritance due him upon the death of his non-Jewish parent.[36] In other words, the Rabbis did not consider a child's association with his non-Jewish parents to be completely severed.

Recognizing that there is no law in Judaism more important than the fifth of the Ten Commandments, which demands that one accord respect to his parents ("Honor thy father and thy mother" [Exodus 20:12]), rabbis throughout the centuries have insisted that this commandment be followed in letter and in spirit. They considered it fully applicable to a born Jew and to a proselyte alike. This attitude was emphasized in the twelfth-century by Moses Maimonides, who wrote that a convert to Judaism must not cease respecting his Gentile father. And although the proselyte begins a whole new life and is like a newborn, the blood ties that once existed have not disappeared.

The sixteenth-century code of Joseph Caro repeats the admonition that a proselyte is obligated to treat his parents respectfully.[37]

Generally, authorities are of the opinion that while not *all* mourning rites should be observed by a proselyte for his non-Jewish parents, some should be observed as a sign of respect. They suggest, for example, that during the week of *Shiva* the proselyte continue to wear shoes instead of changing to slippers as born Jews do. These authorities feel that those who visit the proselyte mourner and see that not *all* the mourning rites are observed will understand that a *Jewish* parent is not being mourned.

In a recent responsum[38] Rabbi Moshe Feinstein responds to a question in which a sick non-Jewish mother of a proselyte requests that her (now Jewish) daughter visit her with her children. There has been no contact between mother and daughter for twenty years despite the fact that they live in the same city. Rabbi Feinstein's response is that the proselyte should visit with her children so as to fulfill the commandment of honoring parents.

Why may a proselyte say *Kaddish* for his non-Jewish parents?

While rabbinic authorities do not all agree that a Jew—whether by birth or by conversion—should observe all the mourning rites for non-Jewish parents, there is general agreement that *Kaddish* should be recited for them. In addition to the explanation offered in the answer to the previous question, scholars have noted that *Kaddish* is, for the most part, a universal prayer. Through it the mourner reaffirms his belief in God's goodness and in the worthwhileness of life. It is an expression of hope and faith that can quite properly be voiced by anyone for anyone.

In a 1933 responsum, Rabbi Aaron Walkin of Pinsk wrote that a Jewish proselyte may recite *Kaddish* upon the death of his Christian father. In fact, he says, he is dutybound to do so because one must fulfill the commandment of honoring one's father and mother.[39]

Why does a person who as a baby is converted to Judaism by his parents have the right to renounce the conversion when becoming an adult?

If a baby born to a non-Jewish mother is adopted by a Jewish couple and is converted by them to Judaism, the child is considered to be a full Jew even though he is not old enough to consent to the conversion.

The conversion of a child by a parent is permitted based on the talmudic principle *zachin le'adam shelo befanav,* "one can do another a favor without his knowledge."[40] Jews consider it a privilege to be a Jew and to bring someone into the Jewish fold.

Acknowledging the possibility that persons so converted might wish to renounce Judaism when they grow up, the Talmud (in the above cited reference) reserves for them the right to do so when they reach adulthood (twelve years of age for a girl and thirteen for a boy). (No formal announcement is required of the young man or young woman if they wish to continue to be Jews after they have reached maturity.) Once that point has passed, Jewish law considers them to be like all proselytes who were converted to Judaism as adults, none of whom has the right to annul his conversion.

A proselyte remains a Jew in the eyes of Jewish law even if he becomes an apostate.[41]

Why does a proselyte who reverts to Christianity still retain his status as a Jew?

If a proselyte who converted to Judaism as an adult later has a change of heart and reverts to his former practices and beliefs, in the eyes of Jewish law he does not cease to be a Jew. His defection may be looked upon with scorn by the Jewish community; he may be denied an *aliya* (Tora honor) should he ever attend a synagogue service; he may no longer be counted as part of a *minyan* (a quorum of ten male adults for a religious service)—but all obligations pertaining to Jewish marriage and divorce remain his. If, for example, the defector abandons a wife whom he married after he had become a Jew, she is still legally married to him, and she cannot remarry unless he grants her a Jewish divorce (*get*).

Why can an apostate return to Judaism without undergoing a reinitiation ceremony?

There is general agreement among authorities that if an apostate decides to return to Judaism, he is not required to undergo any ritual. Moses Isseries, in his Notes to the *Shulchan Aruch,* emphasizes the point that even when a Jew abandons Judaism, he is still a Jew.[42] In fact, Jewish law insists that those who return to Judaism are to be treated with kindness and consideration; they are not to be embarrassed by being reminded of their defection.

Why did the practice of sitting *Shiva* for a family member immediately following his or her conversion to another faith gain wide acceptance?

This custom is based on a misunderstanding that dates back to the publication in the twelfth century of *Or Zarua,* by Rabbi Isaac of Vienna. In this book, Rabbi Isaac reported that the great eleventh-century scholar Rabbenu Gershom ben Yehuda, known as the Luminary of the Diaspora *(Meor Hagola),* sat *Shiva* for his son who had converted to Christianity. Upon publication of the book, it became widespread practice to sit *Shiva* for one's child who converts, despite the fact that outstanding scholars, including Joseph Caro, author of the *Code of Jewish Law,* insisted that doing so is not the law and hence is not appropriate conduct.[43]

Why, then, did Rabbenu Gershom sit *Shiva* for his son? Further delving by scholars revealed that Rabbenu Gershom did not sit *Shiva* for his son at the time of the young man's conversion. He sat *Shiva* for him at a later date, at the time of the son's death. And the misunderstanding grew out of the misreading of one word in Isaac of Vienna's work. Isaac wrote that Rabbenu Gershom sat *Shiva* for his son—and he used the Hebrew word *shenishtamed,* meaning "who had converted." Some of the texts erroneously added one letter to the word and spelled it *k'shenishtamed,* meaning *"when* he had converted." Because of the error, it was believed that Rabbenu Gershom sat *Shiva* at the time of his son's conversion.

Sitting *Shiva* for a child who joins another faith has never been a legal requirement for Jews, and authorities do not favor following the practice.[44] Mourning a member of the family who has abandoned Judaism runs counter to the basic talmudic principle that one never loses his Jewish identity and that he may return to the fold, unceremoniously, when he decides to do so. To sit *Shiva* for a family member who converts is, in a sense, consigning him to death, thus precluding the possibility of his ever returning to the faith of his ancestors.

CHAPTER 5

The Personal Dimension

INTRODUCTION

In Jewish tradition man's body is considered of the utmost importance primarily because it houses the soul, and for that reason the body must be kept clean and healthy. Hillel said (Leviticus Rabba 34:3) that it is a religious obligation *(mitzva)* for one to bathe and thereby keep his body—the holy vessel—clean.

Since Bible times, Jews have been concerned with physical and mental health. The Priests were the doctors in primitive society, and in fact several chapters in the Book of Leviticus (12 through 14) are devoted to the control of disease.

The Talmud continues to stress this concern for health. Many statements pertaining to it are found in a number of tractates:

- Shabbat (41a) says that fluids should be drunk during mealtime, that a person should get enough sleep, and that physical exercise should follow every meal.
- Ketubot (110b) warns that one should watch his diet because a change in eating habits may upset one's health.
- Bava Kamma (92b) emphasizes the value of eating breakfast: "Have an early breakfast in the summer because of the heat, and in the winter because of the cold, and people even say that sixty men [a common hyperbolic term] may pursue him who has early meals in the morning and will not overtake him."

• Bava Metzia (107b) lists thirteen advantages that come to one who eats his "morning bread [meal]."

• The tractate Berachot, in particular, devotes many pages to very intimate health concerns.

In Judaism, the obligation to preserve life, especially one's own, is basic. The Talmud[1] says that if any human being saves a single soul of Israel, it is regarded by Scripture as if he has saved the entire world.

The twelfth-century scholar and physician Moses Maimonides points out in his *Eight Chapters* (a preface to the *Ethics of the Fathers)* that prudence demands that every person practice moderation in personal living so that his body will remain strong and healthy. He specifically warns against excesses in eating, drinking, and sex.

Joseph Caro (sixteenth century), in the *Shulchan Aruch,* particularly the Orach Chayim section, devotes many chapters to the care of physical self. Rabbis of subsequent centuries have continued to address this theme.

In the 1960s the sexual revolution began to exert a powerful force on the lives of young and old in every part of the world. By 1970 the revolution was full-blown. Society and the individual became more open, more outspoken, more daring. Sex was no longer a forbidden word, and all religions had no choice but to deal with it. Homosexuals who had been "hiding in closets" began to reveal their attitudes openly, demanding equality and justice. Couples living together unmarried no longer kept their lifestyle secret. Sexual inhibitions were a thing of the past.

Judaism, like all other religions, has had to react to these changes. It has not been easy. Is the new behavior compatible with Jewish tradition? Do the Bible, the Talmud, the Codes, and the Responsa literature have anything of significance to say relative to the new social attitudes and modes of living?

In addition to confronting the sexual revolution, Judaism has had to address itself to the new problems of medical ethics that have exploded in recent years. What guidance, if any, can Jewish tradition offer in attempting to answer questions relating to transplants, transfusions, abortions, artificial insemination, and a score of other issues that have come to the fore in the last two decades?

Matters such as these—all aspects of the personal dimension—are treated in this chapter. Less controversial but also discussed are matters relating to personal grooming. These include the use of cosmetics, the wearing of jewelry, hair styling, and cosmetic surgery.

Why, unlike classical Christianity, has Judaism not characterized sexual activity as sinful?

Until modern times, the Western world, under the influence of Christianity, considered sex and sin to be virtually synonymous. Based on New Testament teachings (I Corinthians 7:19), throughout the centuries Christian scholars have viewed sex as a concession to human weakness and marriage as an "evil" necessary for the propagation of the human race. Celibacy, it was believed, is the ideal state. Galatians (5:24) considers the body a repository of "passions and desires," and Paul supports this view when he says in Romans (7:24-25), "Wretched man that I am! Who will deliver me from this body of death? . . . With the mind I serve the law of God, but with the flesh the law of sin."

In Jewish tradition sex is not considered sinful. Genesis (1:28) stresses man's duty "to be fruitful and multiply" as a *positive* commandment. Man is *obligated* to propagate the race. Isaiah (45:18) later taught that "God formed the earth so that it should be inhabited."

The Rabbis of the Talmud went even further. They declared that, beyond the propagation of the race, sex is to be enjoyed.[2] A man is obligated to satisfy his wife's sexual needs (referred to as *ona* in the Bible [Exodus 21:10]), and this must be done with respect and consideration.[3] To deny one's wife sexual pleasure is grounds for compelling a man to issue a divorce. Maimonides elaborates, emphasizing that just as a man may not deny his wife sexual satisfaction, so may a woman not withhold sex from her husband.[4]

Why do most authorities approve of sexual intercourse with one's spouse even if the purpose is not procreation?

The view that Jewish law approves of sexual intercourse between married people only when there is a possibility of the woman conceiving is clearly incorrect. The *Shulchan Aruch* states that the biblical ban on "wasting seed" (see questions later in this chapter) does not apply to intercourse with a sterile woman so long as the intercourse is normal and artificial barriers (contraceptive devices) are not placed in the womb to bar the seed from entering.[5] Rabbi Moses Isserles (1525-1572), in his Notes, is quite explicit when he comments that although the purpose of marriage is to have children, it is not prohibited to marry a woman who cannot bear children.[6] Several centuries earlier, Rashi (1040-1105) had commented that "a wife has the right not to be ignored [sexually]" even if she is unable to bear children.[7]

Many of Rashi's predecessors, including Saadya Gaon in the tenth century, and many of his successors, including Moses ben Nachman (Nachmanides) in the thirteenth century, agreed that sexual activity is permissible even when procreation is not its immediate purpose. They acknowledged sex as an honest expression of love which deepens the marital bond between husband and wife and provides personal satisfaction for both mates. There can be nothing reprehensible about the sex act, said these rabbis, since God's holy men in the Bible engaged in it with His approval.

Why is the Sabbath considered a special day for cohabitation?

This idea is based on the talmudic recommendation that the frequency of copulation for a scholar should be once per week, and the appropriate time is Friday night.[8] Rashi, in his commentary, suggests that Friday night is ideal because "it is a night of delight, relaxation, and joy." A fourteenth-century document entitled *Iggeret Hakodesh* repeats this idea, explaining that Friday night is a night of heightened spirituality, and sexual union between husband and wife is most suited for this time of the week.

In Jewish tradition, copulation is a joyous, spiritual, and holy act. Because the Sabbath is the holiest and most precious day of the week, Jewish tradition considers it an appropriate time for sexual intercourse between husband and wife.

Why is cohabitation banned on fast days and on days of mourning?

As indicated above, sex in Jewish tradition is considered a pleasurable activity. Since fast days and days of mourning (the *Shiva* period) are sad occasions, sex is banned on those days.

Why do many Orthodox Jews avoid physical contact, particularly kissing, with the opposite sex?

The Bible does not condemn physical contact, particularly kissing, between members of the opposite sex, whether family members or not (Genesis 29:11 and 32:1; Exodus 4:27). The Rabbis of the Talmud, however, generally disapprove of kissing and even consider it obscene.[9] Rabbi Akiba praises the ancient Medes because when they kissed, they kissed only on the hand, not on the lips.[10]

Maimonides established a biblical basis for avoiding physical contact with the opposite sex when he interpreted the verse in Leviticus (18:6), "No one shall approach close relatives to uncover their nakedness," to mean that not only are sexual relations between relatives forbidden, but kissing is forbidden as well, even where it does not cause sexual arousal. But Maimonides and all other authorities excluded from this ban the kissing of one's closest relatives—including one's mother, wife, daughter, sister, and aunt."[11]

Later codifiers of Jewish law have gone beyond the ban on kissing, declaring all physical contact with the opposite sex inappropriate because it can lead to sexual arousal. This ruling, recorded in the *Code of Jewish Law,* forbids a man to smell the scent of a strange woman, to look at her hair, even to gaze upon her little finger.[12] Many Orthodox Jews today, particularly among the ultra-Orthodox, are meticulous about the observance of this law, and accordingly they refuse to hug, kiss, or even shake hands with members of the opposite sex except for their mates.

Why is sex prohibited during a woman's menstrual period?

The prohibition barring a man and woman from having sex during the woman's monthly period is described in the Bible. Leviticus 15:19-24 explains that the woman is in a state of impurity during this period of time, and Leviticus 20:18 says, "If a woman lies with a man in the time of her menstrual flow . . . both shall be cut off [excommunicated] from among their people." Some commentators say that "to be cut off" means "to be ostracized," while others interpret it to mean "to be put to death."

How long does the menstrual period last? Leviticus 15:19 states that "when a woman has a discharge of blood from her body, she shall remain impure for seven days." The Bible requires that abstention from sex last only seven days, to be reckoned from the day menstruation begins. The Rabbis of the Talmud, however, wanting to emphasize the seriousness of the offense of having sex with a menstruant, ruled that the seven-day period of abstention mentioned in the Bible is to begin *after* the actual flow of blood has ceased.

The seven-day period is usually referred to as "clean days" or "white days." Since the flow of blood in most cases lasts from four to five days, the total period of abstinence from sex for the average couple is eleven or twelve days. Each woman notes when the flow of blood has ceased and then counts seven more days of abstinence. Orthodox women follow this practice today. At the end of the period of abstinence, the woman must immerse herself in a ritual bath (mikva) before once again having sex with her husband. (The talmudic laws referred to here were summarized by Maimonides in his Mishneh Torah.[13])

In biblical times, when the period of abstinence came to an end, the menstruant (called the nidda in Hebrew) offered to the Lord a sacrifice of two turtledoves or two young pigeons. No mention is made in the Bible of the requirement that a woman immerse herself in a mikva to achieve purification, but the Rabbis of the Talmud (in the tractates Nidda and Mikvaot) infer this from Leviticus 18, which calls for bathing in water for one to achieve purification. The talmudic laws pertaining to the menstruant are codified in the Shulchan Aruch.[14]

A variety of reasons have been offered by talmudic and later scholars to explain the importance and meaningfulness of sexual abstinence during the menstrual period. One scholar says that it teaches a lesson in patience, and that men who are unable to wait for their wives to be "clean" again and who rush to have sex while they are still menstruants should learn the lesson of patience from young trees whose fruit may not be eaten for the first three years (Leviticus 19:23). Dr. Norman Lamm, president of Yeshiva University, complements this thought. He writes, "Unrestricted approachability leads to overindulgence," which in turn leads to overfamiliarity and can result in "marital disharmony." For this reason, he points out, "Orthodox Jewish homes will have twin beds, never a double bed."[15]

The Talmud expresses these same sentiments when it notes that the enchantment of marriage is heightened if abstinence is observed during the menstrual period.[16] The

Talmud even points out that the Romans considered the menstrual laws the key to the wholesomeness of Jewish family life, and when they attempted to undermine the Jewish faith, they legislated that Jewish men must have intercourse with their menstruating wives.[17] The Rabbis of the Talmud have high praise for women who kept their husbands from transgressing.[18]

The laws of *nidda* and *mikva* are observed primarily by Orthodox Jews.

Why are ritual baths frequented most often at night?

Although a ritual bath *(mikva)*, sometimes called a ritualarium, is visited by some observant Jews to purify themselves before major holidays and particularly before the Day of Atonement (some members of chassidic sects immerse themselves every Friday afternoon to prepare for the Sabbath), the most frequent user of the *mikva* is the woman who has completed her menstrual cycle.

Since the menstruant *(nidda)* and her husband abstain from sex for approximately twelve days each month, and since the period of abstinence ends with nightfall (when the new day begins in the Jewish calendar), most women use the *mikva* in the evening so as to avoid any unnecessary delay in the reunion with their husbands.[19]

Why do some people believe that if a menstruant touches a Tora scroll, the Tora becomes unfit for further use?

Many people mistakenly believe that since a menstruant is unfit *(pesula* in Hebrew) for cohabitation with her husband because she is considered to be in a state of impurity, any holy object touched by her becomes unclean and unfit for use. That this is not the case is derived from the comment of Rabbi Judah ben Bathyra, who says, "Words of the Tora are not susceptible to uncleanness."[20] No individual, even one in a state of impurity, can defile a Tora by touching it or handling it.

Why did talmudic authorities tread lightly in their disapproval of premarital sex?

Recognizing how strong is man's desire for sexual gratification and how powerless he sometimes is to control it, talmudic authorities were not quick to condemn sexually active single persons. Although the Rabbis of the Talmud considered premarital sexual activity sinful, they did display an understanding of man's sexual needs. One tractate, for example, records the rather unorthodox observation of Rabbi Assi: "In the beginning, the evil [sexual] inclination [yetzer hara] is [thin and fragile] like a spider's thread, but in the end [as it continues to spin its thread] it becomes as strong as a rope that pulls a wagon."[21] To Rabbi Assi, sexual need is a force to be reckoned with.

Also in the Talmud we find the view of Rabbi Ela'i the Elder. He believed that a person is not evil if he cannot control his sexual passions, but he also believed that the person should act discreetly. "If a man sees that he is being overwhelmed by sexual desire," said Rabbi Ela'i, "he should go somewhere where he will not be recognized, and there should dress himself in black garments [so he will not be recognized], and do what his heart desires, but let him not defame God by conducting himself in that manner publicly."[22]

Acknowledging the sexual needs of the unmarried, the Sages suggested early marriage. The Ethics of the Fathers (5:25) suggests that "eighteen is the proper age for marriage."

Why does Jewish law disapprove of couples living together as man and wife without being formally married?

Surprisingly, the Bible does not even comment on the propriety of unmarried persons living together as man and wife, and it is interesting that John Calvin (1509-1564), the French Protestant reformer, once expressed amazement at this "omission" from the Bible.[23] Talmudic and later authorities, however, were deeply concerned about the issue of living together.

The Rabbis of the Talmud established the requirement that before a couple could live together it was necessary that the woman receive from her man a *ketuba* (marriage contract).[24] In the fourteenth century, Rabbi Jacob ben Asher, author of the *Tur,* the code of Jewish law upon which the *Shulchan Aruch* is based, wrote (Evan Haezer 26) that if a man lives with a woman merely for sex, this is simple lewdness.

Some contemporary authorities, in expressing their disapproval of unmarried couples living together, cite the talmudic admonition against a man being alone in an enclosure with a woman other than his wife.[25] This is interpreted to mean that a man is forbidden to have sexual relations with anyone except a spouse.

Why does Judaism frown on masturbation?

Based upon the biblical narrative in Genesis 38, the Rabbis of the Talmud and the codifiers of the law have strongly condemned masturbation. The Bible tells the story of Judah, the son of Jacob. Judah had three sons, Er, Onan, and Shelah. Er was wicked and God slew him. (His wickedness is not specified.) Judah told Onan, the elder of the two remaining brothers, that he must fulfill the obligation of Levirate Marriage by marrying his brother's wife because Er had died childless.[26] (Levirate Marriage, or *Yibum* as it is called in Hebrew, was a practice followed by many people in the Near East in biblical times, having been introduced into the area by Indo-Europeans between 2000 and 1000 B.C.E.)[27]

The story in Genesis continues: "And Onan knew that the child would not be his. And it came to pass when he went into [had intercourse with] his brother's wife that he spilled it [his seed] on the ground, lest he should give seed to his brother. And the thing which he did was evil in the sight of the Lord, and God slew him" (Genesis 38:1-10). The Rabbis condemn anyone who "brings forth seed for no purpose" because they considered semen to be a valuable resource reserved for a holy task: to populate the world and thus bring glory to God by his creatures.[28]

Despite these proscriptions, modern rabbis (some Orthodox included) tend to favor a more liberal approach. They do not categorize masturbation as "wasting"—or, as some authorities call it, "destroying"—semen if the semen is used for medical testing or for artificially inseminating a man's wife who would otherwise remain infertile. Others, particularly among the non-Orthodox, agree with physicians and psychologists who do not condemn masturbation as an evil act, but consider it a normal, healthy human release.

It is reasonable to assume that the point of the Onan story in Genesis 38 has been misinterpreted. Traditionally, the story has been taken to be a condemnation of masturbation, but it may very well be no more than a condemnation of the attitude of a selfish brother who refused to carry out the ancient rite of *Yibum*, of marrying the childless widow of a brother in order to produce a child with her so as to carry on the deceased brother's name.[29]

Why is the Bible firmly opposed to homosexuality?

Considering it an unnatural and depraved activity, the Book of Leviticus (18:22) is very explicit on the subject of homosexuality: "Thou shalt not lie [cohabit] with a male as one lies with a woman; it is an abomination." Leviticus 20:13 repeats this characterization, adding, "The two of them shall be put to death."

The consequences of homosexuality are vividly portrayed in the Bible. In Genesis (19:5), a group of the inhabitants of Sodom demanded that Lot, Abraham's nephew, send out of his house male visitors so that they, the Sodomites, could cohabit with them. Lot refused to comply with their demands. Because of the prevalence of homosexuality among the Sodomites, Jewish tradition says, Sodom was eventually destroyed. (Today, the word "sodomy" is generally used to characterize any depraved sex act.)

In the Book of Judges (19:22), members of the tribe of Benjamin from Gibeah demanded that a visitor being housed for the night be sent out of the house "that we may know [cohabit with] him." Gibeah, like Sodom, was destroyed for its homosexual practices.

The Bible does not mention female homosexuality, from which one may infer that lesbianism was not widely practiced, or that if it was, it was not considered a crime. In Jewish law, lesbianism is treated as a minor offense. In fact, the Talmud declares that although female homosexuality is prohibited, if a lesbian should marry a Priest, the marriage is considered valid.[30] Maimonides explains that this leniency in the law was arrived at based on the belief that lesbianism does not involve genital intercourse.[31]

Why is homosexuality condemned by contemporary mainstream Judaism?

Homosexuality was common among the Canaanites and among the early Egyptians. It was part of heathen worship in biblical times and was widely accepted as the norm among the Greeks. In the Athens of Pericles and Plato, love affairs between boys and men were common. In fact, the classical Greek system of education was built on an erotic association between teacher and pupil: the student was to "inspire" the teacher with his good looks, and the teacher in turn was to prove himself a worthy role model.

Even in the first three centuries B.C.E., when Greek influence was strongest, Jews never accepted homosexuality as a way of life. The Talmud notes that Jews did not engage in such activity.[32] Centuries later, Moses Maimonides (1135-1204) and other codifiers of Jewish law also observed that "Jews are not suspected of practicing homosexuality."[33]

Throughout the Middle Ages, until recent times, Jewish sources have focused little attention on the issue of homosexuality. In the past two decades, however, as society in general has been confronted by the demands of homosexuals, so has the Jewish community. Today, synagogues have been established by and for homosexuals; there are rabbis who marry homosexuals; and there are rabbis who are homosexual themselves. The argument offered in defense of the homosexual lifestyle is that although procreation is the primary purpose of Jewish marriage, it is not the sole purpose. Surely, it is argued, homosexuals are made in God's image as everyone else, and they should not be denied the right to a full life.

Halachists (masters of Jewish law) have not had sufficient time to assess the demands of the Jewish homosexual. However, Rabbi Norman Lamm, president of Yeshiva University (Orthodox), has advanced a response to the homosexual community in which he maintains that homosexuality is an abominable act, exactly as the Bible asserts. He argues that if Jews were to condone the practice of homosexuality, they should also condone other acts heretofore held immoral by Jewish tradition.[34]

Most Conservative and Reform rabbis agree with this view. Yet, while homosexuals are considered to be in violation of Jewish law, no one has yet argued in favor of banning them or expelling them from the Jewish community. There has been strong opposition to the establishment of special gay synagogues, but there has been little, if any, opposition to homosexuals freely joining established synagogues.

Why does Jewish law prohibit the male from using contraceptive devices even after he has established a family?

The biblical precept to "be fruitful and multiply" (Genesis 1:28) has been interpreted by the Talmud as addressed to men only. It is they, not their wives, who are obligated to carry out the commandment. Despite the fact that the Talmud says that a man has complied with the law once he has fathered two children,[35] he may not employ birth control devices even after he has done so. Jewish law, as interpreted by all leading authorities, considered the prohibition against "destroying" or "wasting" seed (in Hebrew, *hashchatat zera*) to be an inviolable law in its own right, and the use of a condom by a male is prohibited except in special cases where pregnancy may cause injury or death to the woman.

Why does Jewish law disapprove of vasectomy?

In Jewish law, it is the duty of the male to propagate the race. Since vasectomy prevents the man from fulfilling this duty, submitting to the procedure is considered a direct violation of biblical law.

Opposition to male sterilization is also based on Deuteronomy 23:2, which states: "He whose testes are crushed or whose male organ is cut off may not be admitted to the congregation of the Lord." Intentional castration was practiced by heathens who wished to achieve positions of trust. Jewish tradition considers castration—and by extension any action that permanently damages the male's power of propagation—an affront to human dignity and damaging to the status of Israel as a holy nation. Accordingly, Jewish law condemns it.[36]

In recent years, since the medical profession has learned to perform vasectomies that are reversible, some rabbinic authorities have permitted men to undergo the operation, especially when the health of the wife is a factor.

Why have some rabbinic authorities been reluctant to permit women to use birth control devices?

Although the primary obligation of building a family

belongs to the male (as explained above), the wife may nevertheless not use contraceptive devices even if she and her husband have already established a basic family, which according to the School of Hillel means having a boy and a girl and according to the School of Shammai means having two boys.[37] The sole exception to this rule is the use of the birth control pill. (See next question.)

The main argument advanced in support of this attitude is the talmudic reference to three kinds of woman who according to Rashi "may use" and, according to Rabbenu Tam, "should use" a contraceptive device called a *moch*—a soft tuft of wool or cotton that is inserted into the vagina. The three categories of woman are the minor, the pregnant woman, and the nursing mother. In each case, the reason for permitting (or requiring) the use of the *moch* is to prevent a pregnancy that might be harmful to the health of the mother or the child.[38]

Based on the fact that in the above cases it is the well-being of the mother and child that is the reason for permitting the use of a contraceptive device, the rabbis in post-talmudic times permitted the use of contraceptives only by women in similar kinds of emergency.

Today, almost all rabbinic authorities permit the use of contraceptive devices—even if a family has not already been established—in cases where pregnancy may imperil the life of the mother or where it is certain that the newborn might be afflicted with a serious congenital disease or abnormality. Authorities who are more liberal are generally lenient in taking into account the mental attitude of the woman and the stress to which she might be subject if she were to become pregnant.

Why is there little opposition by rabbinic authorities to women using the birth control pill?

In post-talmudic times rabbinic authorities began to view sex as having a purpose beyond procreation, namely the sexual gratification of both male and female. Authorities such as the thirteenth-century Isaiah di Traini of Italy, the sixteenth-century Solomon Luria of Poland, and the nineteenth-century Moses Sofer of Hungary were among those who propounded the idea that mutual pleasure from intercourse is a legitimate pursuit and that the *moch* (and similar devices) may be used. They believed, however, that contraceptives should not interfere with sexual gratification and should allow for unrestricted penetration by the male.

Practically all rabbinic authorities permit women to use the birth control pill after the birth of a boy and a girl (or two boys) because unlike other contraceptives it does not in any way interfere with the sexual act. Being a nonuterine device, the pill satisfies critics who argue that Jewish law forbids the use by the woman of any device that interferes with the passage of semen or that prevents the husband and wife from achieving direct and full physical contact during cohabitation.[39]

Why do some rabbinic authorities object to the use of fertility drugs?

The use of drugs known to increase fertility in women has been questioned primarily because the drugs frequently have detrimental side effects. However, most rabbinic authorities agree that since fertility medications are more helpful than detrimental, and since they contribute to the fulfillment of the commandment to "be fruitful and multiply" (Genesis 1:28), their use is permissible.

Why is the artificial insemination procedure a controversial subject among rabbinic authorities?

Because there are more than one type of artificial insemination procedure, and because there are many different circumstances under which they can be used, there is no clear-cut attitude toward artificial insemination that is shared by Jewish scholars.

One type of artificial insemination involves injecting the semen of the donor directly into the women's uterus. The egg (ovum) of the woman is fertilized by the sperm of the donor, an embryo develops, and the woman carries the child to term.

A second type of artificial insemination is implemented in situations where the fallopian tubes of the woman are blocked and the egg cannot reach the uterus to be fertilized by the sperm of the male. In these cases the ovum is removed from the woman by means of a minor operation. The egg is placed in a dish or test tube and the male's sperm—freshly obtained or frozen—is introduced. If the fertilization is successful, the resulting embryo is implanted in the uterus of the mother. Babies born as a result of this *in vitro* (in glass) procedure are known as test-tube babies.

In both artificial insemination procedures, the husband of the woman who provides the egg for fertilization may or may not be the donor of the sperm. If he is, the procedure is referred to as AIH (Artificial Insemination Husband). If, for one reason or another, the husband is unable to provide the sperm and the semen of a stranger must be used, the procedure is known as AID (Artificial Insemination Donor).

Many Jewish (as well as Christian) theologians have criticized these procedures on moral grounds. They argue that whatever good may be accomplished by helping infertile couples to have a family is by far outweighed by the danger of allowing humans to "play God." However, the consensus among Jewish scholars is that AIH is a permissible procedure while AID is questionable.

Why is artificial insemination with the husband as the donor (AIH) approved of by most rabbis?

When the donor of semen is the husband (AIH), most rabbinic authorities approve of artificial insemination. They follow the lead of great scholars such as Rabbi Shalom Mordechai Schwadron, the nineteenth-century Galician authority; Aaron Walkin, the celebrated rabbi of Pinsk after

World War I; and Rabbi Eliezer Waldenberg of Israel in the 1950s. All believed that it is quite proper for a woman who cannot otherwise conceive—because the male has difficulty depositing sperm—to be impregnated artificially with the seed of her husband. They did not regard this as "wasting seed" or "destroying seed" (hashchatat zera) because the purpose of the procedure is the propagation of life.[40]

Why is artificial insemination with the husband as donor (AIH) opposed by some rabbinic authorities when it is performed outside the wife's body?

The strong opposition is based on moral considerations. While in 1978 Rabbi Ovadya Yosef, the former Chief Sephardic Rabbi of Israel gave his qualified approval to the procedure,[41] Rabbi Shlomo Goren, the Ashkenazic Chief Rabbi at the time, opposed in vitro fertilization on the ground that it was morally repugnant. He and those who shared his view argued that children who are the product of fertilization outside the female body may be born with physical abnormalities because of the extra handling of the ovum when it is extracted from the womb to be fertilized and then reimplanted.[42]

Why is AID permitted by some rabbinic authorities under certain circumstances?

As a matter of practical law rabbinic authorities are opposed to artificial insemination by a donor other than the husband (AID). While some equate AID with adultery, most oppose it on the ground that it could conceivably lead to a situation where sperm from the same donor might be used to impregnate other women, and the children born from these procedures (who would actually all be half-brothers and half-sisters) might one day meet and marry. Such marriages, say the opponents of AID, would be incestuous and strictly forbidden by biblical law (Leviticus 18).

Opponents of AID also argue that the donor, the stranger, is "wasting seed" if the semen he emits is not used to establish a family for himself. "Wasting seed" (onanism) is a direct violation of traditional Jewish law.

Under certain circumstances, however, rabbinic authorities have permitted artificial insemination in which the semen of a stranger is used. One such case is referred to in a responsum of Rabbi Moshe Feinstein.[43] He ruled that in a case where a married woman has been unable to conceive for ten years, and doctors concur that the husband is sterile, the woman may be impregnated with the semen of a stranger. This conclusion is based on an incident related in the Talmud.[44] While immersing herself in a ritual bath (mikva) that had earlier been used by a man, a virgin was unknowingly impregnated by semen that remained floating in the water. The Talmud explains that a High Priest, who by biblical law (Leviticus 21:13-14) can marry only a virgin, was permitted to marry this woman.

Citing this as a legal precedent, rabbinic authorities have said that to impregnate a woman with the semen of a donor (AID) is permissible as long as there is no direct physical contact between the man and the woman. A child born from such a pregnancy is considered legitimate in every respect. Yet, while theoretically Jewish law permits AID, it does not encourage it in actual practice.

The liberal view is expressed by Rabbi Solomon B. Freehof, who sees no reason not to allow AID. He considers the primary objection to AID—namely, that a child born as a result of the procedure may unknowingly marry a close blood relative and thus violate biblical law—so farfetched that it should not be considered a factor in determining the law.[45]

Why, in Jewish law, is a child born as a result of the AID procedure not considered the child of the mother's husband?

When a child is born from seed provided by a donor

other than the husband, Jewish law considers the child legitimate in every respect. But unlike secular law, Jewish law does not consider the husband of the woman to be the legal father of the child. The donor of the seed is the legitimate father,[46] and the woman's husband has no legal connection with the child because he did not provide the seed. And although the man's wife has had a child while married to him, this child does not satisfy the biblical commandment incumbent upon the husband to beget children.

See the previous answer for the non-Orthodox view.

Why has the use of a host-mother been criticized by many as offensive?

In some cases where a woman is unable to carry a fetus to term (as when she has a tendency to abort), arrangements are made to have the fertilized egg of the woman implanted in the uterus of a second woman. (Sometimes the fertilized egg is extracted from the womb of the first woman and implanted in the second. Sometimes the egg is fertilized in a test tube or dish outside of the womb.) For a fee, the second woman, the host-mother, carries the fetus to term. Upon giving birth, the child is "returned" to the natural mother, the supplier of the ovum.

Rabbinic authorities, including Chief Rabbi Immanuel Jakobovits of England, have condemned this practice as morally offensive. However, since this is sometimes the only way in which a married couple can have a child, the practice is generally approved of as long as the sperm that fertilizes the egg is that of the husband.[47]

Why does the religion of a host-mother not determine the religion of the child she carries to term?

As discussed fully in Chapter One, the religion of a child is determined solely by the mother. If the mother is Jewish, the child is Jewish.

The religion of a child carried to term by a host-mother is in question when a fertilized ovum of a Jewish woman is implanted in the womb of a host-mother who is not Jewish. Who is the real mother of the child? Is it the Jewish woman who supplied the fertilized egg, or is it the non-Jewish host-mother who nurtured the child in her womb and carried the child to term?

It would appear, at this point, that most authorities are of the opinion that it is the supplier of the ovum who is the real mother. But the question is so new and so complex that very few rabbinic authorities have ventured definitive opinions. The issue will be the subject of much debate in the future.[48]

Why does Jewish law permit abortion under certain circumstances?

In the Talmud and later rabbinic literature, the opinion is expressed that an abortion may be performed if the mother's life is in danger. This view has been extended by some authorities to include "indirect" threats to the mother's well-being, meaning that under certain circumstances pregnancies may be aborted for the sake of the woman's mental health or for other familial considerations.[49]

Rabbi Yair Chaim Bachrach, the prominent seventeenth-century German authority, wrote in response to a question that it is not permissible for a married woman who was impregnated by a stranger to have an abortion. Although he agreed that the fetus is not to be considered a human being, he feared that immorality would be encouraged if he granted permission for an abortion.[50] However, in a similar situation, Rabbi Jacob Emden, a leading eighteenth-century authority, permitted aborting a pregnancy that resulted from an adulterous union. He also condoned abortions that would spare the woman great pain or discomfort.[51] The late Sephardic Chief Rabbi of Israel from 1939 to 1953, Ben Zion Uziel (also spelled Ouziel), was of the same opinion as Jacob Emden. He permitted abortions that were in the best interests of the mother, even if not crucial to her health.[52]

Today, many rabbis approve of abortion in cases where there is considerable likelihood that the child will be born deformed (for example, if the mother has contracted a disease such as rubella, known to cause severe malformation). To some authorities, unfavorable indications from an amniocentesis analysis are sufficient grounds for abortion.

In general, both the non-Orthodox rabbinate and the Orthodox rabbinate do not favor indiscriminate abortions, but they do favor abortion when the mother's well-being is at stake. Conservative and Reform rabbis would tend to be more liberal in their interpretation of what constitutes valid therapeutic reasons.[53]

Why is the unborn fetus not considered a "person" in Jewish law?

Perhaps influenced by the teachings of the Greek philosopher Aristotle, who believed that the soul becomes part of the unborn male child on the fortieth day after conception and of the female child on the eightieth, the Rabbis of the Talmud and those of later centuries regarded the fertilized ovum as mere fluid until the fortieth day after conception. On the fortieth day the embryo forms, and from that point until birth the fetus is considered part of the mother, not a separate entity.[54]

Basically, the Sages arrived at their point of view from the statement in the Book of Exodus (21:22) that if a pregnant woman is struck by someone, and her unborn child destroyed, the person who caused the mishap must pay damages. He is not, however, considered a murderer because the unborn child is not a person. The Talmud is quite specific in describing the status of an unborn child: "If a woman is having difficulty giving birth and her life is in danger, the fetus may be removed surgically, limb by limb, because her life takes precedence over the unborn fetus. However, if delivery of the child has already begun, and its head or the greater part of its body has already emerged, the child may not be harmed to save the mother, because one person's life may not be taken to save another."[55] This view was reiterated by Rashi, who said, "So long as the fetus does not enter the 'atmosphere of the world,' it is not to be considered a person [*nefesh* in Hebrew]."[56] However, despite the fact that in Jewish law the unborn child is not considered a person, the law does not approve of abortion unless there is sufficient justification.[57]

Why is a Caesarian section sometimes prohibited in Jewish law?

If a Caesarian section—a surgical operation for delivering a baby by cutting through the mother's abdominal and uterine walls—will not harm the mother and is deemed necessary for the well-being of the child, it is permitted in Jewish law. However, if the operation might endanger the life of the mother, it is prohibited. As indicated in the previous answer, the Talmud states clearly that the mother's life takes precedence over the life of the child. This was codified as law.[58]

Why does the Bible prescribe that a sin-offering be brought by the mother after giving birth?

The Book of Leviticus (12) states that the mother of a newborn boy is considered impure for seven days plus an additional period of thirty-three days, for a total of forty days. For a girl child, the period of impurity is eighty days. (No reason is given for this difference.) When the periods of impurity are over, the Bible says, the mother is to bring a sin-offering. The Talmud explains the reason for the sin-offering: the pain of giving birth (which is ascribed in Genesis 3:16 to Eve's disobedience) is so intense that most women foreswear future sexual relations with their husbands, for which they are later sorry. The sin-offering is for the promise made that will not be kept.[59]

Why do rabbinic authorities differ on the question of using organs from a dead person for transplant purposes?

Based on Deuteronomy 21:22-23, which states that if a criminal is put to death by hanging, "his body shall not remain all night hanging on the tree, but thou shalt surely bury him that same day," the Rabbis conclude that to mistreat or mutilate the body of a deceased (known in Hebrew as *nivul hamet*) is a violation of scriptural law.

Since it is argued that the body of a dead person is in a sense being mutilated when an organ is removed from it for transplant into the body of a living person, strong opposition to the procedure exists. Most authorities agree, however, that when a transplant is likely to save a life, such surgery is permitted. Transplant surgery that results in the saving of a life adds glory and honor to the dead (in Hebrew, *kevod hamet*). Thus, the positive commandment of saving a life, the rabbinic authorities say, is of the highest priority, superseding even the laws of the Sabbath.[60] The talmudic principle that is applied by the advocates of transplant surgery is *zeh ne'heneh vezeh lo chaser,* "one party is helped and the other is not harmed."

Aside from the question of mutilation of the dead, many in the Orthodox community object to organ transplant surgery on the ground that it results in a violation of the Jewish law requiring that all severed parts of a person be buried. When an organ is used for transplant purposes, it is obviously not buried.

This question has been addressed by Rabbi Moshe Feinstein (Orthodox), who counters that when any organ from the body of a deceased is transplanted into a living person, the organ can no longer be considered an organ of the dead. It becomes part of a living body, and the law demanding the burial of all parts of a deceased does not apply.[61] Rabbi Isaac Klein (Conservative) points out that a transplanted organ will eventually be buried, thus satisfying the requirement.[62]

Why are organ transplants from living donors often permitted under Jewish law?

While some Jewish scholars over the centuries have asserted that one is a "pious fool" *(chassid shoteh)* if he endangers his own life in order to save the life of a fellow man, most agree with Moses Maimonides that a person must be willing to place his own life in jeopardy in order to save someone who may die if help is denied him.

Several years ago, the former Sephardic Chief Rabbi of Israel, Ovadya Yosef (who served until 1983), was asked whether one can donate a kidney to a person in critical need of a transplant. His response was that one is obligated to donate a kidney if doctors can assure him that the operation is likely to succeed and that the donor's health will not be jeopardized. By extension, he ruled that all organ transplants that do not put the donor's life at risk or health in danger are permitted under Jewish law. *Pikuach nefesh* ("saving or prolonging a life"), an overriding principle in Jewish law, applies here. Where a transplant will save a life without sacrificing another life, it is generally permitted.[63]

Generally speaking, most rabbinic authorities approve of transplant procedures in cases where the donating of the organ is not likely to in any way shorten the life of the donor and where the chances of success of the transplant are favorable. Thus, the donating of a kidney is permissible because the donor can function normally with just one kidney and because the success rate for kidney transplants is impressive (51 percent graft survival after one year, 40 percent after three years, 31 percent after five years). Furthermore, in cases where the kidney transplant fails, the patient is still able to survive on dialysis.[64]

Why have heart transplants been condemned by the interpreters of Jewish law?

When the heart transplant operation was first introduced by Dr. Christiaan Barnard in Cape Town, South

Africa, in 1967, many rabbinic authorities expressed their approval of the new lifesaving measure. However, as one after another of these operations ended in failure, rabbinic opposition to the heart transplant procedure became virtually unanimous. Strong opposition developed not only because the operations were unsuccessful but also because there was a suspicion—now confirmed—that the heart to be used for transplant is generally removed from the donor before death, which is defined by Jewish law as the time at which respiration ceases.[65]

Orthodox authorities are of the opinion that a minimum of twenty minutes must elapse after breathing has stopped before a person can be declared dead. (Brain death is not accepted as *the* moment of death.) In some cases authorities insist on waiting one-half hour or one hour to make certain no error has been made.[66]

In summary, the view of traditional authorities today is that when one takes a heart from a donor by standard procedure, the donor is technically alive, and is in fact being killed by removing the heart for transplant. Jewish law forbids taking the life of one person to save another.

Why may a valve from the heart of a pig be used for human transplant?

Although Jewish law (Leviticus 11:7) forbids the consumption of a pig as food, it does allow the use of that animal in any other way. For this reason observant Jews do wear pigskin gloves or play with footballs or other balls made of pigskin. For the purpose of saving a life, no part of any nonkosher animal is considered taboo. Not only may parts of the animal be used for transplant purposes, but the animal itself may be consumed as food if prescribed by a physician as necessary for survival.[67]

Why does Jewish law permit medical experimentation on animals for the benefit of man?

While the humane treatment of animals was mandated in the Bible (Exodus 23:5 and Deuteronomy 22:4), man is the central figure in the Jewish tradition. Everything exists for his welfare, and this includes all animal and vegetable life. For this reason, most rabbinic authorities permit experimentation on animals if the purpose is to find a cure for man's ills. They do, however, insist that every precaution be taken to prevent inflicting unnecessary pain on the animals.

Rabbi Ezekiel Landau of Prague (1713-1793) was asked whether one is permitted to hunt animals for sport, and whether if he does so he is violating the law against causing pain to animals. Landau replied that technically there is no violation of Jewish law when one hunts, since man is permitted to slay animals for his own benefit, and this consideration is paramount. But he does condemn the action on moral and ethical grounds, emphasizing that it runs counter to the whole of Jewish tradition, and also that it places a man's own life in jeopardy when he enters the woods to hunt. [68]

Why does Jewish law consider it permissible to take the life of an animal in order to use its organs for transplant purposes?

In October 1984, an infant who came to be known affectionately as Baby Fae, was born with a defective heart and with virtually no chance of survival. When the child was two weeks old, a medical team at the Seventh-Day Adventist Medical Center in Loma Linda, California, with the permission of the parents, replaced Baby Fae's heart with that of a baby baboon. This action became the subject of much debate. Many protested that animal rights were being violated, that it is improper to kill an animal to save a human being. The majority of people, however, applauded the surgical effort, even though the baby lived for only thirty-two days.

As indicated in the above answer, while Jewish tradition considers it improper to inflict pain upon animals or to take their lives for mere sport, it does consider it quite proper to sacrifice an animal for the benefit of man. The entire sacrificial system described in the Bible, which continued until the destruction of the Second Temple in the year 70 C.E., was predicated on the premise that man may take the life of an animal to atone for his sins or to express gratitude to God. Man, in Jewish tradition, is the centerpiece of Creation, and animals were created for no reason other than to serve him.

This belief was expressed in various ways by the Rabbis of old. In one instance, in analyzing the story of Noah, the Talmud asks why the animals were destroyed in the flood.[69] Since man had been sinful, it is understandable why he would have been destroyed in the flood, but why were the animals destroyed as well? What was their sin?

The answer comes in the form of a parable. The Rabbis compare what happened during the flood to a man who prepared an elaborate wedding for his son. During the week of festivities following the ceremony, the son died suddenly. Whereupon the father tore apart the elaborate decorations and cancelled the festivities, sending home all the celebrants. He said, "Did I prepare all this for anyone except my son? Now that he is dead, what need have I for the banquet?"

"Likewise did the Holy One, blessed be He, say [at the time of the flood]: 'Did I create the animals and beasts for any reason other than that they should serve man? Now that man has sinned, what need have I for the animals?' "

The Midrash expresses this same attitude in describing a man who was transporting his animal by boat. A tempest developed and the boat was about to capsize. What should the man do? And the answer given is, the man may throw the animal overboard in order to prevent the boat from sinking. The decision clearly implies that animals are not as important as human beings.[70]

Rabbi Simeon ben Eleazar gave expression to this same belief in the superiority of man over beast when he remarked, "Throughout my entire life I never witnessed a deer gathering fruit, a lion carrying a burden, or a fox acting as a shopkeeper. [None have had to work for a living or plan their lives like man.] Yet, they all manage to live without trouble. Now, if these animals who were created to serve man can be sustained without any effort on their part, how much more so am I entitled to live and be sustained without working and without anxiety."[71]

Tradition, quite clearly, sees man as the most important creature in the universe and finds it proper and moral to sacrifice an animal if necessary to save a human life.

Why does Jewish law permit blood transfusions despite the biblical ban on consuming blood?

The biblical laws (Leviticus 3:17, 17:10-12) prohibiting the consumption of blood have been interpreted by the Rabbis as referring only to blood that is consumed orally, not to blood administered intravenously. This aside, the ruling of the Rabbis is in keeping with the established talmudic principle that the saving of a life supersedes all Tora commandments.

Why do some authorities oppose cosmetic surgery?

Some scholars oppose cosmetic surgery because, unlike other forms of surgery, it involves inflicting a wound upon a person unnecessarily. Jewish law permits cutting into a human's flesh if the purpose is to effect a cure. If done for other reasons, the practice is disapproved of because it may endanger the person's life.[72]

However, most rabbinic authorities permit cosmetic surgery based on the biblical verse (Exodus 21:19), ". . . and he shall cause him [the wounded person] to be thoroughly healed." This has been interpreted to mean that for the purpose of healing a deformed or unattractive part of a person's anatomy a wound may be inflicted, that is, an operation may be performed.

The vast majority of scholars approve of cosmetic surgery when it serves a positive psychological or practical purpose. This would include an operation for a girl to improve her appearance so she might find a husband. It would also include surgery to improve an individual's looks so he or she might be more successful in the business world.[73]

Why do segments of the Orthodox community disagree over whether a *Kohayn* should be permitted to study medicine?

In Temple times, a Priest had to be a proven descendant of the family of Aaron of the tribe of Levi before he could serve at the altar. *Kohanim* today are only "presumed" to be Priests because their pedigree cannot be proven. For this reason, some authorities within the Orthodox community do not consider it a violation of biblical law or talmudic law if a *Kohayn* wishes to study medicine, even though it requires that he be in contact with corpses in the course of his studies. They feel that inasmuch as doctors save lives, and since in Jewish law there is no greater good deed one can perform than that of saving a life (one may even violate the Sabbath to do so), *Kohanim* should be permitted to study medicine.

There are, however, Orthodox authorities who vehemently reject this position. Rabbi Yekutiel Greenwald and Rabbi Moshe Feinstein[74] forbid a *Kohayn* from entering the medical profession. They consider the laws of Levitical purity to be fully in effect as they were in Temple times. Rabbi Greenwald berates Rabbi Bernard Revel, first president of Yeshiva University, for holding a liberal view in this matter.

Non-Orthodox authorities take the position that all *Kohanim* today are Priests only by presumption, and they see no reason for prohibiting them from studying medicine.

Why does biblical law prohibit tattooing?

Leviticus 19:28 states explicitly, "You shall not cut into

your flesh for the dead, nor cut any marks on yourselves; I am the Lord."

Ancient peoples of the Near East often cut into their skin and mutilated their bodies to demonstrate grief. They also cut into their skin and filled the incisions with indelible dyes, creating tattoos of the deities they worshipped. These practices were forbidden to Jews not only because they represented pagan worship, but also because they ran counter to the biblical prohibitions against spilling blood and mistreating man's God-given body.

Since tattooing in modern times involves pricking the skin rather than cutting into it, and since idolatry is no longer practiced among civilized people, there is some doubt whether the biblical ban against it applies today.

Why is it customary for Jews to allow their beards to grow?

The Bible expresses vigorous opposition to all pagan practices. Foremost among these is the ban on removing facial hair (Leviticus 19:27). The Bible forbids the Israelites from "rounding off" or "destroying the sidegrowth [in Hebrew, *payot*] of one's head" because those who ministered to idols were known to shave certain areas of the face with a sharp blade. Aside from the association with idolatry, the Rabbis objected to the use of the blade (in Hebrew, *taar*, meaning "sword") on the ground that it could be used as a lethal weapon and also because the open blade was a symbol of war.

In Jewish tradition, from post-biblical times onward the beard was considered "an adornment to man's face"[75] as well as a symbol of maturity, piety, and distinction. Young Priests who had not yet grown beards were not permitted to bless the people.[76]

Moses Maimonides, in the twelfth century, was probably the first scholar to note five specific areas of the male face which could not be shaved with an open blade; both upper sides of the jaw (next to the ears), both sides of the chin, and the peak of the chin. The penalty for removing hair from these areas with a blade is whipping (in Hebrew, *malkot*), says Maimonides, but there is no punishment if the hair is removed with scissors. According to Maimonides, a blade may be used to remove hair from soft areas of the face, including the upper lip and the area below the chin to the neck.[77]

There has never been unanimity among rabbinic authorities as to which areas of the face are actually meant by Leviticus 19:27, and in the sixteenth century a stricter attitude toward shaving was adopted. Joseph Caro and Moses Isserles ruled that Jews may not remove *any* hair from the face.[78] Later scholars, such as Ezekiel Landau (1713-1793) of Prague, noted that trimming the beard is a violation of sacred Jewish tradition.[79]

After the seventeenth century, however, as they were increasingly drawn into the mainstream of Western society, Jews found it necessary to make their appearance more acceptable to the general population. Since Jewish law permitted the removal of facial hair by means other than a single swordlike blade, Jews began to remove hair from their faces by using scissors, clippers, or chemical depilatories. Today, most Orthodox Jews who shave use electric razors.

Why do male members of the chassidic community crop their hair closely?

While *chassidim* allow the *payot* (sidelocks) to grow long, they do not permit the hair on the top of the head to grow long. The Talmud[80] warns that to grow hair long is one of "the ways of the Amorites" and, as is the rule with all pagan practices, it must be avoided.

Chassidim also take seriously the admonition of the *Zohar*[81] that "[growing] long hair increases the stern decree directed against the world." This is linked to a central concept of mysticism known as *kelipot* (plural of *kelipa*, meaning "shell, husk"). *Kelipot* are barriers and distractions that take a man's mind away from spiritual matters.

To achieve spiritual purity and maturity the mystic believes that he must rid himself of these barriers, which include man's hair.[82]

Why does Jewish law prohibit men from dyeing their hair?

The biblical ban (Deuteronomy 22:5) that prohibits men from wearing the garb of women was extended by the Rabbis to include all practices peculiar to women. Maimonides points out that the commandment in Deuteronomy implies that a man should not wear brightly colored clothing or shiny jewelry if such be the practice among women in his locality. He also points out that a man should not pluck white hairs from his head or face, a habit of women. Nor should a man dye his graying hair, which is a woman's practice as well. The *Code of Jewish Law* prohibits the looking in a mirror by a man and calls it "a woman's way."[83]

Why do some Orthodox women shave their heads?

Before marrying, the extremely Orthodox woman shaves her head and covers her shaven head with a scarf *(tichl)* or with a wig *(shaytl)*. The basis of this practice is biblical. Deuteronomy (21:12) describes what a woman must do when she is taken captive in wartime and becomes her captor's wife: "You shall bring her into your house, and she shall trim [shave] her hair, pare her nails ..." The removal of hair from a woman's head symbolized a change in her status from single to married.

Why is the use of cosmetics by women not considered inconsistent with the Jewish ideal of modesty?

The Bible and Talmud make many references to women using spices and lotions in order to make themselves more attractive. This is evident from verses such as Song of Songs 3:6, which speaks of women "perfumed with myrrh and frankincense," and Esther 2:12, which describes women anointed with "oil of myrrh" and "sweet odors and with other ointments of women."

The Talmud takes note of the special permission Ezra granted peddlers of cosmetics to travel about freely among the women who had returned from the Babylonian captivity so that ointments and beauty aids would be readily available to them.[84] From many other talmudic references,[85] it is clear that Jewish tradition wants a woman to look beautiful before marriage so that she might win a husband and after marriage so that she might keep him.

Until the time of Rabbi Akiba, the second century C.E., women were not permitted to use cosmetics or beauty aids during their menstrual periods so as not to make themselves attractive to their husbands. Akiba lifted this ban because he feared that women might grow accustomed to not using cosmetics and would continue to do so even after their menstrual periods had passed. They might then be unattractive to their husbands at a time when they should be attractive.

Why do some brides refrain from wearing make-up when they are standing under the marriage canopy?

In talmudic times a song sung to the bride at her wedding contained the following verse: "[She wears] neither paint, nor rouge, nor [hair] dye; yet radiates charm."[86] This reflected the attitude that a bride is pure and innocent on her wedding day, and that purity and innocence should not be tainted. Today, many brides still follow the ancient custom of appearing under the canopy unadorned with cosmetics.

Why do some Orthodox rabbinic authorities disapprove of the use of makeup on the Sabbath?

The use of cosmetics is generally approved of in Jewish

law, but the application of eye makeup, lipstick, and rouge is forbidden on the Sabbath because it is considered painting.[87] The use of powder, however, is permitted on the Sabbath.

Why do ultra-Orthodox men refrain from wearing rings and other jewelry?

Rings and other jewelry are categorized as women's garb. According to the Bible (see the next question), a man may not wear a woman's garment, just as a woman may not dress in a man's garment.

Why do some observant Jewish women wear slacks, which are ordinarily considered men's apparel?

The Bible (Deuteronomy 22:5) is quite specific on the question of the sexes wearing each other's garments: "A woman shall not dress in man's apparel, nor shall a man wear a woman's garment . . ." To do so is considered "an abomination to the Lord your God."

Observant women who wear jeans, pantsuits, and the like justify their conduct by arguing that garments made specifically for women—such as designer jeans and slacks, especially those with zippers on the side—cannot be considered men's apparel since they were never intended to be worn by men.

Why in Jewish tradition does one dress up for the Sabbath and holidays?

In the Talmud, Rabbi Yochanan comments that it is important to show respect for the Sabbath (and holidays), and one does so by changing clothes from those worn on weekdays.[88] To strengthen his point, he cites the biblical verse that calls upon a Priest, officiating at the altar, to "remove his garments and put on other garments" (Leviticus 6:4). The implication is that for important occasions one should put on fresh garments.

CHAPTER 6

Death and Dying

INTRODUCTION

In the past several decades, psychologists, psychiatrists, social workers, and other mental health professionals have become increasingly involved in the study of death and dying. Among other things, they have discovered the importance of preparing the terminally ill for death, of learning how to accept the death of a loved one, and of encouraging the mourner to express grief. Grieving openly is considered cathartic, purifying. It helps the bereaved to release emotional tension and return to a state of normalcy.

While the Rabbis of the Talmud were not nearly so sophisticated as our contemporary professionals in matters relating to death and dying, they did show great sensitivity to the problems of the bereaved, and they established meaningful laws to help ease their pain. For example, recognizing the shock experienced by an individual immediately following the death of a loved one, the Rabbis freed him of all religious obligations. (The mourner, during this period extending from death to burial, is known in Hebrew as the *onen* or *onan*, meaning "sad, depressed.") Traditionally the *onen* is not to engage in prayer and therefore does not put on *tefilin* or a *talit*.[1] Prayer, according to the Rabbis, is to be engaged in only by a sober person in full charge of his faculties. An *onen*, who like an inebriated person is governed more by emotion than by reason, is therefore not required to pray. He is also not required to study Tora, which is considered a joyful activity.

Just as the Rabbis were sensitive to the needs of the *onen,* they were also sensitive to the needs of the mourner following the burial. Realizing that the mourner would be disinterested in preparing his own meal when he returned home, they ordered that friends and neighbors assume this obligation. Also realizing that the mourner may require a few days to be alone after the funeral, the Rabbis suggested that friends not pay condolence calls for the first three days of *Shiva.* All in all, the Jewish laws of death and mourning are extremely human, meaningful, and beneficial measures geared to quicken the healing process of mourners burdened by grief.

In the chapter devoted to death and mourning in *The Jewish Book of Why,* the focus is primarily on ritual observances, including questions pertaining to preparing the body for burial, cemetery visitation, reciting *Kaddish* and *Yizkor,* observing *Yahrzeit,* and the unveiling of tombstones. While this chapter elaborates on some of the matters treated in the first volume, it also focuses on some of the broad principles on which the laws of death and mourning are based. It shows how these principles are applied to solving some problems Jews must face as a result of recent scientific advances and changing attitudes in society.

Here, we shall discuss

- euthanasia and how Jewish law views the issue
- the growing trend of rabbinic authority to take a more liberal stance on the matter of autopsy
- the propriety of withholding information from the seriously ill
- the Jewish view on cremation
- the burial of suicides
- honoring requests made by the deceased about how mourning should be conducted
- the problems of the *Kohayn* (Priest), who is forbidden by biblical law to come into contact with the dead

And, lastly, we shall talk about the Jewish-Christian relationship with regard to burial and mourning: May non-Jews serve as pallbearers at a Jewish funeral? May a Jew be buried in a non-Jewish cemetery? Can a Jew say *Kaddish* for parents who have abandoned the Jewish faith?

The subject of death and dying is complex and the issues are wide-ranging, but this chapter, coupled with Chapter Three of the first book, should provide the reader with a good understanding of the laws of mourning and the principles involved in their formulation.

Why is euthanasia forbidden under Jewish law?

Both civil law and Jewish law are in general agreement that euthanasia, or "mercy killing" as it is more popularly called, is murder. Regardless of the severity of the condition or how negative the prognosis, no effort may be made to shorten the life of the patient. Jewish tradition places the decision of who shall live and who shall die in God's hands alone. Joseph Caro's *Code of Jewish Law* says that one is not permitted to remove a pillow from under a dying person's head, nor may one create any kind of disturbance that is likely to hasten an individual's death.[2]

In recent times some Jewish authorities have expressed a more liberal attitude toward euthanasia. In support of their position, they cite an incident described in the Talmud. When the death of Rabbi Judah the Prince (135-219), editor of the Mishna and the most outstanding scholar of the third century, was imminent, his disciples gathered around his bed and prayed continuously for his recovery. However, one of Rabbi Judah's maidservants (who was reputed to be a learned woman), realizing how intense was her master's suffering and how useless it would be to prolong his life, hurled an earthenware jug to the ground. The noise had its expected effect: it attracted the attention of everyone in the room and the praying ceased, whereupon

Judah expired. By her action, Judah's maid hastened his death.[3]

Rabbi Nissim ben Reuven Girondi, an outstanding fourteenth-century Spanish scholar and physician, known by the acronym Ran, used this incident as the basis for his decision that one may refrain from praying for a sick person whose pain is intense and for whom there is no hope for recovery. A number of authorities today cite this same incident as grounds for adopting the passive euthanasia approach. They argue that when a terminally ill patient is living in great pain, doctors are not obliged to keep the patient alive by introducing artificial life-support systems, thus leaving therapeutic intervention in the hands of God. *Active* euthanasia, however, which would include injecting the patient with a drug that would speed his demise, is widely condemned as tantamount to murder.[4]

In recent centuries, the practice among the Jews of Yemen has been to remove the *mezuza* and sacred books from the room of a dying man who is in great pain. The Yemenites believe that the presence of holy objects lessens the power of the Angel of Death, and when they are removed the power of the angel increases. Thus, the Angel of Death is able to take the life of the patient sooner.

Why must one refrain from notifying a sick person that a relative has died when it is likely to aggravate his condition?

In Jewish law, withholding the truth is permitted when it eases the burden of the living. Telling an ill person that a relative has died is forbidden because it might cause him great mental anguish and lead to a worsening of his condition.[5]

Why is it sometimes proper to ignore the funeral and mourning instructions left by an individual?

Based upon the principle that one may not give away

that which is not his, rabbinic authorities are in general agreement that certain requests made by an individual prior to his death may be ignored. The accepted view as stated in the Talmud and codified in the *Code of Jewish Law* is that if a person requests that his funeral service be simple—specifically, that no eulogy be delivered—the request is honored because the eulogy is delivered to praise the deceased. However, Moses Isserles points out that if a person requests that the seven days of mourning *(Shiva)* or the thirty days of mourning *(Sheloshim)* not be observed, the request is not to be honored. These periods of mourning are established by Jewish law, and it is not the individual's prerogative to deny them. Besides, the mourning periods were instituted for the benefit of the living as well as to honor the dead.[6]

Why is the Jewish attitude toward performing autopsies becoming more liberal?

The Rabbis of the Talmud considered any form of mutilation of the body a form of irreverence, and this included all forms of dismemberment and disfigurement. For this reason, the Orthodox to this day strenuously oppose autopsy. They believe that "in the end of days" God will resurrect the dead, and any kind of disfigurement of the body will interfere with the process.

A problem that has continued to plague rabbinical and medical authorities in Israel is how to satisfy the requirements of medical schools and medical researchers if anatomical dissections and post-mortem examinations are prohibited. How can scientists learn more about disease if autopsies are forbidden? How can medical students receive proper training if Jewish law *(halacha)* forbids handling the body of a deceased?

The first breakthrough came in the eighteenth century when Rabbi Ezekiel Landau (1713-1793), the famous rabbi of Prague, responded to a question from a Londoner who asked if it is permissible to perform an autopsy on a Jew in order to ascertain the cause of death in the hope that what is learned might save the lives of others. Rabbi Landau ruled that an autopsy may be performed if there is reason to believe that what doctors may learn as a result may be able to save an actual patient who is nearby and is in dire need of help.[7] This opinion was widely hailed and was instrumental in reversing the argument hitherto advanced by authorities that autopsy must necessarily be considered mutilation of the body and hence offensive. Here, the most respected authority of his age was saying that performing an autopsy in certain cases may aptly be called reverence for the dead *(kevod hamet)* since as a result of the procedure another life might be saved, and in Jewish law nothing is of greater importance than preserving life (known in Hebrew as *pikuach nefesh*).

Since Rabbi Landau's decision was issued, many authorities have begun to view some autopsies as leading to the sanctification of life rather than to its desecration.[8]

Why was a burial society, the *Chevra Kadisha,* formed in the Jewish community?

Preparing the deceased for burial in a dignified manner is of the highest priority in Judaism. In Jewish tradition, a human being is equated with a Tora scroll. Like the scroll, which is treated reverently not only while it is in use but also when it is no longer in use, so is the human being to be treated when his life is over.

When Jewish communities were close-knit, towns or villages and often individual synagogues had their own burial societies. The Jewish burial society, known in Hebrew as the *Chevra Kadisha,* literally meaning "Holy Society," was comprised of individuals who consecrated themselves to the holy task of preparing the dead for burial.

Although the Jewish community is no longer as cohesive as it once was, the *Chevra Kadisha* still functions, either under the aegis of the religious community or under the auspices of the funeral parlor. After the funeral director has arranged for the attending physician to certify the individual's death, and after the body has been transported to the chapel, the *Chevra Kadisha* is called in by the rabbi or the funeral director to attend to the body. A *shomer* ("watcher") stays with the body and recites Psalms, while the other members of the *Chevra Kadisha* wash the body and dress it as prescribed by Jewish law.

Why may shrouds be made of mixed fibers (shaatnez)?

The Bible (Deuteronomy 22:11) prohibits the wearing of garments made from a mixture of wool (animal) and linen or cotton (vegetable) fibers. Such a mixture is called *shaatnez* in Hebrew. (See Chapter Eight.)

Shrouds for the dead may be made of *shaatnez* because the dead are free of all commandments, and laws that apply to the living need not be carried out in behalf of the dead.[9]

Why is a person often buried with the prayer-shawl he used in his lifetime?

The *talit* worn by a man throughout life is buried with him after one of the four fringes *(tzitziot)* is torn off so as to make the *talit* invalid *(pasul).*[10] This is done as a symbolic expression denoting that in the grave one is no longer able or required to abide by Jewish law. The commandment pertaining to *tzitzit* (Numbers 15:37-41) demands that a Jew should "look at them and remember all the commandments of the Lord." The deceased can no longer fulfill this commandment and the *talit,* by being made invalid, reflects this reality.

Where a person does not have a *talit* of his own, the *Chevra Kadisha* (Holy Society) of the community that prepares the body for burial will provide one if that is the wish of the family.

The *atara* ("headband," or more literally, "crown") is removed from the *talit* before burial to symbolize that the "crown" that graced the *talit* of the deceased during life has served its function and must now be retired.

Why are the dead not dressed with shoes?

In Jewish law there is no objection to the dead being buried wearing shoes. In the Talmud it is reported that the prophet Jeremiah is said to have left instructions that when he died he was to be buried in his clothes, with staff in hand and with shoes on his feet,[11] presumably to be fully prepared for resurrection when the Messiah comes. Today, however, when most Jews are buried in simple, white shrouds rather than in their normal street garb, it is quite natural that shoes not be put on their feet.

Why are only the closest relatives of the deceased required to tear their garments (perform *keria*) at the funeral service?

Originally, all who were present in the same room with a person at the moment of death were required to tear their garments and recite the prayer, *Baruch ata ... dayan ha-emet* ("Blessed art Thou, O Lord our God, the Righteous Judge"). In time, these requirements were limited only to close relatives. Had the law not been changed, friends, neighbors, and distant relatives would have been discouraged from visiting the terminally ill lest they be present at the moment of death and would be compelled to tear their garments.

In more recent times the tearing of garments has been shifted to the funeral parlor, where the garments of only the closest relatives are rent. (In some isolated cases *keria* is performed at the cemetery.) While strict observance of the law requires the actual tearing of one's own garment, most mourners—modern Orthodox as well as non-Orthodox—choose to wear a ribbon that is supplied by the funeral parlor and that is torn instead of the garment.

Why is the coffin of a Jew draped with a black cloth embroidered with a Star of David?

There is no specific law regarding this practice, which

probably began as local custom and then grew in popularity. The cloth covering may have been introduced to soften the harsh appearance of an unadorned pine coffin.

The embroidered covering may also be seen as a sign of respect for the dead. The Talmud says that anyone who handles an undressed Tora scroll with his bare hands commits an act of disrespect.[12] Permitting an uncovered casket to remain in full view is often considered a sign of disrespect.

The Star of David is embroidered on the covering for decorative purposes only.

Why are some funeral services held in the synagogue?

Originally, funeral services were held in the home of the deceased, not in the synagogue. Rashi was probably the first to say that an exception could be made in the case of a great scholar or community leader. For him, the funeral may be held in the synagogue because a large number of people will be anxious to attend and the home of the deceased would be too small.[13]

Today, almost all funerals are held in funeral parlors, largely for the convenience of having the funeral director take care of the many necessary details. There is, however, no reason why a funeral may not be conducted in the home of the deceased or in the synagogue if it suits the needs of the family and the congregation. Today, some congregations in the United States have adopted a policy of holding the funerals of all their members in the synagogue, because by so doing the congregation is able to establish procedures and guidelines that best suit the interests of its members, especially in the financial area.[14]

Why do funeral processions occasionally stop in front of a synagogue?

The custom of stopping a funeral procession in front of a synagogue and having the officiating cantor or rabbi recite the *El Malei Rachamim* memorial prayer was common-place in Europe and America before World War II. The custom, believed to have been introduced in some unidenti-fied community during the Middle Ages, was undoubtedly based upon the desire to accord respect to a learned indi-vidual or a communal leader. None of the codes of Jewish law or the classic books dealing with Jewish customs refers to the practice, which is only occasionally observed today.

Why are all customary funeral and mourning rites observed for some suicides?

Suicide in Jewish law is a serious offense. The Talmud says:

> For him who takes his own life with full knowledge of his action [the Hebrew word is *b'daat*] no rites are to be observed . . . There is to be no rending of clothes and no eulogy. But people should line up for him [at the end of the burial ceremony] and the mourner's blessing should be recited [as the family passes through] out of respect for the living. The general rule is: Whatever rites are [normally] performed for the benefit of the survivors should be observed; whatever is [normally] done out of respect for the dead should not be observed.[15]

Jewish law does not, however, place all suicides in the same category. One category of suicide, as stated above, includes those who are in full possession of their physical and mental faculties (*b'daat*) when they take their lives. A second category includes those who act on impulse or who are under severe mental strain or physical pain when com-mitting suicide. Jewish law speaks of an individual in this second category as being an *anuss,* meaning a "person under compulsion," and hence not responsible for his ac-tions. All burial and mourning rites are observed for him.

The first *anuss* in Jewish history was King Saul, who, after being defeated by the Philistines on Mount Gilboa, realized what would have happened to him if he were taken alive. He therefore impaled himself on his sword (I Samuel 31:4). This action gave rise to the expression *anuss k'Shaul,* meaning "as distressed as Saul."

Consequently, Joseph Caro in his *Code of Jewish Law* (*Shulchan Aruch,* Yoreh Deah 345:3) and most authorities of subsequent generations have ruled that the majority of suicides are to be considered as distressed as Saul and as having acted under compulsion when taking their own lives. As such, they are not responsible for their actions and are to be accorded the same courtesies and privileges granted the average Jew who has met a natural death.

Why do most Jews keep their heads covered in a cemetery and in a house of mourning?

In biblical times one sign of mourning was to cover one's head and face. This is how King David expressed his grief upon learning of the death of his son Absalom (II Samuel 19:5). The custom continued to be observed in talmudic times. The Talmud notes that when the third-century Palestinian scholar Bar Kappara mourned the passing of his teacher, Rabbi Judah the Prince, he covered his head.[16]

Even in modern times it has become a strong Jewish custom to show respect for the deceased by keeping one's head covered in all parts of a cemetery, just as most Jews keep their heads covered in a synagogue. Although a cemetery is not considered to have the sanctity of a synagogue, Moses Sofer (1762-1839), the Hungarian legal authority, responded to a question on the subject by saying that just as one may not sleep in a synagogue, so may one not sleep in a cemetery: the two must be treated with equal respect.

The procedure followed in a house of mourning is considered an extension of the procedure followed in the cemetery. One of the caveats found in the *Shulchan Aruch* is that in a cemetery one must not behave disrespectfully.[17] Since it is improper to go with one's head uncovered in a cemetery, the same rule has traditionally been applied to the house of mourning. However, many non-Orthodox Jews who generally do not keep their heads covered while in their homes also go bareheaded during the *Shiva* period.

Why are funerals generally held during the day?

Although Jewish law does not in any way prohibit night funerals, they have generally been avoided by Jews for the following reasons:

1. Based on the verse in Deuteronomy (21:23), "Thou shalt surely bury him the same day," the Rabbis concluded that burial should take place during daylight hours.

2. The first-century historian Flavius Josephus refers to night burials, but he is speaking of disgraced criminals who have been condemned to die.[18] Over the centuries the association of disgrace with night burial came to be made by Jews, and daytime funerals were therefore favored.

3. The sixteenth-century Rabbi Moses Isserles says, "There are some who say that if you bury the dead at night, you may not recite the *Kaddish* or *Tziduk Hadin* prayers."[19] Other authorities have added that one may also not deliver a eulogy at night.[20] Those Jews who accept these restrictions will avoid night burials, although the ultra-Orthodox today will sometimes hold a funeral at night, as has been known to happen in the Mea Shearim section of Jerusalem.

4. Dr. Julian Morgenstern, former president of Hebrew Union College (Reform), writes: "Evil spirits are generally thought by the Semites, ancient and modern, to be dangerous at night. With the rising of the sun their power wánes or departs completely."[21] It was therefore considered inadvisable to hold funerals after dark.

Why is more consideration given to a man's first wife than to his second wife in matters of burial?

Most rabbinic authorities agree that a man who has remarried after the death of his first wife should continue his loyalty to his first wife because the strong bond established in a marriage is not automatically dissolved with the passing of a mate. The Talmud says that a man's first wife is his true love and that when she dies during his lifetime, it is as though the Temple had been destroyed in his lifetime.[22] For this reason, a widower who remarries may be buried next to his first wife, especially if he has had children with her. When the second wife dies, she may also be buried next to her husband if that was her expressed wish. However, if the second wife had been married previously and she had children from that marriage, custom would dictate that she be buried next to her first husband.

None of this, of course, applies to a wife and husband who have been divorced.

Why may a *Kohayn* (Priest) attend the funeral of a Gentile but not of a fellow Jew?

The Bible states (Numbers 19:11) that all Israelites become ritually impure (*tamay* in Hebrew) if they touch a corpse, whether the deceased is a Jew or a non-Jew. A *Kohayn*, however, had special responsibilities and therefore had to measure up to a higher standard. He became impure not only when he touched a corpse but even when he entered an enclosure (*ohel* in Hebrew) that contained a Jewish corpse. When not in an enclosure, the *Kohayn* was also required to stay a minimum distance of six feet from a Jewish corpse (more than six feet is considered outside the domain of the deceased). This rule did not apply if a *Kohayn* simply entered an enclosed area where there was a Gentile corpse. Only by actually touching a Gentile corpse did a *Kohayn* become impure.[23]

For the above reasons a *Kohayn* today may attend the funeral of a non-Jew, and he may visit a non-Jewish cemetery. He may not, however, attend the funeral of a Jew when it is held in an enclosed area, unless that Jew is a member of his immediate family: mother, father, son, daughter, brother, unmarried sister, and wife. The first six are mandated in Leviticus 21:2, the seventh by a ruling of the Rabbis of the Talmud.[24]

A traditional rabbi who is a *Kohayn* may not officiate at a funeral held in any enclosed area. If he wishes to be present at the funeral, he must wait outside the building. The rabbi-*Kohayn* may visit a cemetery because it is not in an enclosure, but he must distance himself at least six feet from all graves.

Non-Orthodox rabbis who are *Kohanim,* by and large, do not follow these proscriptions because they believe that the laws of ritual purity and impurity continued to apply to Priests only as long as there was hope that the Temple and the sacrificial system might be restored.

Why is a *Kohayn* (Priest) usually buried next to the walkways of a cemetery?

As stated in the previous answer, a *Kohayn* becomes impure by touching or coming into close proximity to a corpse. Because according to the Jewish law a *Kohayn* must distance himself a minimum of six feet (four *amot*) from a Jewish corpse, a deceased *Kohayn* must be buried next to a walkway that is at least twelve feet wide, or he may be buried at the edge of the cemetery, making it possible for relatives who are also *Kohanim* to visit the grave without violating the law.[25]

Why are the female members of the family of a *Kohayn* permitted to attend funerals?

Moses Maimonides, in his *Mishneh Torah,* says, "The daughters of Aaron [from whom all Priestly families stem] were not warned to be careful about defiling themselves through contact with the dead, for it is written [Leviticus 21:1]: 'Speak to the Priests, the sons of Aaron . . .' "[26] The fact that no reference is made to the *daughters* of Aaron is proof that female members of a Priestly family are not subject to the same laws of defilement as are the male members of the family, undoubtedly because women were not required to perform in the Temple. They may, therefore, attend funerals and visit cemeteries like every other Jew.

Why is the shovel used to fill a grave not passed from person to person?

Once the coffin has been placed in the ground, it is customary for several of those present to take turns filling it in with earth. When an individual has completed his task, instead of handing the shovel being used to the next person, he pushes it into the earth alongside the grave. The next person then picks up the shovel and in turn repeats the procedure. The practice of not passing the shovel directly from hand to hand has been explained as a symbolic avoidance of passing a sorrow from person to person.[27]

It is for this same reason that when persons wash their hands before leaving a cemetery or before entering the home for *Shiva* after returning from a funeral, they do not pass the washing cup from person to person. Instead, each individual washes and then places the cup on the ground for the next person to pick up.

Why is the back side of the shovel used to fill in the grave at a funeral?

The reason for using the back side of a shovel to fill in a grave is obscure and probably started as local custom. The custom may have been instituted to establish a difference between the ordinary type of shoveling (to fill in a hole) and the occasion of shoveling earth to bury a loved one.

Why do some rabbis insist that the grave must be filled before the mourning period begins?

In ancient times, when bodies were buried in caves, the mourning period officially began when the mouth of the cave was covered with a rock. When caves were no longer used and bodies were buried in the earth, authorities disagreed as to whether mourning was to begin at the moment the corpse was laid in the ground and covered with some earth or when the entire grave was filled with earth. The disagreement stemmed from the interpretation given the words *yisatem hagolel,* which literally means "to seal [or cover] with a rock." This phrase is used in the Talmud[28] to indicate that burial has been completed and mourning has begun.

The great scholar Rashi (eleventh century) believed that the word *golel* refers to the cover (lid) of the coffin, implying that once the corpse is placed in the coffin and the cover closed, mourning begins. His grandson, Rabbenu Tam (twelfth century), argued that just as the stone in early times covered the cave opening completely, so must the coffin be lowered into the grave and be covered completely with earth before mourning begins.

Nachmanides, the famous thirteenth-century authority, agreed with Rashi, but later scholars have largely sided with Rabbenu Tam, and so it has become traditional for the grave to be filled to the top before the mourning period officially begins. In extenuating circumstances, however, such as when a family is extremely distraught or when the hour is late and the Sabbath or a holiday is to begin that evening, only the coffin itself is covered with earth and the burial service is concluded. Non-Orthodox rabbis (siding with Rashi) are satisfied under all circumstances, if it is the desire of the family, to have only several token shovelfuls of earth dropped onto the coffin, after which a grasslike carpet is stretched out over the grave. The cemetery crew fills in the grave after the family has left the graveside.

Why are coffins and graves not adorned with flowers and plants?

Although there is no objection in Jewish law to covering a coffin with flowers or adorning graves with shrubs and plants, Jewish custom has never favored the practice. Rashi, the eleventh-century French scholar, points out that there existed a custom "to place myrtle branches on a coffin to honor the dead."[29] However, this practice did not persist because adorning a coffin in this manner was considered a non-Jewish custom and, as such, one not to be followed by Jews.

A second reason for the custom of not adorning coffins and graves is that in Jewish tradition all people—rich and poor—are equal in death.[30] Just as the burial garment of both the rich and the poor is to be the simple, white shroud, so is the grave of both the rich and the poor to remain simple and unadorned.

During World War II, the chaplaincy committee of the National Jewish Welfare Board (representing Orthodox, Conservative, and Reform rabbis) ruled that on Memorial Day, as a way of honoring the dead, it is permissible to decorate the graves of the military with flowers. The committee did, however, object to permanent plantings.

Among liberal Jews today, flowers are often placed on a coffin and flowers or plants are placed or planted on the grave as a token of "reverence for the dead" (kevod hamet).

Why do those at the graveside form two rows at the conclusion of the service?

The ancient custom requiring those attending a funeral to form two rows at the conclusion of the service is first mentioned in the Mishna.[31] The mourners pass through the rows in order that they may receive the words of condolence, uttered in Hebrew, "May the Lord comfort you along with all the mourners of Zion and Jerusalem."

Why do some people consider it improper to visit the graves of other persons when at the cemetery to attend a funeral?

There is actually no basis in Jewish law for the belief that it is improper to visit other graves when one is at the cemetery to attend a funeral. Nevertheless the belief persists, and the following reasons have been given for it:

1. To visit other graves is an affront to the deceased and to the mourners. It detracts from the attention and respect due the deceased.

2. Those who wander off to visit other graves may be distraught and may accidentally step on graves that block their way.

3. Evil spirits lurk about cemeteries at times of burial, and it is therefore wise for all to leave the cemetery as quickly as possible.[32]

Why is it not permissible to bring religious articles into a cemetery or to pray there?

The *Shulchan Aruch* prohibits one from bringing a Tora scroll into a cemetery as well as from wearing *tefilin* or engaging in formal prayer there.[33] The prohibitions are based on the interpretation of a verse in Proverbs (17:5), "He who mocks the poor [*loeg lerash* in Hebrew, literally meaning 'teasing the dead'] blasphemes God." In Jewish literature a poor man is equated with a dead man. Hence, those lying in their graves are sometimes referred to as "the poor ones." Tradition considers it a mockery of the dead to come into a cemetery with religious articles which the deceased may have once enjoyed but now can no longer enjoy.[34]

Why does Jewish law discourage the serving of food in the cemetery?

The *Shulchan Aruch* cautions that all activities smacking of disrespect (called *kalut rosh* in Hebrew) be avoided in a cemetery.[35] In general, Jews have heeded this caution with one exception: with regard to the serving of food.

When cemeteries were far from cities and a trip to a cemetery might occupy as much as one full day, it was considered proper to feed those who made the long trek. Serving food in the cemetery became a necessity and was not done in a spirit of celebration.[36] Today, with travel time reduced considerably, rabbinic authorities consider it inappropriate for food to be served at the graveside after a funeral or unveiling.

Why were the Rabbis of the Talmud insistent that mourning be observed in moderation?

At one point in history, Jews took the words in the Book of Proverbs (31:6) literally. The author of the book, ascribed to King Solomon, suggested that strong wine should be offered to those who are "bitter of soul." This was taken to mean mourners. But with the destruction of the Second Temple many Jews became ascetic to demonstrate their sense of loss over Israel's most holy place. They purposely refrained from drinking wine and eating meat, which had become symbols both of luxury and of joyful living.

The Rabbis of the Talmud were annoyed at such behavior because they felt it fostered an idea that would be damaging if it spread widely. "We should not mourn excessively," they said, "because we must not impose upon the community a hardship that would be difficult to bear."[37]

In arguing the point with the community of ascetics, Rabbi Joshua said, "My sons, why do you not eat meat or drink wine?"

They replied, "Shall we eat flesh which used to be brought as an offering on the altar, now that this altar is destroyed? Shall we drink wine which used to be poured as a libation on the altar, when it no longer exists?"

"If that is so," Joshua responded, "we should not eat bread either, because the meal-offerings have ceased."

"That is so. We can manage with fruit," replied the ascetics.

"We should not eat fruit either," said Joshua, "because there is no longer an offering of first-fruits."

"Then we can manage with other fruits," they said.

"But," he said, "we should not drink water either, because there is no longer any ceremony of the pouring of water [on the festival of Sukkot]."

To this they could find no answer, so Joshua said to them: "My sons, come and listen to me. Not to mourn at all is impossible, because the blow has fallen. To mourn overmuch is also impossible, because we do not impose on the community a hardship which the majority cannot endure."

Why are mourners sometimes offered a cup of wine upon returning from the cemetery?

The Talmud mentions a "cup of mourners."[38] Apparently, this alludes to the wine that was customarily offered to mourners.

The origin of the custom of giving mourners a cup of wine upon returning home from the cemetery has been attributed to Rabbi Chanin, who interpreted the verse in Proverbs (31:6), "Give strong drink to him that is ready to perish, and wine unto the bitter of soul," as meaning that "wine was created specifically for the purpose of comforting mourners." The practice is rarely, if ever, followed today.

Why do some mourners observe *Shiva* for less than seven days?

Shiva, the seven-day period of mourning (*shiva* is Hebrew for "seven"), although not directly mandated in the Bible, is nevertheless believed by the Rabbis to have the full force of biblical law. This conclusion is based on an interpretation of the verse in Amos (8:10) in which the prophet speaks of feasts (festivals) and mourning in the same sentence. Since the festivals Passover and Sukkot are seven days long, the Rabbis declared that the initial period of mourning for the loss of a loved one should also be seven days.[39] Additional proof that the period of mourning should last seven days is adduced from the Book of Genesis (50:10) where Joseph is said to mourn his father, Jacob, for seven days.

The Rabbis of the Talmud found it necessary to make exceptions to the law and have, in special situations, reduced the number of days Shiva is to be observed. Two basic principles of Jewish law were used in establishing the exceptions:

1. A holiday that falls in the midst (even at the very beginning) of the Shiva period cancels Shiva because the biblical commandment to "rejoice on your festivals" supersedes the Shiva period, which is not directly mandated. Thus the whole week of Shiva is cancelled if burial takes place immediately before Rosh Hashana, Yom Kippur, Passover, Shavuot, or Sukkot. Mourning is not observed on the Sabbath or on Purim (a minor biblical holiday), but these days are counted as one of the seven days of mourning. Chanuka is not a biblical festival and mourning is therefore observed during the eight days of that holiday.

2. The Rabbis established the rule that "part of a day is like the whole of it."[40] Thus, if a burial is completed just before nightfall and the mourner simply removes his shoes in the cemetery as a token sign that mourning has begun, this counts as the first day of mourning even if the mourner arrives home after dark.

A more liberal opinion (discussed earlier in this chapter) considers the period of mourning to have begun once the coffin has been lowered into the grave and covered with earth. Some even consider the mere closing of the coffin (which is sometimes opened momentarily in the funeral chapel for mourners to verify the identity of the deceased) sufficient to consider mourning to have begun.

The Shiva period is also sometimes shortened if full observance will seriously affect the mourner's livelihood. If by observing the full seven days severe financial hardship will ensue, the mourner may return to work even after three days. And since part of a day is considered a full day, the mourner may leave for work immediately after the prayer service on the mourning of the third day.

Why is *Shiva* observed in the home of the deceased?

The Talmud and the *Shulchan Aruch* specify that the proper place for services to be held during the week of mourning is the house in which the deceased lived.[41] Rashi (1040-1105) maintains that the proper place to sit *Shiva* is the house where the deceased died.

Several authorities, among them Abraham Danzig (1774-1820) of Vilna, offer a mystical reason for observing *Shiva* in the home of the deceased. They say that for seven days after death the soul hovers about the house in which the deceased lived. The soul grieves and mourns for the body that it once inhabited and with which it hopes to be reunited. The prayers that emanate from the house three times each day during the period of *Shiva* are a source of consolation to the unhappy spirit.

Nowadays, when families are spread out geographically, and sometimes for other compelling reasons, it is often necessary for *Shiva* to be observed in more than one home. Most rabbis encourage *Shiva* to be observed in the house of the deceased if at all possible.

Why is it sometimes permissible to start the *Shiva* period even if the deceased has not actually been buried?

From time to time inclement weather or strikes by cemetery personnel delay the burial of a deceased. In such cases, the funeral service is held, the coffin sealed, and the body placed in storage for later burial. There are also occasions when a deceased is to be buried in a distant city. After the funeral the coffin is sealed and sent off for burial.

In the above-mentioned instances, mourners do not have to wait until the body is laid in the earth for the official seven-day mourning period to begin. *Shiva* commences immediately upon closing the coffin. This ruling is based upon the view of Rashi, who declared that once the coffin is closed, the body is considered to have been buried.

Why do some authorities permit a mourner to listen to music, watch television, and engage in similar activities during the mourning period?

The Rabbis of the Talmud forbade mourners from participating in pleasurable activities during the designated period of mourning.[42] For a parent, the mourning period extends for twelve months, although *Kaddish* is only recited for eleven months. For a son, daughter, brother, sister, and spouse the mourning period is thirty days.[43]

While the law forbidding pleasurable activities during the mourning period is generally considered inviolable, modern Orthodox and Conservative rabbis have interpreted it liberally. Orthodox rabbis such as Maurice Lamm distinguish between music listened to for sheer pleasure and more subdued mood music that induces contemplation and reflection. He considers the former unacceptable and the latter acceptable.

Rabbi Emanuel Rackman, another Orthodox authority, shares this view and writes: "There is no prohibition against the sound of music as such . . . [It is proper for mourners to listen to classical music] that induces a mood that the laws of mourning promote." He continues to say that the same principle applies to plays and movies: "The light, the gay, the humorous—these are to be avoided. However, a drama or film that would contribute to one's philosophical musing or meditation is precisely what the occasion demands."[44]

Why are there differing opinions as to whether one who has abandoned the Jewish faith should be mourned at the time of his death?

The Talmud[45] says that mourning is not to be observed for any Jew who has become an apostate. In the Talmud a Jewish defector is in the same category as a suicide and an executed criminal.

Scholars have pointed out that when Maimonides, in his *Mishneh Torah,* lists those for whom Jews do not mourn "because they have separated themselves from the community," he mentions "apostates to idolatry."[46] Since today (and for the past eight or more centuries) a Christian is no longer considered to be an idolator in the eyes of Jewish law, the question of whether a family is to sit *Shiva* upon the death of one of its members who had earlier joined the Church is moot.

Of consideration, however, is whether the apostate abandoned Judaism as an act of rebellion toward his family or teachers or whether he truly loved his newly adopted faith. When the motivation of the apostate is spite, some authorities argue, there is always a degree of hope that he may reconsider at a future date and return to the fold. Such an apostate is to be considered a full Jew, and when he dies *Shiva* may be observed for him under the talmudic principle of *"af al pi shechata, Yisrael hu* [a Jew continues to be a Jew even if he has sinned]."[47] Some authorities are of the opinion that one who denounces Judaism publicly should not be mourned. His action, they believe, will encourage others to defect, and it is therefore inexcusable.[48]

Although burial of an apostate in a Jewish cemetery is legally permitted (because a Jew is a Jew forever), it is usually discouraged.

Why may one recite *Kaddish* for parents who have abandoned the Jewish faith?

There is a difference of opinion among authorities as to whether a child may recite the *Kaddish* for deceased parents who were apostates and severed all ties with the Jewish community. Rabbi Moses Isserles (1525-1572) says that a son may recite *Kaddish* for an apostate father who was murdered by idolators because it is presumed that through his death the father has made atonement for his sin, and that in all probability the man repented just before life left his body.[49] Other authorities follow the lead of the famous Rabbi Akiba Eger (1761-1837), rabbi of Posen, Poland, who held that a son is permitted to mourn and say *Kaddish* for an apostate parent even if the death was natural.

Why is it permissible to recite the *Yizkor* prayer without a *minyan* but not to recite the *Kaddish* without a *minyan*?

Some prayers rank higher than others. In order for one to recite the words of the *Kaddish,* a *minyan* (quorum of ten) must be present because the prayer calls for an "Amen" response by a congregation, and especially for the response *Yehay shmay rabba . . ,* which is pronounced by the congregation after the first paragraph (beginning with the words *Yitgadal, veyitkadash*) is recited. For this same reason the *Barchu* and the *Kedusha* may be recited only when one prays with a *minyan.* This is codified as law in the *Shulchan Aruch.*[50]

Since the *Yizkor* prayer does not call for a response from the congregation at any point (in fact, it is recited silently), all rabbinic authorities permit it to be recited at home without a *minyan.* Having been introduced as a formal part of the service during the Crusades of the eleventh century, the *Yizkor* has not yet attained the sanctity of the other major prayers in the Jewish liturgy, which are over two thousand years old.

Why may a person recite *Yizkor* for anyone he chooses?

The recitation of *Yizkor,* which is a universal prayer expressing the belief that acts of piety and virtue can bring honor to the dead, is not a legal requirement as is the *Kaddish. Yizkor* may be recited by anyone wishing to remember any deceased relative or friend.

Often, a widow or widower who remarries will refrain from reciting *Yizkor* lest the new mate be offended. However, this is not demanded by law or custom since the

Yizkor prayer is recited silently and the possibility of offending the current spouse is not a consideration.

Why is it not always proper for a man who has remarried to say *Kaddish* and observe *Yahrzeit* for his first wife?

If a man has remarried after the death of his first wife, it is not proper for him to recite *Kaddish* in the synagogue or light a *Yahrzeit* lamp at home for her lest his new wife be offended. If children of the first marriage are still living with the father, they may observe these rites in the presence of their stepmother, since the Ten Commandments obligate children to respect their mother and their father. However, if the first marriage was childless or if there are no children alive from the first marriage, it becomes the obligation of the remarried husband to recite *Kaddish* for his first wife.

Rabbi Moses Sofer (1762-1832), the Hungarian authority on Jewish law, was of the opinion that when a man remarries after the death and burial of his first wife, his primary obligation is to his second wife, and that his relationship to his first wife has totally ended. Most scholars do not agree.

Conservative, Reconstructionist, and Reform congregations that grant women equal status with men would also apply the above obligations to a woman who has remarried after the death of her husband.

Why is an adopted child sometimes required to say *Kaddish* for his adoptive parents?

An adopted child is not a blood relative of his adoptive parents, and hence technically is not required to say *Kaddish* for them. Nonetheless, many authorities are of the opinion that because of the close emotional ties that develop over the years, it is proper for the adopted child to say *Kaddish* for his or her adoptive parents. In cases where there are no natural sons to fulfill the obligation to say the

Kaddish, many authorities believe that that obligation should be assumed by the adopted son.

This latter view is supported by the Talmud, which says that a person who raises an orphan is considered to be the orphan's father, and in some cases even more important than the natural father.[51] The great thirteenth-century German talmudist Meir of Rothenburg said, "A man who calls his child 'son,' that child [even if adopted] is legally his son." Three centuries later Moses Isserles included this view in his Notes to the *Shulchan Aruch.*[52]

Why is indiscriminate disinterment contrary to Jewish law?

Jewish law is strongly opposed to removing a body from its burial place.[53] Jewish law views a disturbance of the deceased as *nivul hamet,* "an offense to the dead." Once buried, the body must be left at peace, undisturbed.

There are exceptions to the rule, however. If it was clear from the outset that the burial was temporary, and that as soon as arrangements could be made the deceased would be transferred to a family plot or to Israel, such reinterment is permitted. (Burial in Israel's sacred soil has always been looked upon with favor by rabbinic authorities.) Similarly, if a Jew had been buried in a Christian cemetery for one reason or another, it is considered an honorable deed to remove the body of the deceased and to transfer it to a Jewish cemetery so that the body may rest with its ancestors. Generally speaking, disinterment for reasons that are not compelling is forbidden by Jewish law.

Why is a boy often referred to as a *Kaddish* or a *Kaddishl*?

In Jewish law it is the religious obligation of a son (not of a daughter) to recite the *Kaddish* for a parent. Since this is the male's duty, a young boy who is the only son in a family is sometimes referred to as a *Kaddish* or a *Kaddishl* (diminutive form), even during the lifetime of the parent.

CHAPTER 7

Theology and Prayer

INTRODUCTION

Three basic questions must be addressed in man's search for God. First, man asks, "How did God create the world?" Second, "What is God's continuing relationship to the world that He created?" And third, "How does man reach God and relate to Him?"

The Bible, the Talmud, and all subsequent traditional Jewish literature posit the existence of God as axiomatic, as an indisputable fact. When pressed for proof, traditionalists point to the existence of the world and say, "This is God's handiwork, for only God could have the intelligence and power to put such a beautiful and complex world into motion."

How did the world come into being? The traditional answer, the biblical answer, is *Va'yomer Elohim*, "And God said . . ." It was by the word of God, by divine fiat, that the world was formed. Genesis describes God as saying, "Let there be light . . . Let there be a firmament . . . Let the dry land appear . . . Let the waters swarm with living creatures . . ." God spoke and the world came into being.

What is God's continuing relationship to the world? Is He transcendent?—that is, Does he exist apart from the material world? Does He maintain a distance from it and His creations? Yes, answers the Psalmist: "The heaven belongs to God, and the earth He has given to man."[1]

Or is God immanent?—that is, Is he present throughout the universe? Does he stay close to man? This view was endorsed by Rabbi Chama in his interpretation of the text in Deuteronomy (13:5), "You shall walk after the Lord your God." How does a human being walk after God? By emulating Him, said Rabbi Chama: Just as He clothes the naked, so must you clothe the naked. Just as He visits the sick, so must you visit the sick. Just as He comforts mourners, so must you comfort mourners. Just as He buries the dead, so must you bury the dead.[2]

Does a belief in God's transcendence exclude a belief in His immanence? The Rabbis thought not. They found it quite legitimate to speak of God as existing apart from the material universe and yet as being near to all those who reach out to Him and call upon Him.

In attempting to explain the relationship of God to man, some Rabbis of the Talmud expressed the idea that man and God are partners. Just as man is dependent on God, so is God dependent on man. Although God, they say, created the world, and although He alone is sovereign, God needs man to help perfect it.

Other Rabbis of the Talmud reject the idea of a partnership existing between man and God. They present this view in answer to the question Why was Adam the last of all creations? If, as Judaism believes, all of the world was created for man, why was Adam not the first of God's creations? The answer of the Rabbis is, "Man was created on the eve of the Sabbath [making him the last of all creations] so that the Sadducees should not say, 'Man was God's partner in creating the world.' "[3]

Despite the initial aversion of the Rabbis to the idea of linking God to man as partners, this view was, and still is, subscribed to by most traditional theologians. This partnership, they say, is an expression of God's immanence, of God's concern for man, the crown of all His creations. Man, by his faith and actions, contributes to perfecting the world. The Jew, in particular, makes his contribution toward creating an improved world through prayer and study and the observance of the commandments (mitzvot).

How does man reach God and relate to Him? The Rabbis of the Talmud believed that this is accomplished by serving God through the observance of the commandments of the Tora and by praying to Him. The two—observance and prayer—are inextricably intertwined and for that reason prayer is called "service of the heart."[4]

Prayer in the Jewish tradition means more than simply asking God to fulfill one's personal needs. "Whoever has it in his power to pray on behalf of his neighbor and fails to do so is called a sinner," says the Talmud.[5] The needs of one's fellow man and the needs of the community are paramount in Jewish prayer. Said the fourth-century Babylonian scholar Abaye, the correct way to pray is to include the whole congregation of Israel in one's prayers. One should say, "May it be Thy will, O Lord *our* God, to lead *us* forth in peace . . ."[6]

The questions in the first part of this chapter touch upon some of the theological concepts expressed above while answering specific questions such as What does Judaism mean when it teaches that "God is One"? Why does the Bible present God as a corporeal being and especially as a sentient being; as one Who *smells* the savor of sacrifices, Who *sees* man's deeds, Who *speaks* to Moses and *hears* the cries of the Children of Israel? Is it necessary to believe in angels and miracles? Is the belief in life after death a basic Jewish belief? How, after the Holocaust experience, can a Jew continue to believe in God?

The second part of the chapter relates to prayer as it affects many areas of Jewish life, both personal and communal. Here, most of the questions involve legal *(halachik)* principles pertaining to the language of prayer, the validity and propriety of certain prayers, and the manner in which they are to be recited. For questions dealing with the symbols, gestures, and postures of prayer consult Chapter Seven of *The Jewish Book of Why.*

Why is the belief in one God the most basic concept in the Jewish religion?

The German philosopher Arthur Schopenhauer (1788-1860), a vocal critic of most aspects of Judaism, once commented, "Judaism cannot be denied the glory of being the only genuinely monotheistic religion on earth."

The Jewish belief in one God (the doctrine of monotheism) is expressed in the Ten Commandments: "Thou shalt have no other gods before me" (Exodus 20:3). It is reiterated in the *Shema* (Deuteronomy 6:4): "Hear O Israel, the Lord is our God, the Lord is One." This emphasis on the oneness and uniqueness of God, with its implication that God is the father of all mankind and that all men are therefore brothers, runs counter to the concepts advanced by other cultures and religions of the biblical period. The Zoroastrian doctrine of dualism, which states that there are two basic antagonistic principles—good and evil—governing the universe, was propounded in Persia from the seventh to the fifth centuries B.C.E., while the Greeks advanced a pantheistic view of the universe which proposed that God is the total of all the laws, forces, and manifestations of the existing universe. The concept of one God in full control of man and nature was the Jewish contribution to civilization.

The Rabbis of the Talmud considered the belief in one God basic to Judaism and therefore legislated that all Jews recite the *Shema* prayer twice each day, evening and morning.

Why does Judaism not conceive of God as a corporeal being, since the Bible presents Him as such?

Almost all Jewish philosophers and theologians are in agreement that God is not to be conceived of as having human form. This belief is based upon the biblical description of the revelation on Mount Sinai (Deuteronomy 4:12), in which God is described as being without human form: "You heard the sound of words, but you saw no form . . ."

Portraying God as having physical form was a heathen practice, and this the Bible condemns.

Moses Maimonides (1135-1204) was probably the first Jewish philosopher to state categorically that "whoever conceives of God as a corporeal being is an apostate."[7] One of his contemporaries, however, the French talmudist Abraham ben David of Posquières (1120-1190), also known by the acronym Ravad, argued that many good Jews believe that God has human form, and they are not heretics or renegades; they are simply in error for failing to understand that the anthropomorphic passages in Scripture and in rabbinic literature were not meant to be taken literally.

Why are Jewish houses of worship devoid of works of art in which the human form is represented?

The second of the Ten Commandments states (Exodus 20:4), "Thou shalt not make unto thee a graven image, nor any manner of likeness of anything that is in the heaven above or on the earth beneath . . ."

Deuteronomy 4:16-18 repeats this commandment and elaborates upon it, specifying that it is forbidden to make "the form of any figure, the likeness of male or female, the likeness of any beast that is on earth." Verse 19 explains the reason for the prohibition: Nothing must stand in the way of Israel worshipping the one and only God.

The Rabbis of talmudic and post-talmudic times interpreted the Bible to mean that all art forms are permissible if there is no danger that they will be worshipped.[8] Despite the liberal ruling of the Rabbis, in building their synagogues in ancient times Jews, by and large, refrained from using decorations that represented the human form in any way—high relief, bas relief, or flat surface. They believed that all such decorations would interfere with absolute concentration on the spirituality of God.

There were, however, many exceptions to this general rule. The Talmud makes a distinction between images made for the purpose of worship and those made for other reasons. It also tells us that there was a synagogue in Nehardea, Babylonia, in which a statue of the king had been erected, and that in the third century C.E. the great talmudic scholars Rav and Samuel and the father of Samuel used to go there to pray.[9]

In recent times, a number of ancient Palestinian synagogues were excavated, revealing that synagogues were beautified with a considerable amount of art. The most famous of these is the Dura Europos synagogue, which was erected in 245 C.E. on the Euphrates River in Babylonia. Its ruins were discovered in 1932 in a remarkable state of preservation. The synagogue contained a surprising number of exquisite frescoes, mosaics, symbols of the zodiac, and even large panels of biblical scenes showing pictures of the full human form. (In the centuries that followed, using the human form in art was banned as being a violation of the second of the Ten Commandments.)

Maimonides, in his *Mishneh Torah,* summarizes the opinions expressed in the Talmud. He says that the prohibition against making graven images applies only to representations of the human form.[10] Possibly reacting to the ever-increasing appearance of statues of Jesus and the saints, Maimonides emphasizes that a human figure may not be made in high relief (three-dimensional), but it may be rendered in bas relief or may be painted on a flat surface or woven into a tapestry. These views are also codified in the *Shulchan Aruch,* which states that it is permissible to paint, draw, or weave into a tapestry the figures of human beings, but not to make the complete human form.[11] Sculpting a human head alone or a torso alone is permitted, but shaping an entire body is prohibited because it imitates heathen practices.

In 1926, Rabbi Abraham Kook, Chief Rabbi of Palestine, responded to a question by the painter Abraham Neumann by saying that while some pious Jews object to being painted or photographed, the majority follow the *Shulchan Aruch,* which permits it (as noted above).[12]

Why is it permissible to illuminate prayerbooks with renderings of birds and other animals and also human figures?

In one of his responsa, Rabbi Meir of Rothenburg (thirteenth century) responded to this question, which had been posed by his outstanding disciple Rabbi Asher ben Yechiel (1250-1327). Rabbi Meir wrote that the practice of illuminating a prayerbook should be discouraged because the drawings interfere with one's concentration on prayer. He added, however, that since the drawings in books are two-dimensional, they are not absolutely forbidden.

This issue was the subject of debate among rabbinic authorities from talmudic times onward. What was crucial in the debate was the interpretation given to biblical passages that prohibit the making of "graven images and the likeness of male or female . . ." (Deuteronomy 4:16ff.).

Some authorities, such as Meir of Rothenburg, took their lead from the Rabbis of the Talmud[13] who interpreted the words of the Bible (Exodus 5:12), "This is my God and I will glorify Him," to mean that God is glorified when He is worshipped with love in the most beautiful manner humanly possible. It therefore became customary (primarily from the thirteenth century onward) to adorn all ritual objects as artistically as possible, and to illuminate (decorate) prayerbooks and Bibles and religious documents, such as marriage contracts *(ketubot),* with colorful borders and drawings of birds, animals, and even figures of humans.

Why has a belief in angels never been central to the Jewish religion?

Although there are references in the Bible to God and his heavenly court, where celestial beings minister to Him (I Kings 22:19; Isaiah 61ff.), angelology did not originate with Judaism. It was quite common for peoples of the Near East to describe a heavenly world inhabited by beings belonging to a species distinct and separate from humans.

The Talmud addresses itself to angels much more than does the Bible, but neither depicts angels as intermediaries between God and man, as is the case in other religions.

In his twelfth-century *Guide for the Perplexed*, Maimonides downgrades the belief in the existence of angels as corporeal beings.[14] He believed that angels are natural forces placed in the world by God, and that these forces shape and control all that happens in the universe. In the Bible, they are manifested in many different ways. To Abraham angels appeared as messengers of God (Genesis 18:2). In another instance an angel is seen as fire (Genesis 3:2), and in another as a person causing terror (Judges 13:6).

While some Jews with mystic leanings still believe in angels as celestial beings with special access to God, most Jews today subscribe to the attitude of Maimonides.

Why did a belief in heaven and hell gain currency among Jews despite the fact that the Bible makes no reference to either?

The Bible makes no direct reference to a heaven or hell as a place to which people go after death. Chapters 2 and 3 of Genesis as well as Chapter 28 of Ezekiel refer to an earthly Garden of Eden (*Gan Ayden* in Hebrew), but this is not the celestial paradise referred to in later Jewish literature. Only after the destruction of the First Temple in 586 B.C.E. and the subsequent exile of Jews to Babylonia (later conquered by Persia), at which time Jews came under the strong influence of Persian Zoroastrian teachings, did the concept of heaven and hell become the subject of serious discussion among Jews.

In talmudic times, especially during the periods of persecution by the Romans in the early centuries C.E., we find the concept of heaven and hell taking root. Heaven was equated with *Gan Ayden* (the Garden of Eden), or paradise. The Greek translation of the Bible (the Septuagint) calls *Gan Ayden* by the name "paradise," a word some scholars believe to be from the Persian meaning "park" or "garden." The Garden of Eden was considered the place where the righteous would go after death to enjoy the fruits of the good life that they had led while here on earth.

In contradistinction to paradise, the view prevailed in rabbinic (talmudic) times that those who did not live exemplary lives here on earth would be consigned to hell, to *gehinnom*. The Hebrew word *gehinnom* is the same as the Greek *gehenna*. The Books of Joshua (15:8) and II Kings (23:10) describe *gehinnom* as "the valley of the son of Hinnom," a place located south of Jerusalem where children were sacrificed to the god Moloch. The valley was deemed accursed, and the word *gehenna* became a figurative expression for all that is evil and sinful. Hel (Hell), the Old Norse goddess of the underworld, was later associated with *gehenna* and the two words became synonymous.

To many rabbis in talmudic times hell and paradise were real places "created by God."[15] The Talmud says that the illustrious Rabbi Yochanan ben Zakkai wept before his death because he was not sure whether he would go to paradise or to hell.[16] Many talmudic references indicate that *Gan Ayden* and *gehenna* are actual terrestrial places.[17]

To other scholars, such as the third-century Babylonian Abba Aricha (popularly known as Rav), however, paradise (or "the world-to-come," as it is sometimes called) is a spiritual place where there will be "no eating, or drinking, or procreation, or business dealings, or jealousy, or hatred, or competition. The righteous will sit there with crowns on their heads, enjoying the brightness of God's radiance."[18]

Scholars of post-talmudic centuries were less and less inclined to view the hereafter as a physical place. *Gan Ayden* to Rabbi Moses ben Nachman (Nachmanides) of the thirteenth century was a "world of souls" (*olam haneshamot* in Hebrew). It was a place where only the souls, not the bodies, of the departed would enter immediately after death. Maimonides, a century earlier, wrote: "There are neither bodies nor bodily forms in the world-to-come, only the souls of the righteous . . ."[19]

Most Jews today—Orthodox and non-Orthodox—believe in the immortality of the soul, but not all believe in paradise and hell and the physical resurrection of the dead. Reform Judaism and Reconstructionism accept only the idea of immortality of the soul, and their prayerbooks reflect this attitude.

Why are there conflicting views about the nature of the Messiah?

The word "Messiah" is used by some to refer to an actual person and by others to refer to a future time when a perfect world will be established.

The exact nature of the Messiah is not clarified in the Bible, the Talmud, or later rabbinic writings. In fact, these sources contain many vague and contradictory statements.

In the Bible, the Messiah idea is connected with the concept of the world-to-come *(olam haba)*, a time described by several of the prophets as the "end of days." Isaiah refers to the "end of days" a number of times (Isaiah 2:2-4; 27:13; 55:6-7), as does Jeremiah (23:5-6; 30:3). In these prophetic writings the ideal condition of man is portrayed: God will redeem Israel and establish His kingship over all the earth. There will be no war and no want, no struggle and no strife. Righteousness will prevail and eternal peace and prosperity will be the lot of all good people, Jew and Gentile alike. Others, those who deny God—Jew and Gentile alike—will perish.

Beginning with the talmudic period, we find the attitude shifting away from the concept of the Messiah as a period in time. Actual persons began to proclaim themselves or were proclaimed by others to be the Messiah or precursors of the Messiah. Undoubtedly the most famous such person was Bar Kochba, who in the year 132 C.E., during the Jewish revolt against the Roman occupation of Palestine, was proclaimed the Messiah by a figure no less distinguished than Rabbi Akiba.

Throughout history, during periods of persecution and crisis in the Jewish community, Jews in a mood of despair eagerly yearned for a real person who could promise them salvation. From the time of the Crusades (1096) onward many such pseudo-Messiahs appeared on the scene. Among the more prominent ones were David Alroy, who appeared in Mesopotamia in 1147, and Abraham Abulafia, who was active in Sicily in the thirteenth century. In 1391, because of persecution in Spain, Moses Botarel became a popular messianic figure, and following the expulsion of the Jews from Spain in 1492 numerous pseudo-Messiahs surfaced, Shelomo Molcho (1500-1532) being the most famous. Undoubtedly one of the better known and most charismatic of all the false Messiahs was Shabbetai Zevi of Smyrna, Turkey (1626-1676), who in the end converted to Islam. The most recent pseudo-Messiah was Loibele Prossnitz, who appeared in Yemen in 1889.

Maimonides speaks of the Messiah as both an age and a person.[20] He envisions the coming of the Messiah as a time when a serene climate will exist and Jews will be able to devote themselves undisturbed to the study of Tora in order to gain in wisdom and thus serve God better. Maimonides also conceived of the Messiah as a person: as a king who will appear on the scene. This king will be a descendant of King David. He will be wiser than Solomon and possess prophetic powers almost on a par with Moses. He will teach the people and lead them in the way of the Lord.

Why was the prophet Elijah singled out to be the forerunner of the Messiah?

The charismatic prophet Elijah, who burst upon the Jewish scene in the ninth century B.C.E. during the reign of King Ahab and Queen Jezebel, was said to be the forerunner of the Messiah because he, more than any other prophet, battled the pagan foes of Israel who sought to discredit God (I Kings 18:17ff.). For this reason Elijah became the "guardian angel" of the Jewish people. He insisted that Israel must not forsake God, so that the Covenant that was made between God and Abraham may endure.

In the Book of Malachi (3:1) the last of the prophets identified Elijah as "the messenger of the Covenant," and he prophesied that the Messianic Age would be heralded by a reappearance of Elijah: "Behold, I will send you Elijah the Prophet before the coming of the great and terrible day of the Lord" (3:23).

The belief in Elijah as the forerunner of the Messiah has been kept alive over the centuries in the ritual of the Passover Seder. He is the expected guest in every Jewish home where a Seder is held, and at one point in the ritual of the evening the outer door of the house is opened, and Elijah is greeted with a warm welcome.

Why did Rabbi Akiba hail Bar Kochba as the Messiah?

During the decades preceding and following the destruction of the Second Temple in 70 C.E., oppression of Jews by the Romans was intense. Every sign that pointed towards redemption was cherished.

The contemporary historian Josephus, in his *Antiquities*, which records the events of that period, tells of the many people who came forward claiming to be the Messiah or to suggest the name of the Messiah. Rabbi Akiba suggested that Bar Kochba, the Jewish general who in 132 C.E. led an armed rebellion against the Romans, was the Messiah. He brought as proof for this contention the verse in the Book of Numbers (24:17), "There shall come forth a star [kochav] out of [the house of] Jacob." This, he said, refers to Bar Kochba (also spelled Bar Kochva), who is to be the Messiah. Most of Akiba's colleagues ridiculed the idea. One of them, Rabbi Yochanan ben Torta, exclaimed, "Akiba, grass will grow from your cheeks [you will be long dead] and still the Messiah will not have come."[21]

Nevertheless, Akiba clung to his belief and left Palestine, traveling to distant Jewish communities in Babylonia, Egypt, North Africa, and Gaul in order to raise funds and rally support for the man he believed to be the Messiah.

Akiba even permitted his thousands of students to join the fighting forces of Bar Kochba, most of whom were massacred by the Romans. In 135 the rebellion was crushed and Akiba abandoned his belief.

Why in the Jewish tradition is the Messiah identified with King David?

Many of the Rabbis conceived of the Messianic Age as a period of perfection that would be ushered in by a royal personality who had been anointed by God (the word "Messiah," *Mashiach* in Hebrew, means anointed). Since the Anointed One will be a descendant of King David, he is called Mashiach ben David ("son of David") or Tzemach David ("offshoot of David") (Jeremiah 23:5).

Based upon various verses in the Bible, rabbinic authorities concluded that the name of the Messiah will be David. One such verse is Psalms 17:51: "He [God] gives deliverance to His king and shows kindness to His anointed [*Mashiach*], to David, and to his seed forever."

Why has Moses not been deified?

Moses, the great lawgiver and emancipator, was the master prophet in Jewish history. He was the man who, the Bible says, received the Ten Commandments directly from God. Yet, in Jewish tradition Moses is presented as a mortal, with no divine attributes. The Tora (Numbers 12:3) refers to him simply as "the man Moses."

The Jewish Sages explain that the precise burial place of Moses was kept unknown so that future generations would not be tempted to worship at his grave and ultimately deify him. Throughout the ages the Rabbis were concerned about preventing the possible deification of any mortal, particularly Moses. This is why in the entire Passover Haggada, which tells the story of the Exodus, in which Moses is the principal figure, the name of Moses appears only once, and then merely as part of a biblical reference.

Maimonides summed up the traditional Jewish attitude toward Moses the prophet when he wrote that Jews do not believe in the *man* Moses; they believe only in the *prophecy* of the man Moses.

Why did belief in the resurrection of the dead become a cardinal principle of Judaism?

Although belief in the resurrection of the dead first entered Jewish thought in the sixth century B.C.E., under the influence of the Persians who ruled Palestine, it took several centuries for the concept to take root among Jews.

In the Bible itself there are few references to resurrection of the dead. The most famous is the vision of the Prophet Ezekiel (37), which describes a valley of dry bones that will come to life again. The concept is also mentioned in the Book of Daniel (12:2-3):

> And many of those who sleep in the dusty earth shall awake, some to everlasting life, others to everlasting reproach and contempt. Then the knowledgeable shall shine like the brightness of the sky; those who justified the many, like the stars, forever and ever.

Not until the fourth century B.C.E., when the Greeks conquered Palestine and the influence of Plato and others began to be felt, did the doctrine of resurrection begin to emerge and become accepted by Jews. It was embraced particularly by Jews who battled for their lives and honor when they opposed the domination of the Syrian-Greeks in the second century B.C.E. Loss of life was so great during these battles that the survivors found it necessary to cling to a belief in a world-to-come where the righteous would return to life.

At this point in Jewish history, the two major Jewish sects debated whether the doctrine of resurrection should be accepted as a basic article of Jewish faith. The Sadducees believed that only that which is explicitly commanded in the Bible should be accepted, and since belief in the resurrection of the dead is not specifically advocated in the

Pentateuch, they denied the doctrine. The Pharisees, however, believed that the words of the Tora *are* subject to interpretation, and they affirmed the belief in resurrection.

The view of the Pharisees was adopted by the later Rabbis of the Talmud, and this view was stated strongly: "Anyone who denies that the doctrine of the resurrection of the dead is a Tora-based commandment excludes himself from the Jewish fold and will have no share in the world-to-come."[22]

Jewish scholars and theologians were not in agreement as to the precise nature of "resurrection." Would the dead be revived and restored to full physical life, or would only "souls" be revived while bodies remained dust? Maimonides' view left many scholars in a quandary. In his commentary on the Mishna and in his *Mishneh Torah,* Maimonides offered seemingly contradictory opinions, for which he was criticized by some of his contemporaries.[23]

Today, the more liberal wings of Judaism (Reform, Reconstructionist, and part of the Conservative movement) do not believe in physical resurrection of the dead. They have affirmed in its place the concept of immortality of the soul. The prayerbooks of these two groups have been modified accordingly. Orthodox and Conservative prayerbooks have retained references to the resurrection of the dead *(techiyat hamaytim),* and leave it to the worshipper to apply his own interpretation.

Why did some early Jewish scholars believe that the miracles of the Bible were not really "miraculous" events?

George Santayana once wrote: "Miracles are propitious accidents, the natural causes of which are too complicated to be clearly understood."

About 1,800 years ago, a number of talmudic scholars held a somewhat similar view about the miracles described in the Bible, except that they were able to harmonize what was seemingly supernatural activity with the laws of the universe. These rabbis suggested that the unusual events that transpired were indeed miracles, but they were not miracles in the sense that we understand the word. The biblical happenings that we call miracles were actually pre-ordained events that were programmed into nature and were thus part of the natural order. Accordingly, the miracles of the Bible were no longer to be considered a break with the natural order, but a fulfillment of a plan that was set in motion at the very beginning.

Here is how two early talmudic scholars viewed supernatural occurrences:

Rabbi Yochanan: "God made an agreement with the sea [during the time of Creation] that it would split in half when it would be approached by the Israelites [fleeing from Egypt]."

Rabbi Jeremiah: "Not only did God make an agreement with the sea, but He made an agreement with all the other things that were created during the six days of Creation.

"God made an agreement with the sun and the moon that they should stand still in the time of Joshua.

"God made an agreement with the ravens that they should feed Elijah.

"God made an agreement with the fire that it should not harm Hananiah, Mishael, and Azariah—the three friends of Daniel—when they would be thrown into the fiery furnace at the command of Nebuchadnezzar of Babylonia.

"God made an agreement with the fish that it should spit out Jonah alive, after it had swallowed him."[24]

Some talmudic and post-talmudic authorities were of the opinion that miracles are to be taken as allegorical and poetic expressions of God's greatness. This is evident, for example, from the manner in which the Rabbis interpreted the story of Israel's battle with its archenemy, the Amalekites. The Bible says, "And it came to pass, when Moses held up his hand, Israel prevailed; and when he put down his hand, Amalek prevailed" (Exodus 17:11). The Rabbis of the Talmud wondered about this miraculous event, and concluded that the biblical statement is not meant to be taken literally. Rather, it is allegory, with the message that as long as the Children of Israel look up and keep their hearts attuned to their Father in heaven, they will prevail. If they do not look up toward God, they will be defeated.[25]

This manner of interpreting the Bible was widely accepted by the greatest of scholars, among them Saadya Gaon and Moses Maimonides. Maimonides, in fact, stated openly in his *Guide for the Perplexed* that all the miracles described in the Bible in connection with the careers of the prophets must be understood as prophetic visions, not as literal happenings.[26]

Why is public worship considered more important than private devotion?

Prayer in the Jewish tradition is more than communion with a Higher Being; it is also communication with one's fellow Jew. "The king's glory is enhanced by a multitude of people" (Proverbs 14:28) has been interpreted by scholars throughout the ages to mean that God (the King) looks with favor upon congregational (public) prayer, generally referred to in Hebrew as *tefila betzibur*.

To reinforce the importance of congregational prayer, the Rabbis of the Talmud ruled that the most important prayers (which include the *Amida,* the *Kaddish,* and the *Barchu*) may be recited only when a *minyan* (quorum of ten persons) is present.[27] "A man's prayer is heard [by God] only in the synagogue," said the talmudic scholar Abba Binyamin.[28]

Scholars of later centuries concurred with the view that public prayer is preferred over private prayer. In the eleventh century, Rashi expressed the view that a person is *obligated* to pray with a *minyan*. A century later Moses Maimonides expressed a similar view when he wrote:

> God always answers the prayers of a community . . . Therefore, one should always associate himself with the community and, wherever possible, not pray privately.[29]

The thirteenth-century scholar Moses ben Nachman (Nachmanides) agreed with Maimonides but disagreed with Rashi. Nachmanides said that a man should seek out a *minyan* and join them in prayer whenever possible, but that he is not *obligated* to do so.

The Committee on Law and Standards of the Rabbinical Assembly (Conservative), in a majority opinion, agreed with Maimonides and Nachmanides on the importance of worshipping with a *minyan* and permitted riding to the synagogue on the Sabbath in order to attend services (for those who would otherwise be unable to attend public worship). Reform and Reconstructionist Jews agree with this view, but the Orthodox consider it more important not to violate a Sabbath law than to attend a congregational service.

Why are most congregational prayers recited quietly?

The most popular explanation offered for the quiet recitation of prayer is that to the Rabbis of the Talmud prayer is the "service of the heart,"[30] and God knows what goes on in a man's heart without him shouting it aloud. This view is based on the verse in the Book of Deuteronomy (11:13) which speaks of *serving* God "with all your heart and all your mind and all your soul." Serving is identified with prayer. The Rabbis support their conclusion by calling attention to Hannah, the mother of Samuel, who when praying for the birth of a child "spoke in her heart. . . . Only her lips moved, but her voice could not be heard" (I Samuel 1:13).

In the Talmud, the prayer referred to as the *Tefila*,[31] literally meaning "prayer" (also known as the *Shmoneh Esray* and *Amida*), was recited silently, as were all prayers. (Today the *Tefila* prayer is sometimes referred to as the *Silent Devotion*.) The Talmud notes: "He who recites the *Tefila* so it can be heard [by others] is a person of small faith."[32] The implication is that such a person believes that

God will be unable to hear his prayer unless it is recited aloud. Rabbi Huna qualifies this statement by saying that the talmudic statement applies particularly to public prayer, because when one prays aloud in the midst of a congregation he may disturb the concentration of the other congregants.

Another reason why prayers are recited quietly or silently may be traced to the procedure followed when a sin-offering was brought in Second Temple times. The individual bringing the sacrifice would deliver it to the Priest, and it would be offered on the same side of the altar as all other sacrifices. None of the onlookers was able to detect whether the Priest was offering up the sin-offering or one brought by an individual who had come to the Temple with an offering of thanksgiving or any other kind of offering.

This may have led Rabbi Yochanan to ask, "Why was the rule instituted that the *Tefila* should be recited silently?" His answer was, "So as not to put sinners to shame."[33] It was customary for sinners to confess their sins in the course of prayer, and if prayers as a rule were recited aloud, all would hear their confessions. To avoid embarrassment to sinners all prayers were recited quietly.

The practice today, particularly in congregations that follow the Sephardic rite, is to recite most prayers aloud along with the cantor, some of them in unison, and some responsively.

Why does Jewish law consider it proper to pray in any language?

The Hungarian authority Rabbi Moses Sofer (1763-1839), author of the *Chatam Sofer,* believed that it is forbidden to pray in any language other than Hebrew and that it is better to recite prayers in Hebrew even if the individual does not understand their meaning. However, this attitude is certainly not typical of rabbinic scholars. Rabbi Sofer's attitude was undoubtedly part of his uncompromising opposition to Reform Judaism, which was beginning to take root in Europe during his lifetime and which had begun to add prayers in the vernacular to its liturgy.

However, the classic rabbinic view, to which almost all authorities subscribe, is mentioned several times in the Talmud and most directly in Berachot:

> Our Rabbis taught: "The *Shema* must be recited as it is written [in the original Hebrew]." This is the opinion of Rabbi [Judah the Prince]. The Sages, however, say that it may be recited in any language . . . What is the reason of the Sages? It is because the Bible uses the word *hear* in Deuteronomy 6:4 [*"Hear, O Israel . . .*], implying that you can recite it in any language that you understand.[34]

Although Hebrew was always the preferred language of prayer, the Rabbis in talmudic times recognized that Hebrew was not the native tongue of all Jews and was not even familiar to all Jews. For example, the very large Jewish community in Alexandria, Egypt, which was ruled by the Greeks, spoke the Greek language and knew little if any Hebrew. The substantial community of Jews in Babylonia, where the vernacular was Aramaic, also had little knowlege of Hebrew. Even in Palestine Aramaic was the language of the street.

While they were fully aware that Hebrew was not familiar to most Jews, the Rabbis nevertheless did not cease composing prayers in that language, for to them Hebrew was the holy tongue. However, they did acknowledge the validity of prayers recited in the vernacular. This point of view prevailed throughout the ages and in the sixteenth century was codified as law.[35]

Why do only some blessings include the phrase "Who has sanctified us by His commandments"?

As a general rule, only those blessings that are recited before an activity that is biblically mandated include the phrase *asher kideshanu bemitzvotav,* meaning "Who has sanctified us by His commandments." Thus, for example, when one affixes a *mezuza* to a doorpost, as commanded in the Bible (Exodus 6:9), the prayer recited is "Blessed art thou, O Lord our God, Who have sanctified us by Your commandments and commanded us to affix a *mezuza.*" When one eats *matza,* he likewise is observing a biblical commandment (Deuteronomy 16:3), and the blessing recited over the *matza* includes the sanctification phrase.

On the other hand, the blessing recited before eating a piece of bread, "Blessed art thou, O Lord our God, Who bring forth bread from the earth," omits *asher kideshanu bemitzvotav* because there is no biblical commandment to eat bread. The blessing over bread was introduced by the Rabbis of the Talmud. As stated above, blessings over nonbiblically-based actions do not contain the sanctification phrase.

Notable exceptions to the rule are the blessings recited when kindling the Sabbath and Chanuka candles. In both instances *asher kideshanu bemitzvotav* is part of the prayers despite the fact that the kindling of candles on these occasions is not biblically mandated. The Bible requires that the Sabbath be observed but not that candles be lighted. And, of course, there is no reference at all to Chanuka in the Bible because the holiday itself is of post-biblical origin.

To the Rabbis of the Talmud, however, the Sabbath represented the essence of Judaism, and Chanuka represented a victory that saved Judaism from extinction. The candlelighting prayer for each occasion was therefore deemed worthy of containing the words *asher kideshanu bemitzvotav.*

Why do observant Jews refrain from speaking from the time they utter a blessing associated with an activity until after the activity has been performed?

In Jewish law, a blessing associated with an activity must be followed immediately by the activity. Thus, for example, when a person says the prayer before donning a *talit*, he may not pause to carry on a conversation before actually putting on the *talit*. Or, when one recites a prayer over food, he must taste of the food immediately, without interruption. The act of interruption is known as *hafsaka* in Hebrew.[36]

Why are some blessings characterized by the Rabbis as "wasted" or "superfluous"?

Two types of blessings are considered by the Rabbis of the Talmud to be wasted or superfluous because they employ God's name for no legitimate purpose. The third of the Ten Commandments (Exodus 20:7) prohibits one from taking the name of God in vain.

A blessing can become superfluous if it calls for an action but after the blessing is recited no action is taken. For example, Jewish law demands that all unleavened food *(chametz)* be removed from one's house on the night before Passover. To accomplish this, a special ceremony called *bedikat chametz* (searching out the *chametz*), culminating in *biur chametz* (the removal and burning of all *chametz*), was instituted. The master of the house goes from room to room and places a crumb or two on each windowsill. He then recites a blessing over the removal of the *chametz* from the home. Following this, he lights a candle and, guided by its light, again goes from room to room (usually accompanied by his children) and with a feather brushes the crumbs into a wooden spoon. The crumbs and the implements are then all wrapped together and burned the next morning along with any food *(chametz)* left over from the breakfast meal.

Why are crumbs placed on the windowsills after days, perhaps weeks, have been spent cleaning the house thoroughly so there will be no *chametz* in the house during Passover? The answer is, since the head of the household is obligated to recite the *biur chametz* prayer,[37] and since there is the likelihood that the master of the house will find no *chametz* when he conducts his search, crumbs are purposely placed in each room to be collected later. Otherwise, the blessing that he recites might become a *beracha levatala*, a wasted prayer.

For this same reason no blessing was assigned to a number of important positive Tora commandments *(mitzvot)* where one would have expected a blessing to be recited. The first commandment in the Tora is, "Be fruitful and multiply" (Genesis 1:28). To have children is of the highest priority in Jewish law, yet before engaging in sexual intercourse no blessing is recited. Why? Probably because of the principle *beracha levatala*. Should the intercourse not result in a pregnancy, the blessing would have been for nought, wasted.

In this same category is the absence of a prayer before giving charity. *Tzedaka*, the giving of charity, is a primary biblical commandment (Deuteronomy 15:7-8). Why, then, is a blessing not recited before giving charity.? The thirteenth-century scholar Rabbi Solomon ben Adret of Barcelona (also known as the Rashba) responded that the fulfillment of the action of giving charity does not rest with the donor. Since there exists the chance that the person who is offered the charity will refuse to accept it, a blessing that had been recited by the donor could turn out to be a wasted blessing. Hence, a *beracha* ("blessing") is not to be recited when giving charity.

The second type of wasted blessing is uttered by a person who is not required or obligated to pronounce the blessing. If a Gentile were called to the Tora for an *aliya*, and if he knew the Tora blessings and pronounced them properly, each of the blessings would be a *beracha levatala*, a wasted blessing. The blessings are considered wasted because a non-Jew is not eligible to recite a blessing containing the words *"asher kideshanu bemitzvotav vetzivanu . . . ,"* meaning "Who has sanctified us with Your commandments and commanded us to. . . ." Non-Jews, not being part of the Covenant People, were not commanded to observe the *mitzvot* of the Tora.

Why do some congregations omit prayers for the restoration of the sacrificial system?

For centuries after the destruction of the Temple in 70 C.E., all Jews prayed and hoped for the rebuilding of the Temple and the restoration of animal sacrifices. In the twelfth century, Moses Maimonides still firmly believed that the Temple would be rebuilt and the sacrificial system would be reinstituted. He believed this so strongly that in his code of Jewish law, the *Mishneh Torah,* he devotes considerable space to this theme, and includes a full exposition of the sacrificial procedures so that when the Messiah arrives and the Temple service is restored Priests will know how to carry on. On the other hand, another codifier of the law, the sixteenth-century Joseph Caro, devotes no space to this subject in his code of Jewish law, the *Shulchan Aruch.*

While theoretically Orthodox Jews look forward to the restoration of the sacrificial system, and their prayerbooks continue to express this hope, it is not in fact a proposition that is taken seriously. About fifty years ago, when the Chief Rabbi of Palestine, Abraham I. Kook, who believed that the coming of the Messiah was imminent, proposed that a school be established to train Priests in the practical conduct of Temple ritual, he found no support for his idea and he abandoned it.

Reform and Reconstructionist prayerbooks have eliminated all prayers relating to the sacrificial system. Conservative prayerbooks retain these prayers but cast them in the past tense, commemorating the sacrificial system only as an aspect of the Jewish historical past.

Why is the ordination of rabbis called *semicha,* meaning "laying on of hands"?

Semicha, a Hebrew word meaning "laying on" or "leaning," is first used in the Bible in connection with the sacrificial system. When one brings a personal sacrifice of repentance to the Temple, the Bible says (Leviticus 1:4), "He shall lay [in Hebrew, *samach*] his hand upon the head of the [animal] offering." In connection with the offering brought on the Day of Atonement, the Bible (Leviticus 16:21) says that "Aaron [the High Priest] shall lay [*samach*] both his hands upon the head of the live goat . . ."

According to tradition the first ordination took place when Moses ordained Joshua by placing his hands on him. Moses thereby transferred a portion of his power and spirit to his disciple (Numbers 27:22; Deuteronomy 34:9). Moses also ordained seventy elders who assisted him in governing the Children of Israel (Numbers 11:16-17, 24-25). According to Maimonides, these elders ordained their successors, and the chain continued until Second Temple times.[38] Thus, it became the rule that only an ordained person could ordain another, and the ordination could take place only in the Land of Israel. When the Second Temple was destroyed (70 C.E.), the practice of "laying on the hands [*semicha*]" at the time of ordination fell into disuse. Instead, either a document of ordination was issued or the ordination was done orally.

Why do most authorities consider it improper to recite blessings when partaking of a non-kosher meal?

Recognizing that there are emergency situations (times of war, when stranded in a strange city, and the like) when one must eat forbidden food, authorities have addressed the question of whether it is proper to recite a blessing before eating a nonkosher meal. Maimonides (1135-1204) wrote that one should not recite a blessing before or after he has eaten forbidden food.[39] However, his critic, the French talmudist Abraham ben David of Posquières (1120-1198), also known as the Ravad, disagreed. In the Ravad's view a blessing should be recited before eating all food, kosher or nonkosher. He does, however, register his disapproval of eating forbidden food by stating that when two other persons are partaking of the same nonkosher meal, the introductory verses to the *Grace After Meals* should not be recited.

Most contemporary authorities are of the opinion that when one recites the blessing over bread (... *hamotzi lechem min haaretz*) at the beginning of a nonkosher meal, he is in essence condoning the eating of nonkosher food. The blessing, it is believed, should therefore not be said.

Why was the *Shehecheyanu* blessing instituted?

The *Shehecheyanu* blessing—"Praised art Thou, O Lord our God, King of the universe, Who have kept us alive, and sustained us, and enabled us to reach this season"—was introduced to encourage Jews to offer thanks for new and unusual experiences. This prayer of gratitude is recited upon the annual advent of a holiday, when a ritual is observed for the first time in the year, and when a new food is enjoyed (such as eating a fruit for the first time in its season).

The *Shehecheyanu* benediction is also recited when one puts on a new garment, be it a dress, suit, coat, or pair of shoes. The Rabbis, however, made a point of emphasizing that when the article is made from the skin of an animal, a benediction is not to be recited. (See the next question.)

Why is the *Shehecheyanu* not recited when putting on, for the first time, wearing apparel made from the skin of an animal?

The prevention of cruelty to animals is a basic biblical concept that is embodied in several specific laws. These include giving animals a day of rest along with humans (Exodus 20:10); not muzzling an ox while it works in the field, thus denying him food (Deuteronomy 22:4); not harnessing the donkey to the stronger ox in order to plow a field (Deuteronomy 22:12); not removing eggs or fledglings from a nest before the mother bird has been sent away (Deuteronomy 22:28). The Talmud goes so far as to say that before one sits down to eat, he must feed his animals.[40]

Jewish law concedes that while it may be necessary to use an animal for food, it is not permissible to take an animal's life merely to provide man with luxuries. To kill an animal for the purpose of using its fur for a coat or its skin to make leather shoes is considered a violation of the biblical injunction against maltreating animals (called in Hebrew, *tzaar baalay chayim*). Therefore, the *Shehecheyanu* blessing is not recited when wearing such apparel for the first time. (See the previous question.)

Why is the *Kiddush* an independent ceremony that precedes the Sabbath meal?

The Rabbis of the Talmud mandated that the *Kiddush* must be recited and wine drunk before the *Hamotzi* blessing is said and the Sabbath (or holiday) meal begins.[41] If the *Kiddush*, the blessing over wine, were to be pronounced after the *Hamotzi* prayer, the *Kiddush* would be superfluous *(beracha levatala)*. This is so because the *Hamotzi* blessing, which is recited over bread at the beginning of the meal, covers all the food to be eaten in the course of the meal (including wine).

Why do some families sit while reciting the *Kiddush*?

Although it is more common for families to stand rather than sit while the *Kiddush* is recited, this is not and has not been a universal practice.

The Sephardic and chassidic communities generally follow the practice established by Rabbi Isaac Luria (known as the Ari), who lived in Safed, Palestine, from 1570 until his death in 1572. He believed that one should stand during *Kiddush* because it is the ceremony that welcomes the Sabbath. The Ari, comparing the Sabbath to a bride, said that just as when blessings are recited at a marriage ceremony the groom stands next to his bride, so should Jews stand when ushering in the "Sabbath bride."

The Ashkenazic community follows the view of sixteenth-century Joseph Caro, author of the *Shulchan Aruch.* He says that when one recites the first part of the Friday night *Kiddush* (Genesis 2:1-3), he should stand, and thereafter he should sit. Moses Isserles, the Polish-born commentator, says in his Notes that it is acceptable to stand but it is better to sit.[42]

Why is it traditional to use red wine for *Kiddush*?

Since talmudic times there has been much debate over whether only red wine can be used for *Kiddush* or whether white wine is an acceptable alternative. Both the Palestinian and the Jerusalem Talmuds discuss the question, concluding that since only strong wine (the red variety) was used on the altar in Temple times, so must strong (red) wine be used for *Kiddush.* On the other hand, Joseph Caro, in his *Shulchan Aruch,* permits the use of white wine for *Kiddush* but suggests that red wine should be used if possible.[43] In either case, there is no prohibition against using dry wine as opposed to the sweet wines most Jews associate with Jewish ritual.

Why is the cup of wine used for *Kiddush* and other prayers usually filled to overflowing?

It is traditional to fill to overflowing the cup of wine over which *Kiddush, Grace After Meals,* and *Havdala* are recited. This is often explained as an expression of hope that life's goodness and bounty will be as abundant as the wine that is being blessed.

A more basic reason is related to the sacrificial system in Temple times. When burnt- and peace-offerings were made, an entire container of wine was poured onto the altar. After the Temple was destroyed and wine was used in connection with home rituals, a custom developed of filling the cup of wine to its very brim so that some of it would flow over.

Why do *chassidim* wear street hats when reciting the *Kiddush*?

When returning home from synagogue on the Sabbath or holidays, *chassidim*, as well as those who follow chassidic practice, continue to wear their street hats (usually black felt hats) at least until after reciting the *Kiddush*. Sabbath and holiday meals are formal occasions, and one must dress for them accordingly. Some wear a street hat throughout the meal, while others change to a black *yarmulke* after the *Kiddush* has been recited.

Why do some people keep the palms of the hands flat when holding the cup of wine to recite the *Kiddush*, *Grace After Meals*, and *Havdala*?

Those who follow this tradition base it on the verse in the Book of Psalms (145:16), "Thou openest Thine hands and satisfiest every living thing with favor."

Why is the *Kiddush* prayer recited in the synagogue as well as in the home?

After the destruction of the Second Temple in 70 C.E., the size of the Jewish community in Babylonia grew as a result of the emigration from Palestine of large numbers of Jews anxious to avoid Roman persecution. Many of these refugees became itinerant peddlers who often found themselves far from home on the Sabbath. To care for these Jews, synagogues opened their doors and provided meals and lodging.

Up until this time, the *Kiddush*, the prayer of sanctification associated with the Sabbath and holidays, had been recited only in the home. To insure that itinerant Jews who spent the Sabbath away from their families and ate their Sabbath meals in the synagogue would hear the recitation of the *Kiddush*, the prayer was now also recited by the cantor at the conclusion of the synagogue service. (Permanent residents of the town would go home after the service and recite the *Kiddush* privately for their own families.) Thus, in Babylonia and other communities outside of Palestine, it became customary for the *Kiddush* to be recited both in the synagogue and the home. In Palestine itself, where wayfaring strangers were not in abundance and where there was little need for Sabbath synagogue hospitality, *Kiddush* was not recited in the synagogue. To this day, synagogues in Israel do not recite the *Kiddush* at the Friday evening service.

Why are children called up to drink the *Kiddush* and *Havdala* wine in the synagogue?

As pointed out above, the recitation of the *Kiddush* on the Sabbath and holidays was introduced into the synagogue liturgy for the benefit of travelers. Since the cantor chanted the *Kiddush* in the synagogue in their behalf, and since he would soon be going home to recite the *Kiddush* for his family, the cantor did not taste the wine in the synagogue. So that the blessing pronounced by the cantor in the synagogue is not wasted *(beracha levatala),* it became customary to call upon children (usually age six and older) to drink the wine. When there were no children present, the cantor himself would drink at least one quarter of the cupful as prescribed by the *Code of Jewish Law.*

The person who recited the *Havdala* in the synagogue to end the Sabbath also recited the *Havdala* at home. For the same reasons given above, it became customary to call upon children to drink the *Havdala* wine.

Why do bread and wine have their own special blessings?

In almost all cases the blessing recited over a food does not relate specifically to that food. Rather, it relates to the category of food to which that food belongs.

The blessing over fruit of all kinds ends with the words *boray peri ha'etz,* "Who create the fruit of trees"; the blessing over cakes, pastries, and all foods made from flour of the five species of grain mentioned in the Bible (wheat, barley, spelt, oats, and rye) concludes with the words *boray minay mezonot,* "Who create various kinds of food"; and the benediction over liquids and other foods excepting plant life ends with the phrase *shehakol niheyeh bidevaro,* "by whose word all things came into being."

Although bread and wine each fall into one of the above categories, because of their importance in Jewish tradition a special prayer was assigned to them. No Sabbath or holiday meal and no special party meal *(seuda)* is considered complete without bread and wine. Their distinction has been linked to Scripture, which speaks of bread as the food that sustains life and wine as the food that adds joy to life (Psalms 104:14-15).

The special blessing that was created for bread ends with the words *hamotzi lechem min haaretz,* "Who draw forth bread from the earth." The special blessing over wine ends with the phrase *boray peri hagafen,* "Who create the fruit of the vine."

Why is the blessing that is recited over bread not recited over other baked goods?

Logically, it would seem, the same blessing should be recited over bread, cake, cookies, pastries, and other baked goods. All baked goods are made by using all or some of the following ingredients: flour, eggs, shortening, water or another liquid, yeast or another leavening agent, salt, sugar, and flavorings. The different proportions and different ways in which the ingredients are combined determine the nature of the final baked product.

In the Bible (Genesis 21:14) bread is considered a basic food. Therefore, as stated above, the Rabbis instituted a special blessing ending with *hamotzi lechem min haaretz,* "Who bring forth bread from the earth," to be recited before eating bread made from any of the five species of grain. The Rabbis did not consider other types of baked goods basic to a meal, and therefore the blessing ending in *boray minay mezonot,* "Who create all kinds of food," was assigned to it.

Why does the roll served with a kosher meal on an airplane have the Hebrew word *mezonot* printed on the cellophane in which it is wrapped?

The Hebrew word *mezonot* literally means "provisions, foods, nourishment." It is also the name of the prayer recited when one eats food other than bread made from one of the five grains mentioned in the Bible (wheat, barley, spelt, oats, rye). The *mezonot* blessing is recited before eating sweetrolls, cake, noodles, pancakes, dough-covered foods, and the like.

When the word *mezonot* is printed on the cellophane-wrapped hamburger-type roll served with a kosher meal on airplanes, this tells observant Jews that the roll is not considered bread and that the *Hamotzi* blessing normally said over bread need not be recited. The *Mezonot* blessing should be substituted. The word *mezonot* on the wrapper also indicates that since bread is not being served, the repast is not to be considered a meal, and one's hands therefore need not be washed ritually, as one does normally before meals.

The rabbinic authorities responsible for supervising the kosher meals served by the airlines have chosen to label the rolls served as *mezonot*—a legal fiction of sorts—in order to accommodate the religious needs of observant Jews who make long trips and must take their meals on airplanes.[44] It would, Orthodox authorities feel, be an undue hardship for individuals to have to leave their seats in order to wash their hands before meals. In fact, it would be almost impossible because the only place to wash would be in the lavatory, which would be improper.

Why are many prayers preceded by an introductory phrase, sentence, or paragraph?

In early talmudic times, pious Jews were known to prepare for prayer. The Mishna says, "Pious men of old used to meditate for one hour before engaging in prayer so that their thoughts would be properly focused on their Father in heaven."[45] Rabbi Chanina, a first-century Deputy High Priest (whose function it was to stand next to the High Priest on the Day of Atonement, ready to take over should the need arise), said that he would never pray when in a state of agitation.[46] In the third century, the Babylonian teacher Rav (Abba Aricha) issued this ruling: "A person should not pray when his mind is not at ease."[47]

By the time the first authoritative prayerbook was issued by Rabbi Saadya Gaon in the tenth century, a whole series of prayers were already being recited by pious Jews who wanted to prepare themselves for the actual prescribed prayers. These preparatory prayers came to be known as *Pesukay Dezimra,* "Verses of Praise." Saadya included them as an appendix to his *Siddur* (prayerbook), but later prayerbooks grouped them at the beginning of the liturgy, and they became the opening prayers of the morning service. The *Pesukay Dezimra* consist of seven Psalms (100, 145-50) plus other prayer compositions, one of which is the *Baruch She'amar* prayer, "Blessed be He who spoke and the world was created."

In later centuries brief introductions to individual prayers were composed. Most noteworthy were the compositions of the sixteenth-century mystics (kabbalists) living in Safed, Palestine.[48] To reach toward God, to adore Him, to revere Him, to strive to become one with (be part of) Him was the essence of the mystic's existence. Accordingly, the kabbalists, more than other pious Jews, insisted that no prayer should be recited and no ritual performed without proper preparation. Some of the familiar short introductions to prayers composed by them are those beginning with the words *Hineni muchan u'mezuman* ("Behold, I am prepared"), *Yehi ratzon* ("May it be Thy will"), and *Leshaym yichud* ("For the sake of unification").

Why are knives removed from the table before *Grace After Meals* is recited?

After the destruction of the Second Temple in 70 C.E., the table in the home came to represent the altar in the Temple. Since it had been forbidden to place iron implements on the altar (because of their association with war, man's nemesis), it became forbidden to leave knives on the table during the recitation of *Grace After Meals*. In some households, metal spoons and forks are also removed. In others, all metal utensils are covered with a cloth until the recitation of *Grace* is concluded.

Why is it customary to recite specific sections from the Book of Psalms before reciting *Grace After Meals*?

The *Code of Jewish Law* requires every pious person to be ever mindful of the destruction of the Jerusalem Temples (the First Temple by the Babylonians in 586 B.C.E and the Second Temple by the Romans in 70 C.E.) and the devastation of the Land of Israel by enemies of the Jewish nation. Since one eats one or more meals each day, and since one therefore recites *Grace After Meals* at least once each day, mealtime was considered an appropriate occasion to recall these sad times in Jewish history. Thus, as a preamble to the *Grace After Meals,* it became customary to recite or chant verses from the Book of Psalms that address themselves to the destruction of the Temples and the wasting of Zion.

Psalm 137, which begins with the words "By the rivers of Babylon, there we sat and wept as we remembered Zion," is the introduction used before the weekday *Grace After Meals.* However, because the Sabbath and holidays are joyous occasions on which the recitation of this Psalm is inappropriate, Psalm 126 is recited instead. This Psalm, which contains the hopeful words "They that sow in tears shall reap in joy," is generally more joyous and more in keeping with the spirit of festive days.

Why is *Grace After Meals* referred to as *benshn*?

The term *benshn* (also pronounced *benshen*) for *Grace After Meals* was introduced by German Jews. The word derives from the Latin *benedicere,* meaning "bless, pronounce a benediction."

Why is the full *Grace After Meals* recited only if bread has been eaten at the meal?

The requirement to say *Grace* is biblical (Deuteronomy 8:10): "And you shall eat and be satisfied and bless the Lord for the good land that He gave you." This verse is preceded by a description of the good land: "A land wherein you shall eat bread without scarceness and not lack anything." The fact that these two verses appear side by side led the Rabbis to conclude that if one eats bread (considered to be the staff of life), he is then obligated to bless the Lord.

The full *Grace After Meals (Birkat Hamazon),* which consists of four blessings, was designed by the Rabbis to be recited only when a "true" meal has been eaten. At such a meal bread must be consumed. For meals or snacks at which bread has not been served, condensed versions of *Grace* are recited depending on what is eaten. The *Beracha Acharona* (literally, "Last Blessing") is recited when cakes, pastries, fruit, and the like are the essential part of the meal. An even shorter form of *Grace After Meals* known as *Boray Nefashot* is an expression of thanks to God for having created all living things. It is recited whenever neither the full *Grace* nor the *Beracha Acharona* is in order.

Why, after a wedding dinner, do men assemble at a separate table to recite *Grace After Meals*?

At ultra-Orthodox weddings men and women are seated separately, not only during the ceremony but during the meal of celebration that follows. At modern Orthodox weddings, however, women often sit separately during the religious ceremony but not during the meal.

There is a tradition for ten or more men (a *minyan*) to assemble at the head table at the conclusion of the wedding meal. The *Grace After Meals*, concluding with the *Sheva Berachot* (Seven Benedictions), is then recited. Bringing the men to one table insures that the ban against praying in mixed company is being honored.

Why was it decided that three persons must be present to constitute a quorum for *Grace After Meals*?

A quorum of three people is required to recite the introductory prayer to the *Grace After Meals*.[50] The quorum of three is known as a *mezuman*, a name derived from the Hebrew word meaning "to invite." Through the introductory prayer, the *Birkat Zimun*, meaning "prayer of invitation," everyone at the table is invited to recite a prayer of thanksgiving.

Why *three* was established as the requisite number of people to be present to recite the introductory prayer has been related to the fact that the table upon which one eats represents the altar on which sacrifices were offered in Temple times. Three main varieties of sacrifice were brought in the Temple: animal sacrifices (called *zevach* in Hebrew), grain offerings *(mincha),* and libations *(nesech).*

Mystics have explained that the number three was favored because it was the first odd number after the unit (one). Early peoples thought that there is "luck in odd numbers," and this found expression in the talmudic belief that even numbers are not merely unlucky but dangerous.

The number three came to be recognized as having magical qualities.

Why is one not required to recite a blessing before smoking?

In comparatively recent years, rabbis have been concerned with the question of smoking and its effects on health. The debate of earlier centuries did not address the health hazards of smoking but rather did concern itself with the question of whether one must recite a blessing before smoking as one does before eating.

The question was first raised by the talmudist Abraham Gombiner (1635-1683), the rabbi of Kalish, in Poland, who is best remembered for his commentary on the Shulchan Aruch, entitled Magen Avraham. In one of his comments, he discusses whether a person who tastes food while cooking to determine if it is properly seasoned and spits it out before swallowing is required to recite a blessing.[51] He and later commentators were in agreement that only when food is put into one's mouth for the purpose of eating is the recitation of a blessing mandatory. The fact that one who merely tastes food might derive pleasure from it is irrelevant.

Based upon this interpretation of the law, Gombiner concludes that a smoker is not required to recite a prayer before smoking because the inhaling and exhaling of smoke is the equivalent of taking food into the mouth and then spitting it out. The pleasure factor is irrelevant here, as it is in the case of tasting food while cooking.

Most authorities agree with Gombiner's view. Rabbi Israel Meir Hakohayn (1838-1933), for example, points out in his Mishna Berura commentary that no authority of recent centuries has required a person to pronounce a blessing before smoking. However, it should be noted that early disciples of the Baal Shem Tov (1700-1760), the founder of chassidism, have reported that their master smoked a pipe (lulke) and did recite a prayer before doing so.

Why does one utter expressions such as "Gezundheit" (in German, Gesundheit) and "God bless you" upon hearing someone sneeze?

Genesis (2:6) says, "And He [God] blew into his [man's] nostrils the soul of life." It was believed that the nostrils are the apertures through which life enters and leaves man's body.

Jewish legend tells that until the time of the patriarch Jacob people did not become ill before dying. They simply sneezed, then died immediately. Sneezing was believed to signal approaching death.

In early times Jews, as well as other peoples, believed that sneezing was the work of evil spirits determined to take a man's life, and that their plan could be frustrated by uttering biblical quotations or other expressions. Jews have been known to respond to a sneeze with the verse uttered by Jacob on his deathbed, "For Thy salvation have I hoped, O Lord" (Genesis 49:18), or by exclamations such as "God bless you" and "Gezuntheit" ("to your health").

In the Talmud there are two notions about the significance of the sneeze. One is that it is a bad omen; the other, that if one sneezes while praying, he will be blessed.[52]

In the same tractate, the importance of the sneeze is downplayed. The Talmud reports that while studying in the academy, the members of the household of Rabbi Gamaliel did not say "Good health" when someone sneezed, so as not to interrupt their studies.[53] Rashi goes on to explain that when one person blesses another, all must stop what they are doing and listen to the blessing so they can say "Amen." So that time will not be wasted, says Rashi, one does not stop to say "Good health" or "God bless you" during a study period.

Why is the Shema chanted after the Tora is removed from the ark?

The reading from the Tora (and Prophets) is central to most Sabbath and holiday services. The public reading of the Tora affords the congregation an opportunity to fulfill the commandment that imposes upon every Jew the obligation to study Tora. This commandment, mentioned many times in the Bible, is most explicitly stated in the first paragraph of the *Shema* (Deuteronomy 6:7): "And thou shalt teach them [the words of the Tora] unto thy children, and shalt talk of them when thou sittest in thy house, when thou walkest by the way, when thou liest down, and when thou risest up." This important precept is introduced with the words (Deuteronomy 6:4), "Hear, O Israel [*Shema Yisrael*], the Lord our God, the Lord is One." It therefore is most appropriate, when the Tora is removed from the ark for a public reading, that the ritual be introduced with the same words used in the Bible.

Precisely when the ritual of reciting the *Shema* after the Tora is removed from the ark was instituted is not at all certain, and the ritual is not followed by all communities. Ashkenazim do recite the *Shema* at this point, but Sephardic synagogues—with the exception of Egyptian congregations and possibly some others—do not. Instead they chant the verse from Song of Songs (3:11) which declares, "Go forth, O ye daughter of Zion, and gaze upon King Solomon, even upon the crown with which his mother crowned him on the day of his wedding and on the day his heart was so very happy." The daughters of Zion, the bride, symbolizes Israel. King Solomon, the bridegroom, symbolizes God. Just as the bride in this verse greets the bridegroom, so do the members of the congregation welcome the Tora, which represents God.

In Temple times it was customary for the bridegroom to be crowned with flowers prepared by his mother. When the Tora, covered with its silvery crown, is paraded down the aisles of the synagogue, it is showered with kisses by the adoring bride—the congregation of Israel.

Why are two Tora blessings recited by each person who receives an *aliya*?

This practice was a late development in the synagogue

service. In the time of Ezra the Scribe (fifth century B.C.E.), when the reading of the Tora in public was instituted, each person who was called to the Tora read his own portion aloud, but only the first and last reader recited a blessing. The Mishna, which was compiled in the third century C.E., tells us that the first Tora blessing was recited by the person who received the first *aliya,* and the concluding blessing was recited by the recipient of the last *aliya.*[54] Those who were called to the Tora for other *aliyot* read their portions but did not recite blessings.

By the end of the third century C.E. this practice had changed to a degree. The Talmud says, "Nowadays all [who are called to read from the Tora] recite a blessing before and after they read their portions."[55] This was ordained by the Rabbis of the Talmud so that the public should not be misled. The Rabbis were concerned that those who come to the synagogue after the Tora Reading has already begun might notice that some persons (those receiving the second, third, and later *aliyot)* were reading from the Tora without first having pronounced a blessing. The latecomers might be left with the impression that it is not necessary to recite a Tora blessing before one reads from the Tora. Likewise, congregants who leave the synagogue before the Tora Reading has ended, without having heard anyone recite the second (concluding) Tora blessing, might be misled into believing that it is not necessary to recite a blessing after the Tora Reading has been completed.

The Talmud, when saying that "nowadays all recite a blessing before and after" the Tora Reading, was referring to the three who receive *aliyot* at the Sabbath afternoon service, and at the Monday and Thursday morning service. However, this practice did not apply to all other services. The Minor Tractate Soferim, which according to most scholars was compiled in the eighth century C.E.—three centuries after the Talmud was edited in its present form— mentions this practice, but adds that when the Tora is read on Sabbaths and festivals, only the persons called to the Tora for the first and last *aliyot* recite blessings, and that

THEOLOGY AND PRAYER • 241

they recite *both* blessings.[56] The others, who receive the balance of the *aliyot,* recite no blessings.

It would appear that the custom of having all persons called to the Tora recite blessings before and after the reading developed after the ninth century. The reason is not clear, but it may have been introduced to afford members of the congregation an additional opportunity to respond "Amen" to important blessings.

In some Conservative and Reform congregations today two people are called up together for the same *aliya.* At times they recite the blessings in unison, and at other times one person recites the first blessing and the other recites the concluding blessing.

Why is it considered improper to touch the Tora script with bare hands?

Traditionally, when one is called to the Tora and recites the blessings, the Tora Reader points with the Tora pointer to the portion to be read. Before pronouncing the blessing, the person who has received the *aliya* touches the Tora script with the *talit* fringes or with a prayerbook or with the Tora binder *(gartl),* and then kisses the object that touched the script.

In Jewish law the Tora scroll is not subject to impurity, regardless of who touches it.[57] Nevertheless, to ensure that an attitude of respect toward sacred ritual objects would always prevail and that their sanctity would not be compromised, it became a widespread custom to refrain from touching the Tora script with the bare hand.

This desire to show respect toward sacred articles and institutions is evident in the many laws and practices introduced by the Rabbis of the Talmud and later authorities. The manner in which such respect was shown is seen in the way in which the Chanuka menora candles are treated. The Talmud forbids the lighting of one Chanuka candle from another. This is the view of the third-century C.E. Babylonian scholar Rav (also known as Abba Aricha), who explains that to take light from one candle and transfer it to another is robbing light that rightfully belongs to the first candle, thereby detracting from its importance.[58]

An incident described in the Talmud illustrates how Rabbi Joshua, who was on a mission to Rome in behalf of the Jews of Palestine, showed respect for *tefilin*. He was invited to the home of a Roman matron. Before entering, he removed his *tefilin* (in those days many men wore *tefilin* all day long), because commentators explain, there were idols in the house and Joshua did not want to bring sacred articles into such a setting.[59]

Why in some congregations is it customary for the Tora scroll to be closed (rolled together) when the Tora blessings are recited?

The Talmud describes two procedures that were followed in connection with the recitation of the Tora blessings.[60] One procedure was suggested by Rabbi Meir, a second-century Palestinian scholar who said that when a person is called up to the pulpit to read a Tora portion, he should open the scroll, look at the spot where he is to begin reading, roll the scroll closed, recite the blessing, and then open the scroll once again to read from it. Rabbi Meir believed that the words of the Tora should not be exposed while the Tora blessings are being recited because some members of the congregation might then mistakenly conclude that the Tora blessings are written in the Tora.

Rabbi Judah was of a different opinion. He believed that no one would be led to believe that the Tora blessings are written in the Tora if the scroll is left open while the blessings are recited. And although the Rabbis ruled in favor of Rabbi Judah, both procedures have been followed by different communities over the centuries.

Today, for the most part Ashkenazic Jews (primarily those of East European extraction) follow the procedure of Rabbi Meir, or they cover the Tora either with a Tora mantle or a special cloth (called a *mappa* in Hebrew) while the Tora blessings are recited. Sephardic Jews generally do not roll the Tora scroll closed when the blessings are recited, nor do they cover it.

Why is the Tora placed in an upright (vertical) position when read in some congregations, while in others it is placed horizontally on the reading table?

Sephardic congregations whose members have their roots in Eastern countries—Iraq (formerly Babylonia), Syria, Yemen, Iran, Egypt, India, and others—follow the tradition of standing the Tora vertically on the reading table and reading from it while it is in that position. The origin of this custom is not known, and it may simply have evolved out of a practical need.

Ancient Jewish communities were in the habit of adorning each of their Tora scrolls by encasing it in a highly decorated wooden or metal container. The container was hinged, and when it was opened the portion of the Tora to be read was exposed. Handling the Tora and its heavy casing was much easier when the scroll stood upright. The Tora parchment was rolled from section to section by manipulating two finials (atzay chayim) that protruded from the top of the case.

Although reading the Tora while it is in an upright position is probably the older tradition, today the more popular procedure is the one followed by Ashkenazic congregations and by those Sephardic congregations whose roots are not in Eastern countries (this includes communities in North Africa, Europe, America, and elsewhere). The Tora scrolls read in these congregations are not housed in heavy casings with flat bottoms and have finials that protrude from the bottom as well as the top. The Torot are laid flat on the reading table when they are read.

One other reason why the Ashkenazim and Western Sephardim lay the Tora flat on the reading table may be found in a responsum issued by the eminent thirteenth-century scholar Rabbi Meir of Rothenburg. He wrote: "You ask why we do not lay the Tora horizontally in the ark just as the Ten Commandments were laid in the Temple. This is a good question. Rabbenu Tam [the grandson of Rashi] once wrote in a responsum that it would be a good idea to lay the Tora flat in the ark . . . And he [Rabbenu Tam] also wrote that, had he thought of it, when he built an ark he would have made it wider [so as to be able to place the Torot horizontally rather than vertically]."[61]

Why may a Tora scroll not be rolled from one section to another during services?

This prohibition is based on a principle of synagogue etiquette set forth in the Talmud and repeated in the code of Maimonides,[62] both of which stipulate that it is improper to "weary [place an unnecessary burden on]" the congregation. The caveat is derived from the procedure followed by the High Priest, who in Temple times read aloud Leviticus 16 followed by a selection from Leviticus 23 (26-32). The Mishna[63] says that after reading the two selections the High Priest rolled up the scroll, placed it under his arm, and proceeded to recite from memory a selection from the Book of Numbers (29:7-11).

The Talmud asks, "Why did he recite the selection from memory? Why did he not roll the scroll from Leviticus to Numbers and read from it?" Rabbi Huna replies, "Because it is not proper to roll the scroll in public [and to keep the congregation waiting] out of deference to the public."

To this day, except in emergencies (such as when a congregation has only one Tora scroll), synagogue etiquette demands that two scrolls be used when readings are done from different parts of the Pentateuch, which is the case on all holidays.[64]

Why do some congregations honor individuals with *hagbaha* and *gelila* while others do not?

Today, in all Ashkenazic synagogues two separate honors are assigned to be carried out after the reading of the Tora has been completed. One of the honorees raises the Tora from the reading table and holds it aloft so the congregation can see its words. In Hebrew this honor is known as *hagbaha* (usually pronounced *hagba* or *hagbeh*), meaning "raising up [the Tora]." The person so honored is called the *magbiha*. The second honoree rolls the Tora closed, ties it with a binder, and dresses it with a mantle. The person so honored is called the *golel*, and the honor itself is referred to as *gelila*.

Although the word *gelila* is generally translated as "rolling up," this is not the only meaning of the word. The term *gelila* refers to two specific and distinct acts. It can mean "to roll up" the Tora,[65] or "to cover" or "to dress" the Tora.[66]

In Sephardic congregations, whether Eastern (which includes Iraq, Syria, Egypt, Iran, and Yemen) or Western (which includes Spain, England, Holland, and the Americas), special persons are not called up to the pulpit by the names *magbiha* and *golel*. *Before* the reading of the Tora begins, an unannounced person raises the scroll, revealing several columns of the written Tora text. He turns from side to side so congregants in every part of the synagogue can see the words on the parchment, while the Tora Reader *(baal koray)* points to the words where the reading will begin. The congregation then recites the verse from the Bible (Deuteronomy 4:44), "This is the Tora that Moses placed before the Israelites." (Ashkenazim raise the Tora and chant this verse *after* the Tora Reading has been completed.)

The reason why the Sephardic procedure differs from the Ashkenazic one is not readily explained, but it is quite clear that the Sephardic practice is the older. In the Talmud itself no mention is made of a *magbiha,* and exactly when it became customary to call up a special person to raise the Tora is unknown. The Talmud does make reference to the *golel,* but he was never a special person specifically designated for this honor. The Talmud says that the "senior" person among all who have received an *aliya* at a service is the *golel,* which is considered an honor equal in importance to all the Tora honors combined.[67]

Why is the *maftir* section repeated during the Tora Reading?

The Talmud[68] says that the person who reads the *haftara* selection from the Prophets should first read the *maftir* portion from the Tora. The scholar Ulla explains that this is done in order to show respect for the Tora, for by reading from the Tora first the person designated to read the *haftara* is showing deference to the Pentateuch, which is higher in sanctity than the Prophets. And for this reason the *maftir-haftara aliya* is not counted as one of the seven *aliyot* on Sabbath: because the honoree is reading from the Tora only out of respect, not because it is prescribed, since the *maftir* was already read by the person who received the previous *aliya.*

Why is the Tora Reading no longer translated into the vernacular after it is read aloud in Hebrew in the synagogue?

The Talmud requires that every Jew study the Tora Reading for the approaching Sabbath by reviewing, at home, the weekly portion. He is required to read it two times in Hebrew and once in the vernacular.[69] From talmudic times up until the early Middle Ages the vernacular of Palestinian and Babylonian Jews was Aramaic. (The second-century Aramaic translation by Onkelos, called *Targum Onkelos,* was adopted in Babylonia as the official translation of the Bible.)

According to the Rabbis of the Talmud,[70] Ezra (sixth century B.C.E) established the ritual of reading the Tora aloud publicly in Hebrew, one verse at a time. After the recitation of the verse in Hebrew, a translator, called a *meturgeman,* who stood next to the reader, would recite the verse in the vernacular.

The practice of translating the Hebrew into the vernacular was followed in Palestinian synagogues, where the Tora was read over a three-year period (triennial cycle). But the Babylonian custom of reading the Tora in an annual cycle became the common practice of Jews in the Diaspora. And since the weekly Tora portions in the annual cycle are three times as long as the portions read in the triennial cycle, it would be too time-consuming to have the annual Tora portions translated into the vernacular. Therefore, the translator was dispensed with at synagogues following the Babylonian custom, and the practice of reading the Tora in the vernacular was consigned to the home as described above.

By the Middle Ages the practice of translating the Hebrew into the vernacular had all but disappeared, even in the synagogues of Palestine, possibly under the influence of Babylonian immigrants. However, in Israel today there are still a few Yemenite synagogues where the translator stands next to the reader and translates each Hebrew verse into Arabic. Among Reform Jews today only a few verses of the Tora are read each week; the reader (usually the rabbi) reads a verse or part of a verse and follows it with an English translation and explanation.

Why have Reform congregations abbreviated the Tora Reading service?

As a reaction to the restlessness and disorderliness found in many traditional synagogues during the lengthy Tora Reading service, at its inception in the middle nineteenth century the Reform movement changed the entire system of *aliyot*. Quite often, instead of calling members of the congregation to the Tora, *aliyot* are given only to the rabbi, the cantor, and the synagogue officers seated on the pulpit. In some Reform congregations only one *aliya* is awarded, while in others, two or three are given. The number of Tora verses read for each *aliya* varies, and occasionally as little as a single verse is read. It should be noted, however, that in recent years there has been a trend in Reform synagogues toward awarding more Tora honors to members of the congregation, some even offering the full minimum of seven for the Sabbath morning service.

Why is a Tora scroll sometimes set aside, not to be used for public reading?

Once an error has been found in a Tora, that scroll may not be used until the error has been corrected by a scribe. A scribe can correct an ordinary error, such as a misspelling, by scratching off the black lettering with a knife. A pumice stone is then used to smooth the area, after which the correction is made. However, if an error has been made in the spelling of the name of God, the entire Tora scroll is considered invalid for future use, because it is not permissible to erase the name of God. A Tora with a serious error of this kind is buried in a cemetery. In talmudic times, the practice was established to bury invalid Tora scrolls in a grave next to that of a prominent rabbi.

Why is the congregation seated during the reading of the Tora?

Although it is customary for the congregation to rise and remain standing when the Tora is removed from the ark, during the actual reading of the Tora the congregation is seated. Aside from the practical reason that it would be a hardship for congregants to remain standing for the duration of the Tora Reading, standing is not required because the reading of the Tora is considered a form of study, of instruction. Since students normally sit when they study Tora, the congregation sits during the reading of the Tora as well.

For this same reason, in Orthodox synagogues congregants do not rise when the Shema, a selection from the Tora, is recited. Non-Orthodox congregations stand when the first verse of the Shema is chanted because they consider the concept of One God, which is expressed in that verse, to be deserving of special recognition.

In Sephardic congregations members of the immediate family (male and female) stand when a member of the family is honored with an *aliya*, and they remain standing until he returns to his seat.

Why is the second sentence of the *Shema* prayer traditionally recited aloud only on Yom Kippur?

The first verse (sentence) of the *Shema* prayer—"Hear O Israel, the Lord our God, the Lord is One"—is biblical in origin. It affirms that God alone is God and that all loyalty is due Him. The sentence that follows it—*"Baruch Shem kevod malchuto le'olam va'ed,* "Blessed be His glorious sovereign Name forever and ever"—is nonbiblical and hence of lesser sanctity. It appears for the first time in the Talmud in connection with the Yom Kippur afternoon service conducted by the High Priest (known as the *Avoda* service). In the presence of a large congregation, the High Priest, standing in the Temple Court, made confession of his sins. As he did so, he pronounced the sacred and ineffable name of God (Jehovah) which not one but the High Priest ever uttered. Upon hearing this, the congregation responded aloud enthusiastically, "Blessed be His glorious sovereign Name forever and ever." This was repeated three times. [71]

At prayer services conducted in Babylonian synagogues in Temple times, it was customary to intone the second sentence of the *Shema* silently so as not to detract from the importance of the biblical verses that preceded and followed it.[72] This was also the practice of the Jews of Palestine, but when the Christians who lived among them (there were no Christians in Babylonia) accused them of enunciating secret, heretical doctrines, the Jews began to recite the second sentence of the *Shema* aloud.

Today, all Orthodox congregations and a few Conservative ones follow the practice of Babylonian Jewry and recite the *Baruch Shem* silently throughout the year. But on Yom Kippur, as a reminder of the enthusiastic response of the ancient congregation of Israel to the confession of sin by the High Priest, all congregations recite the *Baruch Shem* aloud.[73]

Why do some congregants remain seated when the ark is left open during the Yom Kippur *Neila* service?

Neila, a Hebrew word meaning "closing," is the name given to the last of the five Yom Kippur services. This service is the grand finale of the long Yom Kippur Day, and a tradition evolved whereby the congregation remains standing throughout the entire one- to two-hour service. Although some congregants find it difficult to stand after fasting for almost twenty-four hours, many others find the effort spiritually satisfying, a reverential way of ending the solemn day of meditation. Since standing during the *Neila* service became widespread, congregational leaders decided to further accentuate the importance of this final period of prayer by keeping the ark open throughout the entire *Neila* service. This practice is now followed in almost all synagogues.

Congregants who are unable to stand throughout the *Neila* service have questioned whether they are showing proper respect toward the Tora if they remain seated while the Tora is exposed in the open ark. This question of Tora etiquette was addressed by Joseph Caro and Moses Isserles in the sixteenth-century *Code of Jewish Law.* Caro said that one must stand when a Tora passes in procession before him, and he must stand until the Tora is placed on the reading table or until it is no longer within his field of vision.[74] In a note on this subject, Isserles wrote that when the Tora is placed on the reading table (which is normally on a platform at least ten handbreadths above the floor level of the congregation), the Tora is then considered to be in a different domain or area (the Hebrew word used is *reshut*), and it is therefore not necessary for the congregation to remain standing despite the fact that the Tora is visible.[75]

Using the same reasoning, David ben Samuel Halevi, the seventeenth-century author of *Turay Zahav* (also known by the acronym Taz), the authoritative commentary on the *Shulchan Aruch,* says that when the Tora is in the ark it is considered to be in a different domain, and one therefore does not have to stand even when the ark is open and the Torot are visible. The Taz does take note of the fact that in many congregations worshippers do stand when the ark is open, but he points out that there is no obligation to do so.

Many later authorities have been less permissive in this matter. The eighteenth-century Dutch scholar Meir Eisenstadt is of the opinion that congregants should remain standing when the ark is open and the Torot visible.[76] Moses Sofer, the famous Hungarian authority, agrees. "If the ark is open," he says, "it is forbidden to remain seated."[77] Yechiel Epstein, the nineteenth-century rabbinic authority, says in his code that since *most* people rise for the open ark, *all* people should rise, because although the law does not require that one do so (since the Tora is in another domain), members of the congregation may think that the person who remains seated is acting disrespectfully toward the Tora. Only if a person is known to be weak or ill, adds Epstein, may he or she remain seated.[78]

In congregations today, standing during the *Neila* service is optional, and one finds that congregants generally remain seated except during the more important prayers, such as the *Kedusha,* and when the *shofar* is sounded, concluding the service.

Why is *Half Hallel* recited on some festivals?

In Temple times, the *Full Hallel,* consisting of psalms in praise of God (Psalms 113 through 118), was recited only on the first day of Passover at the Seder, on the eight days of

Sukkot, and on the eight days of Chanuka. After the Temple was destroyed and the psalms of praise that traditionally accompanied the Shavuot offerings of first-fruits were no longer recited, the *Full Hallel* was added to the synagogue liturgy of Shavuot.

Sometime around the beginning of the third century C.E., the Jews of Babylonia added the practice of reciting *Hallel* on the last six days of Passover and on the New Moon days (Rosh Chodesh). To mark a distinction between this new practice and the older one, the first eleven verses of both Psalm 115 and Psalm 116 were omitted on the last six days of Passover and on Rosh Chodesh. This shorter version of the *Hallel* became known as *Half Hallel,* although actually only a very small portion of the *Full Hallel* is omitted.

The *Full Hallel* is also known as the *Egyptian Hallel* because Psalm 114 deals with the Exodus from Egypt.[79] This name was created by the Rabbis of the Talmud to distinguish this *Hallel* from the *Great Hallel,* which consists of Psalm 136 and is recited daily during the *Schacharit* service.

CHAPTER 8

Laws and Customs

INTRODUCTION

Laws and customs are the mortar of Jewish life. They unify the community.

Law derives from the Tora (Bible) and Talmud; custom derives from popular practice. Both are created for the people, and both must serve the needs of the general populace. When, after the destruction of the Second Temple, ascetics proposed legislation that would forbid the consumption of wine and meat as a sign of mourning for the loss of the Temple, Rabbi Joshua said, "No law may be established that the majority of the population cannot accept and live by."[1] This continues to be the prevailing attitude toward Jewish law and custom.

Because serving the needs of the people was the overriding concern of the law, the Rabbis of the Talmud were ever zealous in protecting those needs. And while they were always careful not to issue an erroneous decision that would create a hardship for the people,[2] they were, at the same time, very protective of the law itself. To the Rabbis the law was not only a means to an end but an end in itself. They believed that the commandments (mitzvot) were given to "purify" man[3] and to guide him toward leading the good life, and they also believed, with Ben Azzai, that "the reward of performing a righteous deed [mitzva] is the deed itself."[4]

The satisfaction derived from the performance of the deed is its own reward. And for this reason, they felt strongly that the commandments had to be preserved and protected.

To this end, the Rabbis built safeguards around the law. By establishing "fences" around the commandments, they made it difficult for the people to violate them. The fences became as binding upon Jews as the bibilical law itself, which the Rabbis were protecting.

The commandments in the Tora to which the Rabbis paid the most attention were those concerning the Sabbath. Fences were built around the Sabbath laws to ensure that no "work" would be performed on that day. The playing of musical instruments was banned; dancing was prohibited; swimming was disallowed; the carrying of objects from the private to the public domain was forbidden—all because they might lead to forbidden activities.[5] Later rabbinic authorities, particularly those in modern times, have had to consider whether electricity is to be considered fire and whether and to what extent the use of electric lights, radios and televisions, refrigerators, and similar items is to be permitted. These problems are discussed in this chapter, as are the use of an elevator and travel (driving and riding) in an automobile on the Sabbath.

In addition to questions of Jewish law, the chapter discusses the status of customs that have evolved over the centuries. Unlike law (halacha), which is imposed from without, custom (minhag) takes root and grows from within. That Jews are required to bless the lulav along with the other three species on Sukkot is a biblical ordinance, but how the lulav is to be waved when the blessing is recited is a matter of minhag, of custom, as it evolved within the community. In time, custom takes on an importance of its own, and as far back as talmudic times the warning was issued that custom not be treated lightly. "Do not change [abandon] the custom of your ancestors," says the Talmud.[6] This attitude is repeated in several tractates and is codified as law in the Shulchan Aruch, where custom is equated with law: "The custom of your ancestors is Tora [Law]."[7]

Why is the Oral Law sometimes considered to be equal in status with the Written Law?

According to tradition, the Jewish religion began with the revelation on Mount Sinai (Exodus 19:5-6). God appeared to Moses on the mountaintop, and there He revealed the laws and doctrines Jews were to follow so that they might become a "holy nation." Deuteronomy 29:9-14 elaborates on this theme, asserting that the covenant between God and the Jewish people, which was confirmed at Sinai, includes not only those Jews who were present at the event, but all Jews of future generations.

What is it that was revealed to Moses? The traditional view is that the Tora—referred to in English as the Pentateuch or the Five Books of Moses—was revealed. The Talmud, however, says that more than just the Tora was revealed; the whole Bible was revealed. In addition to the Five Books of Moses (*Chumash* in Hebrew), this includes the Prophetic Writings (*Neviim* in Hebrew) and the Holy Writings (*Ketuvim* or *Kitvay Hakodesh* in Hebrew, and *Hagiographa* in Greek).

The Pentateuch was the primary source from which the prophets and later teachers drew their inspiration. The Talmud words it this way: "Moses received the Tora on Sinai and transmitted it to Joshua. Joshua transmitted it to the elders, and the elders to the prophets, and the prophets to the members of the Great Assembly."[8] All that was transmitted was contained in the twenty-four books of the Bible, called the Written Law or the Written Tora.

The Oral Law (or Oral Tora, as it is sometimes called) consists of the Talmud and Midrash, in which the teachings and laws of the Written Law are explained and interpreted. These explanations and interpretations were transmitted by word-of-mouth from teacher to student for many generations. So venerated were the teachings of the Rabbis that it was claimed that the Oral Tora, along with the Written Tora, was part of the Revelation at Mount Sinai—if not in every last detail, at least in principle. Thus, because both derive from God, the Oral Law was often considered to be equal in importance to the Written Law.[9]

Why was the Oral Law eventually committed to writing?

In the middle of the first century C.E., as the political situation in Palestine deteriorated and the Roman conquerors prohibited Jewish schools from functioning, it became evident that unless the Oral Law was committed to writing it would in time be lost forever.

When Rabbi Yochanan ben Zakkai, the foremost scholar of this period, realized that the destruction of the Jewish commonwealth was imminent, he managed to obtain permission from the Roman ruler to move his school from Jerusalem to Yavneh, a town located between Joppa (present-day Jaffa) and Ashdod. There, a process of collecting the teachings and traditions of the past began. Around the year 200 C.E., Rabbi Yehuda Hanasi (Judah the Prince), the political and religious leader of Palestinian Jewry, took over the project and pursued it vigorously. The result was the Mishna: an orderly compilation of Jewish laws and traditions that had been handed down from generation to generation. In the two and one-half centuries that followed, the Mishna was studied, analyzed, and interpreted, and these interpretations were edited around the year 500 and were set down in final form as the Gemara. The Mishna and Gemara together are known as the Talmud, which is the Oral Law committed to writing.

Why in Jewish tradition does custom often carry the weight of law?

The Talmud states in a number of places that custom is equal in importance to law. One of the strongest statements in this vein is in the tractate Bava Metzia,[10] where Rabbi Tanchum comments, "One should never discard a custom. For, behold, when Moses went up to heaven he ate no bread, and when the Ministering Angels descended to earth they did eat bread." The point is that one must follow local custom.

The importance of deferring to the practices of a particular locality is indicated several times in the Talmud where questions of law are involved. In the tractate Eruvin,[11] when asked which of two blessings should be recited when one drinks water, Rabba ben Chanan replies, "Go out [into the streets] and see what the people are doing [and then you will know which blessing one should recite]." From the Jerusalem Talmud[12] comes the popular maxim, "Do not change the customs of your ancestors." Rabbi Simeon ben Yochai considers the adherence to custom so important that he associates it with the biblical verse (Proverbs 22:28), "Remove not the ancient landmark which your ancestors have set." Thus he indicates that adherence to custom is to be classified as a biblical commandment rather than a rabbinic one.

An important example of how reluctant the Rabbis were to change established laws and customs is mentioned in the Talmud[13] in connection with the holidays. The question is asked, Why do Diaspora Jews observe two days of some festivals while in Palestine only one day is observed? By that time (the fourth century C.E.), after all, the calendar had already been firmly established and there was no longer the need to rely on messengers to report when a New Moon appeared or when holidays should be celebrated. In answer, the Talmud explains that the Diaspora should continue the practice of celebrating a second day of holidays (called in Hebrew *Yom Tov Sheni Shel Galuyot,* meaning "Second Festival Day of the Diaspora") because this custom was established by our ancestors, and we must not deviate from established custom.

Maimonides, in his *Mishneh Torah,*[14] reiterates this point when he says, "Be careful: do not treat the customs of your fathers lightly." This attitude was further reinforced by Moses Isserles who, in his Notes to the *Shulchan Aruch,*[15] says that established custom is equal in importance to established law.

Why were some laws and established customs modified or discarded by Jewish authorities?

Since not all communities had the same needs, some of the basic customs followed in one community differed markedly from those observed in another. For example, one community may have found it easy to assemble a quorum of ten to constitute a *minyan,* whereas another may have found it difficult. For this reason, although the Talmud[16] requires the presence of ten men in order to carry on a full public service, there are many authorities who suggest otherwise. The Jerusalem Talmud[17] says that nine men and a Tora can constitute a *minyan.* The Babylonian Talmud[18] quotes Rabbi Huna as saying, "Nine men and the ark join together [to constitute a *minyan*]." This sounded ridiculous to Rabbi Nachman, who exclaimed, "Is the ark a man?" Suggestions were made by some authorities that nine, eight, seven, even six men can constitute a quorum.[19]

The illustrious twelfth-century French authority Rabbenu Tam, grandson of Rashi, commented on the apparently popular practice of counting a minor as part of a *minyan* if the boy held a *Chumash* (Pentateuch) in his hand. He characterized the practice as ridiculous.[20]

Another example of an established practice being modified to meet a local need can be seen in the action taken by Moses Maimonides (twelfth century) when he was Chief Rabbi of Old Cairo, then called Fostat. Maimonides didn't appreciate the fact that members of the congregation, after finishing the recitation of the *Silent Devotion (Amida),* immediately began talking to one another, creating bedlam in the synagogue. Maimonides learned that Muslims ridiculed Jews for such behavior, and he therefore decided, contrary to talmudic law, to discontinue the long-established practice of having the congregation recite the *Amida* before the cantor recited it aloud. This innovation of Maimonides, which was introduced to solve a local problem, was followed in all Egyptian synagogues and in some Palestinian synagogues for 300 years.

Among the customs that have been accepted by some communities but rejected by others are *Kaparot* and *Tashlich*. *Kaparot*, which seems to have originated in Babylonia some time after 500 C.E., spread to communities in East and West. The ceremony consisted of reciting prescribed prayers on the day before Yom Kippur while waving a chicken over one's head. By means of this ceremony, it was believed, one's illness, pains, guilt, or sins would be transferred to the fowl. While many communities accepted the practice, most rabbinic authorities characterized it as barbaric. Yet, Moses Isserles, the renowned Polish commentator on the *Shulchan Aruch*, approved of it, and because of his great influence among German and Polish Jews *Kaparot* continued to be practiced on the day before Yom Kippur for many centuries. Some Jews practice it even today.

Tashlich, a ceremony through which one rids himself of sins by casting crumbs into a stream or river on the afternoon of the first day of Rosh Hashana, is another example of a custom that was initially widely practiced by Jews and later denounced by rabbinic authorities, who considered it to be of pagan origin. In recent years many congregations have reintroduced the practice.

Why did the Rabbis of the Talmud usually side with Bet Hillel (School of Hillel) rather than with Bet Shammai (School of Shammai) when the two disagreed on Jewish law?

In the first century B.C.E., Babylonian-born Hillel (later known as Hillel the Elder) migrated to Palestine to study, and he eventually became the most influential force in Jewish life. Hillel and his descendants established academies of learning and were the leaders of Palestinian Jewry for several centuries. The Hillel dynasty ended with the death of Hillel II in 365 C.E.

Hillel the Elder's friendly adversary was Palestinian-born Shammai, about whom little is known except that he was a builder. Both lived during the reign of King Herod (37-4

B.C.E.), an oppressive period in Jewish history because of the Roman occupation of Palestine.

Shammai was concerned that if Jews had too much contact with the heathen Romans, the Jewish community would be weakened. This attitude was reflected in his rather strict interpretation of Jewish law. Hillel did not share Shammai's fear and therefore was more liberal in his approach to the law.

Hillel was the more popular of the two scholars, and he was chosen by the Sanhedrin, the supreme Jewish court, to serve as its president. Hillel was respected for his learning and his compassion. He is credited with having enunciated the popular saying, "Do not do unto others what you would not want others to do unto you,"[21] an extension of the Golden Rule (Leviticus 19:18), "Love thy neighbor as thyself."

While Hillel and Shammai themselves did not differ on a great many basic issues of Jewish law, their disciples were often in conflict. The Rabbis of the Talmud generally sided with the rulings of the School of Hillel. Although the Sages believed that the views of both schools were valid and inspired (". . . these and these are the words of the living God" is the way the Talmud[22] expresses it), nevertheless they favored the more liberal School of Hillel. Like their founder, Hillel the Elder, these scholars believed that a lenient approach to the law would in no way lessen or weaken its observance.

Hillel's liberal attitude, which was based on a deep concern for the welfare of the individual, can be seen in his approach to three important issues facing the Jewish community of the first century. Probably the most famous of these was the decision of Hillel to institute the *prosbul* (also spelled *prozbul*). By introducing this legal fiction, the biblical law of Deuteronomy 15 was reinterpreted, making it possible for the poor landowner to obtain a loan prior to a sabbatical year. (See the next question.)

With regard to the remarriage of an *aguna*, whose husband is not known with certainty to be alive or dead, the view of Hillel (and most of his colleagues) was that she can remarry even on the basis of indirect evidence of the husband's death. Bet Shammai, on the other hand, required that witnesses come forth with direct testimony.

Hillel's regard for the sensitivity of the individual can be seen in his attitude toward potential converts. He favored the admission of proselytes even when they made unreasonable demands. One heathen, a prospective proselyte, demanded that he be taught the whole Tora quickly ("while standing on one foot"); Shammai rejected him, but Hillel responded kindly. Another heathen approached Hillel and Shammai, offering to become a proselyte if he could become the High Priest. Shammai dismissed him promptly, while Hillel responded kindly.[23]

Why was the biblical law of the sabbatical year modified?

Although Jewish tradition asserts that the laws of the Tora and Talmud are eternal and immutable, economic and social conditions forced the Sages to make changes, sometimes radical ones, in the law.

One such radical change was made in connection with the sabbatical year (in Hebrew, *shemita*). The Bible (Deuteronomy 15:1-3) demands that every seventh year all debts be cancelled. This law was especially hard on poor people who would not be able to obtain loans when the *shemita* year was approaching. Lenders would certainly not want to lend money if they were not to be repaid.

This law of the sabbatical year was so oppressive that Hillel, the leading scholar of the first century B.C.E., issued a ruling that became known by its Greek name, *prosbul*. A *prosbul* was a declaration made in court at the time of the execution of a loan. Its terms made it clear that the law of *shemita*, which ordinarily cancelled loans, would not apply to the specific loan being transacted.[24]

The Rabbis justified this change in biblical law by explaining that it was done *mipnay tikun ha-olam*, "to improve the human condition." The *prosbul* protected the rich against monetary loss and helped the poor by enabling them to secure loans.

Why was the jubilee year not observed after the destruction of the First Temple?

Leviticus 25 mandates that every fifty years a jubilee year is to be celebrated. During the course of that year all properties are to be returned to their original owners, all Hebrew slaves are to be granted freedom, and all land is to lie fallow. The tenth verse of the chapter, which is inscribed on the Liberty Bell in Philadelphia, is well known: "And ye shall hallow the fiftieth year, and proclaim liberty throughout the land unto all the inhabitants thereof . . ."

The jubilee year was observed during the period of the First Temple, but there is no record of its having been observed in Second Temple times. The Rabbis of the Talmud[25] explained that the biblical law requiring celebration of the jubilee year was no longer enforced after the destruction of the First Temple because Leviticus 25:10 makes specific reference to *"all* the inhabitants" of the Land of Israel. Since some of the Tribes of Israel had been exiled when the First Temple was destroyed, and since not all the Jews lived in Palestine, the jubilee year could no longer be carried out as prescribed by Scripture.

Why are some practices banned or discouraged in Jewish law simply because they may give the wrong impression?

In Jewish law, the concept known as *marit a'yin,* meaning literally "how things appear to the eye," is invoked to avoid situations where a stranger might be led to misconstrue what he observes. For example, margarine, a purely vegetable product, may be served with meat meals, but since its appearance on the table during a meat meal might give someone the idea that butter is being served, those who are extremely meticulous about Jewish observance will avoid serving margarine at a meal where meat is also served. The same would apply to serving a nondairy creamer with coffee at a meat meal. Joseph Caro, compiler of the *Shulchan Aruch* (sixteenth century), did not know about margarine or nondairy creamers, but he was familiar with the use of almond milk (a liquid made from almonds), and he declared that it should not be served with a meat meal on account of *marit a'yin,* "for appearance's sake."[26]

The eminent scholar Rabbi Jacob Emden (1697-1776), in one of his responsa, objects to a woman wearing a wig because, he said, it might appear that it is her actual hair, which ought not be exposed.

As another example, Jewish law states that work may be done for a Jew by a Gentile on the Sabbath if it is not done at the express order of the Jew. Thus, a Jew may make a contract with a Gentile to build him a house. They enter into a type of contract called *kablanut,* which establishes no time limit for completion of the work. The Gentile labors at his own pace and on whatever days he chooses. Such an arrangement is acceptable in Jewish law for the building of a home but not for the building of a synagogue. Why? Because of *marit a'yin,* for appearance's sake. People seeing work being done on the synagogue on the Sabbath might conclude that the leaders of the congregation ordered that the work be performed on the Sabbath, which would be a violation of Jewish law. However, when one observes a house under construction, he does not know whether the house is being built for a Jew or for a non-Jew.

Why do some Jews refrain from using actual numbers when counting to see if enough people are present for a *minyan*?

The tradition of not using actual numbers when counting to see if a sufficient number of people are present for a *minyan* (quorum of ten adults) goes back to the census taken in biblical times. In several places in the Bible, including Numbers 1 and 26, the counting of the Children of Israel was undertaken at the command of God. But in II Samuel 24 David ordered an unauthorized census, and as a result, by way of punishment, a severe plague befell the Israelites and seventy thousand perished.

No explanation is offered in the Bible. However, based on this episode Jewish tradition placed a taboo on using numbers to count people, claiming that this is a privilege that belongs to God alone, and to do so without divine sanction can only result in catastrophe. Therefore, when counting to see if a *minyan* is present, a tradition developed to use a verse from the Book of Psalms (28:9) which in its Hebrew form contains ten words. The verse begins with the words *Hoshia et amecha,* "Save Thy people and bless Thine inheritance, and tend and elevate them forever."

Some follow a different custom: instead of using the verse from Psalms when counting those assembled for a *minyan,* they say in Yiddish, *nisht ayntz, nisht tzvay,* and so on, meaning "not one, not two. . . ." This is a way of pretending that one is not counting.

Why do some Jewish authorities insist that a *minyan* be present at a wedding ceremony?

The Bible (Ruth 4:2) tells us that when Boaz was ready to marry Ruth, he called together ten of the elders of the city. Using this as a basis, the Talmud ruled that a quorum of ten men (a *minyan*) must be present when the *Sheva Berachot* (Seven Benedictions, also referred to in Hebrew as *Birkat Chatanim*) are pronounced at the wedding ceremony.[27] Although the majority of later authorities have agreed that it is preferable that a marriage be performed in the presence of a *minyan,* a ceremony performed without one has not been deemed invalid.[28]

The idea behind the talmudic law is that the *minyan* represents a congregation, and when a wedding takes place in the presence of a congregation, the occasion becomes more solemn. The presence of a *minyan* has additional significance in that it converts a private affair into a public one. This was important in the Middle Ages, when Jews were constantly being expelled from one country or another and marriage records could not be kept. If it became generally known that a marriage took place, there was less chance of misrepresentation (such as a man remarrying without first obtaining a proper divorce from his spouse).

Many contemporary rabbinic scholars in the United States are of the opinion that since a state license must be obtained before a marriage can be solemnized, the chances of misrepresentation have been greatly reduced and there is no longer sufficient reason to insist that a *minyan* be present at the wedding ceremony. However, all agree that wherever possible a *minyan* should be present.

Since today it is often difficult to assemble a *minyan* for small private weddings, most rabbis are willing to perform wedding ceremonies in the absence of a quorum.

Why are the sermons and speeches that are delivered in the synagogue on the Sabbath not applauded?

The Talmud lists several types of activity that are forbidden on the Sabbath (and holidays) because they are not in keeping with the spirit of Sabbath rest *(mishum shevut)*. These are climbing a tree, riding an animal, swimming, applauding, clapping one's hand to one's side, and dancing.[29]

Ovadya of Bertinoro, the fifteenth-century Italian commentator on the Mishna, explains that clapping and dancing are prohibited because these activities involve music. Musical instruments were used to accompany dancing, and people clapped hands and kept beat by slapping their sides. Since a musical instrument might break while the activity was in progress, and one might be tempted to fix it (which would be a serious violation of Sabbath law), dancing and clapping hands were prohibited as a precautionary measure. From this it became customary not to applaud in the synagogue at the conclusion of sermons and speeches on the Sabbath, and this has become a tradition followed by all branches of Judaism. Applauding in the synagogue on the Sabbath has also been discouraged because it is considered unnecessary noise and disturbing of the Sabbath peace.[30]

Why are weddings not celebrated on the intermediate days of Passover and Sukkot?

The intermediate days of Passover and Sukkot, known as Chol Homoed, are semiholidays in which all but extremely Orthodox Jews carry on normal business affairs. Nevertheless, much of the holiday spirit remains in force. As on the full holidays, the Tora is read on each intermediate day, and the *Hallel* (Psalms of Praise) is recited at each service. These secular *(chol)* days of the holiday are considered joyous ones.

With regard to the celebration of weddings on Chol Hamoed, the Rabbis said, *Ayn me'arvin simcha b'simcha,* "It is not proper to intermingle two joys." If two joys are celebrated at one time, the importance of each is diminished. A wedding deserves full celebration, as do the intermediate days of the holiday. Therefore, weddings are never held during the secular days of Passover or Sukkot.

Why is the blessing over the *lulav* and *etrog* considered invalid if it is recited while holding the *etrog* with the *pittom* facing up?

In Jewish law, a blessing must be recited prior to the performance of a religious act. This legal concept is known by the Hebrew term *ovayr laasiyato* (plural; *ovayr laasiyatan*). For example, when one dons a *talit,* he must not put it on until after the blessing has been recited. Should he put on the *talit* before reciting the blessing, the blessing is considered invalid and hence "wasted" (a *beracha levatala*).[31]

The same is true with regard to the blessing recited

when taking up the *etrog* and *lulav*. The *etrog* must not be held in its natural position (the way it grows on the tree) until after the blessing has been recited. Oddly enough, throughout the centuries it was assumed that an *etrog* grows naturally with its protuberance *(pittom)* facing up. This misconception dates back to the German authority Jacob ben Moses Mollin (1360-1427), who in his famous book on customs, *Minhagay Maharil,* describes the procedure of holding the *etrog* with the stem *(ikutz)* up as the blessing is recited and then turning the *etrog* over (so the *pittom* will face up) following the blessing. This practice, codified as law in the *Shulchan Aruch,* is followed to this day.[32] The Maharil and Joseph Caro, author of the *Shulchan Aruch,* erroneously believed that the natural manner of growth of the *etrog* is with *pittom* up.

Although some modern authorities, such as Rabbi Yechiel Epstein (1835-1905)[33] and Rabbi Israel ben Meir Hakohayn (1838-1933),[34] seem to be aware of the fact that an *etrog* grows naturally with the *pittom* facing down, they nevertheless do not recommend that a 500-year-old practice be changed. This is in keeping with the age-old stricture of the Talmud: *Al teshanu minhag avotaychem,* "Do not alter the customs of your ancestors."[35]

Why did the Rabbis of the Talmud find it necessary to prohibit activities on the Sabbath that are not banned in the Tora?

In order to make of the Sabbath a day of complete rest and peace, the Rabbis of the Talmud enacted a law forbidding Jews from engaging in certain activities that even the Tora does not forbid. This ruling, known in Hebrew as *shevut* (derived from the word *shabbat,* meaning "rest"), was introduced in the Talmud with these words: "The following acts are culpable as a *shevut:* one may not climb a tree, nor ride a beast, nor swim, nor clap one's hands, nor slap [the thighs], nor dance."[36] In every case the act is banned not because its enactment would be a violation of the law, but because it might *lead* to a violation of the law.

The Talmud goes on to explain that if one climbs a tree, he might pluck a fruit, and that would be a violation of Sabbath law. If one rides on an animal, he might cut off a branch (to use as a whip), and this would be a violation of the law. The same reasoning applies to other forbidden activities.

Strict constructionists of Jewish law forbid swimming on the Sabbath on the grounds that one might splash some water from the river, lake, or pool. The water overflow might create a furrow or depression in the ground, and this would be a violation of Sabbath law. However, if the swimming is done in a pool which has an overhang that would prevent water from spilling over, swimming is permitted.[37]

Swimming is also banned by some authorities because it might lead to other Sabbath violations. One such violation might be the result of a person sitting in a wet bathing suit and thereby squeezing water from it, an action in breach of Sabbath law. Another violation might arise if waterwings used by a beginner are punctured and one repairs them, which would also be a breach of Sabbath law.[38]

The Orthodox ban on playing baseball, basketball, and similar sports on the Sabbath falls into the same category. It is argued that one might be tempted to carry the ball out of one's private property into the public domain, and such carrying from one domain into the other is a Sabbath violation. Even when played in the private domain (which is permissible), the ball might hit soft earth and create a depression or a hole, which would constitute a violation. For these reasons, Joseph Caro (1488-1575), author of the *Shulchan Aruch,* declares it forbidden to play ball on the Sabbath and holidays.[39]

All of these activities are forbidden on the Sabbath because of *shevut*. In recent years, Orthodox authorities have added the switching on and off of electric lights, appliances, radios, and television sets to the list of activities that fall into this category. The non-Orthodox communities, with some exceptions, do not consider ball playing, carrying objects in public, and similar activities to be in violation of Sabbath law.

Why does the Conservative rabbinate permit travel in a car on the Sabbath and holidays in order to attend synagogue services?

By a majority vote of its Committee on Law and Standards, the Conservative rabbinate granted its constituents permission to "travel" to the synagogue on the Sabbath and holidays in order to attend services, but not for any other purpose.[40] By "travel" the Committee means riding in a vehicle, not driving one. The ruling is based on the fact that travel on the Sabbath does not violate any direct biblical or rabbinic law and that it is better to join fellow Jews in worship than to engage in prayer alone.

Those who oppose the ruling argue that traveling on the Sabbath and holidays violates the spirit of holiness associated with these days, and that granting permission to travel in a car may lead to violations of Jewish law. If one is permitted to travel to the synagogue on these days, they fear, he may grow accustomed to the idea of traveling and eventually will travel for other purposes, including shopping and doing business. Some also argue that riding in a car may lead to *driving* a car, and when one drives he must turn the ignition key to start the motor, which involves starting a fire (combustion), and making a fire is a violation of biblical law.

Why is travel on a ship on the Sabbath permitted by the Rabbis of the Talmud?

From very early talmudic times, the Rabbis recognized that if Jews were to be able to maintain contact with the outside world, it would be necessary for them to travel on the Sabbath. Because of the distances between the great cities and the length of time required to cross large bodies of water, it would have been impossible for Jews to carry on normal business dealings or to engage in social or charitable activities if they had not been able to travel on the Sabbath.

The Talmud stipulates that one may not set out on a journey by ship unless he boards the ship at least three days before the Sabbath begins.[41] This applies only to trips made for business or social purposes. If the purpose of the trip is charitable—to raise funds for a Tora institution, to collect funds for orphans and widows, to ransom one being held captive, or to carry out similar mitzvot (religious precepts)—the Rabbis permit one to board the ship immediately before the onset of Sabbath (Erev Shabbat).

The Rabbis granted permission to travel on the Sabbath in the above circumstances if the owner of the ship is a Gentile, if the trip is not made specifically for the sake of the Jews on board, and if on the Sabbath there is no work performed by sailors on the ship specifically for the Jews on board. To do so would be a violation of Sabbath law.

The above laws are codified in the Shulchan Aruch,[42] and questions about them are addressed. Why may one board a ship immediately prior to the Sabbath instead of three days prior to the Sabbath if the purpose of the trip is to perform a good deed (mitzva)? The Be'er Hetev commentary responds to these questions by citing the rabbinic principle that when one is engaged in performing a mitzva (in this case helping persons in need), he is exempt from performing another mitzva (in this case, observing the Sabbath fully).

The Mishna Berura explains why one must board a ship three days prior to the Sabbath if he is traveling for social or business reasons. Ship travel is very rocky and one becomes seasick. Also, the odor from the salty waters often induces sickness. After three days on board one becomes more accustomed to conditions, and by the fourth day (which would be the Sabbath) he feels normal and is able to fulfill the commandment of enjoying the Sabbath (Oneg Shabbat).[43]

Why do some observant Jews refrain from riding in a car on the Sabbath and holidays while consenting to ride in an elevator on those days?

The Orthodox rabbinate and a minority of the Conservative rabbinate do not permit riding in a vehicle on the Sabbath or holidays even for the sole purpose of attending religious services. Although the use of electricity is involved, they do permit riding in an elevator *if* the elevator has been preprogrammed to stop and start automatically at specific floors. They also permit the use of an elevator operated by a non-Jewish elevator operator who does not have to be instructed where or when to stop or start the conveyance.

Despite the fact that the activity in both cases is the same, this leniency was allowed by traditionalists to meet a problem faced by those who live in high-rise buildings and hotels. A number of traditional synagogues with sanctuaries on upper floors have installed preprogrammed elevators, or they have a non-Jew on hand to operate the elevators. As long as the rider is not required to press the button that summons the elevator and does not have to press any button inside the elevator, use of an elevator on the Sabbath is permitted.

Why do many observant Jews turn off the electric light in a refrigerator before the Sabbath?

Observant Jews refrain from using electricity on the Sabbath and therefore loosen the refrigerator bulb so it will not go on when they open the door. Orthodox Jews and some Conservative Jews consider electricity to be a form of fire since it is used for heating, cooking, and warmth in much the same way as fire is used. Those who are particularly careful in their observance will not open the door of the refrigerator until they hear the motor go off. By waiting until that point they are assured the motor will stay off for a while and will not be activated when they open the door.

Why is it sometimes permissible to carry money on the Sabbath?

The carrying of money on the Sabbath is strictly forbidden by all rabbinic authorities. The prohibition is based on the rabbinic law known as *muktsa,* meaning "set apart." Certain articles are to be set aside and are not to be handled or touched on the Sabbath. This applies to all objects used as part of the daily workaday routine. Articles such as hammers and pencils are not to be used or even touched on the Sabbath.

The law of *muktsa* applies also to any object that is even indirectly associated with work or business, so that a purse or wallet may not be touched even if it contains no money. The introduction of these rabbinic enactments (called *gezerot* in Hebrew) was precautionary. The Rabbis felt that if a person were to be permitted to touch *muktsa* items on the Sabbath, he might inadvertently forget and actually use them.

Later authorities proved themselves flexible in interpreting the rabbinic law of *muktsa.* Moses Isserles (1525-1572), the Ashkenazic authority whose Notes are part of the *Code of Jewish Law,* remarks that a person may carry money on the Sabbath if he finds himself in a situation where he must spend the Sabbath at an inn and is afraid that the money might be stolen if he leaves it unattended in his room.[44] Contemporary authorities in their responsa have applied this law to the problem of muggings. The elderly, being prime targets, have been permitted by rabbinic authorities to carry money on the Sabbath since it was established that muggers often become violent when they discover that their victims are not carrying money.

Why do some Reform Jews observe dietary laws, wear a headcovering at times, and observe other laws and customs once discarded by Reform Judaism?

A 1979 responsum addressed the question What shall be the attitude of Reform Judaism toward practices once discarded? The Committee on Responsa of the Central Conference of American Rabbis expressed the opinion that since the *Code of Jewish Law* and its commentaries have "adopted, omitted, and sometimes readopted" many laws, customs, and ceremonies, there is nothing to prevent Reform Jews from doing likewise. If a new generation finds old, discarded practices meaningful and useful once again, there is no reason why they should not be reintroduced. This applies both to private practices and to synagogue practices.[45] Thus, today, many Reform Jews wear a headcovering *(kipa)* in the synagogue, wear a *talit*, put on *tefilin*, and observe the dietary laws *(kashrut)*—all to varying degrees.

Reconstructionism shares this approach to Jewish law and custom.

Why are most traditionalists not opposed to Sabbath violators participating in Jewish religious life?

Despite the fact that the Talmud categorizes anyone who violates the Sabbath in public (the Aramaic word used is *befarhesya*) as an apostate,[46] and despite the fact that the *Shulchan Aruch* labels the violator an idolator,[47] in practice virtually no authorities have banned such Jews from participation in Jewish religious and social life. While Orthodox authorities will not allow a non-Orthodox Jew (especially one reputed to be a Sabbath violator) to sign as a witness on a *ketuba*, they will count a non-Orthodox Jew as part of a *minyan*.[48]

Rabbinic authorities have made a distinction between Jews who violate the Sabbath publicly to display their spite and aversion to Jewish law and those who violate the Sabbath for personal gain or satisfaction. The former are vigorously condemned. The latter are tolerated because their actions are without malice.

The outstanding Hungarian rabbinic authority Eliezer Deutsch (1850-1916), author of many volumes of legal discussions and responsa, was once asked whether a Sabbath violator is to be permitted to participate in the consecration ceremony (*Siyum Hasefer* in Hebrew) for a newly written

Tora. The custom is for the scribe, after he has handwritten the entire Tora, to leave the letters of the last verses of the Tora in outline form—that is, not filled in with ink. Then, at the Tora dedication ceremony, persons donate money to the synagogue for the honor of filling in one or more letters. Sometimes a donor buys several Hebrew letters to honor someone. For example, if his mother's name is Rachel, he will buy three letters. The scribe finds a *resh, chet,* and *lamed* and guides the donor's hand as he fills in the open-faced letters that spell Rachel in Hebrew. The question addressed to Rabbi Deutsch involved Sabbath violators who had purchased letters and filled them in. May such a Tora be read in the synagogue? Aren't these Sabbath violators apostates, and isn't it the law that a Tora written by an apostate is invalid?[49]

Rabbi Deutsch replied that a Tora in which a Sabbath violator has filled in a letter is not necessarily invalid. He declared that there are two types of Sabbath violators. Some violate the Sabbath purposely, maliciously, spitefully. They want to upset and anger observant Jews (the Hebrew word is *lehachis*). Such people, Rabbi Deutsch says, must be classified as idolators and as apostates, and any Tora that they have helped to write is invalid. However, the vast majority of Jews who violate the Sabbath do not do so out of spite. They do so out of a desire for personal gain (called *l'tay'avon* in Hebrew). Jews of this second category are not to be classified as apostates, and a Tora which they have helped consecrate is perfectly valid.

Why do Reform congregations light candles after dark at their late Friday evening services?

While recognizing that biblical law (Exodus 35:3) forbids the making of a fire on the Sabbath, the Reform rabbinate favors the lighting of Sabbath candles at their congregational late Friday evening services, reasoning that the spiritual benefits of the ceremony by far outweigh the violation of the biblical law concerning the making of fire on the Sabbath.[50]

Why is it permissible to use electric candles in place of wax candles on the Sabbath and holidays?

In many households, especially those of senior citizens, electric candles are used for safety reasons. This has been permitted by rabbinic authorities because the prayer for Sabbath candlelighting does not specifically indicate that there must be a flame on the candle. The prayer reads, "Blessed art Thou, O Lord our God, King of the universe, who have commanded us to kindle the Sabbath lights [ner shel Shabbat]." The word ner, mentioned in the blessing, means "light" or "candle," not "fire" or "flame." In the Havdala ceremony, where a candle with an actual flame is required, the Hebrew word aysh ("fire") is used in the blessing.

Why do many observant Jews feel justified in using electricity on the Sabbath?

All Orthodox and Conservative Jews consider inviolable the biblical ban on kindling a fire on the Sabbath (Exodus 35:3). There is a difference of opinion, however, among Conservative Jews as to whether electricity may be used on the Sabbath. The traditional position is that electricity is fire because, like fire, electricity is used to heat, illuminate, and cook. Accordingly, its use on the Sabbath is forbidden.

While a minority of the Committee on Law and Standards of the Rabbinical Assembly (Conservative) agrees with the traditional position, the majority believes that electricity is not fire and that its use is therefore not a violation of Sabbath law. The Reconstructionist movement shares this view. It permits the turning on and putting off of electric lights, radios, television sets, and the like because use of these modern inventions enhances the joy of the Sabbath and reduces personal discomfort. Permission to turn on electric stoves or appliances to warm food is not included in this decision, because the use of such heating devices can result in cooking.

Almost all observant Jews agree that it is permissible to program a timer in advance of the Sabbath to turn lights on and off during the Sabbath. Some also program their radios and television sets.

Recognizing the need to perform certain essentials on the Sabbath, such as milking cows, turning on sprinklers in the fields, and so on, Orthodox *kibbutzim* in Israel use a preprogrammed system of timing devices that turn machines on and off automatically, thus avoiding any unnecessary violation of the Sabbath.

Reform Jews do not feel bound by the biblical or rabbinic Sabbath prohibitions.

Why are some authorities opposed to the general use of a Sabbath clock (timer)?

While all authorities agree that a timer may be used to put lights on and off on the Sabbath, not all agree that one may be used for other purposes. Rabbi Moshe Feinstein, in his book of responsa,[51] permits the use of a timer to put electric lights on and off on the Sabbath only because it is now a widely accepted practice among Orthodox Jews. But he opposes its use for preprogramming an electric stove or food warmer to heat precooked food on the Sabbath—this despite the fact that the warming of precooked food is permissible on the Sabbath. Feinstein is apprehensive that use of the timer in connection with the warming of food might ultimately lead to use of the timer to set some sort of work process into motion on the Sabbath.

Why are some religious articles treated with greater respect than others?

Not all religious articles are equal in sanctity. Articles such as a Tora, a *mezuza,* and *tefilin* are intrinsically holy. In Hebrew they are called *tashmishay kedusha,* "appurtenances of holiness," and they must always be treated with respect: they must be buried or stored away when no longer usable. Other religious articles, such as a *lulav, talit* (and *tzitzit*), *shofar, sukka,* and the special knife used by a *mohel* or *shochet,* do not have intrinsic holiness and may therefore be discarded in any mamner when no longer serviceable. Religious articles such as these, which are merely used as vehicles to fulfill a commandment *(mitzva)* but are not intrinsically holy, are called *tashmishay mitzva,* "aids in the performing of a *mitzva."*

The Talmud (Megilla 26a,b) spells out how various items of sanctity are to be disposed of or converted to other uses when no longer needed. For example, an eternal light or a *menora* can be sold in order to earn money to commission a scribe to write a Tora, but a Tora cannot be sold to buy an eternal light or a *menora,* because these articles are of lesser sanctity.

The principle of Jewish law that is generally followed was first stated in the Mishna: "One may elevate [upgrade] sacred articles [to a higher degree of sanctity], but one may not lower [downgrade] them."[52] Thus, the minor talmudic tractate Soferim,[53] after pointing out that a *mezuza* has lesser sanctity than *tefilin,* states that one may not use the parchment of tefilin to make a *mezuza,* but one may use a wornout *mezuza* parchment to make *tefilin. Tefilin* parchment is considered more important than *mezuza* parchment because *tefillin* is worn on one's body. *Tefilin* parchment is also more important because it contains four biblical passages whereas *mezuza* parchment contains only two.

Why was the concept of *eruv* introduced into Jewish law?

In the popular mind, as a result of stories carried by the news media, the *eruv* is thought to be a wire or nylon cord that is extended around the perimeter of a geographic location to permit Jews to carry objects within that area on the Sabbath. While this is true, it is only one aspect of the overall concept of *eruv.*

Eruv (plural, *eruvin*) in its literal sense means "mixture, merging, amalgamation, or blending of activities and rights." The term in its legal sense refers to an instrument which permits an activity that is normally forbidden on the Sabbath or holidays to be performed. Appropriate prayers are recited when the instrumentality of *eruv* is enacted.

The Rabbis of the Talmud considered the laws of *eruv* to be biblical in orgin, and they point to verses in Exodus (16:29) and Jeremiah (17:27) as the sources.[55] Three types of *eruv* were introduced in order to alleviate Sabbath hardships:

- the *eruv* of cooked foods *(eruv tavshilin)*, which permits one to cook on a holiday falling on a Friday for the Sabbath that follows it
- the *eruv* of boundaries (called *eruv techumim* in Hebrew), which enables one to walk more than one is normally permitted on the Sabbath
- the *eruv* of yards *(eruv chatzayrot)*, which permits one to carry objects in the public domain on the Sabbath

The three types of *eruv*—all of which are legal fictions—will be explained in the questions that follow.[56]

Why was Jewish law reinterpreted to permit cooking on a festival for the Sabbath that follows it?

The most widely used *eruv* is known as *eruv tavshilin*, meaning "mixture (or amalgamation) of cooked foods." It was established so as to permit a person to cook food on a Jewish festival that falls on a Friday for the Sabbath that follows it. Without executing an *eruv*, it is forbidden on a holiday to cook food that is not to be eaten that same day.

To implement the *eruv*, the homemaker prepares a dish of cooked food before the holiday has begun. The dish may simply be an egg or a piece of roasted chicken along with bread (or Passover *matza* is used). The food is set aside and a special *eruv* prayer is recited. By performing this *eruv* ceremony, one may cook on the holiday for the Sabbath that follows it because the cooking process was started before the holiday began.

Why was Jewish law reinterpreted in order to extend the distance one may walk on Sabbaths and holidays?

Jewish law considers it "work" if on a Sabbath or a festival one walks more than 2,000 cubits (about three-fifths of a mile) beyond the city limits or beyond the inhabited area of one's town. This restriction imposes a hardship on persons who might want to visit a neighboring town to listen to a preacher or to socialize with friends.

To overcome the hardship, a concept known as *eruv techumim,* meaning "fusion (amalgamation) of boundaries," was introduced. To effect this type of *eruv,* a person intending to walk more than 2,000 cubits on a Sabbath or festival selects a spot (perhaps a tree or some such landmark) where he places some food before the onset of the holy day. This new location, for purpose of law, becomes a new "residence" for him, entitling him to walk an additional 2,000 cubits without being in violation of Jewish law, the reasoning being that the place where one eats a meal may be considered a residence.[57]

Why was Jewish law reinterpreted to permit one to carry articles in the public domain on the Sabbath?

A third type of *eruv* is known as *eruv chatzayrot,* meaning "mixture (pooling) of yards." This type of *eruv* involves persons who live in a enclosed area consisting of a group of homes opening on a common courtyard. Since the courtyard is public property, none of the residents of the homes bordering the yard are permitted to carry objects there on the Sabbath. In order to overcome this hardship, before the Sabbath each family brings a dish of food (or some flour for the baking of a large loaf of bread) to a designated home in the compound. Since all families bordering the courtyard contribute food, all have equal rights to the food, and they have joint "ownership" of the courtyard. Thus, the yard that was once considered public property becomes "mixed" or "pooled" (that is, an *eruv* is established), and the yard is considered private property in which all residents may carry objects without being in violation of Sabbath law.

The *eruv* that is created today by extending a wire or nylon cord around the perimeter of a community (by connecting the wire to telephone or utility poles) is an extension of the *eruv chatzayrot* described above. Besides allowing observant Jews to carry objects within the perimeter of the community, it permits them to push baby carriages, an activity hitherto forbidden because in Jewish law pushing an object is the equivalent of carrying an object.

Why, on the Sabbath, may Orthodox women wheel a baby carriage in some public places but not in others?

Many small towns with substantial Orthodox populations have arranged to have *eruvin* erected so as to permit mothers to wheel perambulators in their streets on the Sabbath. This also applies to well-defined areas of large cities, such as Kew Gardens Hills, in New York City.

According to most authorities, any public area in which more than 600,000 people live or work is too large to have an *eruv*. This conclusion was reached because Exodus 12:37 mentions 600,000 as the number of "men on foot" who fled Egypt during the Exodus. And the verse that follows uses the words *ayrev rav* (*ayrev* is a form of *eruv*) to explain that "a mixed multitude" also left Egypt with them. Use of a form of the word *eruv* immediately following reference to the 600,000 was the criterion for determining the maximum population of an area that may have an *eruv*.

Why do some Jews fast on days other than those in the Jewish calendar?

Besides the fast of Yom Kippur, which is prescribed in the Bible, and the other fasts instituted in post-biblical times—Tisha B'Av, Asara B'Tevet, Shiva Asar B'Tammuz, Taanit Esther, and Tzom Gedalia being the primary ones— private fast days are observed by individuals, families, and communities to commemorate special events.

Fasting, in addition to offering prayers, was considered an effective way of reaching God so as to make Him more attentive to one's needs. It also served as an expression of atonement for wrongs committed.

Among the more common private observances are the following:

- Fasting on the anniversary of death *(Yahrzeit)* of one's parent or teacher.[58]
- Fasting by the bride and groom on their wedding day, unless it occurs on a Rosh Chodesh.[59]
- Fasting when a Tora scroll is dropped. This custom was not known in talmudic times but was widespread in the Middle Ages. The *Shulchan Aruch* says that if one drops his *tefilin* on the ground he must fast.[60] Abraham Gombiner, in his commentary Magen Avraham, infers from this that if a *Sefer Tora* is dropped one must also fast. In certain communities all who are present also fast.

In addition to these personal fasts, there are occasions on which a community as a whole will engage in fasting. Each such occasion became known as a Purim Katan (Minor Purim) because it is reminiscent of the Fast of Esther (Taanit Esther), which precedes the Purim holiday. These communal fasts include:

- The Purim of Algiers, first observed on the fourth day of Cheshvan in the year 1540 C.E. to commemorate the community's having been saved from destruction during the Spanish-Algerian Wars of 1516-1517.
- The Purim of Baghdad, established on the eleventh of Av in the year 1773 C.E., on the occasion of the community having been freed from Persian oppression.
- The Purim of Fossano (Italy), established on the eighteenth of Nissan in the year 1796 C.E., on the occasion of the city having been saved from destruction by a bomb explosion.

- The Purim of Rhodes, established in 1840 C.E., on the fourteenth of Adar, on the occasion of the community having been spared annihilation.
- The Purim of Casablanca (called Purim Hitler), established in 1943 C.E. on the second of Kislev, on the occasion of Jews having been saved from Nazi occupation.

Why does Jewish law maintain that one should not sacrifice one's life to save that of another person?

Jewish law has always operated on the principle that one's own life is more precious than anyone else's. The principle was affirmed in the Talmud, which says, "Your life is more important than your neighbor's."[61] The Talmud emphasizes its position by adding, "What makes you think his blood is more red than yours?"

The famous sixteenth-century scholar Rabbi David ben Zimra said that anyone who puts his life in jeopardy to save his friend is a *chassid shoteh*, "a pious fool." Recent authorities, such as Rabbi Eliezer Judah Waldenberg of Jerusalem, have expressed the opinion that one must draw a distinction between times of peace and times of war. In wartime, soldiers in the field operate as a unit, and each must treasure the life of his buddy as he does his own. Every effort must be made to rescue the life of one's fellow soldier, even if that involves placing one's own life in jeopardy.

Why, despite biblical law, were the Rabbis of the Talmud reluctant to carry out the death penalty?

Despite the fact that the Bible explicitly calls for the death penalty for crimes such as insulting or beating one's parents (Exodus 21:15,17), adultery by a woman (Leviticus 20:10), incest (Leviticus 20:11-18), kidnapping (Exodus 21:16), Sabbath violation (Exodus 35:3), and murder (Exodus 21:12), most Rabbis of the Talmud were not in favor of capital punishment. The Talmud calls a court that executes a criminal even once in seven years "a wicked Sanhedrin [court]."[62] Rabbi Eliezer ben Azariah said that such a court deserves that appellation if it executes a criminal even once in seventy years.

Rabbi Akiba, a first-century Palestinian scholar, and Rabbi Tarphon, a second-century Palestinian scholar, opposed capital punishment under all circumstances. Rabbi Simeon ben Gamaliel, president of the Sanhedrin in the second century, disagreed, saying that not to execute a criminal guilty of a capital offense encourages criminal activity.

Generally speaking, the gravity with which members of the Sanhedrin viewed the responsibility of imposing the death penalty upon a criminal is evidenced by the fact that individual members fasted on the day on which they sentenced a person to death.[63]

Since the Rabbis of the Talmud could not summarily disregard laws of the Tora, they searched for verses in Scripture that would justify their opposition to capital punishment. Careful study of the Bible led them to the verse in Exodus (21:15) which concludes with the words *mot yumat,* "that man shall surely be put to death." Since the word for death is repeated in the Hebrew phrase (both *mot* and *yumat* are forms of the word for death), the Rabbis concluded that this was intended to teach that the death penalty is to be imposed only by God, not by man. For, when the Bible wishes to indicate death at the hands of a human tribunal (as in Exodus 35:3), the word *mot* is used alone.

Why is it forbidden to call parents by their first names?

In Jewish tradition, calling one's parent, specifically one's father, by his first name is a violation of the law. It is considered a sign of disrespect, says the *Code of Jewish Law,* adding that it is also a sign of disrespect to occupy one's father's seat and to contradict him publicly.[64]

Why are Jews today permitted to lend money to fellow Jews at interest even though the practice is forbidden in the Bible?

There are three references in the Bible to the lending of money and the taking of interest. Exodus (22:24) and Leviticus (25:36) state that if a Jew lends money to a fellow Jew (or Hebrew, as a Jew was then called), he must not take interest. Deuteronomy (23:20-21) forbids the taking of interest from a fellow Jew but permits taking it from others.

Scholars such as Maimonides insist that taking interest from a Gentile is a positive commandment of the Tora. Maimonides believed that the practice would minimize intermarriage. The reasoning is that if a Jew lends money to a Gentile at no interest, he encourages social contact. Gentiles would eagerly befriend Jews so that they might obtain interest-free loans. As a consequence of the close friendships that would develop, Jews might be influenced to adopt Gentile practices, which would in turn weaken Judaism.

How did it happen that Jews ignored the biblical commandments and began to take interest from fellow Jews as well as Gentiles? In the post-talmudic period (after 500 C.E.), the Church became a powerful political force in Europe. Monarchs were guided by the will of the Church, and Church and State joined hands in denying Jews the right to own land. Forbidden to own land, for their livelihood Jews turned to commerce and industry and particularly to banking. They were practically forced into banking by the Church when, in 1179, based on Luke 6:35 ("But love your enemies, and do good, and lend, expecting nothing in return . . ."), Pope Alexander III issued a ban prohibiting all Christians from lending money at interest.

The Church, which controlled government policy in most countries, did not apply the ban to Jews, for Jews were not "believers." In time, as Jews became more immersed in commerce, they traveled from marketplace to marketplace, from country to country, buying and selling merchandise. Since they had to pay cash when buying,

Jews were forced to borrow money. But since Christians were unwilling to lend money (because they could take no interest), Jews were forced to turn to fellow Jews. Rabbinic authorities realized that it would become impossible for Jews to make a living if they could not borrow money, so they allowed Jews to charge fellow Jews interest. Although this is, in effect, a violation of biblical law, it was deemed justified on the grounds that the livelihood of Jews was at stake.

Why is the smoking of tobacco not prohibited in Jewish law?

The smoking of tobacco is not mentioned in the Bible, in the Talmud, or in early post-talmudic literature. And when smoking was first introduced to Europe in the fifteenth century, no one so much as suspected that smoking might be harmful to health, so we find no condemnation of the practice.[65]

The modern rabbinate, aware of the hazards to health posed by smoking, has addressed the issue. Rabbi Moshe Feinstein, while acknowledging the ill effects of smoking, writes that "there is no Jewish law that forbids smoking and no law that forbids offering a smoker a match." He adds, "Many past and present Tora scholars have smoked."[66] However, the Lubavitcher Rebbe has aggressively condemned smoking, declaring it hazardous to human health and therefore a violation of Jewish law.

At its 1982 convention the Rabbinical Assembly (the association of Conservative rabbis) took up the issue of smoking for the first time. Noting the biblical injunction, "I have set before you life and death, the blessing and the curse, therefore choose life that you may live" (Deuteronomy 30:19), and also noting the proven dangers to health posed by smoking, the organization passed a resolution banning smoking "at public sessions and in dining areas at future Rabbinical Assembly conventions." The resolution was based on the talmudic view that pollution of the public domain constitutes a breach of law.[67]

Why are *chassidim* fond of smoking?

Chassidim are known to be heavy smokers. Their fondness for tobacco stems from the kabbalistic notion that a person is successful in ascending the ladder of spirituality and reaching God in proportion to his ability to release "holy sparks" *(nitzotzot)*. These "sparks," said to be present in all things, are waiting to be redeemed and released. Smoking was believed to be one of the methods of releasing "holy sparks."[68]

Why are *shaatnez*-free garments manufactured?

Although scholars are not certain of the origin of the word *shaatnez* (some believe it is from the Greek), in the Hebrew Bible the term refers to a mixture of diverse species.

In Leviticus (19:19) we find the first reference to *shaatnez:*

> You shall not permit your cattle to mate with a different species of animal; you shall not sow your field with two varieties of seeds; and you shall not wear garments made of a mixture of two kinds of material [fibers].

The Book of Deuteronomy (22:11) specifies what mixture of fibers is prohibited: "You shall not wear a garment containing wool and linen." Because of this specification, the Rabbis of the Talmud ruled that the law of *shaatnez* refers only to garments made of an admixture of these two specific animal and vegetable fibers. However, wool or linen may be mixed with cotton, silk, and other fibers in the manufacture of products other than clothing.[69]

A few small clothing manufacturers who cater to an ultra-Orthodox clientele are careful to produce garments that do not contain the forbidden mixture of fibers. There is also a segment of the Orthodox community that buys off-the-rack garments in general clothing stores and then replaces all threads that are not of the same species as the material itself.

Why does the Bible include the law prohibiting the use of garments made of mixed fibers (shaatnez)?

Certain biblical laws cannot be explained logically, and the law of mixing species (shaatnez) is one of them. (See the previous question.)

Rashi, the great eleventh-century French commentator on the Bible, says in his comment on Leviticus 19:19 that the law pertaining to the mixing of breeds defies logic and must be obeyed without question, just as one obeys a king's command. On the other hand, Maimonides (twelfth century), Nachmanides (thirteenth century), and other scholars have offered explanations.

Maimonides says that the wearing of mixed garments is forbidden because heathen priests wore garments containing vegetable and animal materials.[70] This has been described as a strange explanation since Jewish Priests (Kohanim) wore garments made of wool and linen.[71] According to Josephus, the use of garments of mixed fibers was reserved for Priests and forbidden to others.[72]

Nachmanides, in his commentary on Leviticus 19:19, suggests that all species were made by God at the time of Creation and that any attempt to create a new species by mixing breeds is a defiance of God's will and is therefore forbidden.

CHAPTER 9

The Jewish Woman

INTRODUCTION

Society in biblical times was patriarchal. In that world the Jewish woman occupied a position subordinate to that of the Jewish male. The function of woman, it was thought, was to serve man. When a woman married, she became the property of her husband. In fact, the original word for marriage was *kinyan,* meaning "acquisition," while the word used today is *kiddushin,* meaning "sanctification." Jacob may have loved Rachel when he married her, but he had to buy her from his father-in-law, Laban, by working for him for seven years (Genesis 29:18). A family in biblical times was called *bet avot,* a term literally meaning "house of the fathers" (Exodus 12:3). The Bible states clearly (Genesis 2:18) that woman was created to be a helpmate to her husband.

During the days of the First and Second Temples (the first millenium B.C.E.), women did not participate in Temple rituals. Unlike men, they did not sing in the Temple choir, nor were they permitted to enter the inner court of the Temple when they brought a sacrifice. A woman had to hand the animal offering to the Priest at the entrance of the Tent of Meeting (*Ohel Moed* in Hebrew); the Priest would take the animal and offer it up for her.

The status of Jewish women improved in post-biblical and talmudic times, especially as compared with the lot of women in society at large. Nevertheless, the Jewish woman was far from equal with the Jewish man. The first-century C.E. Jewish historian Josephus, in *Against Apion* (2:24), notes, "Woman, says the Law, is in all things inferior to man. Let her accordingly be submissive, not for humiliation, but that she may be directed; for authority has been given by God to man." Throughout the Talmud we find this same attitude expressed.

Despite the deprecatory statements that are found, it must be emphasized that although considered inferior, women were nevertheless respected and were not abused. This is reflected in statements such as, "Israel was redeemed from Egypt through the merit of its righteous women"; "Women are endowed with more intelligence than men"; "A man should love his wife as himself and respect her more than himself."[1]

The status of women in Jewish life continued virtually unchanged for centuries, through the talmudic and post-talmudic periods, until Rabbenu Gershom of Mainz, Germany, a leading rabbi of the tenth and eleventh centuries, convened a synod of prominent rabbis in the year 1000 which enacted legislation prohibiting a man from having more than one wife at one time and from divorcing a wife without her consent. (She could refuse to accept the *get*, the divorce document.) But despite this monumental change in the law, little new legislation was enacted over many centuries to improve the status of women. Even the liberal pronouncements of Reform Judaism in the middle of the nineteenth century and Conservative Judaism at the end of that century resulted in no practical change in the status of women.

In 1846, at their conference in Breslau, Germany, Reform rabbis favored the granting of religious equality to women, yet it was not until 1972 that a Reform seminary, Hebrew Union College–Jewish Institute of Religion, ordained a woman as a rabbi. By 1984 it had ordained a total of seventy-two women rabbis. The Conservative movement, which also aspired toward greater equality, did not grant women the right to be candidates for ordination at the Jewish Theological Seminary until 1984. In 1985, it ordained the first woman rabbi. Henrietta Szold, who later founded Hadassah, the women's Zionist organization, had been permitted in 1903 to attend classes at the Jewish Theological Seminary, but only on condition that she would not be ordained and that she would not use her knowledge to function as a rabbi. The Reconstructionist Rabbinical College, which was founded in Philadelphia in 1968 by disciples of Rabbi Mordecai Kaplan, stands for granting women full equality with men "in all matters of ritual." In 1974 it ordained its first woman rabbi.

Today, Jewish feminists, many of whom are Orthodox, have become vocal protagonists for change in Jewish law so that women may share with men the privileges and obligations of Jewish living. The manner in which the desired changes should be accomplished is being grappled with by all branches of Judaism. Many of the problems and issues being confronted are discussed in this chapter.

Why does the Talmud group women with slaves and minors?

Women are considered on a par with slaves and minors because, unlike men, none of the three classes is obligated to fulfill all of the 613 commandments (mitzvot). According to the Talmud, women are exempt from reciting the Shema and from putting on tefilin, but they are not exempt from reciting the Tefila (Amida) prayer, or from placing a mezuza on the doors of their homes, or from saying Grace After Meals.[2]

Another probable reason for the linking of women with slaves and minors is that the individuals within these groups are not totally independent persons. Women were tied to their husbands in marriage and in a sense were the property of their spouses; slaves owed total allegiance to their masters; and minors, of course, were under the control of their parents.[3]

Why in Jewish religious life are women traditionally not equal to men?

Genesis 1:27 speaks of both man and woman as having been created independently in the image of God, but Genesis 2:21-23 describes woman as having been fashioned from one of man's ribs, and from this it has been inferred that women are not equal to men.

Although in the Bible many women—for example, Miriam, Esther, Ruth, Deborah, and Hulda—appear as heroines, the number is negligible compared to the many heroes mentioned. This imbalance is clearly a reflection of the position occupied by women in society-at-large in biblical times. Jews were an integral part of that Near Eastern society, and it was only natural that the attitudes and practices prevalent among other nations and cultures would influence Jewish life. Males in general were regarded as more important than females, and the laws and concepts expressed in the Bible must be understood in that context. Men were the inheritors of property, and with few exceptions women were not. If a woman married outside her tribe, she became a member of her husband's tribe. Her status was always subordinate to that of her husband, and her function was to serve him.[4]

That women were considered unequal to men is clearly evident from the fact that although their testimony did not carry as much weight as that of men,[5] there were special instances when a woman could testify (as in the case of an *aguna*). We may assume that a woman's ineligibility in most cases was because her primary obligation was to the home and family, which often would render her undependable as a witness or a judge.

Why in Jewish tradition is a male baby generally preferred to a female?

The Talmud indicates quite clearly that in talmudic times when a male was born all rejoiced, but when a female was born parents and relatives were less happy. At the birth of a male child a prayer of thanksgiving was recited,[6] not only by the father but by the mother as well. Rabbi Chisda, a third-century talmudic scholar, stands alone as one who preferred daughters to sons. "Daughters are dearer to me than sons,"[7] he said. Undoubtedly he arrived at this view because his daughters married the greatest scholars of his day (Raba, Rami ben Chama, and Mar Ukba ben Chama).

Male offspring have traditionally been wished for over female offspring because it is through the male that the family name is perpetuated. Males have also been preferred to females because sons are counted as part of a *minyan* (quorum of ten adults). Women are not obligated by Jewish law to attend public services and are not counted as part of the *minyan*.

Why does a woman not have the same obligation as a man to pray?

Women are obligated to observe all the negative commandments in the Tora *(mitzvot lo taaseh)*. These are commandments that begin with the words "Thou shalt not . . ." However, women are exempt from some of the positive commandments in the Tora *(mitzvot asay)*. The Talmud ruled that women are not obligated to observe "positive commandments dependent upon time [*mitzvot asay she'hazeman gerama*]," commandments that must be observed at a specific time of day or year.[8]

The law was enacted to free women of obligations that they would be unable to meet without hardship. For example, for women to recite prayers in the morning when they are preoccupied with their homes and children would be unduly difficult. Hence, the Rabbis ruled that women, unlike men, are not *obligated* to recite all prayers, although they are free to do so if they wish.

There is no unanimity of opinion among the Rabbis of the Talmud or later scholars as to which positive, time-bound commandments women are not obligated to observe. Generally, however, the view of Maimonides is accepted. He lists (in *Sefer Hamitzvot*) the following *mitzvot* from which women are exempt: recital of the *Shema*, wearing *tefilin*, wearing *tzitzit*, counting the *Omer* (Nachmanides obligates women to count the *Omer*), living in a *sukka*, reciting the *lulav* prayer, and listening to the blasts of the *shofar*.

Why are women obligated to light Chanuka candles?

The primary obligation to light Chanuka candles rests with the master of the house.[9] However, despite the fact that the lighting ceremony must be performed at a given time, and (as discussed above) despite the fact that women are exempt from performing time-bound positive commandments, Chanuka candlelighting is an exception to the rule.[10] Women are said to be obligated to light Chanuka candles because women as well as men witnessed the miracle of Chanuka.[11]

The lighting of Chanuka candles is only one of several time-bound positive commandments from which early talmudic scholars had exempted women but which later Rabbis considered mandatory. Among them are reciting the *Kiddush* on the Sabbath (Berachot 20a), fasting on Yom Kippur,[12] eating *matza* on Passover and celebrating festivals,[13] reading the Scroll of Esther on Purim,[14] and drinking four cups of wine on Passover.[15]

Why do Orthodox prayerbooks contain a morning prayer in which man expresses thanks for "not being created a woman"?

In the Jewish prayerbook, one of the first blessings of the morning service reads, "Blessed are Thou, O Lord our God, for not making me a woman." (The prayer ends with the Hebrew words *shelo asani isha*.) Over the centuries, this prayer has been viewed by most Jews as an expression of thanks on the part of man for the good fortune of having been born male and thus for being privileged to perform so many more commandments *(mitzvot)* than a woman.

It is interesting to note that the first reference to this prayer is in the Talmud, where Rabbi Judah is quoted as saying, "A man is bound to say three blessings each day: (1) Blessed art Thou . . . for not making me a heathen; (2) Blessed are Thou . . . for not making me a woman; (3) Blessed art Thou . . . for not making me a scoundrel."[16]

Today, the Conservative and Reform movements consider this prayer offensive to women and have therefore eliminated it from the liturgy.

Why are women not required to observe the biblical commandment pertaining to the wearing of fringes *(tzitziot)* on their garments?

One would expect women, like men, to be obligated to carry out the biblical commandment of wearing fringes on one's garment, since it would not interfere with their daily routine. In fact, some Rabbis in the Talmud believed that women are indeed so obligated.[17] Rabbi Judah attached *tzitziot* to the aprons of all women in his household. However, since women in ancient times generally did not wear the type of four-cornered garment *(talit)* worn by men—the type on which fringes *(tzitziot)* could be sewn—the wearing of *tzitziot* by women never took root. In addition, most authorities consider the law of *tzitziot* to belong to the category of commandments that must be performed at a specific time of day (during daylight hours) and from which women are therefore exempt.

Through the ages women now and again have voluntarily taken upon themselves the obligation of wearing *tzitziot*. Today, in some Conservative and Reconstructionist synagogues women do occasionally wear prayer shawls *(talitot)* with fringes during services, although this is not a common practice.

In some Reform congregations *B'not Mitzva* wear a *talit,* as do women who are called to the Tora.

Why are women obligated to recite the prayer over wine *(Kiddush)* on the Sabbath?

Despite the fact that women are generally exempt from observing positive commandments that must be performed at a specific time (see earlier questions), the Talmud requires them to recite the prayer over wine *(Kiddush)* on the Sabbath.[18] The Talmud bases the reason for this exception on two different words used in reference to the Sabbath in the two versions of the Ten Commandments. Exodus 20:8 commands the Children of Israel to *"remember* the Sabbath Day,"* while Deuteronomy 5:12 commands them to *"observe* the Sabbath Day."* Based upon the words selected, the Rabbis of the Talmud established the principle that whoever has to *observe* also has to *remember,* and since women have to observe the Sabbath by abstaining from work, so must they remember the Sabbath by reciting the prayer of sanctification over wine.

In many homes, only the head of the household recites the *Kiddush,* while all present (wife included) fulfill their obligation to recite the *Kiddush* by responding with "Amen" and then tasting the wine.[19] In some households everyone present recites the *Kiddush* individually, while in others only males do. In many modern Jewish homes girls as well as boys recite the *Kiddush.* In still others everyone present recites the *Kiddush* in unison.

Why are women kept separate from men at Orthodox weddings and other social gatherings?

In the Orthodox synagogue, men and women are seated in separate sections in order not to subject men to sexual distraction or temptation. This tradition of separating the sexes is also followed at weddings and other social gatherings, even when not held in the synagogue. At some Orthodox weddings held in hotels or catering places, a divider *(mechitza)* is set up to separate the men from the women, who are seated on opposite sides of the room. In many cases, a divider is not used, however.[20]

The ultra-Orthodox, particularly *chassidim*, go much further by requiring that men and women be seated separately even at the festive meal following the wedding ceremony. A movable partition is stretched down the center of the hall and men eat and dance between courses on their side of the divider, while women do the same on their side.

Why does the Orthodox community differ over whether a woman may wear a wig?

As discussed in Chapter One, it is customary for a married Orthodox woman to wear a headcovering at all times because the sight of her hair (as well as her voice and skin) by men is sexually arousing.[21] The question arose whether a wig may be worn with no additional headcovering, such as a veil, hat, or kerchief.

Some scholars permit the wearing of a wig on the ground that the Talmud only disapproves of a woman displaying her *own* hair, and a wig is not *her* hair. However, the majority of Orthodox scholars are of the opinion that a woman may not wear a wig without covering it, because of "the appearance factor" (in Hebrew, *marit a'yin*). A man might be misled into thinking that he is looking at the woman's own hair and is thereby violating the talmudic prohibition against gazing upon the hair of a woman.[22]

Why do some Conservative congregations count women as part of a *minyan* while others do not?

In 1973, the Rabbinical Assembly Committee on Law and Standards (Conservative) voted that the decision on whether to count women as part of a *minyan* be made by the individual congregation and its rabbi. Many Conservative rabbis prefer to follow the law as enunciated in the *Shulchan Aruch*, which states that a *minyan* for a prayer service must consist of ten adult males.[23] Other Conservative rabbis favor counting women as part of a *minyan* and base their attitude on another passage in the same code, where it is stated, "All are to be counted in the *minyan* of seven [who may be called up to read the Tora on Sabbath], even a woman and a minor . . ."[24]

Although liberal rabbis acknowledge that this statement refers only to the *minyan* (quorum) required for the Sabbath Tora Reading, they emphasize that the Reading is an essential part of the synagogue service; and since women once enjoyed the honor of receiving *aliyot* and reading from the Tora, this privilege of being counted as equals with men should be restored and should even be extended to include women as equals when counting individuals as part of a *minyan* for a prayer service.

Orthodox congregations do not count women as part of a *minyan,* while Reform and Reconstructionist congregations do.

Why are women traditionally not counted along with men as part of a quorum for Grace After Meals?

At least three adult persons must be present if the preamble to the *Grace After Meals* is to be recited. For this quorum of three *(mezuman)* to satisfy Jewish law, it must be composed of all women or all men; the sexes cannot be mixed.[25] The Talmud offers as a reason for this requirement that close proximity between men and women is to be avoided because it may lead to immorality.

The law committee of the Rabbinical Assembly (Conservative) has taken a more liberal approach. It permits women to be counted along with men to form a *mezuman* (quorum). Reform Judaism does not require a *mezuman*.

Why are women traditionally not permitted to officiate at religious services?

Jewish law and tradition have always been strongly

opposed to women participating as officiants at religious services. The reason generally given is that women's participation at such events is not in keeping with the "respect [honor] due the public," referred to in Hebrew as *kevod tzibur,*[26] or *kevod haberiot,* or *torach tzibur.* The dignity of the public is jeopardized if a man listens to a woman's voice during the prayer service. The Talmud states that the voice of a woman can cause sexual arousal in men and can therefore interfere with concentration on prayer.[27]

A second reason is advanced as well. Since women are not *required* to participate in public prayer, they are not permitted to lead a congregation in prayer. The talmudic principle employed in arriving at this conclusion is that only a person who himself is *obligated* to perform a *mitzva* may perform that *mitzva* in behalf of a second party.[28]

Today, Orthodox congregations do not permit women to officiate at or participate in the synagogue service at all, while all Reform and Reconstructionist congregations allow them full participation. Conservative congregations are divided on the question and follow different practices. Most do not permit a female to serve as a cantor or Tora Reader, while others do permit a girl to do so on the occasion of her Bat Mitzva or on other special occasions.

Congregations that allow women full participation in the synagogue service note that the concept of *kevod tzibur* did not originally relate to women at all. The term was used by the Rabbis to express their concern over any undue hardship or inconvenience or some impropriety that might be imposed upon a congregation.

This is clearly evident in one striking description of the conduct of the illustrious Rabbi Akiba. Rabbi Judah reported, "This was the practice of Rabbi Akiba: When he prayed with the congregation, he used to cut it short [referring to the lengthy *Shmoneh Esray* prayer, also known as the *Tefila*] in order not to inconvenience [the term *mipnay torach tzibur* is used here] the congregation. But when he prayed privately, one might leave Akiba's room when he was standing in one corner and praying, and later, upon his return, find him in another, so energetic were the many genuflections and prostrations that Akiba indulged in."[29]

By shortening his prayer, Akiba displayed concern for the congregation, who out of respect would wait for the saintly scholar to complete his prayers. It is this kind of respect for the congregation as a whole that the Rabbis had in mind when they used the terms *kevod tzibur, kevod haberiot,* and *torach tzibur.*[30]

Why do most non-Orthodox congregations honor women with *aliyot*?

In talmudic times women who were sufficiently educated received *aliyot* and read from the Tora just as men did.[31] In that period (first centuries C.E.), those who were called to the Tora not only recited the Tora blessings but also read their own individual portions from the Tora. However, the Rabbis were concerned that if a woman were given an *aliya* while some men present in the congregation had not received one, the impression might be left that the men did not know how to read from the Tora, which would cause them and the congregation embarrassment. The Rabbis therefore invoked the "honor of the public" *(kevod tzibur)* principle and denied women the privilege of being awarded *aliyot.*

Today, non-Orthodox congregations do not consider this principle applicable. Rarely does one called to the Tora read his own portion. Rabbi Meir of Rothenburg (thirteenth century) ruled that if a congregation consists only of *Kohanim* (Priests), then women and children may be called to the Tora. And if there are no women or children present, the Tora may not be read because a *Kohayn* may not be given the third, fourth, fifth, sixth, or seventh *aliyot* on Sabbath. If one of those *aliyot* were given to a *Kohayn*, an observer might be misled into thinking that these *aliyot* were awarded to them because their Priestly lineage is in doubt.[32]

Why do some congregations award women *aliyot* but not count them as part of a *minyan*?

Congregations that award *aliyot* to women but do not

count them as part of a *minyan* argue that a woman's right to be called to the Tora has nothing to do with her being counted as part of a *minyan*. Her right to be called to the Tora is specified in the Talmud,[33] and it was only later that she was denied this privilege, as the Rabbis put it, "out of respect for the congregation."

The Talmud, however, never discusses whether a woman may be counted as part of a *minyan*. It is only in the codes that appeared many centuries later that she is denied this right.[34] The reason given is that women have important responsibilities toward home and family that exempt her from attending public prayer services. Since she is exempt from this responsibility, eligibility to be counted in the quorum *(minyan)* is denied her.

In 1973 a majority of the Rabbinical Assembly Committee on Law and Standards (Conservative) voted in favor of counting women as part of a *minyan*. However, each Conservative congregation was granted the option of following the majority or minority view. Reform Judaism has granted women full equality with men since its inception. In Orthodox congregations women are neither granted *aliyot* nor counted as part of a *minyan*.

Why do some rabbinical seminaries ordain women while others do not?

In October 1983 the faculty of the Jewish Theological Seminary of America (Conservative) voted by an overwhelming margin to admit women to the rabbinical school as candidates for ordination. Until that time, only Reform and Reconstructionist seminaries in the United States had granted women this privilege. Orthodox seminaries do not accept women as rabbinical students.

The arguments of those who oppose the ordination of women are primarily these:

1. Women may not be witnesses in Jewish law, and therefore a woman rabbi would not be able to sign as a witness on a *ketuba* (Jewish marriage contract) or on a

divorce document *(get)* or on a conversion document.

2. In the past, and occasionally today, rabbis have been called upon to act as judges. There is a principle in Jewish law that he who is not qualified to be a witness may not serve as a judge. This disqualifies women.

3. In Jewish law, women are not obligated to participate in public prayer because their obligations in the home sometimes conflict with the specific times at which prayer should be recited. Since in Jewish law one can carry out a function for others only when he himself is *obligated* to perform that function, a woman is unable to lead a group in prayer. Today many rabbis are called upon to lead their congregations in prayer. (In January 1984, the Jewish Theological Seminary made it mandatory for all women who apply for admission to its rabbinical school to take upon themselves the obligation to observe *mitzvot* such as *talit* and *tefilin*.)

4. Women officiating at a religious service may detract from the prayer mood because, says the Talmud, a woman's hair, voice, and skin arouse sexual passion in men.[35]

Proponents of the ordination of women do not consider these objections valid. They are unwilling to accept the argument that because women have not served as rabbis in the past, they should not be given the privilege of serving in that capacity today, when women are struggling to attain equal rights with men. Many believe that the time has come to actively grant those rights.

Why do some Conservative congregations often hold the Bat Mitzva ceremony on Friday night rather than on Saturday morning?

Congregations that favor calling women to the Tora generally conduct the Bat Mitzva ceremony during the Sabbath morning service. The Tora is read during the service, and the young lady being inducted into the Jewish fold receives an *aliya* and often reads from the Tora.

Congregations that do not honor a woman with an *aliya*

often hold the Bat Mitzva celebration at the Friday evening service, when the Tora is not normally read. Generally, at a Friday night Bat Mitzva service the young lady chants from the Prophetic portion scheduled to be read the next morning. Some Conservative rabbis who conduct a Friday night Bat Mitzva do not permit the *haftara* blessings to be recited, arguing that these would be wasted blessings *(berachot levatala)* since the reading of the Prophetic portion is not required by law.

In Reform congregations, where the Tora itself is read on Friday night, the Bat Mitzva reads from the Tora and from the Prophets.

Why are some Orthodox rabbis vehemently opposed to celebrating a Bat Mitzva?

Although Orthodox Jews generally do not hold a Bat Mitzva ceremony for their daughters, they do join others in their celebrations. While some may not wish to attend the synagogue service at which the Bat Mitzva takes place, they do attend the ceremonies and parties that are held outside the synagogue.

Among the ultra-Orthodox there is a wide range of attitudes on the subject. Rabbi Moshe Feinstein is opposed to anyone attending either the Bat Mitzva service (which he refers to as *hevel,* meaning "nonsense") or the party that follows.[36] Other ultra-Orthodox authorities—such as René-Samuel Sirat, the Chief Rabbi of France, a Sephardic Jew—oppose the ritual as well but with less vituperation.

The former Sephardic Chief Rabbi of Israel, Ovadya Yosef, is much more liberal in his approach. While he does not advocate calling a girl to the Tora, he does believe that inasmuch as she has reached her twelfth birthday and is obligated to assume all religious responsibilities like all other adult women, the day should be marked by a festive meal which may legitimately be called a *seudat mitzva* (religious meal of celebration).[37]

Why were girls traditionally given less Jewish education than boys?

Since women were tied to the home and, unlike men, were not obligated to perform all the positive commandments of the Tora, their need for a formal education was not pressing. For girls, the primary place of learning was the home. They learned, unsystematically, by observing and helping their mothers and by listening in on lessons taught to the boys of the family by their father or a private tutor.

Over the centuries, various authorities have urged that girls be given a thorough Jewish education. The Mishna presents one such authority, the second-century scholar Ben Azzai, who argued that a man is obligated to teach his daughter Tora.[38] But aside from the legendary Beruriah, wife of the second-century Palestinian talmudic scholar Rabbi Meir (and the daughter of the illustrious scholar Chanina ben Teradyon), few women achieved stature as learned persons or scholars. The Talmud was so enchanted by Beruriah that it exaggerated her accomplishments and astuteness by claiming that "she learned three hundred laws from three hundred teachers in one day."[39] But as a matter of fact, many of the scholars in talmudic times did not think highly of the educational level and character of women and described them as lightheaded,[40] gossipy,[41] and incapable of learning.[42]

In Jewish tradition, the role of women was to foster education, not to become educated. It was her responsibility to ensure that her sons attended classes and that her husband was cared for upon returning home from work or from studying in the academy.[43] Women who filled this role well were highly praised. For the guidance they gave the family and the support they lent their husbands they were called "righteous women." And, say the Rabbis, for the sake of righteous women the Israelites merited redemption from Egyptian bondage.[44]

Although over the centuries individual girls have on occasion received a private Jewish education, it was not until after World War I that the Orthodox establishment recognized the need for a formal education for women. In 1917, the first school for girls was organized in Cracow, Poland, with the aid of the ultra-Orthodox Agudat Israel. This was the beginning of the Beth Jacob School educational system, which now boasts of an international network of schools including teacher training institutes.

Most modern *yeshivot* provide a full Jewish education for girls as well as boys.

Why does Jewish law prohibit women from serving as witnesses and offering testimony?

The Talmud states that "an oath of testimony applies to men but not to women."[45] This refers to the biblical law (Leviticus 5:1) that requires that a man who can offer testimony but refuses must bring a sin-offering. The question is asked (Shevuot 30a), "How do we know [that women are ineligible as witnesses]?" And the answer is that because the verse in Deuteronomy (19:17) that refers to witnesses says, "And the two *men* shall stand," we know that witnesses must be men.

Moses Maimonides, in his *Mishneh Torah*, comments that when the Bible refers to witnesses, it uses the masculine form, implying that it is only men who can serve as witnesses.[46] (This is evident in Deuteronomy 17:6 as well as 19:17.) Authorities such as Joseph Caro, the sixteenth-century author of the *Code of Jewish Law*, disagree, pointing out that often when the Tora uses the masculine form, it is really referring to both sexes.

Some scholars believe that Jewish law prohibits women from serving as witnesses and offering testimony because in most cases in talmudic times women owned no property and were supported totally by their husbands. Therefore, if a woman had been allowed to testify and her testimony proved inaccurate, damages could not be collected from her, as would be done in the case of a man who gave incorrect testimony.

A second reason offered is that because women have

traditionally borne home responsibilities, they cannot always be counted on to be dependable witnesses.

It should be noted that in talmudic and later times women were called upon as witnesses in matters in which they were particularly knowledgeable, such as women's purity, and in cases where a husband was missing and only a woman was available to offer testimony.[47]

In Reform and Reconstructionist Judaism women have full equality. They are counted as part of a *minyan,* act as rabbis and cantors, and may sign as witnesses on all religious documents. Conservative Judaism has granted women many of these rights, but not the right to sign as a witness.

Why is the woman given a marriage contract by her husband?

In biblical times and for several centuries thereafter, Jewish women, like other women in society, were considered the property of their husbands. The Rabbis were concerned about the total dependency of wives on husbands and, to rectify the situation, in the year 80 B.C.E. the *ketuba* (marriage contract) was introduced by Simeon ben Shetach, a leading Pharisee and president of the Sanhedrin. With the introduction of the *ketuba,* for the first time wives were guaranteed some protection in marriage.

The *ketuba* is a written document in which the groom promises to pay his bride a stipulated amount of money should the marriage end in divorce or should the husband not live up to his marital obligations. It also guarantees that the husband's estate will pay the wife a stipulated amount should the husband die. In Jewish law, the wife does not inherit her husband's estate; she merely collects the monies stipulated in the *ketuba.* Upon divorce, she returns to her father's home.

Why did the Conservative rabbinate find it necessary to add a clause to the standard *ketuba*?

To alleviate the problem faced by the Jewish woman

who has been divorced in civil court but whose husband refuses to give her a Jewish divorce *(get)*, the Conservative movement has formulated a document which is signed by the couple in advance of the marriage ceremony. The essence of the agreement is expressed in a clause that is added to the marriage contract *(ketuba)* that is read under the canopy.

The clause stipulates that in the event that the marriage is to be dissolved, the husband and wife agree to abide by the decisions of the *Bet Din* (court) of the Rabbinical Assembly, and that the court may impose terms of compensation "for failure to respond to its summons or to carry out its decisions." The fuller agreement, which is signed by the couple at an earlier date, states that the husband authorizes the court to be his agent and to write and to deliver a *get* to his wife should the need arise.

The need for the court to intercede may arise when a husband is spiteful and refuses to issue a *get* to his wife unless he receives compensation. But the need may also arise when a husband has not returned from a trip and it is assumed that he is dead but there is no positive proof. The same situation exists when soldiers are missing in action in wartime.

In all these cases a wife is not free to remarry because her husband may be alive, and in the eyes of Jewish law she continues to be a married woman. She is called an *aguna,* a chained woman, a woman tied to her husband. In such cases, the prenuptial agreement that was signed by the couple becomes operative, and the *Bet Din* of the Rabbinical Assembly, acting as the husband's agent, issues a divorce to the wife.

The Orthodox rabbinate does not consider the new *ketuba* of the Conservative movement to be in full compliance with Jewish law.

Rabbi Yitzchak Elchanan Spektor (1817-1896) of Kovno, Lithuania (for whom the rabbinical school at Yeshiva University was later named), was anxious to relieve the burden carried by the *aguna.* One method he employed was quite unconventional: he visited drafted soldiers before they left for military duty to persuade them to write an actual *get* which would *not* be delivered to the wife but would be held in safekeeping by the *Bet Din*. The *Bet Din* was authorized by the soldier to serve the divorce on the soldier's wife only in the event that he be missing in action and presumed dead.

Why did Hillel believe a family should have at least one daughter to be complete?

How many children must one have in order to comply with the biblical commandment, "Be fruitful and multiply and populate the earth" (Genesis 1:28)? This was discussed in the Talmud by Hillel and Shammai, the two friendly first-century protagonists. Hillel and his followers believed that a married couple must have one boy and one girl in order to satisfy the commandment. The School of Shammai contended that it was necessary to have two boys.[48]

The Hillelites based their view on the verse in the Bible, "And God created man in his own image . . . male and female created He them" (Genesis 1.27). This verse, they said, emphasizes the equality of the sexes as perceived by God. The Shammaites did not accept this interpretation, reasoning instead that since Moses, the great Lawgiver, had two sons and no daughters, having two sons should be seen as the requirement for satisfying the biblical commandment.

Generally, the opinion of Hillel is followed, and rabbinic authorities are quite unanimous in considering that one has fulfilled his religious obligation if his family consists of not less than one son and one daughter.

Why did the Bible not grant daughters the same inheritance rights as sons?

When the Land of Israel was divided among the Twelve Tribes, the territory of each tribe had to be protected against encroachment by another tribe, and the Tora was careful to enact legislation to prevent this from happening. One aspect of this legislation involved the inheritance rights of daughters.[49]

To minimize the loss of land by tribes, women were not permitted to inherit property. This law was enacted because when a woman married a man of a tribe other than her own, she too became a member of that tribe, and any property inherited by the woman would belong to her new tribe. The Bible (Numbers 26:33 and 27:1-8) reports that the five daughters of Zelophehad of the tribe of Manasseh were unhappy with this law and protested to Moses that they were being treated unfairly. Their father had no sons, so why should they not inherit his property! Moses presented their case to God, and their claim was upheld. Henceforth, the Bible decreed that where there are no male heirs, daughters may inherit the property of their father.[50]

Why is the concept of family purity central to Jewish tradition?

The wife and mother of the family sets the tone for family life. How she cares for her husband and children is of great importance. Even more crucial is how she adheres to the laws of family purity (in Hebrew, *taharat hamishpacha*). Basically, this pertains to her observance of the *mikva* ritual.

A woman is required to immerse herself in a ritual bath (*mikva*) when her monthly menstrual period ends. (See Chapter Five, The Personal Dimension, for a full discussion of this matter.) How meticulously she observes this biblical law is generally considered a mark of her piety, and pious women have been labeled the backbone of the Jewish people. The Rabbis said: "Israel was redeemed from Egypt because of the merit of pious women."[51]

Most Orthodox women follow the laws of *taharat hamishpacha* to this day, as do a small number of Conservative women. Reconstructionists as well as Reform Jews find the laws incompatible with modern living.

Why are menstruant women, who are forbidden to have physical contact with their husbands, permitted to touch and kiss the Tora?

Although an impure woman may not have contact with her husband during the period of her impurity (some Orthodox Jews do not even permit the passing of a common article such as a house key from one to the other during this period), her state of impurity does not prohibit the woman from holding, touching, or kissing a Tora or a *mezuza* (which contains a parchment with writings from the Tora). Jewish law states that the words of the Tora are not subject to defilement.[52] So high is the Tora on the ladder of spirituality that nothing can affect its holiness.

Why are women permitted to perform circumcisions?

There are many Jewish rituals that women do not practice even though they are legally permitted to do so. For example, although Jewish law in theory allows a woman to act as a ritual slaughterer (shochet), this is traditionally a male occupation and women are discouraged from entering it.[53]

The same is true of circumcision. Jewish law permits a Jewish woman to act as a *mohel*,[54] although tradition does not consider it a proper female occupation because it might offend the public's sensibility. This attitude prevails despite the fact that early in the Bible (Exodus 4:25) Tzipora, the wife of Moses, circumcised her son.

Why is the mother's name, rather than the father's, used when reciting a prayer for the recovery from illness?

As a rule, a person is identified by his or her father's name, as "FIRST NAME son of FATHER'S NAME" or as "FIRST NAME daughter of FATHER'S NAME." This is how an individual is identified when called up to the Tora and how the bride and groom's names are written in the marriage contract *(ketuba)*. Only during times of illness, when a prayer for recovery is recited, is a different form of identification used. Then, the individual is referred to as "FIRST NAME son or daughter of MOTHER'S NAME."

Using the mother's name on the occasion of illness was already in vogue in talmudic times. The fourth-century talmudic scholar Abaye said, "My mother told me that all incantations [prayers for recovery] ... must contain the name of the mother."[55]

The *Zohar,* on the Bible portion Lech Lecha (Genesis 12–17), makes a similar point when it says that all appeals to supernatural beings must be made in the name of the mother.

For biblical justification of using the mother's name, the Sages pointed to the verse, "I am Thy servant, the son of Thy handmaid. Thou hast loosened my bonds [saved me]" (Psalms 116:16). The inference drawn from the word "handmaid" in this verse is that in an emergency, when one prays to be saved, the matronymic rather than the patronymic form should be used.

CHAPTER 10

Jewish Foods
and Mealtime Rituals

INTRODUCTION

The Bible, the Talmud, and later writings devote considerable attention to food and the important role it plays in life. Abba Aricha (also known as Rav), the outstanding third-century Babylonian scholar, said that the time will come when one will have to render an account for all the food he has seen but not tasted.[1] Eating in moderation was considered a wholesome and pleasurable activity. Food was meant to be enjoyed, and it occupied a central position in the celebration of the Sabbath and holidays.

The wide variety of dishes created to celebrate the special days in the calendar has been a positive element in keeping the family together and in making religion an exciting adventure. Jewish housewives seem to have taken seriously the answer to a question posed in the Talmud, "How does one prove that he delights in the Sabbath?" To which Rabbi Judah replied, "He proves it by preparing a dish of beets, a large fish, and cloves of garlic."[2] (Meat was also a Sabbath favorite, but only the rich could afford it.)

The tradition of celebrating Sabbaths, holidays, and the happy occasions in one's personal life with specially prepared foods has added spice to Judaism. It has in fact been a factor in making Jewish living more meaningful.

It is evident from study of the Talmud and other early sources that the Rabbis were aware of the health values of certain foods. Rabbi Jose the son of Bun said, "One should not live in a city that does not have a vegetable garden."[3] Two reasons have been offered in explanation of this statement. First, if there are no vegetables available in the city, a person's cost of living will be much higher because more of this diet will have to consist of meat and dairy products, which are more expensive. Second, vegetables provide nourishment for the body, and it is wise to live in a location where such food is plentiful.

In talmudic times, the weekday diet of the majority of people was vegetarian; meat was eaten only on Sabbaths, holidays, and special occasions. There was a difference of opinion among the Rabbis as to whether it is better to eat vegetables raw or cooked,[4] and the Talmud recommends some vegetables over others. Cabbage is considered a nourishing food, and beets are said to be healthful. Lentils, if eaten once in thirty days, protect one from respiratory problems.[5] Of garlic it is said, "It satisfies, it warms the body, it makes the face shine, it increases seminal fluid, and it cures tapeworm."[6] Radishes are good for one's health,[7] and onions should be avoided because of the pungent fluid they contain.[8]

Olives were extremely popular in talmudic times. White olives, it is said, cause one to forget what he has learned,[9] but olive oil is said to be good for old men. A talmudic aphorism counsels, "Bread for young men, oil for old men, and honey for children."[10]

Many talmudic references are to be found relating to the influence of foods on sexual activity.[11] The view is expressed that such foods as eggs, fish, garlic, wine, milk, cheese, and fat meat increase sexual potency. On the other hand, salt and egg barley are said to diminish it.

In the twelfth century, scholar and physician Moses Maimonides wrote a health book called *Sefer Refuot (Book of Remedies)*, and his idea of what is good and bad for one's well-being is not always in agreement with the ideas expressed in the Talmud. He recommends bread baked from flour that is neither too old nor too fine. He considers cheese and butter, white-meated fish with firm flesh, and the meat of the goat, sheep, and chicken to be healthful. Wine and dried fruits are also wholesome foods in his eyes, but fresh fruits are considered unwholesome. In *Sefer Refuot,* Maimonides does not recommend garlic or onions.

While Jewish tradition has much to say about all aspects of food, this chapter deals particularly with dietary laws and attitudes, mealtime rituals, foods especially favored in Jewish life, and Passover foods and dietary laws.

For information about specific holiday foods and holiday rituals pertaining to these foods, much of which is explained in *The Jewish Book of Why,* consult the Index.

———— ☐ ————

Why are there separate meat and dairy dishes and utensils in a kosher home?

Based on the commandment in the Bible (Exodus 23:19 and Deuteronomy 14:21), "Thou shalt not seethe [cook] a kid in its mother's milk," the Rabbis of the Talmud legislated not only that meat and milk products not be *cooked* together, but that they not be *eaten* together at one meal. They went further and ruled that the same cooking and eating *utensils* must not be used for preparing or serving meat and dairy meals. Undoubtedly, it was the absorbent nature of pottery, from which most dishes were made in early times, that led the Rabbis to prohibit using meat and dairy dishes and utensils at one meal.

Rabbinic laws of this type, which far exceed biblical requirements, were instituted in many areas to serve as a "fence around the Law [*seyag laTora*]" and thus protect biblical ordinances from being violated. In this case it is a basic dietary law that is being protected.

Why is it widely believed that glass dishes can be used for meat and milk indiscriminately?

Because glass dishes (which includes Pyrex and Corningware) are not absorbent, it is widely believed that they may be used interchangeably at meat and dairy meals. While this is technically correct,[12] the intent of the law is to keep separate sets of dishes, whether made of glass or other materials, for dairy and meat.

Jewish law makes a distinction between *a priori* actions (called *lechatchila* in Hebrew, meaning "from the outset,") and *a posteriori* actions (called *bediavad* in Hebrew, meaning "from what comes later" or "after the fact"). Certain actions are forbidden at the outset, but once they have taken place they are considered valid. This applies to the interchanging of glass dishes at meat and dairy meals.

Thus, the serving of a dairy meal on glass dishes that have previously been used for meat is not censured in Jewish law, provided that it is not done knowingly or intentionally. If, however, from the outset one plans to use only one set of dishes for both meat and dairy meals, it is considered contrary to the spirit of the law.

It should be noted that Jewish law permits drinking glasses to be used interchangeably at meat and milk meals.[13]

Why can some utensils be made kosher *(kashered)* while others cannot?

Generally speaking, if a dish, pot, or serving utensil that is designated for use with meat only is inadvertently used to cook or serve dairy products (or vice versa), it becomes nonkosher. If a cooking or serving vessel or implement is unintentionally used to cook or serve nonkosher *(terayfa)* food, it becomes nonkosher as well. In some cases, a vessel or implement that has been made nonkosher can be made kosher *(kashered)* once again. This depends on whether the foods involved were hot or cold, for how long the contact was made, whether actual cooking has taken place, and the material from which the vessel or implement is made.

Pots, pans, dishes, and utensils made of absorbent materials such as earthenware or plastic cannot be *kashered* because some of the food that makes contact with them is absorbed—as are its odors—and cannot be removed. All other cooking and eating vessels and utensils can be *kashered* by one of several processes.

The *Code of Jewish Law*[14] describes the *kashering* practice followed by many. The utensils are immersed in a pot filled to the brim with boiling water. Some people then place a red-hot stone in the water so that the heat will be retained and so that the water will overflow, thus cleansing the outside of the container as well.

Cookware that has been used for broiling, baking, frying, and the like may be *kashered* by subjecting it to an open fire until it becomes red-hot. In some instances silverware and serving utensils can be *kashered* by sticking them into the earth.

The length of time that various cookware and utensils must be subjected to a given procedure ranges from one hour to 72 hours, depending upon the circumstances and the authority consulted. Joseph Caro[15] and later authorities describe the requirements in detail in their writings. For example, recognizing that the practice of *kashering* is basically symbolic and subject to local custom, Rabbi Solomon ben Adret (1235-1310), the renowned Spanish authority, indicated in one of his responsa that in *kashering* dishes the amount of time the dishes should be boiled should be left to the individual. Later authorities were not so liberal in their interpretation, and we therefore find many variations in practice.

Why is it not required that a period of time elapse before one eats meat after having eaten dairy products?

There is a requirement that one wait a period of time after eating a meat product before eating a dairy product. Depending on the rabbinic authority, the waiting period extends from one hour to six hours. Observant Jews in

Holland wait 72 minutes, German Jews wait three hours, and the East European practice is to wait six hours. Some authorities base the waiting period on how much time is required for the breakdown of the fatty meat residue that clings to the palate and the particles of meat that are trapped between the teeth. Other authorities base the waiting period on how long it takes for the food to be digested.

Because dairy products generally do not leave the same residue in one's mouth as meat products do, and because they require less time to be digested, a waiting period between eating dairy and eating meat was not considered necessary. However, when the dairy product eaten is hard cheese, which tends to cling to the palate and, like meat, requires a longer period of time for digestion, many authorities require the full waiting period to be observed.[16]

Why has Reform Judaism's attitude toward the observance of dietary laws changed in recent years?

Early on in its history Reform Judaism took a negative view of the dietary laws. Two prominent American Reform leaders, Rabbis David Einhorn (1809-1879) and Kaufmann Kohler (1843-1926), argued that with the destruction of the Jerusalem Temple in the first century there was no longer reason to observe the laws of *kashrut*. These laws, they said, had ceased to be relevant because they were instituted in connection with the Temple sacrificial system.

Accordingly, at their conference in Pittsburgh in 1885, American Reform rabbis nullified the dietary laws, and for decades afterward no discussion regarding dietary laws took place at Reform conferences. Even the noteworthy conference in 1937 in Columbus, which introduced new Reform ideas, made no mention of the dietary laws, and the subject ceased to be a matter of concern to Reform Judaism.

In recent years, however, the attitude has changed and

today there are Reform Jews who have made *kashrut* observance, to one degree or another and for a variety of reasons, part of their lives. Some believe it is an expression of their personal attachment to Judaism, and to others it is the link that joins Jews of the present to the Jews of the past. Still others believe that adherence to dietary laws is a discipline worth preserving, at least in some modified form, and observance ranges from full compliance to compliance only with certain biblical laws, such as the ban against eating pork or shellfish. In general, the Reform movement today regards the observance of the dietary laws as a matter of personal preference, not of law.[17]

Why is the eating of fish together with meat prohibited in Jewish law?

In talmudic times, Jews believed that the eating of fish together with meat was harmful to one's health, specifically that it predisposed one to leprosy. For that reason the Rabbis forbade the cooking of fish and meat together in the same pot and the serving of fish and meat on the same plate.[18] The *Code of Jewish Law,* written many centuries later, also warns against eating fish and meat together, considering it harmful to one's health.[19] Moses Isserles, in his Notes, adds: "One should also not roast the two together because the fragrance of one penetrates the other, but if it was done inadvertently the food may be eaten." The paragraph that follows in the code does not suggest a waiting period between the eating of meat and the eating of fish but does suggest that one rinse the mouth or chew on something hard, such as bread, after eating meat to help dislodge any food trapped in the teeth.

In many traditional homes, at Sabbath and holiday meals soup (usually chicken soup) is served between the fish and the meat courses. The original reason for serving soup was probably to cleanse the palate.

Why is the *kashrut* of swordfish and sturgeon disputed?

For a fish to be considered kosher it must have fins and scales, as indicated in the Bible (Leviticus 11:9-10 and Deuteronomy 14:9-10). The reason is not given. All fish have fins, so what is important is ascertaining whether the fish to be eaten has, or ever did have, scales. While some fish, such as catfish, don't have scales, species such as swordfish and sturgeon have scales in the course of their development but lose them at some point. According to the *Code of Jewish Law*, any fish that has scales at some point in its lifetime is considered kosher.[20] Many in the Orthodox rabbinate are not convinced that the scales swordfish and sturgeon have in the early stages of their development can truly be called scales, and they therefore do not consider these fish kosher. The Conservative rabbinate, following a responsum issued by Rabbi Isaac Klein, classifies both swordfish and sturgeon as kosher.[21]

Why is pork more objectionable to Jews than is the meat of other nonkosher animals?

Although the pig should be no more objectionable to Jews than are any of the other prohibited animals (see Leviticus 11) that have split hooves but do not chew their cud, Jews in fact do find the pig more abhorrent than other nonkosher animals. To this day, many Jews who do not observe the dietary laws as a whole still avoid eating the meat of swine (called *chazir* in Hebrew).

The Talmud says, "It is not proper to raise pigs," adding, "Cursed is he who raises pigs."[22] The reason is not given, but scholars have associated the deep Jewish aversion to the pig with the Hasmonean period in Jewish history (second century B.C.E.) when the Syrian-Greeks, led by Antiochus Epiphanes, dominated the Palestine scene and tried to force Jews to sacrifice pigs in the Temple and to eat of their flesh.[23]

A second reason for the Jewish aversion to the animal is that during the early centuries of the Common Era the Romans dominated Palestine and the pig was one of their accepted symbols. The Romans destroyed the Second Temple in 70 C.E. and treated Jews harshly for many years thereafter. To the Jews, the pig became a reminder of the Roman reign of terror, and the animal consequently was considered more repugnant than other nonkosher animals.

Why is bee honey considered kosher?

The Bible (Leviticus 11:20-23) indicates that most insects are not kosher. Exceptions are "the locust after its kinds, and the bald locust after its kinds, and the cricket after its kinds, and the grasshopper after its kinds." The bee is not listed as kosher. Why, then, is the honey that comes from the bee considered kosher?

The Rabbis of the Talmud[24] asked this question because they were aware of an earlier Mishnaic law which states that that which is produced by a nonkosher animal is nonkosher.[25] (The milk of a pig is not kosher even though milk in itself is kosher.) The Talmud answers that honey is kosher even though it comes from a nonkosher insect because the bee itself does not produce the honey. It merely stores the honey in its body while it carries it from the flower to the beehive. (This is, of course, at variance with modern scientific knowledge. It is now known that during the time that the nectar is being carried by the worker bee to the beehive, a chemical reaction takes place in which the nectar is converted into a sweet and thick liquid. Rashi seems to have understood this, although he was under the impression that the bee eats the whole blossom rather than merely extracts the nectar.)

Why is honey important in Jewish tradition?

Honey derived from fruits (dates, figs, grapes, carob) is

mentioned often in the Bible. Canaan, later called Palestine, is frequently referred to as a land "flowing with milk and honey" (Exodus 3:8). Deuteronomy (8:8) lists honey as one of the seven foods with which the Land of Israel is blessed (the others are wheat, barley, grapes, figs, pomegranates, and olives).

To render "a sweet savor on the altar," honey was brought to the Temple Priests as an offering of first-fruits (Leviticus 2:12). The Talmud speaks of honey as one of the "seven healing substances."[26] Another passage praises it highly as a food for children: "Bread for young men, oil for old men, and honey for children."[27] Centuries later, Maimonides, in his *Sefer Refuot (Book of Remedies)*, wrote that honey is good for old people.

Bee honey, also mentioned in the Bible (Deuteronomy 32:13; Judges 14:14), became a favorite Rosh Hashana food, for on that holiday Jews greet each other with words that express hope for a good, healthy, and *sweet* New Year.

Why have the laws regarding growing food in Israel during sabbatical years *(shemita)* been modified?

According to the Bible (Exodus 23:10-11; Leviticus 25:1-7), the Land of Israel must be allowed to lie fallow every seventh year. The seventh year is called *shemita,* from the Hebrew verb meaning "to abandon, to leave alone." The fiftieth year (after seven sabbatical years) is called the *yovel* (literally "ram's horn") or jubilee year (Leviticus 25:8ff.); it is ushered in by the blowing of the ram's horn (Leviticus 25:9).

Exodus 23:12 and Leviticus 25:4 explain that the *shemita* year is to be a rest period (a Sabbath) both for the land and for the people who work it. Whatever grows in unattended fields during *shemita* is to be left for the poor.

The Rabbis of the Talmud regard the sabbatical year and the jubilee year as applying only to the Land of Israel. This interpretation is based on Leviticus 25:2: "When you come into the land which I give you . . ."

In modern times, the need for Jews to grow food in Israel became acute, and observance of the sabbatical year became a problem. To cope with the situation rabbinic authorities have permitted Jewish farmers, via a legal fiction, to sell their land to non-Jews for the *shemita* period. This allows them to cultivate the land as nonowners. The chief proponent of this innovation was Rabbi Isaac Elchanan Spektor of Kovno (1817-1896), the foremost authority of his age, and Rabbi A.I. Kook (1865-1935), Chief Rabbi of Palestine. Most, but not all, rabbinic authorities subscribe to this approach to the problem.

Why was the ban on the force-feeding of geese lifted?

In the early part of the twentieth century a dispute developed between rabbinic authorities in Eastern Europe over the question of whether Jewish farmers are permitted to force-feed geese in order to fatten them and thus enlarge their livers. From goose livers an expensive delicacy known as *pâté de foie gras* ("goose liver paste") is made, and the livers were therefore an important source of income for East European Jews. The prevailing rabbinic view was that the force-feeding of geese violates the biblical principles of *tzaar baalay chayim,* meaning "concern for the pain caused living creatures," and must therefore be avoided.

After the state was established in 1948, raising fowl, including geese, became a big industry in Israel. The Israelis discovered that they could increase their balance of payments considerably by fattening geese through force-feeding and selling the enlarged livers to European markets. The legality of this practice was brought before the Chief Rabbinate, and the ban on force-feeding was lifted on purely economic grounds. This decision was in keeping with the talmudic principle, *HaTora chasa al mamonam shel Yisrael,* "The Tora protects [is concerned with] the money [economic interests] of Israel."[28]

Why do some Jews place a hand on their heads before drinking or eating?

When an observant Jew does not have his hat or skull-cap handy, he will often cover his head with a hand and recite the prayer over the drink or food he is about to consume. Rabbi Yisrael Meir ben Aryeh Hakohayn (also known as the Chafetz Chayim) characterized this practice as improper because, as he explains it, one part of the body cannot serve as a covering for another part. He adds, however, that in an emergency this practice is permitted. What constitutes an emergency? If one awakens in the middle of the night and must drink water, he can cover his head with his hand while reciting the blessing.[29]

Why is the washing of hands required before eating a meal at which bread is served?

The origin of this law is biblical (Exodus 30:17-21). Moses was commanded to make a copper laver and to place it at the entrance to the altar area so that Aaron and his sons (the Priestly family) could wash their hands before approaching the altar to offer sacrifices. Verse 20 concludes, ". . . and it shall be for them a statute forever."

In Jewish law, one must wash the hands ritually (with a vessel) before eating a regular meal, that is, a meal at which bread is served. One is not required to wash before eating a meal at which no bread is served.

One reason for the washing of the hands is the purely mundane one: to cleanse them before eating. The second, and more important, reason is to render the hands ritually pure, for the hands are forever touching impure objects. This symbolic expression of washing away impurity from one's hands dates back to Temple times, when Priests (Kohanim) devoted their lives to the Temple and its sacrificial system. The Priests had to be in a constant state of readiness to accept the animal and vegetable offerings that were brought to the Temple by the public to be offered on the altar as sacrifices to God. In his normal state, a Kohayn

(Priest), like all other individuals, was considered impure *(tamay)*, ritually unclean, and before performing a ritual act he was therefore required to wash his hands.

In the fifth century B.C.E. Ezra and his fellow scribes *(soferim* in Hebrew; singular, *sofer)* of the post-biblical period insisted that Priests wash their hands before accepting the first-fruits of grain brought to the Temple as an offering, a practice that was apparently being neglected by the Priests.

When the Temple was destroyed in 70 C.E., the table in the home came to represent the Temple altar. The bread placed on it came to symbolize the offerings that had once been brought to the Priests. The Sages, who believed that the Temple and the functions of the Priesthood would one day be restored, did not want the practice of washing the hands before handling an offering to be forgotten, and so the washing of hands before eating a meal was strictly enforced. And just as Priests did not partake of the offerings brought to them without first washing the hands, so was bread, the basic food, not to be eaten without first washing and pronouncing the blessing, "Blessed art Thou . . . Who commanded us to raise up hands and to pour water over them."

So widespread was the practice of ritual handwashing in talmudic times that the Midrash reports that an innkeeper once said to a Jew, "When I saw that you ate without washing your hands and without a blessing, I thought you were a heathen."[30]

The Rabbis of the Talmud,[31] in defining what constitutes a meal, indicate that there is a difference between a regular meal *(seudat keva)* and a temporary (light) meal *(achilat ara'i)*. For a repast to be classified as a regular meal bread must be served and eaten.[32]

Why, in ritual handwashing, is water poured over the right hand before the left?

"The right hand of the Lord doeth valiantly," says the

Psalmist (118:15,16). In Jewish tradition the right hand is accorded higher status than the left. For this reason pious Jews put on their right shoe first in the morning.

It is the function of the left hand to serve the right hand. That is why the *tefilin* are placed on the left hand (by right-handed persons): so that the right hand can have the honor of winding the leather strap around the arm. The same is true of the handwashing ritual. Water is poured over the right hand so that the left hand can serve the right hand.[33]

Why, in ritual handwashing, is water poured over each hand three times?

The *Code of Jewish Law*[34] explains that in ritual handwashing it is necessary to pour water over each hand three times. The first pouring cleanses the hand; the second removes the ritual impurity (*tuma* in Hebrew); and since the water of the second pouring becomes impure when it comes into contact with the (impure) hand, a third pouring is required to restore the hand to a condition of ritual purity (*tahara* in Hebrew).

Why, when washing before meals, do some Jews raise their hands after pouring on the water?

The raising of hands was part of the washing ritual from the very beginning, as is evident from the prayer recited when the hands are washed. The prayer ends with the words "to raise our hands" (in Hebrew, *al netilat yada'yim*).

The purpose of washing the hands is to remove ritual impurity, and to accomplish this the water must reach all parts of the hand including the area between the fingers, and the palm up to the wrist. In order to distribute the water, the hands are raised. This custom is described in the *Shulchan Aruch*.[35]

Why do people refrain from speaking from the time of washing the hands until after reciting the *Hamotzi* blessing and eating the first bite of bread?

Despite the fact that the *Netilat Yada'yim* prayer, which is recited when washing the hands, is totally separate from the *Hamotzi* blessing, which is recited over the bread to be eaten, the two prayers and the two actions over which they are pronounced are closely related. So as not to diminish one's concentration, the Rabbis urged that no words be uttered between the time one begins to say the handwashing blessing and the time one finishes eating the first morsel of bread.[36] This custom is generally followed by observant Jews today.

Why is bread the most important food in Jewish tradition?

In Jewish tradition, no food is more important than bread. Proof of this is usually adduced from the verse in the Bible (Deuteronomy 8:8) in which bread (or, to be more specific, wheat from which most bread is made) is mentioned before all other foods. It is for this reason that when the blessing over bread *(Hamotzi)* is recited at the beginning of a meal, it covers all foods to be eaten during the course of the meal. Individual blessings need not be recited over the foods eaten, unless the foods are not considered integral to the meal—such as grapes, dates, and other fruit.[37]

In many passages throughout the Bible, the significance of bread is indicated. Whenever a guest is invited for a meal, bread is served (Genesis 18:5). In fact, so highly regarded is bread in the Jewish tradition that the Talmud makes this statement: "Four things have been said in connection with bread: (1) Raw meat should not be placed on it (the meat might spoil the bread); (2) a full cup (of wine) should not be passed over it (some wine might spill on the bread); (3) it should not be thrown around; and (4) it should not be used as a prop for a dish."[38]

Why, after the *Hamotzi* blessing is recited, do many observant heads of household "break" the bread and distribute it to those at the table?

With the destruction of the Second Temple and the discontinuance of the sacrificial system, the Rabbis of the Talmud began to think of the table in the home as representing the altar in the Temple: "As long as the Temple existed, the altar atoned for Israel, but now a man's table atones for him," says the Talmud.[39] It was then that the bread served at mealtime began to take on new meaning as a symbol of and a replacement for the sacrifice that was brought in Temple times—a sacrifice consisting of a mixture of fine flour, oil, and frankincense, often baked into loaves. The Priest burned up some of these loaves of bread on the altar to serve as a memorial to God, and the remainder were for his personal use. (When bakers make bread today, a portion of dough is removed prior to baking [this piece of dough is known as *challa*] and is thrown into the oven and burned as a reminder of the dough given to the Priests in ancient times. This procedure is referred to as "[the] taking [of] challa." *Challa*—plural, *challot*—is also the name by which the special loaf of bread eaten on the Sabbath is known.)

In post-Temple times (after 70 C.E.), it became customary for the head of the household to break off pieces of bread after the *Hamotzi* blessing was recited and to pass the bread to those at the table. The custom is described in the Talmud: Rabbi Abbahu, a third-century Palestinian scholar, made a dinner for Rabbi Zeira, the most distinguished rabbinic authority in Palestine. Abbahu said to Zeira when they sat down to eat, "Will your honor please commence [meaning 'break bread'] for us?" Zeira replied, "Doesn't your honor accept the ruling of Rabbi Yochanan, that the host should break bread?" So Rabbi Abbahu broke the bread for those assembled at the dinner.[40]

In many homes today, particularly on the Sabbath, after cutting the loaf of bread part way through, the head of the household *breaks* off pieces of bread *(challa)* with the hard crust and passes a piece to each family member. Ashkenazim often score the loaf top and bottom before breaking off pieces for distribution to family members.[41]

Why is a blessing not recited when washing the hands at the conclusion of a meal?

It is customary to wash the hands, particularly the fingers, after the meal has been eaten and before *Grace After Meals* is recited. The water that is poured on the fingers is known as *ma'yim acharonim,* meaning "final waters."

Maimonides, in his code, the *Mishneh Torah,* explains that unlike the washing of hands at the beginning of a meal, which is a religious obligation, the washing of hands at the end of the meal is done for health reasons only. In early times, it was customary to use salt freely. Salt was taken in hand and sprinkled over the food. A residue of salt always remained on the diner's fingers when the meal was over, and if the diner rubbed his eyes, he could cause serious damage. It therefore became customary among Jews to wash the fingers at the end of the meal, and since this was only a precautionary health measure, not a religious obligation, no prayer was assigned to the act.

Why is the word *l'chayim* used when raising a glass and making a toast?

L'chayim is a Hebrew word meaning "to life." According to an incident described in the Talmud, it would appear that in the Jewish tradition the custom of toasting someone with the word *l'chayim* has its origin with the great scholar Akiba who, at a banquet he gave in honor of his son Shimon, is said to have offered each guest a glass of wine and to have saluted them with the words, "To the life and health of the Rabbis and their disciples!"[42]

Why is salt important in Jewish tradition?

The Bible (Leviticus 2:13) commands, "On all your meal-offerings shall you sprinkle salt," and the Talmud (Menachot 20a, b) extended the requirement to all sacrifices. Salt is a preservative, and since sacrifices were not always eaten immediately by the Priest or the offerer, it was necessary to use salt to retard food spoilage.

Salt in general was important throughout biblical and later times. Treaties were sealed with salt. The Bible (Numbers 18:19) speaks of "an everlasting covenant of salt." The Talmud says, "The world can get along without pepper, but it cannot get along without salt."[43]

In present-day Israel, the mayor of Jerusalem often greets distinguished visitors at the entrance to the city with an offering of bread and salt. Arabs, to this day, seal agreements with bread and salt.

Why is the apple a popular fruit among Jews?

In Jewish tradition the apple is noted for its healing power as well as its sweetness. The Jewish historian Flavius Josephus (38-100 C.E.), in his *Antiquities* (17:7), notes that whenever King Herod (73-4 B.C.E.) felt faint, he would eat an apple. In early talmudic times it was believed that apples had medicinal value, and apples were often sent as gifts to people in ill-health.

The curative power of the apple is associated with its sweetness. The Hebrew word for apple, *tapuach,* is derived from the word *nafach,* meaning "exhale" or "emit a sweet scent." The Song of Songs (3:3) refers to the sweet taste of the apple (2:3) and to its attractive odor (7:9). The Talmud also regards the apple as a superior fruit, delicious in taste and appealing in fragrance. When the Tora is praised, it is described as being "more delicious and more fragrant than apples."

On the second night of Rosh Hashana it is customary to serve a fruit not yet tasted that year. Many families serve apples dipped in honey. There is also a tradition to eat apples on Shavuot, a holiday on which the first fruits of the field were offered in the Temple. The custom is first mentioned in the post-talmudic collection of homilies entitled *Targum Sheni,* relating to the Book of Esther.

Why are nuts popular in Jewish tradition?

Nuts have always been used in baking by the Jewish homemaker, but they have even been more popularly used as a goody for children, much like candy is today. The Talmud makes a number of references to this. Rabbi Judah said, "It is not fair for a storekeeper to distribute [free of charge] roasted grain kernels or nuts to children in order to get them into the habit of coming to his store [and to bring along their mothers, who would then make purchases]."[44] Rabbi Judah considered this unfair competition, but the majority of the Rabbis did not agree.

In another talmudic reference, we are told that Rabbi Akiba distributed roasted grain kernels and nuts to children on the eve of Passover (prior to the *Seder*) so that the children would be excited from having received the treats and would be alert to recite the Four Questions.[45]

Nuts were not only used for food. The Midrash refers to them as "playthings for children and for kings."[46]

Why has the pomegranate been a favorite Jewish food and symbol?

Along with figs and grapes, pomegranates were favored in Bible times. The pomegranate was one of the foods that the scouts sent out by Moses (Numbers 13:23) brought back with them from Canaan (later called Palestine) as proof that the Promised Land was fertile. The pomegranate in particular was identified with fertility because of its many seeds. (Some students of Jewish law have claimed that a pomegranate has 613 seeds, hence its identification with the 613 commandments [*mitzvot*] that Jews are obliged to observe.)

Because of the popularity of the pomegranate, it has been widely used as a symbol in Jewish art. The two pillars of the First Temple (I Kings 7:18) were ornamented with pomegranate representations. Pomegranates were also embroidered on a garment of the High Priest (Exodus 28:33).

In more recent times ark curtains have often been decorated with embroidered representations of pomegranates, and the shape of the fruit inspired the design of the crowns that are placed on the two finials of a Tora scroll. These crowns are called *rimmonim* (singular, *rimmon*), Hebrew for pomegranates.

Why was garlic once very popular among Jews?

Garlic (*shum* in Hebrew) has long been popular among peoples of the Middle East. The bulb is mentioned in the Bible (Numbers 11:5) as one of the vegetables that the Israelites ate in Egypt and for which they yearned during their long years in the wilderness.

Early Jews believed that garlic possesses aphrodisiac qualities, and according to a tradition mentioned in the Jerusalem Talmud Ezra decreed that garlic be eaten on Friday evenings because "it promotes and arouses sexual desire."[47] The fact that in talmudic times there was a group referred to as "garlic-eaters"[48] indicates how popular this vegetable was among Jews.

Why are figs served on Rosh Hashana?

Figs are served on Rosh Hashana because, like honey and apples, they are known for their sweetness. In the parable of Jotham (Judges 9:1-11), the fig tree refuses to become King of the Trees, arguing, "Shall I forsake my sweetness and good fruitage and go forth to rule over trees?"

The fig was indigenous to the ancient Land of Israel, and along with grapes and pomegranates it was one of the principal fruits of the Promised Land (Numbers 13:23).

Although in the Christian tradition the forbidden fruit in the Garden of Eden is the apple (Genesis 2:17), in Jewish tradition it is the fig, since the leaves from which Adam and Eve made aprons (girdles) to cover their nakedness were taken from the fig tree mentioned in the very next chapter (Genesis 3:7). Since Rosh Hashana is associated with the appearance of the first members of the human species, it is logical that the species of fruit which Adam and Eve tasted in the Garden of Eden would become linked to the holiday.

It should also be pointed out that the *t'ayna* mentioned in Genesis is a variety of fig that is particularly known for its sweetness and that ripens in Israel in August, shortly before the Rosh Hashana holiday. Another variety, *pagim*, ripens later in the year and is not as sweet.

Figs were a great delicacy in ancient Palestine, and it was natural for them to become associated with the holiday that fell on the first day of Tishri (Rosh Hashana), when sweet figs were in abundance.

Why did Ezra order the eating of sweet foods on Rosh Hashana?

The eighth chapter of the Book of Nehemiah speaks of Rosh Hashana as being a holy day on which sweets should be eaten. In that chapter, Ezra and Nehemiah address the congregation of Israel on the first day of Tishri, which is Rosh Hashana, saying to them:

> This day is holy unto the Lord your God; mourn not nor weep . . . Go your way and eat the fat, and drink the sweet, and send portions unto him for whom nothing is prepared, for this day is holy unto our Lord.

The fifteenth-century scholar Rabbi Jacob Levi Mollin of Germany, also known as the Maharil, interpreted the words "drink the sweet" to mean that Jews should use honey at their Rosh Hashana meals on the first day of Tishri. The serving of sweet side dishes and desserts on the holiday is said to stem from the Maharil's interpretation.

Why is *tzimmes* a popular holiday dish?

Tzimmes became popular in Jewish households primarily because it is easy to prepare and can be reheated for repeated servings.

Tzimmes is not the same dish to all people. To some Jews it is a sweet casserole of vegetables or fruit, sometimes in combination with meat. To others it is a vegetable and fruit preparation combined with other ingredients. Carrots, sweet potatoes, and apples are the most common of the vegetables and fruits used. Jews who have roots in Rumania and the Balkan countries serve a *tzimmes* compote made of fresh or dried fruits to which sugar or honey is added.

There are many varieties of *tzimmes*. The word *tzimmes* according to one (unsubstantiated) theory is derived from the Yiddish phrase *tzim essen*, "to eat," as in the expression *Vos host du tzim* (or *tzum) essen?* meaning "What do you have to eat?"

Why must ovens be made kosher for Passover by heating the interior?

The talmudic principle that applies to the ritual cleansing *(kashering)* of utensils and appliances for Passover is, "In the manner that the vessel absorbs *chametz* so should it get rid of the *chametz*."[49] The oven becomes *chametzdik* (unfit for Passover use) because when cooking is done in it, particles of food spatter over the interior. Just as the heat provided by an open fire or an electric element cooks the food, so may it be used to *kasher* the oven. Exceedingly observant Jews suggest that a blowtorch be applied to every surface of the interior of the oven for at least seven minutes to remove all encrustations. Others place a red-hot brick in the oven and leave it there with the heat turned on. Still others require only that the heat be turned on and that it be kept on until the oven is red-hot. When the oven has cooled sufficiently, its interior is scraped and thoroughly cleaned.

Self-cleaning ovens are self-*kashering* and need only be cleaned in a normally thorough fashion.

Why is it not necessary to *kasher* a microwave oven for Passover use?

Unlike a conventional oven, a microwave oven does not cook by fire or by the heat of an electric element. The cooking is done by radiation, and only the food placed in the oven is affected by the heat. The cookware in which the food is cooked becomes warm because of the food that has been heated by the radiation, not because of the radiation itself.

Because a microwave oven operates under different principles than a conventional gas or electric oven, it need not be *kashered* like one. The interior, which is made of steel that has been coated with a nonporous material, does not absorb food as does a conventional oven. Therefore, to *kasher* a microwave oven, all that is required is a thorough cleaning. However, to differentiate between ordinary cleaning and a special Passover cleaning authorities suggest that a pot of steaming water be placed in the oven and the oven be turned on to allow the water to continue to boil for a while so that the steam will reach all the surfaces.

Why does the Talmud specify only five grains from which *matza* can be made?

The Talmud says that a person has fulfilled his biblical obligation to eat *matza* on Passover only if the *matza* he eats has been made from one of five grains: wheat, barley, spelt, oats, rye.[50] These five grains were undoubtedly chosen because they are mentioned in the Bible; but although these grains were indeed used in biblical times, it is only the Talmud, not the Bible, that specifically associates them with the Passover holiday and the baking of *matza*.

It should be pointed out that while Passover *matza* must be made specifically from one of these grains, the grains may not be used for any other food preparations for the duration of the holiday.

What the five grains mentioned above have in common is that they are subject to fermentation when water is added to the flour that is made from them. And this is the essential requirement: the grain used in the making of *matza* must be fermentable. Only by using one of the five grains is the description of *matza* in Exodus 12:39 satisfied: "And they baked unleavened bread [before it had enough time to ferment] from the dough which they brought forth out of Egypt, for they were chased out of Egypt and could not delay."

Since the grain used in the making of *matza* must be susceptible to leavening when water is added to it, that which is generally referred to as pulse or legumes (which includes peas, beans, peanuts, and lentils) cannot be used to make Passover *matza*. The Rabbis of the Talmud and later codifiers of the law believed that the flour made from legumes (which are characterized by pods that enclose edible seeds) would not ferment when water is added to it, though we know today that they were in error.

Maimonides, in his *Mishneh Torah,* adds rice to this group, explaining, "Pulse, such as rice, millet, beans, lentils, and the like, are not subject to the law prohibiting leavened bread. Even if one kneads dough out of rice flour, or the like, with hot water, and covers it with garments until it swells in the same way as ordinary fermented dough, it may still be eaten during Passover because what has taken place is not fermentation but putrefaction [rotting]."[51]

Why do some communities use rice and legumes on Passover?

As indicated above, the Talmud lists five grains that may be used to make *matza* for Passover. Joseph Caro, the Sephardic author of the *Shulchan Aruch,* states that rice and other legumes (*kitnit* or *kitniot* in Hebrew) may be used during Passover.[52] Sephardic Jews follow this ruling.

The Ashkenazic community, following the lead of Moses Isserles, prohibits the use of rice and legumes *not* because Jewish law bans them directly, but because their use might lead to possible confusion in the kitchen. The mixup that is feared is that flour made from rice or legumes might be stored near flour made from the five permissible grains (see previous question), and through an error a homemaker wanting to bake *matza* might use the rice or legume flour, which is not permissible. As a precautionary measure, Ashkenazic authorities have banned the use of rice and legumes totally, in all forms, during Passover while Sephardic authorities have not.[53]

Why is peanut oil permitted on Passover while peanuts themselves have been prohibited?

Peanuts are legumes, just as are peas and beans and similar vegetables. In the case of peanuts the pods grow underground rather than on a vine above ground. Sephardim permit the use of legumes, but Ashkenazim do not because, as pointed out in the previous answer, Ashkenazic authorities fear that if flour were to be made from the peanuts and kept on a shelf along with wheat flour, or one of the other flours from which *matza* may be made, confusion would set in. By error, a baker or a housewife might use the peanut flour to bake *matza* for Passover use—something that the law prohibits.

Peanut oil is permitted because the oil is squeezed directly from the peanuts. Flour is not involved in producing the oil and an error cannot be made.[54]

Why is there so much uncertainty over the use of corn and corn oil on Passover?

Those Ashkenazic authorities who prohibit the use of peanuts on Passover also prohibit the use of corn, and for the same reasons. (See previous questions.) Sephardic authorities, however, do permit the use of corn and corn oil, just as they permit the use of peanuts and peanut oil.

Many Ashkenazic authorities today have placed the use of corn on the "doubtful" list and not on the "prohibited" list of kosher for Passover foods. (See Note to previous question.) The reason for the uncertainty lies in the mistaken conceptions about the nature of corn. For a long time scholars confused ordinary grain with corn. The confusion manifested itself in the mistranslation of biblical and talmudic texts that spoke of *kali* and *dagan.*

It is quite obvious that the early Jewish sources knew nothing about corn (maize) as we know it today. The world-at-large had not heard of corn until Columbus discovered this Indian food in the Americas and brought it back to the Old Country. And so, when the word *dagan,* used often in the Bible (Deuteronomy 18:4) and the Talmud,[55] is translated as "corn," it is not translated accurately. *Dagan* is actually a generic term for grain. And, when the word *kali* (as in Leviticus 23:14) is translated as "roasted corn" when it actually means "roasted grain," it is incorrectly translated as well.

Why is beer as well as scotch, rye, and other hard liquors not kosher for Passover?

All alcoholic beverages made from grain are prohibited for Passover use. If some other ingredient, such as potato or fruit, is substituted for the grain, alcoholic drinks can be made in accordance with Passover rules.

Many Jews will also not use cosmetics or medications containing alcohol made from any of the five prohibited grains (wheat, barley, spelt, rye, and oats), since these grains may be used for the making of *matza* and for no other purpose.

Why is year-'round baking soda permitted for Passover use while year-'round baking powder is prohibited?

Baking soda (sodium bicarbonate), which is an antacid

as well as a leavening agent, is not a fermenting agent and hence is kosher for Passover use.

Baking powder, also not a fermenting agent, is traditionally considered not kosher for Passover only because it contains cornstarch (see earlier question on corn) in addition to its other ingredients (baking soda plus an acid-forming substance such as cream of tartar). Today, kosher-for-Passover baking powder is produced by substituting potato starch for the starch made from prohibited grains. In recent years, one manufacturer (Erba Food Products, Inc., of Brooklyn, New York) has produced such baking powder under the brand name Hadar.

Notes

GENERAL INTRODUCTION

1. Bava Kama 79b; Bava Batra 60b.
2. Bava Kama 84a.
3. Hilchot Melachim 5:7, 8.
4. Yoma 82a.
5. Midrash Pesikta Rabbati 6:26a.
6. Yoma 85a.
7. Pesachim 25b; Sanhedrin 74a.
8. Mishna Bava Kama 8:1 and 91b. See the *Mishneh Torah,* Hilchot Chovel Umazik 5:1 and Hilchot Rotzayach 11:5. See also *Shulchan Aruch,* Choshen Mishpat 426:1, and the *Aruch Hashulchan* on this section which emphasizes the view that one must not be overprotective of oneself and must do everything within one's power to save a life.
9. Pesachim 22b.
10. Bava Metzia 75b.
11. For a full presentation of the responsum of Solomon Luria in English, see Solomon B. Freehof's *The Responsa Literature,* pp. 129ff. For a full legal discussion of the principle of *marit a'yin,* see also Betza 9a.
12. Taanit 27b.
13. A report of this ruling appeared in the October 1983 bimonthly *Torah World,* published by United Orthodox Services, Inc., Brookline, MA 02146.

Chapter 1
WHO IS A JEW?
WHO IS A GOOD JEW?

1. See Chapter Three for further elaboration on the concept of Covenant People.
2. Avoda Zara 2b.
3. Ibid.
4. Yevamot 45b.
5. Kiddushin 68b.
6. Rabbi Shaye J.D. Cohen, in *Conservative Judaism*, Summer 1983, Vol. XXXVI, No. 4, argues that the principle of matrilineal descent was not established until the time of Ezra in the fifth century B.C.E.
7. *Shulchan Aruch*, Even Haezer 4:5, 19.
8. Mishna Kiddushin 3:12; Kiddushin 66b, 67a; and Yevamot 54b.
9. *Mishneh Torah*, Hilchot Yibum 3:1.
10. Megilla 13a and Sanhedrin 19b.
11. *Igrot Moshe*, Yoreh Deah II:131.
12. Kiddushin 73a.
13. Ethics of the Fathers 2:6.
14. Mishna Hora'yot 3:8.
15. Yoma 86a.
16. Simeon ben Shetach was a brother-in-law of King Alexander Yannai.
17. Bava Batra 21a.
18. *Shulchan Aruch*, Orach Chayim 282:3, and Notes of Isserles.
    Since official records of marriage are no longer kept by Jewish communities as they were in the past, the issues under discussion are of little practical consequence today.
19. Chagiga 14b.
20. Sanhedrin 44a.
21. This was indicated in the Notes of Moses Isserles on the *Shulchan Aruch*, Even Haezer 37, where he states that marriage between Karaites and other Jews is forbidden.
22. The first Chief Rabbi of Palestine, Rabbi Abraham Isaac Kook (died 1935), referred to the Falashas as "part of the Jewish people who because of trials and tribulations of the Exile have been far removed from us . . ." His successor, Yitzchak Halevi Herzog (died 1959), ruled that the origin and descent of the Falashas is too doubtful for them to be regarded as Jews, and he insisted that they undergo conversion. On February 9, 1973, the Sephardic Chief Rabbi of Israel, Ovadya Yosef, ruled that Falashas are Jews according to *halacha*. The Ashkenazic Chief Rabbi, Shlomo Goren, concurred. Nevertheless, despite their rulings, these two Chief Rabbis still required Falashas to undergo conversion before they could marry Jews, as does the ultra-Orthodox leader Rabbi Eliezer Schach.

23. The minor talmudic tractate Kutim (2:7) ends with these words: "When may we accept them [the Samaritans as Jews]? When they abandon their belief in Mount Gerizim, and acknowledge Jerusalem as the holy city, and believe in the resurrection of the dead." See also Sanhedrin 90b for more on the rabbinic attitude toward Samaritans.
24. Chulin 1:1.
25. Ibid. 4b.
26. Introduction to Lamentations Rabba 2.
27. *Shulchan Aruch,* Yoreh Deah 158:2.
28. Eruvin 69a; *Shulchan Aruch,* Orach Chayim 385:3.
29. *Shulchan Aruch,* Choshen Mishpat 283:2.
30. Exodus Rabba 25:16.
31. Eruvin 69a and 69b.
32. This equation is also made in the *Shulchan Aruch,* Orach Chayim 385:3.
33. Sanhedrin 74b.
34. *Igrot Moshe,* Even Haezer 76.
35. Additional examples of the ultra-Orthodox attitude toward Conservative and Reform rabbis and Judaism are to be found in *Igrot Moshe,* Orach Chayim III:13 and III:30; Yoreh Deah II:106, 125 and III:107; Even Haezer III; 3, 4, 23, 25.
36. The philosophy of Samson Raphael Hirsch, rabbi of the influential German Orthodox community of Frankfurt-am-Main, was expressed in his *Nineteen Letters of Ben Uzziel* and *Horeb.* Rabbis associated with the Rabbi Isaac Elchanan Theological Seminary of Yeshiva University are generally supportive of his views. Hirsch is considered to be the progenitor of neo-Orthodoxy in Western countries.
37. Mechilta to Exodus 14:31.
38. Mechilta d'Rabbi Yishmael on Va'yechi.
39. Sota 14a.
      The Jerusalem Talmud (Shabbat 1:3 [9a]) offers this definition of a good Jew: "Anyone who has settled in the Land of Israel, is careful with regard to the consumption of consecrated food [he does not eat sacrificial animals that belong to the *Kohayn*], and who speaks in the holy tongue [Hebrew] and recites the *Shema* mornings and evenings—it is certain that such a person will merit life in the world-to-come."
40. Berachot 60b.
41. Nedarim 30b.
42. Kiddushin 8a.
43. Kiddushin 30a.
44. Moed Katan 15a and 24a.
45. Soferim 14:15.
46. Orach Chayim 91:3.
47. Kiddushin 31a.
48. Shabbat 118b.

49. Ibid. 156b.
50. Sanhedrin 58b.
51. Berachot 24a.
52. Ketubot 72a.
53. Yoma 47a.
54. *Shulchan Aruch,* Orach Chayim 75:2.
55. Ketubot 111a.
56. Ibid. 110b.
57. Ketubot 111a.
58. The Satmar *chassidim* believe that the establishment of the State of Israel has delayed the coming of the Messiah and the redemption of Israel. The coming of the Messiah, they say, must be accomplished by God through supernatural means. The Satmar do not, however, oppose *aliya* so long as it is done individually rather than as a mass movement.
59. Berachot 19a.

Chapter 2

JUDAISM AND CHRISTIANITY

1. See Shabbat 55a, which says, "There is no death without sin," and Shabbat 55b, which says that even Moses and Aaron died because they had sinned. See also *Judaism and Christianity,* by Trude Weiss-Rosmarin, Chapter Three, "Free Will vs. Original Sin."
2. Genesis Rabba 15.
3. Mishna Sanhedrin 6:11.
4. The Romans were in complete control of Palestine during the first century B.C.E. and the several centuries that followed. The statement in Berachot 58a by the third-century Babylonian scholar Rabbi Shila testifies to how well established was their control. While the Jews conducted their own courts, they were not empowered to execute criminals. When asked why a person found guilty of adultery had been subjected to thirty-nine lashes rather than to the death penalty, as prescribed in Leviticus 20:10, Rabbi Shila replied: "Since we have been exiled from our land, we have no authority to execute people."
5. Sanhedrin 52b.
6. *Mishneh Torah,* Melachim 12:5.
7. See also *Judaism and Christianity,* by Trude Weiss-Rosmarin, pp. 126ff.
8. The Vilna edition of the *Shulchan Aruch* contains the introductory statement, "Let it be known that wherever [in this book] the words *Akum, Goy,* and *Nachri* are used, the reference is to those who did not recognize the True God, who did not believe in His revelation, and were far from morality; but the people on whose land we live and

whose government protects us believe in God and in revelation and in ethics." See also Solomon B. Freehof's *Reform Jewish Practice,* Vol. II, pp. 36ff.

9. Yevamot 63a.

10. Ovadya Yosef, the former Sephardic Chief Rabbi of Israel, in his book of reponsa *Yechaveh Daat* IV:45, continues to adhere to the view of Maimonides despite the fact that almost all authorities are more liberal in their assessment of the Christian Trinity. See *Shulchan Aruch,* Orach Chayim 156, and Yoreh Deah 148:12.

    See also *Jewish Mystical Testimonies,* by Rabbi Louis Jacobs, pp. 58 and 72, for a similar liberal attitude expressed by the thirteenth-century mystic Abraham Abulafia. Abulafia makes reference to the talmudic statement in Chulin 13b that "there are no *minim* [a *min* is a Jew or non-Jew who worships idols] among the Gentiles . . . The Gentiles outside the land [of Israel] are not idolators. They only continue to follow the custom of their ancestors [and their manner of worship is not to be taken as proof that they actually believe what they practice]." Abulafia's contemporary, Meir of Rothenburg, held a similar view. See *Rabbi Meir of Rothenburg,* by Irving Agus, p. 245.

11. In his talmudic commentary on Sanhedrin 63b and Bechorot 2b, Rabbenu Tam maintains that when Christians take oaths in the name of "the Father, the Son, and the Holy Spirit," their intent is actually to take an oath to God alone. (The association of the Son and the Holy Spirit with God [the Father] is called *shituf,* "association" in Hebrew.) Christians, he says, are not bound by the covenant that prohibits Jews from adding personages to the godhead. They are bound only by the Seven Noahide Laws, none of which prohibits *shituf.*

12. Ethics of the Fathers 4:24.

13. Bava Kama 83b-84a.

14. Lamentations Rabba, Introduction 2.

15. Shabbat 31a.

16. Of the four Gospels, only the Gospel of John, which is considered by scholars to be the least historical (it is primarily theological), portrays Jesus as other than a practicing Jew.

17. Taanit 27b.

18. See *Jerry Falwell and the Jews,* by Merrill Simon, pp. 46-47.

19. *The Jewish War* II:160.

20. *Mishneh Torah,* Deot 3:1

21. Mishna Kiddushin 4:12.

22. Mishna Nedarim 9:1.

Chapter 3

JEWS IN A GENTILE WORLD

1. Gittin 61a.
2. Tosefta Bava Kama 10:15.
3. Many of these "fences" or precautionary measures applied to Sabbath observance (such as limiting the distance a person may walk on the Sabbath), and some dealt with a Jew's association with his Gentile neighbors.
4. *Mishneh Torah,* Sefer Kinyan 18.
5. His code was called *Semag,* an acronym for *Sefer Mitzvot Gadol.*
6. Bava Metzia 59b.
7. Gittin 61a. Some commentators note that this does not imply that Gentiles should be permitted to be buried in the same cemetery as Jews. See note in the Soncino translation of the above.
8. *Shulchan Aruch,* Yoreh Deah 367:1.
9. Of all the denominations, to date only Reform Judaism has addressed itself to this question and has stated that the rabbi may officiate at the funeral of a non-Jew. See the responsum of Rabbi Israel Bettan in the 1947 yearbook of the Central Conference of American Rabbis, Volume 52, pp. 136-37. See also *Reform Responsa,* by Rabbi Solomon B. Freehof, p. 146, where the authority Rabbi Simon Sofer of Eger is quoted as affirming that it is a duty to officiate at the burial of, and to eulogize, the Gentile dead.
10. *Igrot Moshe,* Yoreh Deah III:129, section 6.
11. *Yechaveh Daat* IV:45.
12. *Mishneh Torah,* Hilchot Teshuva 3:5 and Hilchot Edut 11:10.
13. Bechorot 2b. This opinion has prevailed over the centuries. The great German rabbinic scholar Jacob Israel Emden (1697-1776) expressed the attitude of most scholars when he wrote that Christians cannot be considered idol worshippers and that it is incumbent upon every Jew to befriend Christians in their hour of need, as was taught by the Sages of the Talmud (Gittin 61a).
    On this subject see also *Jewish Folkways in Germanic Lands (1648-1806),* by Herman Pollack, p. 14 and p. 210.
14. See *Reform Responsa,* by Solomon B. Freehof, p. 115.
15. Yoreh Deah 184:12.
16. *Terumat Hadeshen* 195.
17. Berachot 30b and 31a.
18. See *Jewish Folkways in Germanic Lands (1648-1806),* by Herman Pollack, pp. 59ff., for festive celebrations held on Saturday afternoon after the Bar Mitzva.
19. Dr. Trude Weiss-Rosmarin believes that this tendency on the part of some Jews is merely another example of a truism once expressed by the German-Jewish poet Heinrich Heine, who submitted to baptism in 1825: *"Wie es sich Christeled so Judelt es sich,"* meaning

"As Christians act, so do Jews." These Jews feel that it is in the best interests of the Jewish community not to antagonize the Christian majority in the United States and to let them know "that Jews are on the right side." (These views were expressed in an interview with Dr. Rosmarin, editor of *The Jewish Spectator*, by *The Jewish Week* newspaper, in its March 16, 1984 issue.)

In 1984, President Ronald Reagan proposed a Constitutional amendment for voluntary prayer in which he advocated that no child should be denied the right of prayer and no child should be forced to pray, but the proposal met with defeat in the U.S. Senate.

20. Sanhedrin 56a.
21. *Mishneh Torah,* Hilchot Melachim 8:10.
22. *Shulchan Aruch,* Yoreh Deah 254:2.
23. Yearbook XCII, 1982, pp. 215-16.
24. See *Igrot Moshe,* Orach Chayim II:73, by Rabbi Moshe Feinstein. The Rabbinical Council of America holds the more liberal view.
25. Taanit 16a.
26. *Shulchan Aruch,* Orach Chayim 579:3.
27. Bava Batra 112a.
28. *Igrot Moshe,* Yoreh Deah II:131.
29. Normally, when a distinction is to be made, the space left is four cubits *(amot),* or six feet.
30. Gittin 61a.
31. *Shulchan Aruch,* Yoreh Deah 367:1.
32. Bava Batra 112a.
33. Sanhedrin 47a.
34. See Mishna Sanhedrin 5:1.
35. *Ach Letzara,* p. 34.
36. Yoreh Deah 291:2.
37. Situations that create ill will are described as *mishum ayva* in Hebrew, and situations that encourage good will are characterized as *mipnay darkay shalom.*
38. Berachot 22a.
39. *Mishneh Torah,* Hilchot Sefer Tora 10:8.

Chapter 4

MARRIAGE, INTERMARRIAGE, AND CONVERSION

1. Sanhedrin 21a.
2. Yevamot 65a. See also Ketubot 62b.
3. Kiddushin 7a. Rashi comments that "a woman cannot be a wife to two [men]."

4. See *The Jewish Way in Love and Marriage,* by Maurice Lamm, pp. 73-76, for a full discussion of the subject.
5. Unlike the Christian Church, in which priests and pastors— particularly of the Roman Catholic, Episcopal, Lutheran, and Greek Orthodox sects—are sometimes thought of as being closer to God (they can forgive sins), in Judaism rabbis do not play such a role. Every Jew has equal access to God through prayer, and the prayer of one individual is no more efficacious than that of another. Like any layman, a rabbi must comply with all the requirements of Jewish law.
6. See *Maarchay Lev,* responsum 87, quoted in *Reform Jewish Practice,* Volume I, by Solomon B. Freehof, for a full discussion.
7. Sanhedrin 82.
8. As indicated by Moses Maimonides in his *Mishneh Torah,* Hilchot Teshuva 3:5, and by Joseph Caro in his *Shulchan Aruch,* Yoreh Deah 148:12.
9. See *Jewish Intermarriage: Fact and Fiction,* by Rabbi David Max Eichhorn, pp. 45ff., for a detailed discussion of this position. He argues that it is contrary to traditional Jewish law to convert a non-Jew to Judaism if the sole purpose is to make one eligible to marry a Jew.

    The Midrash (Genesis Rabba 39:21) points out that anyone who draws a Gentile close to Judaism and converts him is equivalent to having created him.
10. Mishna Kiddushin 3:5.
11. *Shulchan Aruch,* Yoreh Deah 268:12.
12. Sanhedrin 44a.
13. See *Igrot Moshe,* Orach Chayim 23, where Rabbi Moshe Feinstein, in an emergency, permits a Sabbath violator to be counted as part of a *minyan.* A Jew married to a non-Jew is certainly less culpable in traditional law than a Jew who violates the Sabbath.
14. Yevamot 46b and 47a.

    According to Yevamot 76a, proselytes were not admitted into the Jewish fold during the reigns of King David and King Solomon because there was good reason to suspect the sincerity of those who wished to convert.

    Louis Ginzberg, in his *Legends of the Jews,* Vol. 6, p. 190, points out that a prospective convert asking to be admitted into the Jewish fold is to be refused until he persists and makes a second request. Accordingly, Naomi refused Ruth's first request but admitted her as a proselyte when she repeated her request, after the laws concerning proselytes were explained to her.
15. Chelbo's comment is to be found in Yevamot 109b, Kiddushin 70b, and Nidda 13b.

    Other rabbis shared the view of Rabbi Chelbo. They, too, were concerned that foreign influences might spread among Jews, as is evident from the comment in Nidda 13b: "Our Rabbis taught:

'Proselytes and those who play with [molest] children delay the advent of the Messiah.' " The Rabbis coupled proselytism with the practice of pederasty (abnormal sexual relations between males, especially by a man with a boy, which was common among heathens), because they believed the proselyte would bring with him these alien homosexual practices into the Jewish community.

Most authorities, however, probably shared the more positive view of Rabbi Eleazar, who believed that Israel was exiled for no other reason than to win over converts. See Pesachim 87b.

16. See *Shulchan Aruch*, Even Haezer 129:20.
17. Yevamot 22a.
18. Mishna Demai 6:10.
19. Bamidbar Rabba 8:2.
20. Berachot 28a.
21. Genesis Rabba 39:14.
22. The centrality of the rite of circumcision in Judaism and the loyalty it symbolizes is pointed up by Rashi in his comment on Genesis 24:2-3. Abraham commissions his servant to find a wife for Isaac from among Abraham's kinfolk and not from among the Canaanites in whose midst they lived. Rashi emphasizes that the phrase used by Abraham is significant. Abraham says to his trusted servant, "Put your hand under my thigh and I will make you swear by the Lord, the God of heaven and the God of earth." The reason for making this demand, says Rashi, is that when one takes an oath he is required to take hold of a sacred object, such as a *Sefer Tora* or *tefilin*, preferably a Tora (as indicated in Shevuot 38b). In Abraham's case, the most sacred "object" in his life was his *mila*, his circumcision. Circumcision was the first religious commandment *(mitzva)* he observed, and since it came to him through pain and suffering, it was all the more dear to him. Abraham therefore asks his servant to hold him "under his thigh," at the point of circumcision, and to take an oath that he will be faithful in carrying out the assigned mission of finding a wife for Abraham's son.
23. Yevamot 46b.
24. Keritot 8b and 9a.
25. Maimonides, in his *Mishneh Torah* (Issuray Biah 13:5), repeats what the Talmud says (Keritot 9a): Since the Temple no longer exists and the sacrificial system is no longer in effect, what is expected of a proselyte is immersion for a woman and immersion plus circumcision for a male. But when the Temple is rebuilt, proselytes will be required to offer up a sacrifice as well.
26. *Shulchan Aruch*, Yoreh Deah 268.
27. See *American Reform Responsa* (1983), edited by Jacob Walter, p. 214.
28. Yevamot 46a and 46b.
29. See Yevamot 47a, where the subject is discussed.
30. See *Shulchan Aruch*, Even Haezer 6:1.

31. The non-Orthodox offer one additional argument: Since Jewish law (Even Haezer 6:1) considers a marriage between a Priest and a proselyte or a divorcee binding once it has taken place (called *bediavad* in Hebrew), there is no valid reason for denying the *Kohayn* and his offspring all Priestly privileges. Such privileges include officiating at a redemption ceremony for the firstborn *(Pidyon Haben)* and being called to the Tora for the first honor *(aliya)*.
32. Yevamot 78a.
33. *Shulchan Aruch*, Yoreh Deah 268:6.
    The Committee on Law and Standards of the Rabbinical Assembly (Conservative) recognizes the fact that in these cases the child is Jewish, but it suggests nevertheless that it undergo immersion *(tevila)*.
34. See the article "Jews by Choice," by Dr. Egon Mayer, in the 1983 *Proceedings of the Rabbinical Assembly*, pp. 57-70.
35. Yevamot 22a. This view is emphasized by Maimonides in his *Mishneh Torah*, Hilchot Avel 2:3.
36. Mishna Demai 6:10.
37. *Shulchan Aruch*, Yoreh Deah 241:9. In a later section (Yoreh Deah 374:5), Caro adds that when authorities say that a proselyte does not have to mourn his parents, it means that he is not *obligated* to do so, but *may* do so.
38. *Igrot Moshe*, Yoreh Deah II:130.
39. *Zekan Aharon*, No. 87.
    This responsum is noted by Rabbi Solomon Freehof in the *Central Conference of American Rabbis Yearbook*, LXVII (1957), pp. 82-85. Rabbi Maurice Lamm, in his *Jewish Way in Death and Mourning*, p. 170, indicates current Orthodox opinion as permitting the recital of *Kaddish* at graveside "for a close friend and also for a worthy Gentile, providing a duly constituted *minyan* is present."
40. Ketubot 11a. See also *Shulchan Aruch*, Yoreh Deah 268:7.
41. *Shulchan Aruch*, Yoreh Deah 268:7, 12.
42. Yoreh Deah 268:12.
43. The *Shulchan Aruch*, Yoreh Deah 345:5, states that "[one] does not mourn for an apostate."
44. See Rabbi Yekutiel Greenwald's *Ach Letzara*, p. 238, for opinions of various authorities. See also Rabbi Solomon B. Freehof's *Recent Reform Responsa*, pp. 132ff., for a wide-ranging discussion on the subject.

Chapter 5
THE PERSONAL DIMENSION

1. Sanhedrin 37a.
2. Ketubot 14a.
3. Ibid. 62b and Pesachim 49b.
4. *Mishneh Torah,* Ishut 15:1.
5. Even Haezer 23:5.
6. Ibid. 1:3.
7. Ketubot 60b.
8. Ibid. 62b.
9. Genesis Rabba 70:12.
10. Berachot 8b.
11. *Mishneh Torah,* Issuray Biah 21:1, 6.
12. *Shulchan Aruch,* Even Haezer 21:1, 2.
13. Issuray Biah 11:2-4.
14. Yoreh Deah 183-200.
15. *A Hedge of Roses,* by Norman Lamm, pp. 58-67. See also *Jewish Woman in Jewish Law,* by Moshe Meiselman, pp. 125ff., where other reasons are given.
16. Nidda 31b.
17. Me'ila 17a.
18. Megilla 13b.
19. See *How to Run a Traditional Jewish Household,* by Blu Greenberg, pp. 120ff., for more information on this subject.
20. Berachot 22a.
21. Sukka 52a.
22. Megilla 16a.
23. See *The Christian Book of Why,* by John C. McCollister, pp. 60-61, 183, for Christian attitudes toward sexual behavior.
24. Sanhedrin 21a.
25. Avoda Zara 36b.
26. Shelah, Judah's third son, was too young at the time to carry out the *Yibum* requirement.
27. See *The World History of the Jewish People: The Judges,* edited by Benjamin Mazur, p. 63. Levirate Marriage was well established in biblical times, as is attested to by the fact that it is mentioned in Indian heroic epics. It was not considered a new marriage, but a continuation of the woman's first marriage, with the second husband merely serving in place of his brother.
28. Even Haezer 23:1-3.

   For detailed discussions of the entire subject of masturbation see Mishna Nidda 2:1 (13a); Nidda 13b; Nidda 43a; Rosh Hashana 12a; and *Shulchan Aruch,* Even Haezer 23:1-3. Nidda 13b reads: "Rabbi Eleazar asked, 'Who is referred to in the verse "Your hands are full of blood" (Isaiah 1:15)?' Those that commit masturbation with their hands."

29. While the "crime" of Onan (from which the term "onanism" derives) is connected with the spilling or wasting of seed, it is not clear from the text of the Bible that by his action Onan was guilty of destroying a future life. The text (Genesis 38:9) says simply, "And Onan knew that the child [to be born from his cohabitation with his sister-in-law, Tamar] would not be his . . . and he spilled it [his seed] on the ground lest he should give seed to his brother." Onan was selfish and did not want to establish a family for his dead brother. That was his crime. The wasting of seed was the manner in which his defiance was expressed and was not necessarily wrong in itself.

Proof that Onan's "crime" was social rather than sexual becomes clear as we examine the reason why Er, Onan's brother, met his death. The Bible says (verse 7) that he was evil and God killed him. No further explanation is given. But Rashi, quoting a Midrash, comments that Er was killed for committing the same wrong of which Onan was guilty: spilling seed. But why would Er have to spill seed? He was not trying to avoid marriage (Yibum) to a widowed sister-in-law. And here Rashi asserts that the motive was selfishness: "Er destroyed his seed at the instigation of his wife, Tamar, who did not desire to become pregnant and thereby mar her beauty." Er's actions were intended purely to accommodate the selfishness of his wife.

There is another reason in Jewish tradition that explains why the act of spilling seed is condemned, and here again the crime is not connected with sexual deviation. The spilling of seed on the part of Onan is called sexually evil because the Rabbis found it to be a convenient way of explaining and excusing the actions of Judah, who later became the father of a child by his daughter-in-law, Tamar. Er, Onan, and Shelah were the children of Judah and his Canaanite wife (Genesis 38:1ff.). The future Messiah was to be a descendant of Judah, but he would have to come from Judaic stock. The lineage of the Messiah would have to be pure, untainted, and of regal stature.

Jacob, in his blessing (Genesis 49:10), promises that "the scepter shall not depart from Judah, nor the ruler's staff from between his feet." And so Judah's non-Jewish children are removed from the scene and he is able to cohabit with Tamar (who according to tradition is the daughter of Shem, the son of Noah, and of Priestly heritage, as it is written (Genesis 14:18): "Melchizedek [whom the Rabbis identified with Shem], king of Salem . . . was a Priest of God." Thus, the stage is set for the ancestors of the future Messiah to have a clean record. Tamar gives birth to twins, one of whom, Peretz, becomes the ancestor of King David and the future Messiah. For the full lineage see Ruth 4:18-22. The spilling of seed is incidental to the story.

See *Encyclopedia of Biblical Interpretation*, by Menachem M. Kasher, pp. 60-82, for a variety of comments on the above subject.

30. Shabbat 65a and Yevamot 65a.

31. *Mishneh Torah*, Issuray Biah 21:8.

32. Kiddushin 82a.

33. *Mishneh Torah*, Issuray Biah 22:2.

34. See article in *Encyclopaedia Judaica Yearbook*, 1974, edited by Cecil Roth, pp. 194 ff.

35. Yevamot 61b. See also later question on the use of birth control devices by women. More on this subject is to be found in *Judaism and Healing*, by Rabbi J. David Bleich, pp. 55ff.; *Birth Control in Jewish Law*, by Rabbi David M. Feldman, pp. 229-30; and *The Jewish Way in Love and Marriage*, by Rabbi Maurice Lamm, pp. 133ff.

36. *Shulchan Aruch*, Even Haezer 5:1-2.

37. Yevamot 61b.

38. This is mentioned five times in the Talmud: Yevamot 12b and 100b, Ketubot 39a, Nidda 45a, and Nedarim 35b.

Yevamot 12b gives the reasons why these three types may use the *moch*. A minor may otherwise become pregnant, and being so young, may die as a result. A pregnant woman may use the device because, it was believed, sperm may cause damage to the fetus.

In the case of nursing women it was felt that should a woman become pregnant while still breastfeeding her first child, the child may have to be weaned prematurely, thus causing harm or even death to the infant. See also *Birth Control in Jewish Law*, by Rabbi David M. Feldman, pp. 169-75, for a full discussion on the *moch* (also spelled *mokh*).

39. Although not all rabbinic authorities agree with these views, it is by far the majority opinion. For a complete discussion of the subject, see Rabbi David M. Feldman's *Birth Control in Jewish Law*.

Probably the first authority to express this view is Rabbi Moses Sofer (1762-1839), who wrote in his book of responsa *(Chatam Sofer)* that contraceptives that do not interfere with sexual gratification and that allow for unrestricted penetration by the male are readily acceptable in Jewish law.

The birth control pill that was introduced in the United States in the late 1950s as an effective oral contraceptive for women is reminiscent of an oral contraceptive mentioned in the Talmud (Shabbat 10a and Yevamot 65b) and in later rabbinic literature. It was referred to as "the potion of sterility," "the cup of sterility," and "the potion of roots" (*kos ikrin* in Hebrew). Depending on the dosage of the concoction (its exact contents are not known), sterility could be prevented or induced. This potion was believed to be effective for both men and women, but the Talmud and the *Shulchan Aruch* (Even Haezer 5:12) permit its use only by the woman so that she might make herself sterile—temporarily or permanently—depend-

ing upon her health requirements and physical condition.
40. See *Judaism and Healing*, by J. David Bleich, pp. 80-84, for a full discussion of artificial insemination. Rabbi Bleich points out that the AIH method preferred by (Orthodox) rabbinic authorities is to retrieve and use the semen from the vagina after intercourse. This eliminates any question of "wasting seed." He also points out that some authorities are opposed to AIH because to achieve pregnancy some physicians have been tempted, in order to assure more potency, to add the semen of a foreign donor to the husband's without disclosing that fact.

See also the discussion in *A Treasury of Responsa*, by Solomon B. Freehof, pp. 307-309.
41. In an address to the annual Torah Sheb'al Peh convocation in Israel, August 1978.
42. See *Jewish Medical Ethics* by Immanuel Jakobovits, pp. 244-50. See also p. 264, where a full account of the 1970 pronouncement by the Office of the Chief Rabbi in London is given on the subject of *in vitro* fertilization. See also *Judaism and Healing*, by J. David Bleich, pp. 85-91.
43. *Igrot Moshe*, Even Haezer I:10.
44. Chagiga 14b-15a.
45. See *Central Conference of American Rabbis Yearbook*, LXII (1952), pp. 123-25. See also pp. 501-504, where Alexander Guttman points out that the incident referring to the High Priest in Chagiga is not analogous to what we mean by artificial insemination. That incident was sheer accident, while we are talking about pregnancy that is wanted and desirable.

See also the discussion on artificial insemination in *Judaism and Healing*, by J. David Bleich, pp. 80-82.
46. In emphasizing the fact that the child is the son of the donor of the semen, Samuel ben Uri Phoebus, the seventeenth-century commentator on the *Shulchan Aruch* (Bet Shemuel on Even Haezer 1, Note 10), says that if this were not the case, Jewish law would not be concerned that the child might marry his own blood sister. We are concerned because the donor is, indeed, the father.
47. See *Jewish Medical Ethics*, by Rabbi Immanuel Jakobovits, pp. 264-65, where the author quotes the views of the office of the Chief Rabbi in London, issued after the 1970 public debate on the subject of test-tube babies and host-mothers.
48. See *Judaism and Healing*, by J. David Bleich, pp. 92ff., for a full discussion on host-mothers.
49. See *Shulchan Aruch*, Choshen Mishpat 425:2.
50. Chavot Yair 31.
51. Sheelot Yavetz 1:43.
52. Mishpetay Uziel 2:47.
53. For the Conservative approach, see *Responsa and Halakhic Studies*, by Rabbi Isaac Klein, pp. 27-33. Solomon B. Freehof presents the Reform approach in his *Recent Reform Responsa*, pp. 188-93,

and in *Reform Responsa for Our Time*, pp. 256-60. J. David Bleich, in *Judaism and Healing*, pp. 96-102, presents the Orthodox point of view.

54. See Yevamot 69b and Nidda 15b.
55. Mishna Oholot 7:6.
56. Sanhedrin 72b. This law is codified in the *Shulchan Aruch*, Choshen Mishpat 423, 425.
57. See the *Tosafot* commentary, Chulin 33a.
58. *Shulchan Aruch*, Choshen Mishpat 425:2.
59. See Nidda 31b.
60. Yoma 85a.
61. *Igrot Moshe*, Yoreh Deah 229, 230.
62. See his responsum on autopsy (1958) in his *Responsa and Halakhic Studies*, pp. 34ff., and his "Teshuvah on Autopsy," *Conservative Judaism*, Fall 1958, pp. 52-58.
63. *Yechaveh Daat* III:84, by Ovadya Yosef.
64. See *Compendium on Medical Ethics*, by Rabbi David Feldman and Dr. Fred Rosner, pp. 67ff., for more information on this subject.
65. There has been considerable rabbinical opposition to the heart transplant procedure as it currently exists, despite 1983 data showing that the success rate of the procedure is now quite high (78 percent patient survival after one year, 58 percent after three years, 42 percent after five years). See *Compendium on Medical Ethics*, p. 69, which states that "cessation of spontaneous respiration and absence of heartbeat for a given time period represents the classical Jewish legal interpretation of death."
66. One contemporary authority, Rabbi Yechiel Tucatzinsky, notes in his book *Gesher Hachayyim* that in Jerusalem today the custom is to wait twenty minutes after an individual is presumed dead before removing the body from the deathbed. See *Judaism and Healing*, by J. David Bleich, for a detailed discussion.
67. See *Shulchan Aruch*, Yoreh Deah 155:3, and the *Mishneh Torah* of Maimonides, Hilchot Yesoday Hatora 5:6. See also *Modern Reform Responsa*, by Rabbi Solomon B. Freehof, pp. 217ff., and *What Does Judaism Say About . . .?* by Rabbi Louis Jacobs, pp. 322-23.
68. See *Noda Biyehuda II*, Yoreh Deah 10, by Rabbi Ezekiel Landau.
69. Sanhedrin 108a.
70. Tanchuma Hayashan, Noach 7.
71. Kiddushin 82b.
72. See *Shulchan Aruch*, Choshen Mishpat 420:31, and *Mishneh Torah*, Hilchot Chovel Umazik 5:1.
73. Rabbi Immanuel Jakobovits, Chief Rabbi of the British Commonwealth, points out in his *Jewish Medical Ethics*, p. 284, that recent responsa permit cosmetic operations, in principle, as long as there is no danger to health, and, in the case of males, where it is commonly practiced in a locality. See also *Judaism and Healing*, by Rabbi J. David Bleich, pp. 126ff., for a discussion of plastic surgery in Jewish law.

74. See *Ach Letzara*, by Rabbi Yekutiel Greenwald, pp. 56-59 (published in 1939), and *Igrot Moshe*, Yoreh Deah III:155, by Rabbi Moshe Feinstein.

Although the non-Orthodox believe that the Priestly status of *Kohanim* is doubtful, most extend special privileges to a *Kohayn* by calling him first to the Tora and having him officiate at a *Pidyon Haben*.

See *A Guide to Jewish Religious Practice*, by Isaac Klein, pp. 387-88. See also Chapter Six for other questions relating to the *Kohayn*.

75. Bava Metzia 84a.
76. Yerushalmi Sukka 3:14.
77. *Mishneh Torah*, Avodat Kochavim 12:7-8.
78. *Shulchan Aruch*, Yoreh Deah 181:10-11.
79. *Noda Biyehuda*, Yoreh Deah II:80.
80. Bava Kama 83a.
81. Behaalotecha 151b.
82. It is of interest that until very recently Catholic monks were obligated to shave the top of the head (or at least the front part) so that nothing would interfere with their thoughts and prayers as they are directed toward God in heaven.
83. *Shulchan Aruch*, Yoreh Deah 182:6.
84. Bava Kama 82a.
85. Ketubot 64b and Mishna Nedarim 9:10.
86. Sanhedrin 14a.
87. *Shulchan Aruch*, Orach Chayim 303:25.
88. Shabbat 114a.

Chapter 6

DEATH AND DYING

1. *Shulchan Aruch*, Yoreh Deah 341:1.
2. The *Shulchan Aruch*, Yoreh Deah 339:1, permits the silencing of any external noise which prevents the departure of the soul, but the person himself may not be touched if that action will hasten his death.
3. Ketubot 104a.
4. See *What Does Judaism Say About . . .?*, by Rabbi Louis Jacobs, pp. 128ff. See also *Jewish Medical Ethics*, by Rabbi Immanuel Jakobovits, pp. 123ff. and 275ff.
5. *Shulchan Aruch*, Yoreh Deah 337:1.
6. Sanhedrin 47a states that "funeral rites are in honor of the dead." See also *Shulchan Aruch*, Yoreh Deah 344:10, and the Notes of Isserles on this citation.

Rabbi Maurice Lamm, in his *Jewish Way in Death and Mourning*, p.56, says: "Even if the deceased expressed a desire to be cremated, his wishes must be ignored in order to observe the will of our Father in Heaven. Biblical law takes precedence over the instructions of the deceased."

7. *Noda Biyehuda* II, Yoreh Deah 210.

8. Rabbi Moses Sofer (1763-1839), in his book of responsa, *Chatam Sofer*, Yoreh Deah 336, concurs with Rabbi Ezekiel Landau. In subsequent years many authorities subscribed to this view, although in 1966 the two Chief Rabbis of Israel prohibited autopsies. They state that "autopsy in any form is prohibited by Tora law." The statement was supported by 356 Orthodox rabbis. For a further discussion of the subject see Jacob Z. Lauterbach's 1925 responsum quoted on p. 278 of *American Reform Responsa*.

9. See *The Jewish Book of Why*, p. 104, for a discussion of *shaatnez*.

10. *Shulchan Aruch*, Yoreh Deah 351:2.

11. Yerushalmi Kila'yim 9:3.

12. Megilla 32a.

13. Ibid. 28b.

14. Adas Israel Congregation, in Washington DC, is one such example.

15. Semachot 2.

16. Yerushalmi Kila'yim 9:4.

17. Yoreh Deah 368:1.

18. *Antiquities* 4:8.

19. *Shulchan Aruch*, Yoreh Deah 401:6.

20. *Ach Letzara*, by Rabbi Yekutiel Greenwald, p. 142.

21. *Rites of Birth, Marriage, and Death Among Semites*, p. 137.

22. Sanhedrin 22a, Rabbi Alexandri adds: "The world becomes dark for him whose wife died in his lifetime."

   The Talmud (Berachot 32b) observes: "When a man takes a second wife after his first, he continues to think of the deeds of the first."

23. *Shulchan Aruch*, Yoreh Deah 371:1 and 373.

24. Yevamot 22b; Yoreh Deah 373:3.

   So that a *Kohayn* may visit patients in the Haddassah Hospital in Jerusalem, where Jewish corpses usually are to be found, double doors were installed to seal off certain areas so that the whole hospital is no longer considered a complete unit, thus enabling *Kohanim* to visit the sick in the hospital without violating the law of *Ohel*.

   See also *Mishneh Torah*, Hilchot Hamet 1:10-15, where Maimonides points out that one becomes "impure by enclosure [ohel]" even if he pokes his hand or a finger into the enclosure. The reason why a Gentile corpse (actually the word *akum*, meaning "idol worshipper," is used) does not cause a *Kohayn* to become impure by enclosure is not explained. Maimonides simply says that this is a tradition (*kabbala*) that has been transmitted to us from the past.

25. See *Shulchan Aruch*, Yoreh Deah 371:5. Some Orthodox and Conservative authorities consider four *amot* to be equal to seven

feet. See *A Guide to Jewish Religious Practice*, by Isaac Klein, p. 82. Generally, an *amah* (a cubit) is the distance from the elbow to the tip of one's fingers, which is approximately eighteen inches.

26. Hilchot Avel 3:11.
27. See *The Jewish Way in Death and Mourning*, by Rabbi Maurice Lamm, p. 65.
28. Shabbat 152b.
29. Betza 6a.
30. Moed Katan 27b.
31. Berachot 3:2.
32. Not all contemporary authorities are pleased or comfortable with explanations that connect Jewish customs, laws, and practices with superstitious actions and beliefs. But these elements are clearly an integral part of the Jewish past. The Talmud does not hesitate to describe actions and attitudes of the Rabbis that are clearly based on superstitions and unequivocally connected with the world of demonology and spirits. The tractate Berachot contains many examples of this fact. On page 55a one finds, for example, the following statement: "Three persons need protection ['against evil spirits' is added by Rashi]: a sick person, a bridegroom, and a bride."

Joshua Trachtenberg's *Jewish Magic and Superstition* contains a great number of examples of magical formulas designed to drive off demons and counteract magical spells. Psalm 91 (which begins with the words *Yoshev beseter* . . .), also known as *Shir Shel Pega'im*, is an antidemonic psalm. It was, and still is, recited at funerals, where spirits were believed to be unusually active. See pp. 112-13 in Trachtenberg's book, where he tells about a *shofar* that refused to function in a Frankfurt synagogue one Rosh Hashana in the thirteenth century. Psalm 91 was recited to dislodge Satan, whom it was believed had settled in the *shofar* and blocked the sound from coming out.

See also Israel Abrahams' *Jewish Life in the Middle Ages*, p. 391, for a description of the prevalence of the belief in evil spirits in the thirteenth century.

See also Irving Agus' *Rabbi Meir of Rothenburg*, p. 265, where the thirteenth-century scholar exhorts people to fasten *mezuzot* to their doors. He says, "I am convinced that no demon can harm a house properly provided with a *mezuza*."

33. Yoreh Deah 367. *Tefilin*, in talmudic times, were often worn all day long, not only when one was engaged in prayer.
34. Nevertheless, the Talmud (Taanit 16a) discusses the ancient custom of visiting the cemetery on fast days. It was believed that praying at graveside would be more meaningful than praying elsewhere.
35. Yoreh Deah 368:1.
36. Whiskey was usually one of the items served in order to refresh the mourners and also because it afforded an opportunity to say

> *L'chayim!* ("to life") even while standing in the midst of the dead. The practice continues today even when a lavish spread is not prepared.

37. Bava Batra 60b.
38. Ketubot 8b and Eruvin 5a.
39. Yerushalmi Ketubot 1:1 [2b].
40. Pesachim 4a.
41. Shabbat 152a; Yoreh Deah 376:3.
42. Moed Katan 22b.
43. See *The Jewish Book of Why*, pp. 71-72, for more information.
44. See *The Jewish Way in Death and Mourning*, by Maurice Lamm, p. 179, and Emmanuel Rackman's article in *The Jewish Week*, October 15, 1982.

   The ultra-Orthodox would not agree with this position. They even oppose a mourner's attending a gala function where music is not played. In *Igrot Moshe*, Yoreh Deah 255, Rabbi Moshe Feinstein is asked whether a woman in mourning for her father may attend a synagogue dinner for the benefit of the congregation. Her husband insists that he will not attend the dinner alone, and if his wife does not accompany him family harmony *(shelom bayit)* will be affected. Feinstein makes a concession in this case and permits the woman to attend the function with her husband.

45. Mishna Semachot 2:8.
46. Hilchot Avel 1:10.
47. Sanhedrin 44a.
48. See *The Jewish Way in Death and Mourning*, by Maurice Lamm, p. 83.
49. See his note on *Shulchan Aruch*, Yoreh Deah 340:5.
50. Orach Chayim 54:1. More on the congregational responses and the requirement of having a quorum of ten will be found in *Jewish Worship*, by Abraham Millgram, pp. 134-37 and 342-44.
51. See Sanhedrin 19b and Exodus Rabba 46:6.
52. Chosen Mishpat 42:15.
53. *Shulchan Aruch*, Yoreh Deah 363.

Chapter 7
THEOLOGY AND PRAYER

1. Psalm 115:16.
2. Sota 14a.
3. Sanhedrin 38a.
4. Taanit 2a.

5. Berachot 12b.
6. Ibid. 29b-30a.
7. *Mishneh Torah,* Hilchot Teshuva 3:7.
8. Avoda Zara 43b.
9. Rosh Hashana 24b.
10. Avodat Kochavim 3:10, 11.
11. Yoreh Deah 141:4-7.
12. Rabbi Kook's responsum number 66 is quoted in *What Does Judaism Say About . . .?* by Rabbi Louis Jacobs, p.41.
13. Shabbat 133b.
14. 1:49; 2:6.
15. Sota 22a.
16. Berachot 28b.
17. Taanit 10a, Bava Kama 84a, Eruvin 19a.
18. Berachot 17a.
19. *Mishneh Torah,* Hilchot Teshuva 8.
20. Ibid. 9:2.
21. Yerushalmi Taanit 4:3.
22. Sanhedrin 90a.
23. Compare his commentary on Sanhedrin 10:1 to the *Mishneh Torah,* Hilchot Teshuva 8:2.
24. Genesis Rabba 5:5 and Exodus Rabba 21:6.
25. Rosh Hashana 21a.
26. III:46.
27. Megilla 32b.
    A quorum (*minyan* is the Hebrew word for a quorum of ten; *mezuman* is the Hebrew word for a quorum of three) represents the "community." When something of importance transpires in Jewish life, it must take place in the midst of people, not in isolation; and the fact that members of the family of Jews are present when it happens marks its importance.
28. Berachot 6a.
29. *Mishneh Torah,* Hilchot Tefila 8:1. Maimonides summarized this general view, which was held by Rabbis of the Talmud, when he wrote, "Even if there were sinners among them [the ten members of the *minyan*], God would not despise the prayer of the group," so important is communal prayer.
30. Taanit 2a.
31. Mishna Berachot 3:3 and 4:3.
32. Berachot 24b.
33. Sota 32b.
34. 13a.
35. *Shulchan Aruch,* Orach Chayim 62:2 and 101:4.
36. See *Shulchan Aruch,* Orach Chayim 162, for a more detailed discussion.
37. *Shulchan Aruch,* Orach Chayim 432:1.
38. *Mishneh Torah,* Hilchot Sanhedrin 4:2.

39. Ibid. Hilchot Berachot 1:19.
40. Berachot 40a.
41. Pesachim 105a.
42. Orach Chayim 271:10.
43. Ibid. 272:4
44. *Shulchan Aruch,* Orach Chayim 269, discusses this custom. Classifying a roll that is served as an essential part of a meal as anything other than bread, and therefore unworthy of the *Hamotzi* prayer, seems to be at variance with the law stated in the *Shulchan Aruch,* Orach Chayim 158:1.
45. Berachot 5:1.
46. Eruvin 65a.
47. Ibid. See also Berachot 31a, where the Rabbis taught that a person should not stand up to pray (to recite the *Tefila* or *Amida)* when he was in a sad, listless, silly, or gossipy mood, but only when in a joyful or somber mood that had been reached through the performance of a meritorious deed. Giving charity is one such meritorious deed and is probably the reason why a charity box was traditionally placed at the entrance of the synagogue and also why a charity box *(pushke)* was passed around at weekday services.
48. These mystics had formerly lived in Spain and Portugal, where they had suffered severe persecution. Expelled from those countries in 1492 and 1497 respectively, many settled in Palestine, where they began the search for a life that would be more meaningful and less painful. They were led to mysticism, which involved regular periods of fasting and concentrated prayer.
49. *Shulchan Aruch,* Orach Chayim 1:3.
50. Mishna Berachot 7:1.
51. Orach Chayim 210:2.
52. Berachot 24a, b.
53. Ibid. 53a.
54. Megilla 3:1 [21a].
55. Ibid. 21b.
56. 10:5, 6.
57. Berachot 22a: "The words of the Tora are not susceptible to uncleanness."
58. Shabbat 22a.
59. Ibid. 127b.
60. Megilla 32a. This is repeated in the *Mishneh Torah,* Hilchot Tefila 12:5.
61. This quotation is found in the commentary of Rabbi Meir Hakohayn, Hagahot Maimoniyot, on the *Mishneh Torah,* Hilchot Sefer Torah 10:8. Meir Hakohayn was a disciple of Rabbi Meir of Rothenburg, and many of his master's responsa were preserved in his commentary on the code of Maimonides.
62. Yoma 70a and *Mishneh Torah,* Hilchot Sefer Tora 12:33.
63. Yoma 7:1 [68b].

64. Three Torot are read on four separate occasions, two of which are specified in the Talmud (Yoma 70a and Megilla 29b):

a) When the New Moon (Rosh Chodesh) of Adar falls on a Sabbath, one reading is from the regular weekly portion, the second from the portion normally read on Rosh Chodesh (Numbers 28:1-15), and the third is the portion in Exodus (30:12ff.) which refers to the paying of a half shekel, because in ancient times on the first of Adar an announcement was made concerning this tax.

b) When the Sabbath of Chanuka falls on Rosh Chodesh Tevet, one reading is from the regular weekly portion, the second is the regular Rosh Chodesh reading, and the third is a selection from Numbers 7 which refers to the dedication of the tabernacle in the desert and which by inference is associated with Chanuka.

c) The third occasion is Simchat Tora, at which time one reading is from the last *sidra* in the Tora (Deuteronomy 33:1-34:12), the second reading is from Numbers 29:35-30:1, and the final reading is from Genesis 1:1-2:3. Megilla 31a mentions the reading from the first and second Tora, but not the third. Simchat Tora emerged as a holiday in post-talmudic times when the annual cycle that developed in Babylonia replaced the triennial cycle of Palestine.

d) Finally, three Torot are used for the readings on Parashat Hachodesh when it occurs on Shabbat Rosh Chodesh Nissan.

65. As used in the Talmud (Yoma 7:1 [68b] and 70a) where the High Priest is described as rolling up the Tora.

66. As used in the Talmud (Sota 39b) where Rabbi Tanchum says, "The person who is to recite the *maftir* does not begin until the *gelila* has taken place." Rashi explains this to mean that the *maftir* is not recited until the Tora has been covered with its dressings *(bemitpechotav).*

The word *golel* is used to mean "cover" in connection with the burial procedure. In ancient times, when persons were buried in caves, the final act was to roll a stone over the cave opening, thus "covering" the grave. Therefore the word *golel,* which in the Talmud (Shabbat 142b and Oholot 2:4) is used to mean "rock," took on the meaning of "covering." Rashi (Shabbat 152b) was of the opinion that the word *golel* (in connection with the later burial procedure in which persons were laid to rest in coffins that were placed in the ground and covered with earth) meant the top or "covering" of the coffin itself. This view was accepted by later authorities, such as Nachmanides, who ruled that mourning *(Shiva)* actually begins when the coffin is closed with its cover.

67. Megilla 32a.

Rabbi Solomon B. Freehof, in a private communication (1984), observed that the seventeenth-century Turkish talmudist Chayim Beneviste (1603-1673), in his guide to *halacha, Shiuray Knesset Hagedola,* conjectures that *hagbaha* was transferred from before the Tora reading to *after* the Tora Reading so as to discourage persons from leaving the synagogue early. Many ignorant people, said Beneviste, believe that *hagbaha* is more important than the Tora Reading itself and would therefore leave the synagogue immediately after the Tora was raised. If the *hagbaha* were transferred to the end of the reading, people would stay and listen to the reading, waiting for *hagbaha*.

Apparently *hagbaha* and *gelila* were originally performed by the reader himself. Note the commentary by the Ramban to Deuteronomy 17:26 on the verse, "Cursed be he who will not maintain this Tora." The word for maintain, *yakim*, can be translated as "hold up aloft," and Nachmanides says it means, "Cursed be the *chazzan* who does not hold up the Tora for the people to see it." The Sephardim follow the older custom and often have the reader do the *hagbaha*, and they do not call upon a special person as is the Ashkenazic practice. The laws of *hagbaha* are given in the *Shulchan Aruch*, Orach Chayim 134, and these *precede* the laws pertaining to the actual reading of the Tora, which begins section 135. This was probably the order in which things happened in the sixteenth century. Although Isserles does add that the custom as he knows it (in Poland and surrounding areas) is to have *hagbaha* after the Tora Reading.

68. Megilla 23a.
69. Berachot 8a.
70. Megilla 3a.
71. Yoma 35b.
72. The first sentence of the *Shema* is derived from Deuteronomy 6:4. The second is a nonbiblical sentence. The third section, beginning "And thou shalt love . . .," is from Deuteronomy 11:13-21. The final section is from Numbers 15:37-41.
73. A fanciful explanation for reciting the second sentence of the *Shema* aloud only on Yom Kippur has been offered by mystics. They say that when Moses went to heaven to receive the Ten Commandments, he heard the angels responding aloud to the first sentence of the *Shema* with the words *Baruch Shem kevod*. When the angels discovered that men on earth had been doing likewise, they objected, arguing that earthlings are sinners and they are not entitled to the privilege of responding to the *Shema* as do sinless angels. However, say the mystics, since Yom Kippur is a day on which sins are forgiven and men become like angels, all may respond aloud to the *Shema*.
74. *Shulchan Aruch*, Yoreh Deah 282:2.
75. Ibid. 242:18.
76. *Panim Meirot* 1:74.
77. *Chatam Sofer*, Choshen Mishpat 73.
78. *Aruch Hashulchan*, Yoreh Deah 282:13.
79. Pesachim 118a. See also Megilla 10b and Taanit 28b for another explanation of the *Half Hallel* tradition.

Chapter 8
LAWS AND CUSTOMS

1. Bava Kama 79b and Bava Batra 60b.
2. Berachot 28b.
3. Genesis Rabba 44:1.
4. Ethics of the Fathers 4:2.
5. To offset the possibility of carrying in the public domain on the Sabbath, the *shofar* is not blown, nor is *Tashlich* permitted.
6. Yerushalmi Pesachim 4:1.
7. Yoreh Deah 376:4.
8. Ethics of the Fathers 1:1.
9. This view was unacceptable to Sadducees, Samaritans, Karaites, and other groups. The prohibition against committing to writing teachings that had been transmitted orally is mentioned in Gittin 60b.
10. 86b.
11. 14b.
12. Pesachim 4:1.
13. Betza 4b.
14. Kiddush Hachodesh 5:5.
15. Yoreh Deah 376:4.
16. Megilla 23b.
17. Mishna Berachot 7:2.
18. Berachot 47b.
19. Ibid. 48a.
20. Ibid.
21. Shabbat 31a.
22. Eruvin 13b.
23. Shabbat 31a.
24. Mishna Sheviit 10:3ff. and Gittin 37a.
25. Arachin 32b.
26. Yoreh Deah 87:3.
27. Ketubot 7b. The Talmud also says that a *minyan* must be present when the *Sheva Berachot* are pronounced at the festive meal following the wedding ceremony and again at each of the festive meals held on the six days following the wedding.
28. According to Ezekiel Landau (*Noda Biyehuda*, Even Haezer 1:56), most authorities do not consider a marriage to be invalid if a quorum of ten is not present at the *Sheva Berachot*.

    See *The Jewish Way in Love and Marriage*, by Maurice Lamm, pp. 154 and 185-86, for a fuller discussion. See also *Reform Jewish Practice*, by Rabbi Solomon B. Freehof, p. 89. The basic law is codified in the *Shulchan Aruch*, Even Haezer 34:4 and 62:4.
29. Mishna Betza 5:2.
30. Making noise on the Sabbath is discussed in Eruvin 104a, where Ulla

reprimands a man knocking on the door on the Sabbath. Ulla said, "May his bòdy be desecrated just as he has desecrated the Sabbath [by knocking on the door and making a noise]." Rabba disagreed with Ulla and said, "One is only forbidden to make a *musical* sound on the Sabbath." Making other noises is not forbidden, and one may, for example, make noise to chase away birds attacking his fruit trees. Later authorities are not in agreement.

See also Hagahot Maimoniyot, the commentary of Rabbi Meir Hakohayn on the *Mishneh Torah* of Maimonides, Hilchot Shabbat 23:2, in which the view of Rabbi Meir of Rothenburg is presented.

31. See Pesachim 7b.

For the same reason, a woman covers her eyes when blessing the Sabbath candles. See *The Jewish Book of Why*, pp. 169-70.

32. Orach Chayim 651:1.
33. See his *Aruch Hashulchan* 651:12-13.
34. See his *Mishna Berura* 651:2.
35. Yerushalmi Pesachim 4:1.
36. Mishna Betza 5:2.
37. *Shulchan Aruch,* Orach Chayim 339:2.
38. Betza 36b.
39. Orach Chayim 308:45.
40. The responsum on Sabbath observance is reported in full in the 1950 *Proceedings of the Rabbinical Assembly.*

In her book *The Bene Israel of Bombay,* p. 110, Schifra Strizower, in describing the Orthodox community of Bombay, says that most Bene Israel travel on the Sabbath and festivals. When determining which synagogue to belong to, they do not pick the one closest to their homes so as to avoid travel. At one time, arrangements were made for Jews to be able to buy tramway tickets on Friday so they might travel on the Sabbath without handling money. Most Jews did not take advantage of this arrangement, and as of 1974 tickets were no longer issued.

41. Shabbat 19a.
42. Orach Chayim 248:1-2.
43. Ibid.
44. *Shulchan Aruch,* Orach Chayim 301:33.
45. See *American Reform Responsa,* pp. 3-4.
46. Eruvin 69a.
47. Orach Chayim 385:3.
48. *Igrot Moshe,* Orach Chayim 23.
49. *Shulchan Aruch,* Yoreh Deah 281.
50. See *Reform Responsa for Our Time,* by Solomon B. Freehof, pp. 9ff., for a suggestion on how the candlelighting is handled when there is objection to lighting candles after dark on Friday night.
51. *Igrot Moshe,* Orach Chayim IV:60.
52. In Hebrew, *maalin bakodesh velo moridin.* See Menachot 11:7 [99b].

53. 14:20 [41a]. See also *Shulchan Aruch,* Yoreh Deah 290:1.
54. Abraham Gombiner, in his commentary on the *Shulchan Aruch,* Orach Chayim 38:12, makes this point, calling the obligation of putting on *tefilin* a *chovat haguf,* "a personal [bodily] obligation."
55. The laws of *eruv,* established by the Rabbis of the Talmud, are based on their interpretation of the verse in Exodus (16:29), "Let no man leave his place [domain] on the seventh day." This warning to the Israelites not to leave their homes to gather manna on the Sabbath was taken to mean that it is forbidden to carry an object on the Sabbath from the private domain into the public domain or from the public domain into the private domain. Maimonides maintains this verse to be the basis for limiting the distance one may walk on the Sabbath. See note 57.

    A more direct statement is found in Jeremiah 17:27: "If you will not harken to Me to keep the Sabbath holy, and not to bear a burden and enter in at the gates of Jerusalem on the Sabbath Day, then will I kindle a fire in the gates thereof and it shall devour the palaces of Jerusalem . . ."

    Gittin 60b discusses which of the domiciles is to house the *eruv chatzayrot.*
56. In the *Mishneh Torah,* Hilchot Shabbat 14, Maimonides summarizes the many laws of *eruv* and the extensive discussions that appear in the talmudic tractates Shabbat and Eruvin.
57. See Eruvin 50b-51a. The earliest mention of 2,000 cubits as a noteworthy distance is to be found in Joshua 3:4. See also *Mishneh Torah,* Hilchot Shabbat 27:1-2.
58. Isserles' Notes on the *Shulchan Aruch,* Orach Chayim 376:4.
59. Magen Avraham commentary on Orach Chayim 573:1.
60. Orach Chayim 44:1.
61. Pesachim 25b and Sanhedrin 74a. The Hebrew reads, *Cha'yecha kodmin l'cha'yay chavercha.*
62. Makkot 1:10.
63. Sanhedrin 63a.
64. *Shulchan Aruch,* Yoreh Deah 240 and 241.
65. One of the earliest commentators on the subject is Rabbi Abraham Gombiner (1635-1683), who in his Magen Avraham commentary on the *Shulchan Aruch* says that in his day some Jews were so addicted to smoking that they were impatient for the Sabbath to end so they might indulge once again.
66. *Igrot Moshe,* Yoreh Deah II:49.
67. Bava Kama 30a.
68. In 1876, the chassidic leader Rabbi Meir son of Eliezer of Dzikov died with a pipe in his mouth while sitting in his chair. In a scholarly dissertation, Professor Yaffa Eliach, of Brooklyn College, suggests the interesting possibility that the frequent use of the *lulke* (pipe) by the Baal Shem Tov (1700-1760), the founder of chassidism, may involve the use of a narcotic similar to marijuana. See Basil Herring's

Jewish Ethics and Halakhah for Our Time for a full discussion of smoking and drugs.

69. See Mishna Kila'yim 8:1 and *Shulchan Aruch,* Yoreh Deah 298:1.
70. *Guide for the Perplexed* III:37.
71. Mishna Kila'yim 8:1.
72. *Antiquities* IV:208.

Chapter 9

THE JEWISH WOMAN

1. Sota 11b, Nidda 45b, and Yevamot 62b respectively.
2. Mishna Berachot 3:3 [20a].
3. In biblical and talmudic times, slaves owned by Jews were considered to be members of the household. They were circumcised (Exodus 12:44) and were expected to observe many of the commandments, such as keeping the Sabbath (Exodus 20:10) and holidays (Deuteronomy 16:11). In talmudic times, the most noted slave was Tebi (also spelled Tavi) of the household of Rabban Gamaliel (Berachot 2:7 and Sukka 2:1).
4. The Babylonian scholar Rav elaborated on this thought and observed: "Whereby do women earn merit? By making their children go to synagogue to learn Bible and their husbands go to the *Bet Hamidrash* to study Mishna, and by waiting for their husbands until they return."
5. Sota 47b states that women are not eligible to appear in court as witnesses or judges.
6. See Berachot 59b and Nidda 31b.
7. Bava Batra 141a.
8. Mishna Kiddushin 1:7.
9. *Shulchan Aruch,* Orach Chayim 671.
10. Shabbat 23a.
11. *Shulchan Aruch,* Orach Chayim 675:4.

    The Polish talmudist Abraham Gombiner (1635-1683) elaborates in his authoritative Magen Avraham commentary on the *Shulchan Aruch,* stating that this means that a woman may light Chanuka candles not only in her own behalf but in behalf of her entire family as well.
12. Sukka 28a.
13. Kiddushin 34a.
14. Megilla 4a.
15. Pesachim 108a.
16. Menachot 43b.
17. Ibid. 43a.

18. Berachot 20b.
19. This is consistent with the talmudic law (Rosh Hashana 29a) that permits an individual to perform a religious act in behalf of another as long as both are obligated to perform that act.
20. See Index for further references to *mechitza*.
21. Berachot 24a.
22. See also *Shulchan Aruch,* Orach Chayim 75:1-2.
23. Orach Chayim 55:1.
24. Ibid. 282:3.
25. Berachot 45b.
26. Megilla 23a: "A woman should not read a Tora portion out of respect for the congregation."
27. The text, in Berachot 24a, says: "Rabbi Chisda said, 'A woman's leg is sexually provocative' . . . Rabbi Samuel said, 'A woman's voice is sexually provocative' . . . Rabbi Sheshet said, 'A woman's hair is sexually provocative' . . ."
28. Mishna Rosh Hashana 3:5 [29a].
29. Berachot 31a.
30. The Talmud (Yoma 70a) explains that *kevod tzibur* is also cited as the principal reason for a congregation's removing more than one Tora from the ark for the Tora Reading on certain Sabbaths and holidays. This practice grew out of the procedure followed by the High Priest on Yom Kippur in Temple times. First he read two selections from the Book of Leviticus and then he rolled up the scroll, tucked it under his arm, and recited the *maftir* portion (from the Book of Numbers) from memory. The Rabbis asked why the High Priest did not roll the Tora from Leviticus to Numbers and then read the *maftir* portion from the scroll instead of reciting it from memory. The answer given is *mipnay kevod tzibur,* out of consideration for the feelings of the public. The congregation might have become impatient if it had to sit and wait while the scroll was being rolled.
31. Megilla 23a.
32. This responsum of Rabbi Meir of Rothenburg is found in Hagahot Maimoniyot, the commentary on the *Mishneh Torah* (Hilchot Tefila 2:19) written by Rabbi Meir Hakohayn of Rothenburg, a disciple of Rabbi Meir.
    Today, many Conservative and all Reform and Reconstructionist congregations award *aliyot* to women because they no longer regard as valid the prohibition based on *kevod tzibur.* Since the individual who is called to the Tora no longer reads the Tora portion, they consider the original reason of causing embarrassment to oneself or the congregation no longer applicable.
33. Megilla 23a.
34. *Shulchan Aruch,* Orach Chayim 55:1.
35. Berachot 24a and Kiddushin 70a.
36. *Igrot Moshe,* Orach Chayim 104.

37. *Yechaveh Daat* II:29.
38. Sota 3:4.
39. Pesachim 62b.
40. Shabbat 33b.
41. Berachot 48b.
42. Yerushalmi Pesachim 1:4.
43. Berachot 17a.
44. Sota 11b.
45. Mishna Shevuot 4:1.
46. Hilchot Edut 9:2.
47. See Isserles on Choshen Mishpat 35:14.

   A responsum issued by thirteenth-century Rabbi Meir of Rothenburg, quoted in *Rabbi Meir of Rothenburg*, by Irving Agus, says that if a man was murdered and his wife is the sole witness who can identify the body, and she testifies that a mole on the body of the corpse is identical to a mole on her husband's body, her testimony is accepted, and on that basis she (who is an *aguna*) can remarry.
48. Yevamot 61b.
49. If a member of one tribe borrowed money from a member of another tribe, often he had to put up his land as collateral. If the loan were not repaid, the land would be confiscated by the lender and fall into the hands of his tribe.
50. The Talmud (Bava Batra 116a-119b) discusses the legal argument presented by the five daughters of Zelophehad, who were reputed to be pious and learned. They pointed out to Moses that as daughters they were entitled to be considered equal to sons because when a man died after having sired a son or a daughter, the brother of the deceased is no longer obligated to fulfill the law of Levirate Marriage *(Yibum)*. And if they are not equals, the daughters persisted, and are not considered the offspring of their father in every sense, then their father's brother should be obligated to marry their mother, to establish a family for him (as prescribed in Deuteronomy 25:5ff.). Moses was baffled by the argument and turned to God, who replied that the daughters of Zelophehad were in the right and were entitled to inherit their father's estate.

   According to one rabbinic comment, Moses also addressed God with an emotional appeal expressed by the five women: "Surely, God's love is not like the love of a mortal father. A mortal father prefers sons to daughters, but He who created the world extends love to women as well as to men."
51. Sota 11b.
52. Berachot 22a.

   According to the Bible (Leviticus 15:19), a woman is ritually impure during her menstrual period, and whoever touches her or whatever she touches becomes unclean. She must have no sexual contact with a male during this period, and the penalty for this violation is that both parties are subject to the penalty of *karet*, literally meaning "cutting off" (Leviticus 20:18). In most cases *karet* means one is cut off from the Jewish people (excommunication), but in the main it involves divine punishment, "death at the hands of heaven" (called *mita biyeday shama'yim* in Hebrew).

53. *Shulchan Aruch,* Yoreh Deah 1.
54. Ibid. 264:1.
55. Shabbat 66b.

Chapter 10

JEWISH FOODS AND MEALTIME RITUALS

1. Yerushalmi Kiddushin 4:12.
2. Shabbat 118b.
3. Yerushalmi Kiddushin 4:12.
4. Berachot 44b and Eruvin 55b.
5. Berachot 40a.
6. Bava Kama 82a.
7. Eruvin 56a.
8. Ibid. 29b.
9. Hora'yot 13b.
10. Yoma 75b.
11. See Berachot 40a, Sota 11b, Yoma 18a, and Bava Kama 82a.
12. See *Shulchan Aruch,* Orach Chayim 451:27.
13. See responsum of G. Deutsch, "Use of Pyrex Dishes for Meat and Milk," in *American Reform Responsa,* pp. 135-36.
14. *Shulchan Aruch,* Orach Chayim 452: 6,7.
15. Ibid. 451, 452.
16. Ibid. Yoreh Deah 89 and commentaries.
17. See the report of the Responsa Committee of the Central Conference of American Rabbis in *American Reform Responsa,* pp. 128ff., which explains the Reform attitude toward *kashrut.*
18. Pesachim 76b.
19. *Shulchan Aruch,* Yoreh Deah 116:2.
20. Ibid. 83:1.
21. See *A Guide to Jewish Religious Practice,* by Isaac Klein, p. 305.
22. Bava Kama 79b and 82b respectively.
23. I Maccabees 1:47.
24. Bechorot 7b.
25. Mishna Bechorot 1:4.
26. Berachot 44b.
27. Yoma 75b.
28. Chulin 49b.
Not all Orthodox communities accept the rulings of The Chief

Rabbinate because they believe that as appointees of the government, their *halachic* decisions are not totally unbiased and are sometimes politically motivated. They refer to the Chief Rabbinate as "Rav Mitaam."

29. See the Chafetz Chaim's comment in the Mishna Berura on Orach Chayim 2:6.
30. Numbers Rabba 20:21.
31. Yoma 79b.
32. The nonanimal offerings brought on the altar in Temple times were primarily made of flour derived from the five basic grains (wheat, barley, spelt, oats, rye). When the table of the home assumed the symbolic role of the altar of Temple times, bread made of the five grains took on special significance. Therefore, if bread is to be eaten, the hands must be ritually washed and the *Hamotzi* blessing must be recited. Conversely, if bread is not to be eaten at the meal, the hands need not be ritually washed. The *Shulchan Aruch*, Orach Chayim 177, codifies these requirements.
33. See the Beer Hetev commentary of Rabbi Judah Ashkenazi (eighteenth century) on the *Shulchan Aruch*, Orach Chayim 158:1.
34. *Shulchan Aruch*, Orach Chayim 162:2.
35. Ibid.
36. Ibid.
37. Ibid. 177.
38. Berachot 50b.
39. Ibid. 55a.
40. Berachot 46a.
41. The *Code of Jewish Law* (*Shulchan Aruch*, Orach Chayim 167:1) suggests that the piece of bread *(challa)* that is first tasted after the *Hamotzi* prayer is pronounced should include part of the crust of the *challa*. This, the most baked part of the bread, is a reminder of the meal-offering that was burned on the Temple altar.

   Rabbi Meir Hakohayn, in his commentary *Hagahot Maimoniyot*, Chapter 7, on Maimonides' *Hilchot Berachot*, records the view of his teacher, Rabbi Meir of Rothenburg (thirteenth-century). Noting that the French custom was to cut the bread on the bottom and break it upward, while the German practice was to cut the bread on top and break it downward, Meir of Rothenburg avoided slighting either group by cutting the loaf part way through, top and bottom, and then breaking off pieces.

   See also *Modern Reform Responsa*, by Rabbi Solomon B. Freehof, pp. 97-99, for additional discussion.
42. Shabbat 67b.
43. Yerushalmi Hora'yot 3:5.

   In ancient Rome salt was used as a medium of exchange. In fact, our word "salary" comes from the Latin *salarium*, which is derived from *sal*, meaning "salt." Roman soldiers received part of their pay in salt.

44. Bava Metzia 60a.
45. Pesachim 109a.
46. Song of Songs 6.
47. Megilla 4:1.
48. Nedarim 3:10.
49. Pesachim 30a.
50. Mishna Pesachim 2:5.
51. Hilchot Chametz Umatza 5:1.
52. Orach Chayim 453:1.
53. Jerusalem's Michlelet Bruria, an academy of higher learning (yeshiva) for women, is the counterpart of Yeshivat Hamivtar, founded by Yeshiva University graduate Rabbi Chaim Brovender. The students are adult women who come from diverse backgrounds and cultures—Ashkenazic and Sephardic—and all of whom live in the same dormitory. On Passover, the Sephardic women eat rice, while the Ashkenazic women do not. Both use the same kitchen, and Sephardic women cook their rice (forbidden to Ashkenazic women) in the same pots used by the Ashkenazic women when they prepare their meals. Once the pot used for rice is rinsed, it is considered kosher for use by Ashkenazic women.

See the article by Greer Fay Cashman in the June 10-17, 1984, International Edition of The Jerusalem Post.

The Passover Handbook (1981), written by Rabbi Jacob J. Hecht and issued by the National Committee for Furtherance of Jewish Education, lists foods that are doubtful for Passover use and that should be used only after an "Orthodox rabbi [is] consulted." These include beans, corn kernels, garlic, lima beans, peanuts, peas, rice, split peas, string beans, and spices. Other lists issued by Orthodox rabbis specify that spices such as saffron, cloves, and mustard not be used. All of these prohibitions are based on local custom rather than law and are not shared by the entire Jewish community.

54. Rabbi Shalom Mordecai Schwadron (the twentieth-century Polish authority known by the acronym Maharsham), in responsum 183 in Volume One of his six volumes of responsa (She'elot Uteshuvot Maharsham), says that oil made from legumes is permitted. See also Mishna Berura of Rabbi Israel Meir Hakohayn, Orach Chayim 442.

Rabbi Moshe Feinstein, who follows the Ashkenazic discipline, is not overly concerned that the flour made from peanuts may be inadvertently mixed with the flour of permissible grains. He advises caution, but he does not prohibit the consumption of peanuts outright. See Igrot Moshe, Orach Chayim III:63.

55. Mishna Challa 1:2 and Menachot 66a-66b.

The new JPS translation of the Bible offers the correct translation. Other translations, such as the Soncino translation of the Talmud and the Danby translation of the Mishna, are not correct.

In translations of Pesachim 109a, the word *kali* is invariably mistranslated. It describes the practice of Rabbi Akiba, who used to distribute roasted *kali* and nuts to children on the eve of Passover. (These were favorite goodies of children and his purpose was to keep them excited so they would be wide awake to join in the *Seder* and be alert to ask the Four Questions.) The translation of *kali*, which was always rendered as "roasted corn," is obviously incorrect, since corn did not exist at that time. It is known, however, that roasted kernels of grain were a delicacy loved by children.

Bibliography

Abrahams, Israel. *Jewish Life in the Middle Ages*. London: Edward Goldston, 1932.

Abramov, S. Zalman. *Perpetual Dilemma*. New Jersey: Fairleigh Dickinson University Press, 1976.

Agus, Irving. *Rabbi Meir of Rothenburg*. New York: Ktav Publishing House, 1970.

Arian, Philip, and Eisenberg, Azriel. *The Story of the Prayerbook*. Hartford, Connecticut: Prayer Book Press, 1968.

Arzt, Max. *Justice and Mercy*. New York: Holt, Rinehart and Winston, 1963.

The Babylonian Talmud (Hebrew). Twenty volumes. Vilna: Romm, 1922.

The Babylonian Talmud (English). Thirty-five volumes. London: Soncino Press, 1935.

Bader, Gershom. *Jewish Spiritual Heroes*. New York: Pardes, 1940.

Badi, Joseph, editor. *Fundamental Laws of the State of Israel*. New York: Twayne Publishers, 1961.

Baeck, Leo. *The Pharisees and Other Essays*. New York: Schocken Books, 1947.

Bea, Augustin Cardinal. *The Church and the Jewish People*. New York: Harper & Row, 1966.

Bleich, J. David. *Judaism and Healing*. New York: Ktav Publishing House, 1981.

———. *Contemporary Halakhic Problems I*. New York: Ktav Publishing House, 1977.

371

——. *Contemporary Halakhic Problems II.* New York: Ktav Publishing House, 1983.

Caro, Joseph. *Shulchan Aruch (Code of Jewish Law).* Eight volumes. Probably a reprint of the 1874 Vilna edition. New York: Abraham Isaac Friedman, n.d.

Cohen, A. *Everyman's Talmud.* New York: E.P. Dutton, 1949.

Danby, Herbert. *The Mishna.* Oxford, England: Clarendon Press, 1933.

Davis, Eli and Elise. *Hats and Caps of the Jew.* Jerusalem: Massada Ltd., 1983.

Donin, Hayim. *To Be a Jew.* New York: Basic Books, 1972.

——. *To Pray as a Jew.* New York: Basic Books, 1980.

Eichhorn, David Max. *Conversion to Judaism.* New York: Ktav Publishing House, 1965.

——. *Jewish Intermarriage: Fact and Fiction.* Satellite Beach, Florida: Satellite Books, 1974.

Eisenstein, Ira, editor. *A Guide to Jewish Ritual.* New York: Reconstructionist Press, 1962.

Eisenstein, J.D. *Otzar Dinim Uminhagim.* New York: Hebrew Publishing Co., 1938.

——. *Otzar Maamarei Chazal.* New York: Hebrew Publishing Co., 1929.

Eliach, Yaffa. *Hasidic Tales of the Holocaust.* New York: Avon Books, 1982.

Epstein, Isidore. *The Responsa of Rabbi Solomon ben Adreth of Barcelona (1235-1310).* New York: Ktav Publishing House, 1968.

Epstein, Yechiel. *Aruch Hashulchan.* Eight volumes. Warsaw, 1900-12.

Even Shoshan, Abraham. *Milon Chadash.* Four volumes. Twelfth edition. Jerusalem: Kiryat Sepher, 1964.

——. *A New Concordance of the Bible.* Four volumes. Jerusalem: Kiryat Sepher, 1980.

Feinstein, Moshe. *Igrot Moshe.* Six volumes. New York: Moriah Offset, 1959-81.

Feldman, David M. *Birth Control in Jewish Law.* New York: New York University Press, 1968.

Feldman, David M., and Rosner, Fred. *Compendium on*

Ethics. New York: Federation of Jewish Philanthropies, 1984.

Freehof, Solomon B. *Contemporary Reform Responsa.* Cincinnati: Hebrew Union College Press, 1974.

————. *Current Reform Responsa.* Cincinnati: Hebrew Union College Press, 1969.

————. *Modern Reform Responsa.* Cincinnati: Hebrew Union College Press, 1971.

————. *New Reform Responsa.* Cincinnati: Hebrew Union College Press, 1980.

————. *Reform Jewish Practice,* Volumes I and II. Augmented edition. This is a revised and enlarged edition of *Reform Jewish Practice* with material from *Reform Responsa.* Ktav Publishing House, 1976.

————. *Reform Responsa* and *Recent Reform Responsa.* Two vols. in one. New York: Ktav Publishing House, 1973.

————. *Reform Responsa for Our Time.* Cincinnati: Hebrew Union College Press, 1977.

————. *The Responsa Literature* and *A Treasury of Responsa.* Two volumes in one. New York: Ktav Publishing House, 1973.

Ginzberg, Louis. *Legends of the Jews.* Seven volumes. Philadelphia: Jewish Publication Society, 1956.

Graetz, Heinrich. *History of the Jews.* Six volumes. Philadelphia: Jewish Publication Society, 1891.

Greenberg, Blu. *How to Run a Traditional Jewish Household.* New York: Simon and Schuster, 1983.

Greenwald, Yekutiel. *Ach Letzara.* St. Louis, Missouri: Quality Printing and Publishing Co., 1939.

Gribetz, Donald I., and Tendler, Moshe. *The Mount Sinai Journal of Medicine,* Volume 51, Number 1. New York: Mount Sinai Medical Center of New York, 1984.

Herring, Basil F. *Jewish Ethics and Halakah for Our Times.* New York: Ktav Publishing House, 1983.

Heschel, Susannah, editor. *On Being a Jewish Feminist.* New York: Schocken Books, 1983.

Himmelfarb, Milton, editor. *The Condition of Jewish Belief.* New York: Macmillan, 1966.

Hirshowitz, Abraham. *Otzar Kol Minhagei Yeshurun.* Pittsburgh: Moinester Printing Co., 1918.

Hoffman, Edward. *The Way of Splendor*. Boulder, Colorado: Shambhala Publications, 1981.

Hyamson, Moses. *The Mishneh Torah*. Two volumes. New York: Bloch Publishing Co., 1937, 1949.

Hyman, Aaron. *Otzar Divrei Chachamim Ufisgameihem*. Tel Aviv: Dvir, 1933.

Ibn Chaviv (Habib), Jacob. *En Yaakov*. Translated by S.H. Glick. Six volumes. New York: Hebrew Publishing Co., 1916.

Idelsohn, Abraham. *Jewish Liturgy*. New York: Henry Holt, 1932.

Isaac of Troki. *Chizuk Emuna*. New York: Ktav Publishing House, 1970.

Israel Meir Hakohayn (Chafetz Chayim). *Mishna Berura*. Six volumes. New York, n.d.

Jacobs, Louis. *Jewish Law*. New York: Behrman House, 1968.

———. *Jewish Mystical Testimonies*. New York: Schocken Books, 1977.

———. *What Does Judaism Say About . . . ?* Jerusalem: Keter, 1976.

Jakobovits, Immanuel. *Jewish Medical Ethics*. New York: Bloch Publishing Co., 1959.

The Jewish Encyclopedia. Twelve volumes. New York: Funk and Wagnalls, 1912.

Judaism, Issue Number 129, Volume 33, Number 1, Winter 1984. New York: American Jewish Congress.

Kasher, Menachem M. *Encyclopedia of Biblical Interpretation*. Seven volumes. New York: American Biblical Encyclopedia Society, 1953.

Katsch, Abraham I. *Judaism and the Koran*. New York: A S Barnes & Co., 1954.

Kaufman, Walter. *Religion in Four Dimensions*. New York: Reader's Digest Press, 1976.

Klein, Isaac. *A Guide to Jewish Religious Practice*. New York: Jewish Theological Seminary, 1979.

———. *Responsa and Halakhic Studies*. New York: Ktav Publishing House, 1975.

Kolatch, Alfred J. *Complete Dictionary of English and He-*

brew First Names. New York: Jonathan David Publishers, 1984.

————. *The Jewish Book of Why.* New York: Jonathan David Publishers, 1981.

————. *Who's Who in the Talmud.* New York: Jonathan David Publishers, 1964.

Koltun, Elizabeth, editor. *The Jewish Woman: New Perspectives.* New York: Schocken Books, 1976.

Lamm, Maurice. *The Jewish Way in Death and Mourning.* New York: Jonathan David Publishers, 1972.

————. *The Jewish Way in Love and Marriage.* New York: Harper & Row, 1980.

Lamm, Norman. *A Hedge of Roses.* New York: Philipp Feldheim, 1966.

Landau, Ezekiel. *Noda Biyehuda.* Two volumes. Jerusalem: Books Export Enterprises Ltd., n.d.

Lieberman, Saul. *Tosephta.* Jerusalem: Wahrmann Books, 1970.

Maimonides, Moses. *The Guide for the Perplexed.* Two volumes, Translated by Shlomo Pines. Chicago: University of Chicago Press, 1974.

————. *The Mishnah Torah.* Five volumes. Warsaw, 1881.

Marcus, Jacob R. *The Jew in the Medieval World.* Cincinnati: Union of American Hebrew Congregations, 1938.

Mazur, Benjamin, editor. *The World History of the Jewish People: The Judges.* New Brunswick, New Jersey: Rutgers University Press, 1971.

Meiselman, Moshe. *The Jewish Woman in Jewish Law.* New York: Yeshiva University Press, 1978.

Midrash Rabba. Two volumes. Vilna: Romm, 1938.

Millgram, Abraham. *Jewish Worship.* Philadelphia: Jewish Publication Society, 1971.

Morgenstern, Julian. *Rites of Birth, Marriage, and Death Among Semites.* Chicago: Quadrangle Books, 1966.

Neusner, Jacob. *Judaism in Society.* Chicago: University of Chicago Press, 1983.

Oshry, Ephraim, *Responsa From the Holocaust.* New York: Judaica Press, 1983.

Plaut, Gunther, editor. *The Rise of Reform Judaism.* New York: World Union for Progressive Judaism, 1963.

————. *The Torah.* New York: Union of American Hebrew Congregations, 1975.

Pollack, Herman. *Jewish Folkways in Germanic Lands (1648-1806).* Cambridge, Massachusetts: M.I.T. Press, 1971.

Riemer, Jack, editor. *Jewish Reflections on Death.* New York: Schocken Books, 1974.

Rosenblatt, Samuel. *Saadia Gaon: The Book of Beliefs and Opinions.* New Haven: Yale University Press, 1984.

Roth, Cecil, editor. *Encyclopaedia Judaica.* Sixteen volumes. Jerusalem: Keter, 1972.

Shereshevsky, Esra. *Rashi: The Man and His World.* New York: Sepher-Hermon Press, 1982.

Siegel, Seymour, editor. *Conservative Judaism and the Law.* New York: Rabbinical Assembly, 1977.

Simon, Merrill. *Jerry Falwell and the Jews.* New York: Jonathan David Publishers, 1984.

Steinsaltz, Adin. *The Essential Talmud.* New York: Basic Books, 1976.

Strizower, Schifra. *The Bene Israel of Bombay.* New York: Schocken Books, 1971.

————. *Exotic Jewish Communities.* New York: Yoseloff, 1962.

Tchernowitz Chayim. *The Talmud.* Warsaw: Hasefer, 1912.

Trachtenberg, Joshua. *Jewish Magic and Superstition.* New York: Behrman House, 1939.

Trepp, Leo. *The Complete Book of Jewish Observance.* New York: Behrman House, 1980.

Twersky, Isadore. *Introduction to the Code of Maimonides.* New Haven: Yale University Press, 1980.

Walter, Jacob, editor. *American Reform Responsa.* New York: Central Conference of American Rabbis, 1983.

Weiss-Rosmarin, Trude. *Judaism and Christianity: The Differences.* New York: Jonathan David Publishers, 1965.

Yosef, Ovadya. *Yechaveh Daat.* Four volumes. Jerusalem: Chazon Ovadya Rabbinical Seminary, 1937.

Zlotnick, Dov. *The Tractate: Mourning.* Yale Judaica Series. New Haven: Yale University Press, 1966.

Index

This index covers *The Jewish Book of Why* and *The Second Jewish Book of Why*. The roman numerals in boldface type refer to the volume number.

Bet Midrash, I 125
Betoch shelo, II 104
Betrayal of Jesus, II 69
Betrothal. See Engagement.
Bettan, Rabbi Israel, II 343
Betula, II 67
B'ezrat haShem, I 295
Bialik, Chaim Nachman, I 176
Bible, I, 2, 4. See also New Testament and
Old Testament.
burning of, II 67
commentaries on, I 6
Jewish holidays in, I 11
Judeo-Christian ethic and, II 83
laws of, I 3
literal vs. figurative interpretation, II
215-17
ordinances, II 254
verses in mezuza, I 113
verses in tefilin, I 107
Bima, I 125, 133
Birkat Chatanim, II 264
Birkat Hamazon, II 235. See also Grace
After Meals.
Birkat Kohanim. See Priestly Benediction.
Birkat Levana, I 281
Birkat Zimun, II 236
in Conservative and Reform syna-
gogues, I 141
Birth control
Isaac di Trani on, II 154
Jewish law on, II 152-54
Moses Sofer on, II 154
Rabbenu Tam on, II 153
Rashi on, II 153
Solomon Luria on, II 154
use of fertility drugs, II 154
use of moch, II 153-54
use of pill, II 153-54
when life of mother in peril, II 153
Birth, virgin. See Virgin birth.
Bitter herbs, I 199-200
Biur chametz, II 222-23
Blech, I 166
Bleich, Rabbi J.D., II 351
Blessings. See also Prayers.
over baked goods, II 231
beracha levatala, I 236. II 222-23
over bread, II 227, 230-31
boray minay mezonot, II 232
boray pri hagafen, II 231
followed by action, II 221-22
over fruit, II 231
hamotzi, II 227
l'chayim, II 327
lulav and etrog, II 266-67
mezonot, II 232
shehakol, II 231
smoking and, II 237
superfluous, I 236. II 222
Tora, II 239-42

types of, II 220-22
over nonkosher food, II 225-26
over wine, II 227, 230-31
Blintzes, I 220
Blood
biblical ban on use, II 167
consumption of, II 165
of the Covenant, II 132
of fish, I 94
hatafat dam brit, II 132
of human dead, I 52
intravenous feeding, II 167
removing from meat, I 88, 93-94
spilling of, II 168
for symbolic circumcision, II 132
transfusions, II 165, 167
whose is redder, II 12
B'nai Mitzva (sing., Bar Mitzva). See Bar
Mitzva.
B'not Mitzva (sing., Bat Mitzva), II 295.
See also Bat Mitzva.
Boaz, I 35, 217. II 264
Bokser (carob), I 289
Book-burning
the Bible by Fundamentalists, II 67
the Talmud in Paris, II 61
works of Maimonides, II 57
Book of Death, I 232
Book of Esther. See Esther, Book of.
Book of Life, I 232, 238
Book of Maccabees, II 74
Book of Principles, II 62
Book of Remedies, II 313
Books, respect for, II 60
Booth. See Sukka.
Boray minay mezonot, II 232
Boray Nefashot, II 235
Boray pri haetz, II 231
Boray pri hagafen, II 231
Botarel, Moses, II 211
Bowing, I 153
Brain death, II 164
Bread, II 312
blessing over, II 221, 230-32, 235
breaking, II 326, 368
essence of meal, II 322-23, 358
Grace After Meals and, II 235
in the sacrificial system, II 326
washing hands before eating, II 322-23
Breakfast, II 139-40
Breast-beating, I 159, 243
Breastplates, I 128-29
Bride, I 28, 31. See also Marriage.
covering face at wedding, I 36
fasting on wedding day, I 34
position under canopy, I 38
Bridesmaid, II 108
Brit. See Circumcision.
Broiling meat, I 92-93
Brother Daniel, II 19
Burial. See also Cemetery and Funeral.

on Chanuka, I 265
on Rosh Hashana, I 235
on Shemini Atzeret, I 256
when prohibited, II 227
Shekel (pl., shekalim), I 20-22
Shelah, II 148, 349
Shelo asani isha, II 293
Shelom bayit, II 356
Sheloshim, I 79. II 178
Shema, I 102, 110. II 204, 360
  Baruch shem kevod, II 249-50, 360
  and belief in one God, II 204
  on mezuza parchment, I 114
  recitation
    before brit, I 18
    covering eyes, I 155
    posture during, I 154. II 248-49
  reason for, II 204
  women's exemption from, II 293
  Sephardic rites relating to, II 238-39
  on tefilin parchment, I 107
  type of lettering, I 155
  on Yom Kippur, II 249-50
Shemini Atzeret, I 246ff.
Shemita, II 261
  Kook, Abraham, on, II 321
  Spektor, Isaac Elchanan, on, II 321
Shemoneh Esrei. See Shmoneh Esrei.
Shemura matza. See Matza.
Sherer, Rabbi Moshe, II 47
Sherira Gaon, II 4
Sheva Berachot, I 43
  and minyan, I 45-46. II 236, 361
Shevarim, I 229
Shevat, I 10, 12
Shevut, I 165. II 265
Shiksa, I 296
Shir shel pega'im, II 355
Shisha Sedarim, II 75. See also Mishna.
Shituf, II 342
Shiva. See also Mourning.
  for apostate, II 36, 137-38, 197
  commencement of, II 195
  Danzig, Abraham, on, II 195
  legal status of, II 178
  occasions when cancelled, II 193-94
  occasions when curtailed, II 193-94
  period of, I 60, 63-64
  Rabbenu Gershom on, II 138
  Rashi on, II 195
  removal of shoes, II 194
  sex during, II 143
  starting before burial, II 195
  visiting during, I 50, 67, 68. II 175
  where observed, II 195
Shiva Asar B'Tammuz, I 11, 33-34, 285-86.
  II 280
Shiva call. See Condolence call.
Shloshet Yemei Hagbala, I 214
Shmoneh Esrei (Esray). See also Amida
  and Silent Devotion.

Akiba's custom, II 298-99
  silent recitation of, II 218
Shochet, I 88-89, 97
  woman as, II 309
Shoes, II 324
  burial without, II 181
  removal in synagogue, I 142-43
  use of leather, II 227
Shofar, I 2
  blowing pattern, I 229-30
  during Elul, I 221, 224
  Falasha practice, II 40
  hundred blasts, I 231
  after Neila, I 222. II 251
  ram's horn used, I 228
  on Rosh Hashana, I 225
  on Sabbath, I 2, 228
  in the Temple, I 281
  that wouldn't function, II 355
  women's obligation to listen to, II 293
Shofrot, I 230
Shomer, I 51. II 180
Shomron, II 41
Shomronim. See Samaritans.
Shoshanta (pittom), I 251
Shovel, use of during burial, II 188.
Showbreads (shewbreads) in Temple, I
  173
Shroud, I 52-53
Shtreiml, I 2
Shuckling. See Swaying.
Shulchan Aruch (Code of Jewish Law), I
  6-7, 13. II 6-7. See also Law, Jewish.
Shushan, I 270, 272
Shushan Purim, I 12, 272
Siddur, I 146-47
Siddur of Saadya Gaon, II 233
Sidelocks, I 122. II 170
Silberg, Moshe, II 19
Silent Devotion, I 110-11, 153-56, 265. II
  217-19
  Maimonides on, II 258
Siman tov, I 44
Simcha ben Samuel, Rabbi, I 81
Simchat Bet Hasho'ayva, I 139, 248
Simchat Tora, I 133, 247
  date, I 11
  origin, I 258
  why celebrated, I 258
Simeon ben Gamaliel, II 283
Simeon ben Shetach, I 40. II 33, 305
Simeon (Simon) bar (ben) Yochai, I 151,
  284. II 257
Sin, I 159, 243. II 35
  absolution from, I 150
  Adam and Eve, II 64
  in Christian theology, II 64
  of conversion to Christianity, II 35
  death and, II 341
  Garden of Eden and, II 63-64
  of Golden Calf, II 65

About the Author

ALFRED J. KOLATCH, a graduate of the Teacher's Institute of Yeshiva University and its College of Liberal Arts, was ordained by the Jewish Theological Seminary of America, which subsequently awarded him the Doctor of Divinity Degree, *honoris causa*. From 1941 to 1948 he served as rabbi of congregations in Columbia, South Carolina, and Kew Gardens, New York, and as chaplain in the United States Army. In 1948 he founded Jonathan David Publishers, of which he has since been president and editor-in-chief.

Rabbi Kolatch has authored numerous books, the most popular of which are *Great Jewish Quotations*, *The Jewish Home Advisor*, *This Is the Torah*, and the best-selling *Jewish Book of Why* and its sequel, *The Second Jewish Book of Why*. Several of the author's works deal with nomenclature, about which he is an acknowledged authority. *The New Name Dictionary* and *The Complete Dictionary of English and Hebrew First Names* are his most recent books on the subject. Other books by the author include *The Jewish Child's First Book of Why*, *Classic Bible Stories for Jewish Children*, *The Jewish Heritage Quiz Book*, *The Jewish Mourner's Book of Why*, *Who's Who in the Talmud*, and *The Family Seder*.

In addition to his scholarly work, Rabbi Kolatch is interested in the work of the military chaplaincy and has served as president of the Association of Jewish Chaplains of the Armed Forces and as vice-president of the interdenominational Military Chaplains Association of the United States.